SY 0126592 X

D1613346

# Educating Artists for the Future:
## Learning at the Intersections of Art, Science, Technology and Culture

Mel Alexenberg
Editor

**intellect** Bristol, UK / Chicago, USA

First Published in the UK in 2008 by
Intellect Books, The Mill, Parnall Road, Fishponds, Bristol, BS16 3JG, UK

First published in the USA in 2008 by
Intellect Books, The University of Chicago Press, 1427 E. 60th Street, Chicago,
IL 60637, USA

A catalogue record for this book is available from the British Library.

Front Cover: Based upon a painting by Mel Alexenberg in his "Digitized Homage to
Rembrandt" series

Cover Design: Gabriel Solomons
Copy Editor: Holly Spradling
Typesetting: Mac Style, Nafferton, E. Yorkshire

ISBN 978-1-84150-191-8

Printed and bound by Gutenberg Press, Malta.

# CONTENTS

*Introduction: Education for a Conceptual Age*                                9

**Learning at the Intersections of Art, Science, Technology and Culture**     11
*Mel Alexenberg*
Professor of Art and Founding Dean, School of Art and Multimedia,
Netanya Academic College, Netanya, Israel, (author of *The Future of Art in a
Digital Age: From Hellenistic to Hebraic Consciousness*, Intellect Books, 2006)

*Beyond the Digital*                                                          27

**Beyond the Digital: Preparing Artists to Work at the Frontiers of Technoculture**  29
*Stephen Wilson*
Professor and Director of Conceptual/Information Arts Program, San Francisco
State University, California, USA, (author of *Information Arts: Intersections of Art,
Science, and Technology*, MIT Press, 2002)

**Pixels and Particles: The Path to Syncretism**                             47
*Roy Ascott*
President, Planetary Collegium and Professor, University of Plymouth, UK,
(author of *Telematic Embrace: Visionary Theories of Art, Technology and
Consciousness*, University of California Press, 2003, and editor of *Technoetic Arts:
A Journal of Speculative Research*)

**Sustaining Creativity and Losing the Wild**                                61
*Carol Gigliotti*
Associate Professor of New Media, Emily Carr Institute of Art and Design,
Vancouver, British Columbia, Canada

**Making Space for the Artist**                                                    75
*Mark Amerika*
Associate Professor of Art and Art History, University of Colorado, Boulder,
CO, USA, (author of *META/DATA: A Digital Poetics*, MIT Press, 2007)

*Networked Times*                                                                  83

**Unthinkable Complexity: Art Education in Networked Times**                       85
*Robert Sweeny*
Assistant Professor of Art and Art Education, Indiana University of Pennsylvania,
Indiana, PA, USA

**Art/Science & Education**                                                        103
*Stefan Sonvilla-Weiss*
Professor and Head of the International M.A. Program ePedagogy Design – Visual
Knowledge Building, University of Art and Design, Helsinki, Finland, (author of
*(e)Pedagogy-Visual Knowledge Building: Rethinking  Art and New Media in Education*,
Peter Lang, 2005)

**Learning, Education, and the Arts in a Digital World**                           115
*Ron Burnett*
President of Emily Carr Institute of Art and Design, Vancouver, British Columbia,
Canada, (author of *How Images Think*, MIT Press, 2004)

**Afference and Efference: Encouraging Social Impact through Art and Science
Education**                                                                        127
*Jill Scott*
Research Professor: Institute for Cultural Studies in Art, Media and Design,
Hochschule für Gestaltung und Kunst Zürich, Switzerland, and Vice Director,
Z-Node, Planetary Collegium, (author of *Artistsinlabs: Exploring the Interface
between Art and Science*, Springer, 2006)

*Polycultural Perspectives*                                                        139

**Expressing with Grey Cells: Indian Perspectives on New Media Arts**              141
*Vinod Vidwans*
Professor and Head of Departments of New Media and Software User Interface
Design, National Institute of Design, Ahmedabad, India

**New Media Art as Embodiment of Tao**                                             155
*Wengao Huang*
Associate Professor of Media Art, College of Information Science and Engineering,
Shandong University at Weihai, China

**Between Hyper-Images and Aniconism: New Perspectives on Islamic Art in the Education of Artists** 169
*Ismail Ozgur Soganci*
Assistant Professor of Fine Art Education, Anadolu University, Eskisehir, Turkey

**Touching Light: Post-Traditional Immersion in Interactive Artistic Environments** 175
*Diane Gromala*
Professor and Associate Director of the School of Interactive Arts and Technology at Simon Fraser University, British Columbia, Canada, co-author of *Windows and Mirrors: Interaction Design, Digital Art and the Myth of Transparency* (MIT Press 2005) and
*Jinsil Seo*
Ph.D. Candidate, School of Interactive Arts and Technology, Simon Fraser University

***Reflective Inquiry*** 191

**Media Golem: Between Prague and ZKM** 193
*Michael Bielicky*
Professor and Head of the Department of InfoArt/Digital Media, Hochschule für Gestaltung, ZKM Center for Art and Media, Karlsruhe, Germany, and Academy of Fine Arts, Prague, Czech Republic

**Life Transformation – Art Mutation** 203
*Eduardo Kac*
Professor and Chairman, Art and Technology Department, School of the Art Institute of Chicago, USA, (author of *Telepresence & Bio Art*, University of Michigan Press, 2005; editor of *Signs of Life: Bio Art and Beyond*, MIT Press, 2007)

**Learning Through the Re-embodiment of the Digital Self** 217
*Yacov Sharir*
Associate Professor of Dance and Multimedia Art, University of Texas at Austin, USA

**My Journey: From Physics to Graphic Design to User-Interface/Information-Visualization Design** 229
*Aaron Marcus*
President Aaron Marcus and Associates (AM+A), and Visiting Professor of Media Design, Illinois Institute of Technology, Chicago, IL, USA, (author of *Graphic Design for Electronic Documents and User Interfaces*, Addison-Wesley, 1991)

*Emergent Praxis*                                                                                   243

**Entwined Histories: Reflections on Teaching Art, Science, and Technological Media**                245
*Edward A. Shanken*
Senior Researcher, UCLA Art/Science Center and Lab, Los Angeles, CA, and
Professor of Art History, Savanah College of Art and Design, Georgia, USA
(editor of *Telematic Embrace: Visionary Theories of Art, Technology, and
Consciousness*, University of California Press, 2003)

**A Generative Emergent Approach to Graduate Education**                                             253
*Bill Seaman*
Professor and Head of Department of Digital Media, Rhode Island School of
Design, Providence, RI, USA

**Media Literacy: Reading and Writing Images in a Digital Age**                                      271
*Shlomo Lee Abrahmov*
Senior Lecturer in Design and Instructional Systems Technologies, Holon
Institute of Technology, Holon, Israel

**The Creative Spirit in the Age of Digital Technologies: Seven Tactical Exercises**                 291
*Lucia Leao*
Professor of Art and Technology, Department of Computer Science, Sao Paulo
Catholic University, and SENAC, Brazil, (author of *Derivas: Cartografias do
Ciberespaço*, Annablume, 2004)

*Epilogue: Realms of Learning*                                                                       303

**From Awesome Immersion to Holistic Integration**                                                   305
*Mel Alexenberg*
Former Associate Professor of Art and Education, Columbia University, Chairman
of Fine Arts, Pratt Institute, Dean of Visual Arts, New World School of the Arts,
Miami, and Research Fellow, MIT Center for Advanced Visual Studies, USA

**About the Authors**                                                                                337

# INTRODUCTION: EDUCATION FOR A CONCEPTUAL AGE

# LEARNING AT THE INTERSECTIONS OF ART, SCIENCE, TECHNOLOGY AND CULTURE

## Mel Alexenberg

The genesis of this book was an invitation by the renowned mathematicians Tzvi Arad and Bernard Pinchik to create a new School of Art and Multimedia at Netanya Academic College in Israel. I began to develop a proposal for a school in which students redefine art in creative ways at the interdisciplinary interface where scientific inquiry and new technologies shape aesthetic and cultural values – both local and global. Although I have had years of experience in both science and art education, I knew that I needed to explore fresh directions for educating artists for the future in a rapidly changing world where the boundaries between art, science, technology, and culture are becoming diaphanous. What better way to discern these new directions, I thought, than to invite some of the world's most innovative thinkers in higher education in the arts to advise me. This book is their advice. It not only offers invaluable advice for creating new schools, but it provides alternative paths for upgrading and refreshing existing art schools and university art departments worldwide for a post-digital future.

As I studied the diverse chapters exploring alternative futures for educating artists that I received from artists/researchers/teachers working in Brazil, Canada, China, Czech Republic, Finland, Germany, India, Israel, South Korea, Switzerland, Turkey, United Kingdom, and the United States, I began to search for a conceptual framework for organizing this book. My search was interrupted by a meeting in Holland with Charles Esche, Director of the Van Abbemuseum in Eindhoven, and Richard Flood, Chief Curator of the New Museum of Contemporary Art in New York. We were charged with awarding an artist the coveted Wolf Prize, the equivalent in the arts of the Nobel Prize, from among numerous nominations received from throughout the world. The three of us unanimously agreed to award Michaelangelo Pistoletto the prize because of his inventive career as an artist, educator, and activist, whose restless intelligence has created prescient forms of art that address the major technological and cultural changes of our era. In his hometown, Biella, Italy, he established Cittadellarte as a center to inspire artists to produce responsible change in society through transdisciplinary ideas and creative projects. Pistoletto asserts, "Artists have a unique and totally free way of understanding and analyzing society, and consequently of being engaged with it. Cittadellarte firmly believes that art can interact among all the diverse spheres of human activity that form society, and is thereby a generator for responsible transformation of society."

At Schiphol Airport, waiting for my flight home to Tel Aviv, I was struck by four books sharing the main display rack in the airport bookshop: *A Whole New Mind*, *Intelligence Reframed*, *The Lexus and the Olive Tree*, and *Machine Beauty*. They explore some of the same concepts that I had discussed with Esche and Flood in Eindhoven. Browsing through them gave me further food for thought about how to group the chapters in the book and write the introduction for it. It is significant that none of these books were art books. Glancing at the back covers, I saw that they were classified as books in the areas of business, psychology, current affairs, and computer science. It is apparent that new ways for educating artists for the future will be found in a global fabric woven with colorful threads from all fields of human endeavor. Significant threads are revealed in subtitles of the four books.

The subtitles of *A Whole New Mind* by business consultant Daniel Pink (2006) are "Why Right-brainers will Rule the Future" and "Moving from the Information Age to the Conceptual Age." Pink proposes that we are witnessing a paradigm shift beyond the digital culture of the Information Age to a Conceptual Age in which people in all walks of life will succeed when they behave like artists who integrate left-brain with right-brain thinking. Industrial Age factory workers and Information Age knowledge workers are being superseded by Conceptual Age creators and empathizers who integrate high-tech abilities with high-touch and high-concept abilities. When the president of General Motors states that he is in the art business selling mobile sculpture that incidentally provides transportation, the M.F.A. degree has become more valuable to corporate recruiters than the M.B.A.

"Multiple Intelligences for the 21st Century" is the subtitle of Harvard psychology professor Howard Gardner's book, *Intelligence Reframed* (1999), that describes how artists have always needed to develop their spatial intelligence. Artists of the future, however, will realize that this pattern-recognition mode of thinking is not enough. Spatial intelligence will have to be combined in multiple configurations with bodily-kinesthetic, logical-mathematical, linguistic, musical, naturalist, intrapersonal, interpersonal, spiritual, and existential intelligences.

*The Lexus and the Olive Tree* by Pulitzer Prize–winning author Thomas Friedman (2000) is subtitled "Understanding Globalization." He dramatizes the conflict between manufacturing the luxury car Lexus and attachment to deeply rooted olive trees – the tension between the globalization system and the ancient forces of culture, geography, tradition, and community. His analysis of our global future makes us understand that artists faced with the challenge of finding a healthy balance between preserving a sense of identity and community in an era of globalization will need to learn to create artworks that combine pride in roots with an overview of the world as shared by others.

Yale University computer science professor David Gelernter (1998) subtitled his book, *Machine Beauty*, "Elegance and the Heart of Technology." Artists educated for the future will need to enter into the heart of the technology they are using to locate its inner beauty as a powerful source for their artistic creativity. Gelernter emphasizes that the scientific and engineering geniuses in the computer field are the people with the keenest aesthetic senses, the ones who are capable of creating beauty at every level, in the most important interfaces and programming languages and the winning algorithms.

**Beyond the Digital**
Stephen Wilson's chapter, "Beyond the Digital: Preparing Artists to Work at the Frontiers of Technoculture" sets the tone for the first section of this book and gives it its title. He proposes that although the impact of digital technology is significant, it forms part of something much more momentous that is intertwined with the aesthetic, ethical, cultural, and social-economic. Scientific research and technological development are radically transforming basic philosophical ideas about the nature of the physical world, time and space, the nature of life and intelligence, and the limits in our abilities to transform the world and humanity. Art redefined by a digital revolution linked to revolutions brewing in the realms of biology, neurophysiology, materials science, and cosmology require new methods for educating artists at the intersections of art, science, technology, and culture.

Roy Ascott, in his chapter, "Pixels and Particles: The Path to Syncretism," also proposes that the digital moment has passed in the sense that interfaces are migrating from a cabled, box-bound environment to wireless multi-sensory, multi-modal, mobile, wearable forms, and eventually with biochips implanted in our bodies. He coins the word "moistmedia" as the symbiosis between dry pixels and wet biomolecules. Our artistic inquiry and design skills will be devoted to creating moistmedia artworks from which new metaphors, new language, and new methodologies will arise. The dynamic interplay between digital, biological, and cultural systems calls for a syncretic approach to arts education realized through connectivity, immersion, interaction, transformation, and emergence. Ascott explains that young artists face the challenge of creating a syncretic art that explores telematics (planetary connectivity), nanotechnology (bottom-up construction), quantum computing (augmented cyberception), cognitive science and pharmacology (field consciousness), and esoterica (psychic instrumentality).

In "Sustaining Creativity and Losing the Wild," Carol Gigliotti, who teaches media courses as well as environmental ethics for art, design and media students, discusses metaphoric approaches in new media art and design education that envisions natural and human creativity as integrated components in a universal creative process, both of which need to be sustained. She argues that new media art students cannot ignore, for instance, how the mining of coltan in Africa needed in the manufacture of laptop computers wrecks havoc on the environment and creates political conflict and violence. Her chapter explores the deep connections between the suppression and destruction of creativity in natural systems and the corrosive effects of that destruction on sustained human creativity. Gigliotti argues that embedding this kind of information in a digital art curriculum is the key for placing the medium in a critical cultural context, one in which the social and political implications of the digital medium are made transparent. What this means for educating artists for the future is that we learn to avoid contributing to the destruction of our own creativity by our failure to see the connection of that creativity to the natural world.

Mark Amerika in his chapter, "Making Space for the Artist," refers not to the ecological space of the biosphere, but to the space of mind that *digital-artists-to-be* shape into artistic personas through their own unique creative paths. He tells his students that there is no proper straightforward path for constructing the "right" set of digital personas or sure-fire way for creating their own one-person "art-making machine." Amerika characterizes his own path as being full of aimless drifting, a multi-linear narrative of freeform nomadic excursions. This technomadic journey of writing, performing, hacking, and directing "takes place" in a networked "space of flows" littered with the remains of his collective failures and – much to his total surprise – a few successes. He teaches through example how to enter a space of mind where the *artist-as-medium* improvisationally composes on and in the open playing fields of potential artistic development, while pointing to the radical, intersubjective experiences we are always filtering, tracing, remixing, and otherwise conjuring into multiple and hybridized works of art when tapping into our unconscious potential. His students learn what it takes to participate in a highly technologized, social process of self-motivated personal discovery, social networking, and artistic invention, so that they can step into the fold and "play themselves" – even if that means having to reinvent their artistic personas over and over again.

### Networked Times
Robert W. Sweeny's chapter, "Unthinkable Complexity: Art Education in Networked Times," explores the challenges and possibilities for educating artists in a network society, looking to connections between multidisciplinary complexity theory, art theory fusing physical and virtual space, and educational theory that was put into practice in open classrooms a half-century ago. Sweeny proposes a form of networked pedagogy that is informed by and responsive to complex networks of unthinkable complexity. Teaching in the network society, through hybrid networks consisting of traditional physical spaces and cyberspaces, offers art educators opportunities to address the potential for complex networks in the service of developing new forms of pedagogy and art. Based upon complexity theory, characteristics of both networked art and learning

are: differentiation, interaction, self-organization, and emergence. As differentiated networks and artworks interact, self-organize, and emerge, educators have the opportunity to think the unthinkable, working the 'net through educational practices that are creative, critical, and complex. The structure of the Internet, composed of research tools, interactive social space, communication channel, and art gallery, parallels the structure of open classrooms in which students gained access to a variety of forms of information and took part in social exchanges. The open classroom in networked times offers an educational model for educating artists in a hybrid environment of real and virtual spaces.

In his chapter, "Art/Science and Education," Stefan Sonvilla-Weiss focuses on how cultural, intellectual, and spiritual fields are prerequisite to evolutions in art, science, and technology. He identifies the main question for educating artists in a digital network culture as how the increased recognition of interconnections in differing fields of knowledge, systems, and ecology theories is perceived in light of learning tasks. Chaos theory and self-organization and social network theories suggest that we acquire learning competences from forming connections between disparate ideas and fields in which links between them represent survival in an interconnected world. Amplification of learning, knowledge, and understanding through the extension of a personal network into a global network is the epitome of a new learning culture. The task of tomorrow's artist is that of an intermediary, a catalyst between diverse fields of knowledge, ways of thinking, social models, and solution strategies based upon cooperation, communication, and interaction. Digital network culture not only changes modes of media production and distribution, but it transforms art from object making to art as processes of creating "immaterial" rhizome-like structures of remotely connected individuals in online communities. "Print and radio tell; stage and film show; cyberspace embodies."

Sonvilla-Weiss suggests that pedagogical strategies to encourage more student-centered, self-regulated, participative and active learning include learning modules that are more responsive to change than full courses, projects that emphasize explorative learning and research-based design, and internships in diverse scientific, economic, artistic, public, and administrative fields. In addition, he develops a curricular topography addressing three realms of learning: 1) sensual, mental, and reflexive media perception and usage; 2) spatio-temporal perception and contextualization in creative processes; and 3) contextualization of forms of knowledge and design.

Ron Burnett argues in his chapter, "Learning, Education and the Arts in a Digital World," that digital networks of communication and the speed with which artists and designers have made use of these networks has led to a broadening of all fields that make it necessary for art and design schools and departments to radically alter not only their practices, but also their disciplinary structures. The institutional infrastructure upon which so much education in art and design has depended – discipline-specific departments, specialized educational models, classroom lectures, studios as sites of teaching and practice, learning as training and vice versa, no longer operate with the same authority for students who do schoolwork and create music on computers, chat, surf, and post their videos on the Internet, use iPods, take photos with cell phones, and create their own blogs. Art students need to be challenged to understand the impact of these activities on themselves and on society and analyze whether they open up critical discourses or shut down serious thinking. There is no question that the depth of involvement and commitment of students to these media have changed them and their views of the world. It is, however, essential that learning about these phenomena is framed by a self-reflexive understanding of their structure, function, and role as tools of communication and interaction. Digital technologies can be change agents when they encourage new kinds of interdisciplinary learning that provide students with tools to evaluate alternative ideas, practices, and vantage points and create revolutionary ways of seeing beyond works of art to seeing the world that surrounds and enframes them.

Jill Scott directs a doctoral program in Zurich in which students work with mentors from both the fields of art and science. This program is a node in the global network of the Planetary Collegium headed by Roy Ascott, author of the 'Pixels and Particles' chapter in this book. In her paper, 'Afference and Efference: Encouraging Social Impact through Art and Science Education', Scott explores new forms of social advocacy education emerging from sharing of knowledge between the arts and the sciences in research laboratories and facilitated environments. She uses the neuroscience terms *afferent* and *efferent* to describe somatosensory perceptual processes our bodies undergo in relation to the perception of our immediate environment. While *afferent* is the process of carrying information inward to a central organ, *efferent* processes are those which proceed outward from the center, carrying sensation back to the peripheral parts of the body. She expands these terms from neuroscience into the field of higher education by developing *efferent education* as a socially responsive form of active learning to aid artists in developing unique voices about ethics and science in relation to public understanding. Immersive strategies for learning in the context of laboratories and trans-disciplinary seminars not only facilitate learning for artists, but also help scientists find new ways of communicating with the general public.

**Polycultural Perspectives**
The first two sections of the book primarily explored educating artists in networked times of global reach and transnational interconnectivity. Art, however, has always been an expression of a particular community's cultural values. Thomas Freidman symbolizes globalization and technological progress by the luxurious Lexus sedans that he saw being built entirely by robots in Toyota City and local cultural values by centuries-old olive trees rooted in the Land of Israel.

> Olive trees are important. They represent everything that roots us, anchors us, identifies us and locates us in this world – whether it be belonging to a family, a community, a tribe, a nation, a religion or, most of all, a place called home. Olive trees are what give us the warmth of family, the joy of individuality, the intimacy of personal

rituals, the depths of private relationships, and well as the confidence and security to reach out and encounter others...So what does the Lexus represent? It represents an equally fundamental, age-old human drive – the drive for sustenance, improvement, prosperity, modernization – as it is played out in today's globalization system. (Friedman 2000: 31–33)

Although the emphasis of the chapters in this section is on the olive tree, the authors create a lively dialogue between the forces of globalization represented by digital media art and cultural values – ancient and contemporary – of India, China, and Turkey. The concluding chapter in this section is a transcultural dialogue between a professor of interactive arts and technology in Canada, who grew up in a remote part of the U.S. raised by her grandfather, a folk healer in the tradition of the Carpathian Mountains of Poland, and her South Korean doctoral student whose background of Buddhism and Eastern philosophy related to mind-body interconnectivity shaped her interactive immersive artworks.

The first chapter in the Polycultural Perspectives section, "Expressing with Grey Cells: Indian Perspectives on New Media Art," begins with Vinod Vidwans' erudite overview of a tradition of creativity in the arts that spans millennia on the Indian subcontinent. This overview forms the theoretical foundation for his description of the multifaceted confluence between traditional Indian perspectives and directions in art and education shaped by new media technologies. Art in both ancient India and the post-digital age share profound computational and mathematical foundations, convergence and interdependence between fields, and an aesthetics of virtual reality. The Sanskrit word for art is *kala*, etymologically derived from the root that means counting, calculating or computation, indicates a deep level of correlation between artistic quantification and the quality of aesthetic experience. Art, science, and technology in India were integrated activities shaped by awe, curiosity, primordial quest, magic, and mystery. The contemporary orchestration of art, science, and technology in a symphony of new media art mirrors the interdependent flow that guided art students in ancient India from learning sculpture, image-making, painting, architecture, to theatrical arts, dance, instrumental music, vocal music, composing songs, prose and poetry, literature, languages, grammar, logic, and mathematics. Mathematical aesthetics coupled with the interdependence of various fields of human endeavor and the consequent educational necessity of learning them together indicate a living pedagogy of arts in the civilization of India that resonates powerfully in the education of artists for a post-digital future in which the formal logic of algorithms offers infinite creative possibilities, ineffable corollaries of timelessness, and unfolding of hidden metaphors in the unfathomable depths of structures of space and time.

Wengao Huang's chapter, "New Media Art as Embodiment of the Tao," reinforces through Chinese philosophy the contemporary significance of Asian traditions at the intersections of art, science, and technology that Vinod Vidwans presents through his Indian perspective. When I first encountered a paper that Wengao Huang wrote on the resonance between ancient Chinese philosophy and new media art, I was intrigued by the parallels between his explorations of art as the embodiment of Tao and my work on the confluence between ancient Jewish philosophy and new media art as expressed through kabbalah, a down-to-earth mystical tradition of Western civilization (Alexenberg 2006b). Although we live and work at opposite ends of Asia – China and Israel – I had the opportunity to meet Wengao Huang at the 2006 Consciousness Reframed conference in England and discuss his chapter for this book and our common background of being scientists-turned-artists exploring spiritual dimensions of the post-digital age derived from two very different cultures. We were both amazed that ancient spiritual traditions arising simultaneously on the east and west coasts of Asia millennia ago addressed creativity and the arts with a common language perhaps encoded in the shared consciousness of all humanity. Our dialogue prompted me to write "Ancient Schema and Technoetic Creativity" in the journal *Technoetic Arts* (Alexenberg 2006a), in which I explore how schematic systems originating in Chinese and Jewish traditions offer fresh insights into the structure of human consciousness and its creative expression in technoetic art.

In his chapter, "New Media Art as Embodiment of the Tao," Wengao Huang presents evidence of how the natural sciences are creating a new paradigm that demonstrate what the ancient Chinese perceived as the Tao – dynamic monism in which matter is not concrete and the self not centered and unified. New media arts are embracing this holistic paradigm derived from complexity science that finds parallels in the traditional Chinese spirit's emphasis on connections, transformations, and emergence. Generative and interactive art utilizing emerging technologies have great potential to vividly demonstrate the transforming spirit of the Tao and give new meanings to the saying within the traditional Chinese art world: "Art is the embodiment of the Tao." He describes his artwork on interactive morphogenesis that derives from his research in biotechnology, computer graphics, and ancient Chinese philosophy. The virtual creatures that he creates in artificial evolutionary developmental systems are based upon a biologically plausible developmental model guided by interactions between genes and a morphogenetic field of protein gradients. Artistic expression in new media does not fit within boundaries of areas of conventional specialization. Traditional Chinese education has aimed to produce generalists. Various artistic talents, from painting, calligraphy, music, literature, to chess playing, have been considered necessary for an intellectual to cultivate himself toward the Tao. Underlying various art forms there is a unifying aesthetics based on *Ch'i*, which links the arts, humanity, and the universe in a great whole that promotes artistic creativity. New media art education also calls for generalists rather than specialists. Wengao Huang emphasizes that new media art is the alchemy of our time, bringing technology, consciousness, and culture into a global crucible that leads to the only reality – the Tao, transforming diversity within coherence.

Ismail Ozgur Soganci discusses in his chapter, "Between Hyper-Images and Aniconism: New Perspectives on Islamic Art in the Education of Artists," the curricular neglect in Turkish art schooling of the aniconic tradition in traditional Ottoman visual culture.

This negligence stems from the wholesale adoption of Eurocentric models for educating artists that emphasized figurative art and modernist movements as part of the revolution to Westernize Turkey in the first quarter of the twentieth century. Today, the blind adherence to these adopted aesthetic values make new media art forms unwelcome in most Turkish art schools and university art departments where the rich aniconic past almost always remains unmentioned. Soganci presents a highly original thesis that the aniconic tradition of Islamic art with its emphasis on mathematical beauty, geometric design, and abstract ornamentation can counterbalance the excessive hyper-image bombardment of contemporary media. Aniconism has untouched potentials for enlightening prospective artists about the negative, unwanted, and alienating consequences of the constant barrage of hyper-images and the exhibitionist urges so common among the current generation. He invites not only Turkish art educators, but educators in new media art worldwide, to evaluate the consensus reached by Abrahamic/Byzantine/Islamic visual traditions as possible cures for today's societies of spectacle by quieting the media blitz with the meditative patterns of an art of non-figurative mathematical geometries conceptually linked to the algorithmic power of digital media.

"Touching Light: Post-Traditional Immersion in Interactive Artistic Environments" is a transcultural dialogue between Diane Gromala, a Polish-American professor of interactive arts and technology at a Canadian university, and her Korean doctoral student, Jinsil Seo, who explores the artistic significance of immersion in responsive and interactive spaces. This chapter presents examples of Seo's art-research work in which her cultural background colors her explorations of ambient immersive space, body interaction with environment, ephemeral and transient states of consciousness, and Ch'i as the flow of energy, in creating artworks in which bodily movements trigger interaction and immersion. Seo describes how her research and artmaking is influenced by growing up in South Korea where she developed a deep level of understanding of the conceptual connectivity between consciousness and immersion related to space and time derived from Buddhist thought. In counterpoint to Seo's description, Gromala comments on the interplay between her cultural background, her experience as an artist exploring interactive technologies, and her educational philosophy. Gromala relates how her pedagogical orientation is shaped by being raised in a remote part of the United States by her folk-healer grandfather from the Carpathian Mountains, early Montessori training, a ruinous stint in a Catholic school, and outsider suspicions evoked by her Ivy League education. She attempts to create enough space for her students to work independently, to advise them on how to hunt for what they need, how to build intellectual frameworks and connections with their work, how academia works, and how to creatively navigate around the limitations that new forms of technology and new ways of knowing provoke.

## Reflective Inquiry

There is a growing literature in art education and curriculum theory that employs the qualitative research methodology autoethnography. Rita Irwin calls this autoethnographic methodology in the life of an *A*rtist/*R*esearcher/*T*eacher "a/r/tography," a hybrid form of action research creating its rigor through continuous reflexivity, discourse analysis, and hermeneutic inquiry" (Irwin 2006, p. 78). Artists-researchers-teachers inhabit and explore the borderlands between art, science, and education, integrating knowing, doing, making through aesthetic experiences that elegantly flow between intellect, feeling, and practice to create and convey meaning. A/r/tographers search for new ways to understand realms of learning at the interface between their artmaking, research, and teaching through attention to memory, identity, reflection, meditation, storytelling, interpretation, and representation (Irwin and de Cosson 2004). In the "Reflective Inquiry" section of this book, the autobiographical discourses of a diverse group of artists/researchers/teachers highlight episodes in their lives that offer lessons of significance for the education of artists for the future.

Michael Bielicky's autoethnographic narrative, "Media Golem: Between Prague and ZKM," forms a transition between the Polycultural Perspectives and Reflective Inquiry sections of this book. His polycultural perspective had its origins in his overnight transition from a young Communist pioneer to a Western hippie when his Jewish family ran from the advance of Russian tanks into Czechoslovakia to live in Germany. Three decades later, after having studied medicine and art in Dusseldorf, he was encouraged by his mentor, video art pioneer Nam June Paik, to return to Prague and create a new media department in the art academy there. During his sixteen years teaching in Prague, Bielicky was also instrumental in creating centers for new media arts throughout the former Communist world from Bucharest, Odessa, and Moscow to Alma-Ata in Kazakhstan. He discovered that the newfound freedom in Eastern Europe produced a level of energy and creative potential that was stronger than what was happening in Western Europe. Currently back in Germany as professor of new media art at the Hochschule für Gestaltung, linked to the ZKM Center for Art and Media in Karlsruhe, Bielicky reflects on how living at the intersections of Czech and German cultures triggers high levels of creative thought and action.

Bielicky sees the challenge in educating future generations in the new media arts in dealing with the rapidly changing conditions that make today's media theory stale tomorrow. The most significant change is the democratization of technologies that makes everyone a potential artist when powerful media tools that are cheap enough and compact enough for anyone to create serious digital artworks at home. Although primarily conceptual in orientation, his department in Prague was a laboratory for his students to experiment freely. They became more his partners than his students. Bielicky's experience taught him that project-centered study motivates students more and is generally a more efficient educational methodology than more formal methods. He believes that students should be encouraged to break out of institutionalized frameworks and ask if the so-called art system (art school, gallery, museum, art critic, curator, art magazine, art fair, etc.) is meaningful for a new media artist in a post-digital era.

He describes how his own most recent artwork in collaboration with his wife operates completely outside of the art system. Equipped with a car, a laptop, a compact powerful projector, and a small power generator, they are able to create an instant presence in the urban landscape. They transform city architecture into dynamic and living organisms. Without any on-site preparation and without any permits, they create guerrilla-theater style projections. Within less than ten minutes, they can illuminate giant buildings with their computer-animated urban screening project reaching huge audiences that would probably never walk into a gallery or museum.

In his narrative, "Learning through the Re-embodiment of the Digital Self," Yacov Sharir develops his educational philosophy and practice by tracing his artistic journey from learning music, ceramics, sculpture, and dance in Israel to teaching dance, improvisation, choreography, multi-disciplinary art/technology, and virtual reality/ cyberspace at the University of Texas. Sharir's artistic quest that led to the immersion of his wired body in virtual environments had its origins in his childhood studies with a violin teacher whose way of playing made him feel as if his teacher was wearing the music, as if the music had become his second skin. He taught young Yacov that technological success playing the right notes was not enough without learning to embody the overall mood, the atmosphere, the colors, and the appreciation of meaning. "Tell me your story through your music," his violin teacher insisted. This early learning experience deeply influenced his artistic development and his ways of working and teaching.

After studying art and dance in Jerusalem, he lived two professional lives simultaneously – shaping raw earth into works of clay art while transforming his body into art material as a dancer with the renowned Bat Sheva Dance Company. His trans-disciplinary life also became a trans-cultural life as he moved to Texas to found the American Deaf Dance Company, which pioneered in including deaf artists in professional dance, and the Sharir Dance Company, for which he choreographed and created original technologically mediated compositions using wearable computers, technologically charged interactive systems, virtual reality, interactive video art, and computer-animated cyber human performers. He teaches his students how to build content and meaning through collaborative creation of interactive art that explores how the disembodied digital self is re-embodied in cyber-bodies occupying increasingly immersive cyber-worlds.

Eduardo Kac's chapter, "Life Transformation – Art Mutation," traces two decades of his work as an artist exploring the boundaries between humans, animals, and robots. In his artworks, he appropriates and subverts contemporary technologies to *enact* critical views rather than making detached comments on social change. He makes present in the physical world new transgenic organisms which seek to open a new space for both emotional and intellectual aesthetic experience. The implications of this ongoing work have aesthetic, social, and educational ramifications, crossing disciplines and providing material for further reflection and dialogue. His transgenic art using genetic engineering to create unique living beings was a natural development from his biotelematic art in which biology and networking are coupled to produce a hybrid of the living and the telematic, and from his earlier telepresence art in which humans coexist with other humans and non-human animals through telerobotic bodies. Kac appropriates the techniques of biotechnology to critique the language of science and its inherent ideologies, while developing transgenic art as an alternative means for individual expression. As an artist and as an educator heading a department of art and technology, he explores multiple social implications of genetics, from unacceptable abuse to its hopeful promises, from the notion of "code" to the question of translation, from the synthesis of genes to the process of mutation, from the metaphors employed by biotechnology to the fetishization of genes and proteins, from simple reductive narratives to complex views that account for environmental influences.

Aaron Marcus develops guidelines for educating designers and artists for the future by considering past issues and their resolution in his extensive career that evolved from physics at Princeton to art and graphic design at Yale to user-interface/information-visualization design at Aaron Marcus and Associates (AM+A), the leading-edge international design firm that he founded in 1982 and currently heads. His pioneering work using digital technologies in art and design at AT&T Bell Labs in the 1960s and Lawrence Berkeley Laboratory's Computer Science and Mathematics Department in the early 1980s, coupled with his decades of teaching and practice make his recommendations relevant to the education of students for an age of ubiquitous computing, virtual social networks, cross-national cultures, and access from one's current location to almost any text, image, sound, and experience from any time and place. Marcus proposes educating designers for a worldwide sensorium, a world of unimaginable size, density, variety, intensity, and activity, in which much is changing rapidly even while powerful economic and political forces grind slowly, relentlessly onward, challenging all that we have as human, corporeal, mental, cognitive, spiritual, and emotional beings. His creative journey from young cartoonist and photographer to university professor, from conceptual artist and computer graphics artist to graphic designer, from corporate designer to information-designer, from print designer to user-interface designer was a bumpy road with many unexpected twists and turns that taught him lessons significant in preparing students for an unknown future. They should learn to not to be so immersed in tools and techniques that they forget the larger issues of theory and practice, to expect the unexpected, to realize that help may come when most needed from unexpected sources, to facilitate people making smarter decisions faster, to think about other cultures and times, to conceptualize everything in a system of interrelated parts, to scan the horizon to discern future developments in knowledge-oriented communications, and to cultivate a terminology to quickly, efficiently, and successfully describe their work.

### Emerging Praxis
Art historian Edward A. Shanken reflects on teaching about the entwined histories of art, science, and technological media. In the absence of faculty in art history departments

to teach these entwined histories, studio faculty are often entrusted with providing students with a strong grounding in the history and theory of art, science, and technological media in order to become effective practitioners. The traditional use of slides or other still images to teach art history is inadequate given the time-based and interactive nature of much work in this interdisciplinary field. The conceptual and technical richness of the best artworks, exciting and inspiring for scholars, are difficult to teach given the absence of canonical literature and media resources. Shanken has found a media-archaeological approach to be an effective pedagogical tool, as historical attempts to create surrogates, simulations, and immersive environments can be mapped onto more recent artworks involving technologies such as robotics, artificial life, and virtual reality. Shanken argues further that students who do not develop a firm grasp of the pluralism that characterizes contemporary art practice and similar command over the concepts and histories of information theory, cybernetics, computing, networking, and media cannot hope to have anything but a superficial understanding and appreciation of the contributions of art-science-technology to discourses on the future of art and visual culture. It is important, moreover, to emphasize the particular contexts in which historical and contemporary works emerge, for it is these conditions that make those works distinctive and significant statements about the epistemological and ontological circumstances of the cultures that produce them. Shanken teaches his students how to develop strategies for thinking about systems and systemic behavior illustrated with examples from art history that function as visual markers of parallel cultural developments. In this way, he helps his students "learn how to think with their eyes and see with their minds."

Bill Seaman describes a generative emergent approach to graduate education in the Digital+Media department that he created at Rhode Island School of Design. This exemplary educational program fosters a richly focused liberal arts/conceptual/social agenda in relation to a digital practice in counter distinction to a set of common practices that are passed on to students in a "cookie cutter" manner. His teaching methods articulate a core set of concepts and approaches by providing essential texts and central technological methodologies augmented with a broad range of study related to more individual, eclectic practices and research potentials. The curriculum at the Digital+Media department begins with a "Continuum Studio" where students explore the continuum from the physical to the digital while simultaneously building a space for conceptual exchange, critique, and reflection. Students develop a vocabulary of relevant processes to help them define their own working processes. Along with the Continuum Studio, students participate in a course in the history of digital media focusing on interactivity, in a seminar/tutorial that Seaman teaches, and in lectures by prominent guest artists. Students also choose between a variety of "Node" classes, borrowing a navigational concept from the structure of the Internet. These classes balance the study of technology and art (or design) with inquiry that is conceptual, social, and cultural. They bring core Digital+Media department students together with a broad range of students from other disciplines to facilitate understanding and communicating multiple approaches to contemporary creative technological practice.

Central is a multi-perspective approach to knowledge acquisition where students develop a bridging language and articulate relationships that are relevant to their own fields.

Shlomo Lee Abrahmov demonstrates how visual literacy is developed in his students by combining *reading* and *writing* images. He suggests a set of common categories for both activities based on observing and creating three levels of meaning in images: Factual, Interpretive, and Conceptual. Abrahmov proposes that an effective strategy for teaching visual literacy is a blended approach where the writing of images is through face-to-face teaching on campus and the reading of images is through e-Learning using a web-based teaching platform. Such an approach creates synergy between theoretical and practical activities in a digital age when images become fluid and are used to convey messages and intentions with ease. E-Learning has been shown to be more effective than traditional methods in teaching the reading of images since it provides opportunities for individual students to engage in interpretation and analysis at their own pace. An open submission model in which students post their assignments on a course website and participate in a group discussion board allows them to learn from peer examples.

In "The Creative Spirit in the Age of Digital Technologies," Lucia Leão proposes seven tactical exercises to enhance the creative potential of her students of technoetic arts and new media in Brazil. She traces parallels between the sacred dimensions of education as the search for meaning, creativity as a path to self-discovery, the search for a personal sacred meaning, and new technologies as tools to stimulate interconnected consciousness. The seven learning exercises Leao describes follow mythic movements of the labyrinth path that challenge her students to develop aesthetic dimensions of human experience that make the learning process a path to creative liberation. She invites students: 1) to follow an inner trajectory into a spiritual realm as a creative path to self-discovery; 2) to reflect on non-sense aspects of their lives to discover and appreciate dichotomies, complexities, and ambivalences; 3) to visualize complex systems by mapping their multiple affiliations; 4) to get in touch with the collective unconscious and its archetypes while exploring authorship in an information society by using digital systems for collective writing; 5) to experience their own bodies in relation to the collective body of their class, the Gaia body of Planet Earth, and the expansive body of the Universe; 6) to develop the ability to see inspiration everywhere as the basis for exercising the creative spirit; 7) to go back to the world, sharing knowledge, developing the art of listening and the art of tolerance, and becoming an agent for integrative coexistence.

### Realms of Learning
The concluding section identifies realms of learning that weave together the complex issues of theory and practice in a post-digital Conceptual Age by reflecting on episodes in my self-education as an artist/researcher/teacher in the complex playing field where art, science, technology, education, culture, and consciousness intersect and interact. Through reflective inquiry, I discern realms of learning emerging from my learning path

that spans more than a half-century from my childhood summers in the Catskill Mountains of upstate New York, when I had no clue that art and science were different fields of human endeavor, to my current work creating a new school of art and multimedia design in Israel. These pedagogically relevant episodes include: immersion in the life of a barn swallow, designing hands-on science experiments for children to learn about their senses, researching the psychology of aesthetic experience in the creative work of scientists and artists, developing an integrated art-science curriculum for Israeli youth from diverse cultural backgrounds, revealing beauty hidden in the cellular structure of a blade of grass, constructing a semiotic taxonomy of contemporary art forms, creating a biofeedback digital imaging system generating mind-body self-portraits, producing an art exhibition to explore the spiritual dimensions of the electronic age, sending cyberangels on a circumglobal flight using communications satellites, collaborating with elders of different ethnic communities in creating monumental works of environmental public art, working with students in the Everglades on creating ecological artworks, creating a responsive digital artwork for blind people to "see" images through their fingers, creating a website inviting people to photograph God revealed in their everyday lives, creating an Internet artwork that expresses moral outrage in the tradition of *Guernica*, and integrating theory and practice in a new school for learning at the intersections of art, science, technology and culture.

Realms of learning for educating artists that I identify from these episodes in my journey are: awesome immersion, playful exploration, aesthetic creativity, morphological analysis, interdisciplinary imagination, morphodynamic beauty, semiotic communication, cybersomatic interactivity, global connectivity, polycultural collaboration, ecological perspective, responsive compassion, spiritual emergence, moral courage, and holistic integration.

## Works Cited

Alexenberg, M. (2006a). "Ancient Schema and Technoetic Creativity." *Technoetic Art: A Journal of Speculative Research*. Vol. 4, No. 1.

Alexenberg, M. (2006b). *The Future of Art in a Digital Age: From Hellenistic to Hebraic Consciousness*. Bristol, U.K.: Intellect Books.

Freidman, T. L. (2000). *The Lexus and the Olive Tree: Understanding Globalization*. New York: Ancor Books/Random House.

Gardner, H. (1999). *Intelligence Reframed: Multiple Intelligences for the 21st Century*. New York: Basic Books.

Gelernter, D. (1998). *Machine Beauty: Elegance and the Heart of Technology*. New York: Basic Books.

Pink, D. H. (2006). *A Whole New Mind: Why Right-brainers will Rule the Future*. New York: Riverhead Books.

# BEYOND THE DIGITAL

# Beyond the Digital: Preparing Artists to Work at the Frontiers of Technoculture

## Stephen Wilson

What kind of preparation do artists need? Some would emphasize cultivation of personal vision and creativity, emotional self-knowledge, intuition, and spiritual awareness. Others highlight technical skills of working with media, finding powerful ways to communicate, exposure to the great works of the past, and a strong grounding in art history. Still others stress skills of socio-political analysis, sensitivity to one's own cultural identity, and awareness of critical themes in understanding culture and media.

These emphases are quite different and their relative importance varies with ideas about what is art. In the contemporary postmodern world, the nature of art is greatly contested as is the question of how to prepare artists. Framing the question as "how does one educate artists for a digital age" focuses the challenge a bit. Highlighting "digital age" implies a special attention to what might be needed for artists to function and respond to a technologically oriented world. Although the meta-themes in educating artists suggested above are important and under-analyzed, this essay focuses on the special issues of educating artists in a technological age.

### More than Digital

The term "digital age" is misleading. Digital technology is significant but it is part of something much more momentous. Scientific research and technological development are doing much more than creating new gadgets and media. They are radically transforming basic philosophical ideas about the nature of the physical world, time, and space; the nature of life and intelligence; and the limits in our abilities to transform the world and humanity. The technological is intertwined with the ethical, cultural, and social-economic. The impact of the digital revolution has been enormous, but it is only one of many revolutions that are brewing – for example, the biological, materials science, neurological, and cosmological. It is critical to consider how to educate artists for a scientific/technological age, not just a digital age.

Historically, the arts alerted people to emerging developments, examined the unspoken implications, and explored alternative futures. As the centers of cultural imagination and foment of the times have moved to the technology labs, the arts have not understood the challenge. It is a critical error to conceptualize research as merely some narrow, technical, specialized inquiry. Merely assimilating the new gizmos to create new media is a timid response.

The arts have a much more profound calling. They can become an independent zone of research – pursuing agendas ignored by commercial interests and scientific disciplines and integrating critical commentary with the search for new knowledge and the elaboration of new technical possibilities. Those who believe that the arts are now up to date because they pay attention to digital technology have misunderstood the course of history because the research goes on – investigating many other fields in which the arts should be proactive pioneers rather than merely consumers of the results.

This essay examines this challenge: Assume a definition of art that sees keeping watch on the cultural frontier as one of its central functions. Assume an analysis that scientific and technological research and all their associated implications are critical drivers of culture. The question, then, is how to prepare artists not only to master the historical issues for all artists, but also the special challenges of becoming a strong, independent voice who is competent and innovative in the worlds of both art and research.

The following sections will consider an idiosyncratic selection of historical approaches to this challenge, identify dimensions of variation that art curricula might address, and describe how the Conceptual Information Arts program, which I have been associated with, addresses these dimensions. The discussion is based on my experience as an artist working with emerging technologies, research conducted for my Information Arts book (Wilson 2002), and the 25-year history of the CIA program, which was one of the pioneering curricula preparing artists for technological research.

## An Abbreviated History of Art and Technology Programs

It is no wonder there is uncertainly about how to design art programs to respond to technological culture. The arts in general have been confused and slow to address technological change. It was only a few years ago that museums, curators, and collectors began to accept photography or video as valid art forms. Now there is beginning to be interest in computers, the Internet, and biology. Art influenced by science/technology has mostly been considered outside the mainstream. Most university art programs ignored these themes until the last decade.

The following section provides a brief idiosyncratic history of programs that addressed the challenge of preparing artists for a technological age. It considers the Bauhaus and then two pioneering programs I had personal contact with – Generative Systems and Conceptual Design.

## Bauhaus

The Bauhaus is often identified as a landmark in technological education for artists. This early-twentieth-century European institution brought together an illustrious faculty of artists, architects, designers, technology experimenters, theatre experts, etc. Rather than ignoring technological changes, it felt that artists and designers must embrace the new developments and work with them. All students were required to take part in a series of interdisciplinary workshops. They were not afraid to work with new materials – machinery, electricity, light, sound, factories, and industrial culture. The official Bauhaus history site gives a little flavor of that period.

> At a time when industrial society was in the grip of a crisis, the Bauhaus stood almost alone in asking how the modernization process could be mastered by means of design. Founded in Weimar in 1919, the Bauhaus rallied masters and students who sought to reverse the split between art and production by returning to the crafts as the foundation of all artistic activity and developing exemplary designs for objects and spaces that were to form part of a more humane future society. (Bauhaus-Dessau 2006)

Although most would acknowledge the conceptual leaps and significant innovations introduced at the Bauhaus, contemporary analysts note several problematic aspects. The philosophy was dominated by a modernist faith in rational design to fix the world, which from a postmodernist perspective seems quite naive and unsophisticated in its understanding of the complexities of modern techno-industrial culture. Activities were often dominated by utilitarian goals which may have de-emphasized more speculative art directions. Faculty and students were encouraged to work with industry and serve its purposes, perhaps without enough distance. As my upcoming book, *Great Moments in Art and Science* (Wilson in press), points out, there were many other artistic responses to the developments of science and technology in that era – for example, deep consideration of new scientific paradigms such as relativity, uncertainty, and the unconscious, emotional embrace, irreverence, skepticism, and resistance. As discussed in later sections, many of the Bauhaus themes continue as issues for contemporary curricula.

## Generative Systems

An extraordinary artist and educator named Sonia Sheridan introduced an innovative program called Generative Systems at the School of the Art Institute of Chicago in the 1970s. Sheridan had established her artistic reputation for her early experiments with color copier machines, which were just then becoming available. For example, she created a series of leaves which were synthetically colored by the machine to suggest the passing of seasons. Her work was collected widely by museums. She was also famous for taking on research residencies in industrial research labs (Sheridan 2006).

Students (including me) came from all over the world to study with her in relation to these new artistic technologies. But Sheridan held that the specific technologies should not be the focus. Much more interesting were the processes by which ideas could be transformed (the generative systems) and their philosophical and artistic implications. She felt the scope of interest must stretch from historical art practices to the latest technologies and research. She taught students to tear the machines apart in order to get at core understandings. She taught lessons in light, heat, time, sound, magnetics, etc. She taught courses called Process I and Process II. She noted the Bauhaus as a source of ideas but without the utilitarian preoccupation. In one famous move, she unplugged the machines for a year so students could overcome surface infatuation with the technologies. Years later, she wrote an article describing the curriculum in a special issue of the art/science journal *Leonardo* – "Mind/Senses/Hand: The Generative Systems Program at the Art Institute of Chicago 1970–1980". Here are some excerpts.

> At first we taught extensions of traditional art processes, but later we developed a full program of investigation into the transformative process occurring in art as a result of the impact of the communications revolution on the society at large. Generative systems was a research center; a resource and energy bank; a self-generating center where communication tools came and went while people remained; a nurturing ground for the Electronic Printout Systems (ESP); an extension into the future of photography, drawing, textiles and so on; a time machine from instant real time back to mechanical time; an attitude; an interactive force between industry, education and the public; and finally a viable alternative to the present art education system.
>
> From 67 to 77 we were occupied with exploring many communications systems, which we gathered in a great variety of unusual ways too numerous to discuss here. The communications technology that emerged in the 1960s validated the dreams of the most imaginative minds. Objects could be stretched in time, layered in time, scanned in time, filtered in time, metamorphosed and synchronized in time, in a matter of seconds, on the new electronic copiers, telecopiers, and computers and their moving lights, lenses, thermal and/or steel rollers and electronic gates...
>
> GS was an open system, an ever-changing system, in which the machines would come and go, but the humans would remain the constant factor. Courses would not be named for a specific and therefore static technological process – as had been done before with the standard art courses of printing, painting, photography and video – but rather for a dynamic process encompassing change, metamorphosis, inconsistency and chaos. (Sheridan 2002)

Many students remember the time fondly; it was an exhilarating place. Curiosity and inquiry ruled. Any source of ideas – e.g. from art, commerce, technology, or science, was welcome. She brought in guest speakers from outside the closed circle of art and art history. Sheridan was famous for her long, two-foot-long technician's screwdriver. Students brought in strange devices and she would enthusiastically take them apart to understand how they worked. It was clear that she was investigating and learning right along with the students. When a few advanced graduate students got interested in microcomputers, which were just then becoming available, she offered to change the budget for the department for that year so she could buy one to experiment with. M.F.A. students undertook highly speculative projects – for example, one experimented with growing mold as an image-generating system; another tried to understand fax technology sufficiently that he could create images by singing into the machine. Generative Systems was an influential source in shaping approaches to educating artists for a technological age.

**Conceptual Design**

Working within the Art Department at San Francisco State University, Bryan Rogers and James Storey created another pioneering program that attempted to define a relevant education for artists in the contemporary technological era. Storey was an inventor and product design researcher who worked in art education and Rogers was an artist who had a joint M.F.A. and Ph.D. in engineering from UC Berkeley. Rogers felt that most art programs clung to traditional formats that did not respond to the cultural foment of the scientific and technological worlds and to the innovations of art movements such as the conceptual, electronics, performance, and earth art, which challenged conventional notions. The program had several important features:

- Emphasis on ideas, not media (students were encouraged to work in whatever media served their agendas and to invent new media if necessary)
- Rigorous sequence of common core courses focused on processes and systems analysis. The sequence was stepped, growing more ambitious in its scope as students moved through the program
- Attention focused on the latest developments both in art and science/technology
- Use of geometry as a meta-language and skeleton for inquiries

Here are some excerpts from the SFSU catalog course descriptions from that era that described the core courses, designed and taught by Rogers.

Art 410...Process concepts; structure concepts; and geometrical form-language correlated with a variety of modes of art expression

Art 510...Continuation of Art 410 with emphasis on complex systems and environmental scale. (SFSU 1986)

Rogers noted that Buckminster Fuller was a significant intellectual resource for his thinking. He seemed influenced by Fuller's cross disciplinary philosophy that integrated art, design, engineering, and many other disciplines. Also important was Fuller's visionary "comprehensive anticipatory design" which stressed systems thinking and exhortation to avoid disciplinary blinders. For Fuller, artists, when functioning at their best, were exemplars of the open-minded, expansive innovators that the culture desperately needed. Here is an excerpt from Fuller's *Operating Manual for Spaceship Earth* (Fuller 1973) that gives a flavor of this thinking.

> The great aesthetic which will inaugurate the twenty-first century will be the utterly invisible quality of intellectual integrity; the integrity of the individual dealing with his scientific discoveries; the integrity of the individual in dealing with conceptual realization of comprehensive interrelatedness of all events; the integrity of the individual dealing with the only experimentally arrived at information regarding invisible phenomena; and finally integrity of all those who formulate invisibly within their respective minds and invisibly with the only mathematically dimensionable, advanced technologies, on the behalf of their fellow men. (Quoted in Vesna 2006.)

Conceptual Design hired me to help develop computer and technology-related aspects of the program. In 1980 the program offered one of the first computer graphics courses in the country aimed at artists and designers. A total of 150 potential students showed up for the first day trying to get in. We were amazed at the hunger of people outside technical professions for exposure to this technology. Gradually the program expanded the technology curriculum. Storey soon retired, and Rogers resigned to go to Carnegie Mellon to serve as chair of the art department. There he expanded his ideas to encompass the whole department and founded the Studio for Creative Inquiry. Later he moved on to expand on the ideas even further as dean of the School of Arts and Design at the University of Michigan. Those interested in arts education in a digital age should consult the descriptions of these models available online. Here are excerpts from the prospectus prepared by Rogers for the UM's new M.F.A. program.

> Today, viability in the larger cultural context requires that creative work engage a broader intellectual and social context. Context must be intentionally expanded beyond the self-referential assumptions of the 20th century. In an effort to address this requirement, the School of Art & Design has developed a graduate program in which all students develop a robust, intense engagement with one or more fields of knowledge in addition to art and design. The School intends that graduates of this program have the capability to thrive in a variety of public and private roles and to become cultural leaders in a rapidly changing global culture.

> The University of Michigan offers a panoply of intellectual resources matched by few institutions of higher learning. Many of these offerings are at the forefront of the nation's intellectual life – engaging the critical issues of our time. They address such domains as social justice, the life sciences and medicine, the environment, information-communication technologies, visual culture, law and business. These arenas, individually and in combination, are available at the University to inform creative work. They provide unparalleled opportunities for artists and designers to contribute to the comprehensive culture. (Rogers, 2002)

## Conceptual/Information Arts (CIA)

Conceptual Design eventually morphed into Conceptual/Information Arts (CIA). The name changed because many potential students, confused by term "design," came looking for traditional commercial design and because critical discourse stressed the ideological baggage and modernist assumptions of the term design. CIA is one of longest running programs that has directly addressed the issue of educating artists for a scientific/technological age. Since 1987 I have directed the program. This section briefly describes the curriculum and underlying rationale. The next section analyzes the educational issues that have been confronted and extracts dimensions of variability relevant to all similar programs. Over the years several colleagues have held positions in the department and helped define the curriculum, including George Legrady and Paula Levine. Legrady went on to help found the joint art/engineering MAT (Masters in Art & Technology) program at UC Santa Barbara. Levine is still the other core faculty of the CIA program.

Here is an excerpt from the CIA core concepts web page that presents the basic rationale and foci for the program and suggests some curricular issues to be addressed in technological arts education.

> CIA emphasizes systematic and structured processes of inquiry as an underlying support to the experimental searching at the fringes of the art world...CIA encourages students to supercede, question, and challenge traditional notions of what constitutes valid art media, contexts, and approaches. Students are encouraged to bring ideas, materials, and experiences from outside the art world to become focuses for their art. Students are challenged to combine traditional media and to incorporate new media. They are encouraged to follow their ideas and artistic impulses even if they don't take them into traditional validated art directions.

> Contemporary science and technology are radically transforming the world. The culture desperately needs artists to address these developments. The program encourages students to become knowledgeable about world views, ideas, and tools of these fields and to incorporate them in a non-superficial way into their art making. Students are expected to achieve expertise in technological areas in which most artists only superficially venture.

> Electronic technology and mediated information distribution seem on the surface value-free, but in fact, are causing major shifts in social interaction and the way we perceive ourselves and reality. Artworks generated through digital technology require some knowledge of strategies learned from semiotics, communications studies, and cultural theory for critically understanding technology's impact on culture. (CIA 2006a)

## Dimensions of Variability in Design of Curricula

Designers of programs to prepare students to function in a scientific/technological age face a variety of challenging philosophical and curricular questions. Here are some of questions to be confronted:

**Established Media versus Emerging Research**
Even within the technological arts there is a continuum stretching from established forms such as digital video, web design, animation to emerging research fields not yet established as media such as art & biology, alternative interfaces, etc. What range of this continuum does a curriculum propose to address? How does it propose to prepare students? Many new programs focus on digital media. They teach the latest software skills, digital aesthetics, and theoretical background. They claim that they have prepared artists for the digital age.

As explained earlier, this may not be enough. The research world is moving so fast that today's latest technology may soon be out of date. Even more importantly areas of research in science and technology that now seem esoteric and remote may end up being the core of cultural and media focus. Ironically, those focused on today's digital media may be making the same kind of mistake of complacency that art programs did in 1980 when they thought video was the end state of electronic media. Most art colleagues thought I was crazy to be interested as an artist and teacher in the computer; they dismissed it as only relevant to science and business. Similarly, in 1988, they dismissed our desire to start an Internet art course; the Internet was seen as only pertinent to the military and advanced computer science researchers.

If one defines an artist's role as innovator and anticipator, then the curriculum must reach out beyond today's new media. Indeed, in our kind of culture every area of scientific and technological research is a potential focus for the arts. This approach poses major challenges. How does one decide which emerging fields are worth investigating? How does one prepare to teach in such rapidly developing fields? How does one reconcile the need to teach students mastery of contemporary media while also preparing for more imminent futures?

As described in a later section, one strategy is to teach students meta-skills of how to learn. Still one must also address the concrete curriculum. CIA tries to mix contemporary skills with emergent fields. Most courses include elements that teach students to master current applications to as deep a level as possible. Students are warned, however, that in ten years they will probably be working with application environments that might be quite different. The courses ask them to penetrate deeper than surface software manipulations and to analyze the underlying structures of what they work with. For example, in an Interactive Events course, everyone is required to learn programming rather than just using canned behaviors because that helps to demystify the underlying bases of the application and prepares them to work with unrelated fields. In digital video, students are encouraged to think about the relative ease with which various kinds of narrative structures are supported and excluded in the applications.

But it is important to reach even further than deconstructing today's media. Core faculty in CIA are constantly investigating new areas of research and inventing new courses even while still in the midst of their own research. Faculty hope to model this ongoing investigative stance and make discussions of the research process part of the course. Operationally, it is quite a challenge for faculty to constantly design new courses, and many colleagues teaching in more conventional areas do not appreciate the professional load of constantly reinventing the curriculum. Within a limited budget, CIA also invites visiting artists to teach semester courses in new fields. Examples of the experimental courses taught by core and visiting faculty over the years include: Electronics, Robotics, Physical Computing, Art & Biology, Locative Media & GPS, Interactive Web, Gestural Interfaces, Interactive Video, Tactical Web Media, Interventionist Art, and Cartography.

In addition, CIA tries to take full advantage of university and community contexts. Many art students consider their university general education requirements an annoyance. CIA converts these requirements to an advantage by explicitly strategizing with students to make courses taken elsewhere in the university serve the research interests of their art practice. It also tries to teach students to see the research resources of the larger community as artistic resources by field trips and by bringing in guest speakers from outside of art. One advanced course requires all students to serve internships in art and/or research settings. For more on these approaches, see the later section describing the art & research course.

## Media Skills vs. Meta Skills

What should be the balance of teaching students specific digital applications and skills versus teaching more general orientations and knowledge? What is the ultimate future role imagined for the student – work within media companies, independent artist, member of research teams, some other yet undefined roles? Some programs believe that professional/vocational preparation in the skills needed today is the best way to serve students and the larger community and should be the agenda of higher education. Even many without a vocational emphasis believe the best preparation for artists is intensive hands-on training in the latest technical skills supplemented with some history, aesthetics, and theory. In this view practice is the core of being an artist and art is best learned through doing.

Others reverse the balance – believing that the best training is teaching meta-skills that can transcend the inevitable flux of change. They believe that it is impossible to predict what skills and perspectives will be essential a few years hence and that the student can be prepared by learning inquiry and analytical skills so they can cope with inevitable new developments whatever they may be. The term 'digital age' implies that one expects the technological world artists will deal with to be in flux and constant reinvention and, hence, a world where today's skills and perspectives can be rapidly out of date. Remember the thousands of students in 1900 preparing for a lifelong trade in blacksmithing. Indeed, this debate is at the core of liberal arts education, which is premised on the value of teaching fundamental non-discipline specific knowledge and intellectual skills as preparation for lifelong learning.

Focusing on meta-skills was a feature of Generative Systems and Conceptual Design programs described earlier. Others propose critical theory as the central meta-skill of the contemporary age (see section below). So, what are the meta-skills to best prepare students for a scientific/technological age?

CIA attempts a balance. The challenge may even be more complicated because SFSU is not a research university. Many CIA students are first-generation college students; even though they have chosen the arts, they (and their parents) still are searching for marketable skills on leaving. CIA teaches current state of the art applications but does as part of a conceptual, artistic inquiry. There are no courses named for applications. Nonetheless, students are expected to master these applications and to create works that show the highest level of technical excellence. For example, they learn digital video applications such as Final Cut Pro; yet they do in courses focused on art and history of narrative. They take conceptual strategies courses focused on abstract concepts such as time, randomness, and mapping in conjunction with the more technical courses. Every course includes critical analysis such as how the media produced with the software fits into a larger cultural and media context and a push to understand underlying structures of the software. Ironically, employers like their portfolios because they combine technical competence with unorthodox vision.

As described earlier, CIA also teaches courses focused on emerging research fields – for example, locative media, art & biology, interactive Internet, robotics, and physical computing. Also, a course called art & research focuses on highly experimental research fields (see description below). Working at this edge means there are few consumer applications available. Students must invent their own working environments and work with beta software and hardware still in development. When they have technical questions they must often go to sources outside of the art and media world. The meta-skills in these courses focus on processes of research and development.

Combining these speculative courses with those focused on more commonplace applications has unexpected benefits. Students who have constructed prototypes are much more enterprising and empowered in their approach to troubleshooting and innovation even when working with conventional applications and environments. This comfort and initiative often has benefits in conventional settings because supervisors chose them for challenging new assignments and it also prepares some to be entrepreneurs, starting their own businesses. For those working in the arts, this research background results in a productive skepticism about digital tools and a repertoire of ideas that help them keep their art fresh and compelling.

The balance is difficult. Small programs like CIA must juggle scope versus depth, and they must reassure students that the speculative courses will have long-term benefits. It is difficult for some students to accept the ultimate benefits of speculative courses like art & biology over courses which include training in common applications. This move to teach research skills has begun to spread. For more examples check out the ACE program at UC Irvine, the MAT program at UC Santa Barbara and the DX program at the University of Washington (ACE 2006; MAT 2006; DX 2006).

## Relationship to Traditional Art Curriculum and to Other Disciplines

What is the relative balance between education in traditional art practice and special preparation for work in experimental art practices? Digital/Technological Arts programs can be situated in many different places in the university – for example, cinema/film, design, art, communications, or in their own administrative entities. All programs face the challenge of defining their relationship to established curricula and their integration into other art and media forms. How much conventional history and practice should be required of students in experimental programs? Ideally students would take a full curriculum in both the historical and new forms but often there is not time and choices must be made.

The CIA program sits within the Art Department at San Francisco State University. This has been both an asset and a liability. Undergraduate students are required to fulfill the general requirements of the art department, which includes courses in art forms outside the CIA concentration and art history courses. M.F.A.'s similarly take courses along with students from historical media. It has been an asset in that students see the CIA grounded in the experimental traditions of the arts. Their visual work is informed by the centuries of practice and history of previous artwork. Because the faculty and fellow students they encounter in general art department courses may not be familiar with or may be skeptical or even hostile to experimental technology-based work, they are forced to articulate and explain their work to these audiences. Colleagues from historical art forms sometimes ask fresh questions and suggest connections that do not come up from those working exclusively with technology-based forms.

The link to the traditional art curriculum can also be a liability. Students working with experimental technology arts go in many directions and hence draw on many media traditions besides art – for example, theater, cinema, broadcast, music. For some, the most important sources may even be outside media and art; for example, computer science, engineering, or biology. For example, given limited time, an experimental sound artist might be better served by taking courses in the history of music or the physics of sound than conventional art courses. Also, other students and faculty members' unfamiliarity with issues of culture and technology/science and lack of interest can be demoralizing.

Art departments have a long-standing problem with the experimental forms of visual arts that do not fit into traditional media such as painting or sculpture – for example, conceptual, electronic, installation, ecological, performance, and interventionist art. Some "new genre" and "interdisciplinary" programs have been attempted although they never became an established feature of art programs.

For a long time, technological arts were placed in the same miscellaneous category outside of historical media. Programs such as Generative Systems and Conceptual Design often became a refuge for these kinds of arts because they did not give primacy to conventional media. These alternative traditions can be important resources for those working with technology. For example, CIA teaches these connections: dada, happenings, and performance art for those interested in interactivity, conceptual art for those interested in digital text or coding-based art, installation and kinetics art for those interested in robotics or physical computing, and situationist and interventionist art for those interested in locative media and tactical web interventions. All new technology programs (including those in disciplines such as cinema or music) must establish this balance – how much to emphasize historical connections versus how much to focus on the new developments.

**Cultural Theory**
Some programs believe that critical theory and analysis of the relationships among culture, media, and science and technology may be an extremely important tool for artists and media workers. What should be the balance of emphasis between theory and hands-on skills?

The last decades have seen a revolution in thinking about the relationship of theory to artistic practice and preparation. Some believe it is essential that artists be aware of semiotics, the sociocultural context of the art and media worlds and the meta-narratives that underlie their work – for example, in areas of representation, identity, and the body. In this view, skills in postmodern analysis are even more critical for artists who work with new media. Technology-based artists inevitably encounter issues such as the relationship of popular culture to high culture; virtuality and its impact on time, space and the body; the cultural context of technology developers' claims to progress; and the narratives of science such as objectivity, access to universal truth and immunity from cultural bias.

Preparing artists requires an explicit focus on theory. Conventional programs that emphasize self-expression and technical concerns are seen as romantically self-indulgent, naive, and out of touch with the present-day realities of cultural workers. Theory-based programs claim the work will be stronger if more time between teacher and student is spent on issues such as media archaeology and critiques of popular media and power structures than on technical production skills, which can be left to assistants.

The Technoculture program at UC Davis is a program well known for its emphasis on theory. Here is an excerpt from its website.

We concentrate on transdisciplinary approaches to artistic, cultural and scholarly production in contemporary media and digital arts, community media, and mutual concerns of the arts with the scientific and technological disciplines. In contrast to programs which see technology as the primary driving force, we place questions of poetics, aesthetics, history, politics and the environment at the core of our mission. In other words, we emphasize the "culture" in Technoculture. (Technoculture Program 2006)

The media studies program in the Literature, Communications, and Culture program at Georgia Tech University is another program well known for its theory emphasis. Here is an excerpt from the website for their STAC (Science, Technology & Culture) program.

Georgia Tech's STAC program is unique in its emphasis on communication skills, cultural interpretation, and textual analysis. Unlike similar programs, which look at science, technology, and the humanities as separate entities, STAC examines the modes of communication and understanding common to them all. As a result, students learn to master the range of methodologies of literary and cultural analysis needed to understand and interpret the "texts" ranging from novels and films to scientific journals and web pages that our society to communicate and to understand itself. STAC students pursue a course of study that is genuinely multidisciplinary and international, and that draws upon the multiple strengths of the Georgia Tech faculty. (STAC Program 2006)

Many contemporary programs see this theoretical literacy as the key meta-skill for preparing artists in a technological era. Others think the theory emphasis can sometimes be overemphasized. Every curriculum must determine a relevant balance.

### CIA's Art and Research Course
What are the best ways to build artists' curiosity, competence, and comfort with scientific research and emerging technologies? What should be the relationship of established scientific and technological disciplines to artistic practice? What are the meta skills artists need to flourish in this border area between the arts and research.

The previous sections discussed several approaches. Many of the CIA research-oriented courses include relevant skills such as critical theory, learning what is involved in developing prototypes, and working in areas of inquiry that are in the process of being defined. CIA also offered a course, called Art & Research, specifically aimed at the research meta skills. It asked students to familiarize themselves with information resources that could alert them to developments in the research world, develop competencies in interpreting scientific research, define areas of interest, develop art ideas related to those areas, establish contact with researchers, and to develop working styles necessary to move the research-based art projects along. They read articles and books exploring the relationships between research and culture, went on field trips, and heard visiting lecturers. Here is the description of the course from the Syllabus.

- What will be the art of the future?
- What is going on in scientific research labs?
- How can artists penetrate the secrets?
- How can artists build on research to create new art and media?

This course aims to prepare artists and new media professionals to become innovators in the development of emerging technologies. The past decades have shown that scientific and technological research that seemed esoteric and outside artistic or media realms can quickly become the core of new cultural trends and industries (for example, the basic ideas of the World Wide Web were considered wild, unrealizable ideas when first promulgated by Ted Nelson). Artists who want to help shape future cultural development and new media must become adept at understanding the worlds of research. This approach is critical for those who want to stay ahead of the current pace of change.

This course teaches students skills of monitoring scientific research and emerging technologies. It presents several areas of research that promise to be important in the future. It demonstrates the artistic possibilities by studying the pioneering work of artists around the world who work with concepts, tools, and information contexts not usually defined as art. It explores cultural theory that relates to the development of new technologies. It helps students to reconsider the interrelationships of science, technology, media, and art (CIA 2006b: Research Course Syllabus)

Several assignments focus on cultivating curiosity, awareness of sources of research information, skills at navigating these new information networks, and understanding their possible connections with artworks. The course uses my book *Information Arts: Intersections of Art, Science, and Technology* (Wilson, 2002) and the associated art and research websites as launching points for this work. (CIA 2006c: Art & Science Resource Web Sites). Here are samples of these assignments:

- Journal Search: Students are asked to go to the university library and browse the periodical section to find journals and magazines in topics they were not familiar with. They meet to report on the findings, explaining their understanding of the journal's mission and audience and presenting articles that intrigued them.
- Think Tank Presentation: Students are asked to conduct web research to investigate research think tanks working in innovative areas. They are asked to study the conceptual frameworks the think tanks use to organize their work and to present several particular projects they found interesting.
- Artist Presentation: Students are asked to find artist web sites for artists working with experimental areas of research and to make presentations on several. They are asked to try to understand how the research functions in the artist's work and to read whatever the artist wrote on the topic.
- Trade shows/ scientific meetings: Students are asked to become aware of what trade shows and scientific meetings are taking place in town. They are asked to arrange to attend one that stimulates their interest.
- Patents: They are taught how the patent system works and asked to browse patents via the patent office web page.
- Articles: Students are asked to find and report on cultural theory oriented articles that provide perspective on research fields they are interested in.

Several assignments ask students to actually create art project mock-ups based on emerging areas of scientific and technological research. These projects aim to teach students several skills: identification of cultural theory relevant to their interests, learning the language, history, and conceptual structure necessary to work in unfamiliar fields, identification of web and other sources of information on the research, surveying artists working in related fields, formulation of an art project that might build on that research, identification of researchers with information relevant to the project, initiation of contacts with those researchers or vendors, visits to labs or technology companies if feasible, conceptual mock-up of the art project with background material about the research, and building of models or prototypes if feasible. Here are some examples of projects students developed:

- A skywriter painting system based on understanding of local weather patterns and skywriting technology
- A method to record the sensations of sexual encounter
- An autonomous bat robot
- A system that would allow you to dance with a real time animated image of your skeleton
- An interface to computers that was good for your health
- An artificial 3-d audience that responded appropriately to your performance
- A system for generating sculptures that look like authentic feces
- A "road rage" system that sensed developing rage and calmed drivers
- A system to record dreams
- A teleportation system

Another project asked students to investigate the patent system. Patents are an amazing repository of technological innovation as well as a snapshot of cultural history about changing technological interests. They studied the patent system's rationale and history, its procedures, how to conduct patent searches, and the rudiments of how to compose a patent. They browsed the archives of past patents and considered the relationship of patents to artistic innovation. Here is the description of the assignment from the syllabus.

New Invention Proposal: Propose a new invention that could be produced. The idea should not be strictly utilitarian. It should have some element of cultural commentary or artistic or conceptual experimentation. Conduct a patent search for similar inventions. Present a prototype patent application with text description, discussion of related inventions, and diagrams or mock up images done in the line drawing style of regular patents.

Here are some examples of mock patents that students developed:

- Dream recorder and dream imagery reconstruction device
- A powerful electronic device which simulates a crowd so the neighbors don't have to know how lonely you really are

- Recently broke up? Have an ex? send them a gift they'll never forget- bad flower revenge system
- A lighted, enclosed shelving unit featuring electro-luminescent lighting panels!!
- Projection system that allows people to see different projections based on position
- Evolving autonomous house
- Bicycle system to power personal electronics
- Invisible tattoo system
- "Nanny Helmet" gives rewards and punishments to children based on their behavior
- A "safe" fire that burns cool

The course achieved many of its goals. It awakened young artists to vast reaches of scientific and technological research calling out for artistic attention. It helped demystify these areas, teaching them ways to find resources, to interpret the materials they found, to initiate discussions with researchers, to find critical literature relevant to the research, and to create art that responded to the research. It also illustrated some challenges in this approach. It showed students the difficulty of undertaking to learn new areas of technology or science simultaneous with pursuing art goals. It awakened a hunger for supplemental education in missing areas in their background. Since it promoted an independent approach to research that urged artists to question paradigmatic boundaries handed down from science disciplines and marketplace definitions of importance, it confronted them with the difficulties of differentiating quackery from lines of inquiry that were worth pursuing.

## Summary

Science and technology are transforming culture at its core. How should the arts participate in this transformation? How should they integrate the ancient magic of art with the magic of science? Answering this question will require courage and experimentation in the next decades. Creating programs to prepare artists for these revolutionary times will itself be a significant challenge.

## Works Cited

ACE (2006), (Arts, Computation Engineering Program – UC Irvine). http://www.ace.uci.edu/.

Bauhaus-dessau. (2006), "Bauhaus History," http://www.bauhaus-dessau.de/en/history.asp?p=history.*

CIA (2006a), (Conceptual Information Arts – SFSU). "Program Description." http://userwww.sfsu.edu/%7Einfoarts/core.html.*

CIA (2006b), "Art & Research Course Syllabus." http://userwww.sfsu.edu/%7Einfoarts/cdmain/res/a511.research.syllabus.html.*

CIA (2006c), "Art & Science Resource Web Sites." http://userwww.sfsu.edu/%7Einfoarts/links/wilson.artlinks2.html.*

DX (2006), (University of Washington – Center for Digital Arts and Experimental Media). "Program Description." http://www.washington.edu/dxarts/.*

MAT (2006), (Masters in Art & Technology – UC Santa Barbara). "Program Description." http://www.mat.ucsb.edu.*

Rogers, Bryan (2002), "Prospectus for MFA program School of Arts and Design at the University of Michigan." http://www.art-design.umich.edu.*

San Francisco State University (1985), "Art Department Course Description." *College Catalog.*

Sheridan, Sonia (2002), "Mind/Senses/Hand: The Generative Systems Program at the Art Institute of Chicago 1970–1980." Journal Leonardo. Volume 23, numbers 2 and 3. 2002.

Sheridan, Sonia (2006), "Biography." http://www.sonart.org.*

Studio for Creative Inquiry – CMU (2006), "Program Description." (http://www.cmu.edu/studio/).*

Technoculture Program (2006), (UC Davis). http://technoculture.ucdavis.edu/.*

Vesna, Victoria (2006), "Buckminster Fuller: Illusive Mutant Artist." Excerpt quoted from R. Buckminster Fuller. *Operating Manual for Spaceship Earth.* Penguin, New York: 1973. http://vv.arts.ucla.edu/publications/publications/98-99/bucky/bucky.htm.*

Wilson, Stephen (2002), *Information Arts: Intersections of Art, Science, and Technology.* Cambridge, MIT Press.

*All websites were accessed April 2, 2006.

# PIXELS AND PARTICLES: THE PATH TO SYNCRETISM

## Roy Ascott

Telematic connectivity is about the connectivity of minds, the potentiality of being distributed beyond the constraints of space and time, in asynchronic communication. It means a kind of entanglement at the social level. Central to this is the Web's hyperlink: a kind of semiotic black hole that instantly brings one into other universes of discourse, other worlds, other constructions of reality. Just as wormholes are described as tunneling in quantum foam, connecting widely separated locations in the galaxy, we tunnel through data foam from hyperlink to hyperlink across our planetary Web. This is telematic mind – collective intelligence reaching a level of complexity which suggests the emergence of a kind of hypercortex, now at the core of our reality engine.

The digital moment has passed – at least in the sense that the interface is disappearing, or certainly migrating, from a cabled, box-bound environment to a wireless multi-sensory, multi-modal, mobile form. Already the handheld has taken ascendancy over the laptop for many users engaged in social rituals of exchange and communication. We look to a future symbiosis, in which we wear the computer, and hope for the breakthrough in biochip design, which allows us to carry it, if not directly in the brain, at least within some part of the body. At the leading edge of artistic inquiry, our interest is moving from the pixels to particles. It will be moistmedia that is likely to challenge our artistic and design skills and aspirations. In all of this, a syncretic approach to arts education is called for. We can be sure that over the coming decades, new metaphors, new language, and new methodologies will arise.

Hans-Peter Durr (2002) of the Max-Plank-Institut fuer Physic in Munich, has written about immaterial connectedness as the physical basis of life. In this he argues that quantum physics reveals that matter is not composed of matter, but reality is merely potentiality. In his view "the world has a holistic structure, based on fundamental relations and not material objects, admitting more open, indeterministic developments." In this more flexible causal framework, inanimate and animate nature is not to be considered as fundamentally different, but as different order structures of the same immaterial entity. In a stable configuration effectively all the uncertainties are statistically averaged out, thus exhibiting the unique and deterministic behaviour of ordinary inanimate matter.

It can be argued that an education for art in the present post-biological era should be developed across two principle axes. One comes from our technological development, the other from our cultural development. The axes are those of connectivity and syncretism. It's possible to imagine that the nexus could become a point of transcendence, possibly under special circumstances providing a conduit to a higher level of consciousness. The special circumstances are likely to be within the field of consciousness research that, as will be argued later, should itself syncretize new developments in the chemical mapping of the brain and older models of mind embedded in cultural practices lying outside the Western paradigm.

Syncretism, which has been seen historically as an attempt to reconcile and analogize disparate religious and cultural practices, may contribute today to our understanding of the multi-layered worldviews – material and metaphysical – that are emerging with our engagement in, amongst other things, ubiquitous computing and post-biological technology. The education of the artists will focus on the syncretic reality that can be both construed and constructed by art practice. It will be about breaking boundaries while maintaining cohesion, that subtle attribute that is as necessary in the aesthetic as in the social sphere.

In the syncretic context, extreme differences are upheld but aligned such that likeness is found amongst unlike things, the power of each element enriching the power of all others within the array of their differences. Standing in emphatic distinction to binary opposition, syncretism is a process between different elements, the in-between condition of 'being both', evoking Marilyn Ferguson's memorable phrase "both both and and either or". Etymologically, syncretism relates to the ancient Cretan's decision to unite in the face of a common enemy (sun-kretismos). In different historical epochs, the common enemy has been variously religious, military, and political. In present-day cultural terms the enemy is habit – the passive, uncritical repetition or acceptance of behaviors, opinions, perceptions, and values, and the enshrining as verities, metaphors that have passed their sell-by date. Habit is the enemy of art, impeding the search for new ways of being. In art today, computer-mediated systems are inherently interactive and transformative and largely defy docile stability while bringing novelty to the dynamic equilibrium of living and cultural systems. However, established tropes, often embodied in packaged software, can be traps if students are not positioned to seek out the construction and expression of what is authentic to them and true to their subjective inclinations.

Understanding contemporary reality as syncretic may lead to significant changes in the way students regard their own identity, their relationship to others, and the phenomenology of time and space. Syncretism not only destabilizes orthodoxies and changes language, it may also result in the release of the self from the constraints of overweening rationality and totalizing dogma. In religious or spiritual contexts, syncretism has meant combining rituals, psychic instruments, psychotropic plants and herbs into new forms of sacred communion. In contemporary society, syncretism may involve a parallel process of gathering together disparate technologies (interactive and digital, reactive and mechanical, psychoactive and chemical), and new rituals of communication (mobile, online), and emergent communities (the Net), and should probably be aware of aspects of the holistic practices of older cultures, embracing across a wide spectrum of cultural knowledge what is more classically seen as unfamiliar, alien, or proscribed. Syncretic thinking is associative and non-linear: associative thought and non-linear inquiry inevitably breaches boundaries and subverts protocols. Art education can, and probably should, be understood as a dangerous business. Thinking out of the box, searching for the limits of perception, testing the limits of language, expression and construction, puts the artist out on the edge of social and cultural norms, which in our present, heavily circumscribed society is a dangerous place to be.

There are a number of questions and unknowns that arguably confront any attempt to discuss the issue of art education at the beginning of the twenty-first century. First, it seems necessary to ask whether our drive to create wider and deeper and faster telematic networks is an evolutionary impulse to engage more fully with universal mind. Will cyberception (Ascott 1994), the emerging human faculty that is enabling us to enter into both inner and outer worlds more deeply than our unaided natural senses hitherto permitted, augment our awareness and, eventually, perhaps our understanding of the field of consciousness? Is our interest in the hybridization of forms and materials related to the hybridization of space? Are we able to develop a syncretic reality that merges mixed reality technology, the realities governed by metaphors of biology and quantum physics, language and social habit, as well as those known in altered states of consciousness, into a more or less continuous, seamless whole? Can the education of artists be pursued without the informed study and critique of global conflicts and insight into local cultural norms? Is there sufficient cultural stability or unanimity in any country now, to be able to propose principles or procedures in the education of artists that hold from country to country, or even from year to year?

Against these questions, we have to recognize that science has so far failed to understand or explain the nature of 96 percent of the universe, which it refers to as dark matter and dark energy. We are also in the dark completely in our understanding of consciousness, even though our knowledge of the organization of the brain is becoming increasingly transparent. We have no idea whatsoever of the location of mind, or how consciousness arises. In neuroscience, the hard question (as Chalmers has named it) of the nature of qualia is as intractable as ever. Despite the vigour of conflicting claims and assertions, our evolutionary purpose remains unknown, if indeed there is one, while our evolutionary trajectory is increasingly influenced by technology. At the same time, controversies in science over reductionist and subjective methodologies, and the emergence of controversial field theories (e.g. in biophysics), may lead to a more fluid and less materialist view of nature and of ourselves.

However, while the context of art may shift, it can be argued that there are a number of objectives which probably hold in no matter what environment the education of artists is undertaken.

- amplifying thought: concept development
- sharing consciousness: collaborative processes
- seeding structures: self-organizing systems
- making metaphors: knowledge navigation
- constructing identities: self-creation

Equally, it is possible to follow the sequence of digital art production over the past thirty years. This is a five-stage progression involving connectivity, immersion, interaction, transformation, and emergence. It applies to social and cultural process, as well as to the construction of computer-mediated art, the individual artist's creative process, and to the creation of meaning in the participation of the viewer: connectivity between minds, between minds and machines; immersion in different kinds of (cyber)spaces and locations – sometimes simultaneously; transformation of images, structures, perception; emergence of new forms, new meanings, and new experiences. Given this, it is not difficult to see how new media art is considered to mark a rupture with the plastic arts of the last century. Even when art is not overtly "interactive," as is mostly the case today, we nevertheless recognize that meaning is created in the mind and heart of the viewer and, in the artistic encounter, the viewer completes the work.

The historic vehicle for the education of the artist has been the academy or school of art. These are terms heavy with meanings and practices which have proved resistant to fundamental change for nearly two centuries; in England, for example, go back to the founding of the Government School of Design in South Kensington, London, in 1837. Many would testify to the idea that the *mise-en-scène* of the art school has hardly changed since that time.

To employ the word "collegium," rather than college or academy, may serve to distance our thinking from sclerosis of conventional art education. With the advent of digital technology, in the attempt to graft "the computer" onto studio practice, art educators often lost the plot. The biggest problem was that education got confused with training, almost to the extent of its demise. In the take-up of computer technology, the curriculum became a battlefield between will and will nots. While many design disciplines were early adopters of digital media, fine arts tutors were slow to recognize computer technology as a necessary tool and reluctant at first to embrace it. In consequence, design practices got off to a good start with top-end equipment, while fine art, as a reluctant latecomer, mostly had to do with sparse, inadequate hardware, and very little understanding of the digital environment. This may be of interest now only to education historians, except for the fact that that Johnny-come-lately syndrome may be repeated today in the case of bio-art. Without access to labs, the investigation by art students of moistmedia is doomed. But moistmedia, situated at the convergence of computational systems and living biological processes, is precisely the place where many art students want to be, inspired by investigations into genetic engineering, tissue culture, and nano-biology that are being undertaken by artists in many parts of the world. Art education, always concerned with the provision of tools, will need to find ways to give its student access to the scanning tunnelling microscope and other tools of nano-engineering. As the syncretic way becomes better understood as the route that curriculum developments should take, greater access will be seen to be required to many previously ignored disciplines and resources within the university and in the world more generally.

Another historical perspective suggests that much student work today can be seen as the fruit of seeds planted in the 1960s. Much the same can be said of the "avant-garde" art market more generally. And clearly, the process-based and performative aspects of the art of that decade have been being particularly suited to developing strategies in digital art practice. We see this very positive and productive creativity of art students, even as we observe the dead hand of institutional bureaucracy, which, certainly in the U.K. since the Thatcher years, has become increasingly obsessed with accountability, profitability, and expediency – a shortsighted attitude which infects art teaching institutions in most parts of the world. Shortsighted because without bringing into the world with every generation, imaginative and visionary young people with informed critical sensibilities to new technologies, to complement their (no doubt) necessarily reductionist peers in science and engineering, our current, impoverished social order will persist. This calls for investment in new facilities (actually a complete rethinking, architecturally as well as in educational policy and procedures) that it would be foolish to expect short-term profit and loss accounts to justify.

We see in art schools, also, the fallout from the postmodernist and post-structuralist blitz. While, in terms of student aspirations, relativism has opened the door to a rich infinity of artistic strategies and possibilities, in terms of teaching and evaluation, institutions have found themselves without real authority or credibility. The commercialization of higher education has led to huge gains in real estate but massive inadequacies in resources. Top-down planning leaves the lecturer in a state of bureaucratic stress, endlessly reporting, evaluating, and meeting criteria set from on high. The one-on-one tutorial has virtually disappeared and, indeed, would better serve students if it were really to be virtual; that is, online and accessible to a worldwide network of experts and practitioners who were not constantly disappearing for staff meetings, crisis talks, and admin updates. Instead of showing the cultural way forward with vision and artistic leadership, these institutions are governed by the bottom line. Where this situation persists, students will increasingly find the stimulus for change, transformation, and enterprise on the street rather than in the studio; in the clubs rather than the seminar, in the Net rather than the museum. Art schools for the most part are housed in old nineteenth- and twentieth-century buildings designed for other kinds of practice and older sensibilities. They are incorporated in, but barely tolerated or understood by, the university sector that has absorbed them. There are, of course, significant exceptions, and this paper cannot detail each one except to point to the excellent result of an inquiry by Michael Naimark and Mark Tribe in their Wiki Directory of Academic Art and Technology Programs[1] or the Leonardo Education Forum.[2] These deal largely with the English-speaking world. Much useful information about other such developments, for example, in countries around the Mediterranean rim, is to be found in the online moderated list Yasmin,[3] designed for art-science-technology interactions between artists, scientists, engineers, theoreticians, and institutions promoting communication and collaboration in art, science, and technology in that part of the world.

Since many current attitudes to art practice were first set out in the 1960s (as testified in publications such as Lucy Lippard's Six Years: The Dematerialization of the Art Object (1972), Gene Youngblood's Expanded Cinema (1970), it may be instructive to take a brief look at an example of experiments in art education of that period. The example chosen is the Groundcourse at Ealing School of Art, London in the years 1960 to 1964. The radical, searching nature of the decade is also characterized by such attempts to re-invent the art school, even to redefine what art could be, as those of Victor Pasmore and Richard Hamilton at Newcastle, and Harry Thubron at Leeds. These projects were futures-oriented and dedicated to change, often for its own sake. At Ealing and, subsequently, at Ipswich, the art school was seen as the place where everything was possible, giving licence to rebelliousness, experiment, and dissent.

The teaching at Ealing emphasized foregrounded behaviour, consciousness, conceptual strategy, process, and system over the object-based aesthetic inherited from the European mainstream tradition (Ascott 1964: 37–42). The work was more constructive than responsive; the world was to be built rather than simply observed; the personality of each student was seen as fluid; chance and contingency were celebrated. Cybernetics was at the core of the enterprise. Students came with rather rigid preconceptions about themselves, their limits, what was art and what was not, reflecting the sclerosis of their secondary education. It was thought that only carefully constructed situations designed to elicit amazement, analysis, wonder, deliberation, self-affirmation, enthusiasm, re-evaluation, and delight might shake this hold on their perceptions, release their imagination, and accelerate the acquisition of cognitive and technical skills. The faculty sought to provide the training and pastoral care needed for them to recreate themselves, their relationships, their environment, at whatever level of practicality or poetry they found significant. They saw the art school as a creative organism in which everyone had a stake. To realize these ambitions, cyberneticians, architects, scientists, engineers, writers, musicians, anthropologists, semiologists were sought out and brought directly onto the studio floor rather than to the podium, as part of the mix of minds and methodologies from which new artistic practice might emerge. Analysis, theory, speculation, and social application were valued in equal measure. Later, in 1969, this approach to art education was developed further and applied to the whole of one of the largest art colleges in North America at the time: Ontario College of Art in Toronto (Ascott 1972: 14–16). But it was too radical by far for the rather timid and conservative trustees, and some of the very provincial, older, time-serving faculty, and was soon eradicated, to the protest and dismay of faculty and students (Wolfe 2002). The impact it made, however, was considerable and can still be felt today.

In many ways, the 1970s saw the end of radical experiment and innovative curricular development in art education. The advent of postmodernism was seen by institutions more as a threat to established values than as an impetus to change. Lucy Lippard's *Six Years* (see above) served both to sum up an era that had ended and to lay out the ground for work that would only emerge some thirty years later and, particularly, in the fields of computer-mediated art practices.

Now the future seems to lie in the growing alliance between science and the arts, with the studio more closely associated with the lab, or integrated into wider urban or planetary structures. The training of the artist today must be set in the mixed-reality environment of a distributed, telematic, syncretic network where open-ended research can lead to a visionary pragmatism. The danger, already evident in funding agencies and museum policy, is that art/science has become a mantra, with no real understanding of what it does or could mean. Mostly it's a question of a rather one-way illustration of scientific data by the artist, or a mirroring of scientific attitudes and methodologies, rather than projects built upon dialogue and emergent syncretic discourse. The best advice to the art student must surely be "ask not what science can do for art, but what art can do for science."

For the art education curriculum to embody syncretism would encourage the student artist to look everywhere and anywhere, into any discipline, scientific or spiritual, any view of the world – however esoteric or arcane – any culture, immediate or distant in space or time, in order to find ideas or processes which might engender creativity. There is, after all, no meta-language or meta-system that places one discipline or worldview automatically above all others. It can be argued that a liberated syncretism should inform artistic research at all levels. This is why artists look in all directions for inspiration and understanding: to the East as well as the West; following the left-hand path as well as the right; working with both reason and intuition, sense and nonsense, subtlety and sensibility.

The design or development of any valid collegium at this time will necessarily be bottom up, contingent and always in flux, economically and politically. The only assured stability must lie within the solidarity of its members and associates – internal and external. Since the business of art lies as much in the creation and critique of metaphor as it does in generating structures and media flow, a sufficiently ironic position must be maintained to prevent the sclerosis of practice or the entrenchment of aesthetic or artistic canons. The principles contingency, solidarity and irony are well set out in the book by the pragmatist Richard Rorty (1981), addressing questions and proposing solutions to the problem of value and authenticity in the light of the relativism consequent upon postmodernist discourse.

Most religions, and the worldviews with which they interact, have been syncretic in their formation. There are many examples in early Christianity and in Gnosticism, for example. Syncretism is also a feature of Islam in its least orthodox form, namely in the language of the Sufi. Sufism is a highly syncretic spiritual practice between the tangible and abstract, the known and unknown, the visible and invisible, keeping each distinct yet related in their difference. The Syrian poet Adonis shows a significant link between the syncretism in art, specifically in Surrealism, and in the spiritual domain:

> [Surrealist writing] like Sufi writing, appears for the most part to be filled with strange things, contradictions, obscure references and disjointed images…the anarchic, the astonishing, the baffling and the obscure form the basis for Sufi (and Surrealist) writing…When the poet enters a world of transformations, he can leave it only by transformative writing: waves of illuminating images, which do not bear scrutiny by reasonable or logical means, and through which reality itself is transformed into a dream. (Adonis 2005: 114)

Adonis makes reference to the symbolist poet Rimbaud's dedicated pursuit of "delirium," what would today be called "altered states of consciousness" that is also sought by the Sufi. Syncretic thinking of this kind, entwining different features of different cultures in different time frames, can provide a foundation of ideas from which the student of art can build a personal platform, and without which the manipulation of digital systems can lead only to work that is barren – although vacuity can be obscured with special effects.

There is no doubt that consciousness, in all its forms, is high on the scientific agenda today. But whereas science seeks to explain consciousness, art's role is one of exploration and navigation. This requires training and commitment, as well as the acquisition of ontological understanding. The student artist should not be immune to this. It should be high on the education agenda. The computer is now assimilated into all our cultural norms, to the extent that it is practically invisible in its ubiquity. Notwithstanding the excitement in art generated by the early adoption of biological developments in molecular biology, genetic engineering, and other wetware adventures, and the computational convergence that has led to a moistmedia substrate for art, the mind/brain domain seems to offer the artist particularly enriching and profound lines of inquiry. The part that chemistry can play in this should not be underestimated, and the mapping of the chemical organization of the brain carries rich implications for art, no less perhaps than for cognitive science, as well as for fields beyond biology's current borders.

Particularly iconic in this shift has been the recent move of Thomas S. Ray[4] from Alife research, famously embodied in his 1990 Tierra[5] (evolution in the digital medium), to his current research into the potential of genomic databases for providing a comprehensive understanding of the processes of development and differentiation that generate the architecture of the brain, and how psychedelics interact with the human receptome:

> We can think of [the brain] as a complex dynamical system, in which the trajectory follows high-dimensional orbits, and switches among many "attractors", where the attractors represent the major emotional states and moods, and whatever mental phenomena the chemical systems are mediating. In this dynamic reference frame, drugs will create a perturbation along the binding vector, thereby pushing the system into a new attractor. We want to get to know the pharmacology of the attractors...to begin to map the chemical organization of the human mind. (Ray 2004)

Just as art education has seen the wisdom in exploring how digital systems interact with living systems, so it will begin to see merit in providing its students with the means of navigating the further reaches of the mind, through the syncretic gathering of ideas in neuroscience with those of ethnobotany, chemicals, and plants. Indeed, the separation of advanced technologies of the Valley (Silicon) from the ancient vegetal technologies of the Forest (Amazonia) may become increasingly irrelevant as we look to a kind of syncretic co-evolution of consciousness-changing agencies. There is more for the art student to learn from ancient societies than simply visual form and pattern. For every image, every rhythm, every texture there is usually an equivalent on the psychic plane.

A decade ago, perhaps even just five years ago, contemporary media art meant Western media art. At the same time a distinction between art and entertainment was maintained. Now there is a category shift, the distinction is much more fuzzy, indeed all aesthetic boundaries are eroding. The status of media art in isolation is in doubt. Many interactive artworks can now be seen as no more than menu spinning operations, the viewer trapped in a finite maze. The early intimacy of interactive art experience has been replaced by a very public spectacle and special effects: the mouse goes to Hollywood. This only stiffens the resistance. However, new locations, new cultural groupings are forming wherever the Net reaches. At the very core of any discussion around contemporary art lies the issue of emergence.

Where there is true, open-ended interaction across an interface, there is space for new meaning and authentic vision to emerge. This is so in those former outposts of media art – Brazil, India, Korea, and China. These countries are now each at the centre, there is no periphery in a network, only interacting nodes of greater or lesser energy and intensity. Particularly in non-Western media cultures, a new intentionality is evident, recuperating older cultural norms in new technological contexts. We can expect aesthetic variation across the planet to become more pronounced, the invention of form and behavior to increase and widely diversify. Equally, artistic material is spilling off the screen into the performative arena, just as virtual reality becomes more permeable to its reality environment.

The first lesson to be learned from working in cyberspace, one almost ethical in its formation, is that of immersion. Colonization constitutes a linear, top-down process of cultural erasure through absorption. Immersive environments insist on a holistic perspective, mutuality of interaction, and the sharing of cultural values. In this sense, if in no other, telematic immersive environments employing CAVE (Cave Automatic Virtual Environment) technology can act as both tool and metaphor for bringing together artists and others from radically different cultural positions and geographical locations. Telematic technology, however sophisticated, is only effective and meaningful if it operates in a syncretic intellectual, artistic, spiritual, and political context. Syncretism has to be won through sustained communication and interaction between what may be initially opposed positions, negotiating from an equitable level of power and effect. There is evidence that this is beginning to emerge – certainly the former hegemony of North American and European media artists is giving way to a much more planetary spread of festivals, expositions, media centers, and academies.

There are hopes and ambitions embedded in the Planetary Collegium that has evolved over the past ten years, networking a number sites on the planet, details of which can be examined at www.planetary-collegium.net and which is describe briefly below. But whatever the structure – and it is quite unique in comparison to other centers for advanced research in art and technology – the element of defining importance in the Collegium's evolution is its researchers, doctoral, postdoc and the supervisory teams. Development too takes place as a result of challenges and questions that routinely come forward during the Collegium's many conferences around the world, and those that its members give individually. Taken together, that comprises a spread of countries that include most of Europe, Scandinavia, North, Central and South America, China, Japan, Korea, India, and Australia.

The Collegium grew from the need for art practices involving emergent media (interactive, telematic, technoetic) to be theorized and developed within a community of artists and scholars working at the forward edge of the field. The ethos of the Collegium can perhaps best be understood by the questions it has sought to answer.

■ How might new technologies and the metaphors of science be employed in the education of the artist?
■ How might the insights of the artist contribute to the advancement of knowledge in science and to technological development?
■ How can the accrued wisdom of exotic or ancient cultures be allied to the search for meaning and values in a post-biological society?

- How might new technologies serve to support and sustain cultures that lie beyond the Western paradigm?
- How might the Net serve the needs of interactive, non-linear, syncretic learning, and engender creative thought and constructive action?
- How might new discourses be initiated which will bring critical, aesthetic, and moral perspectives to bear on emergent fields of practice?

While stretching to the full the constructive and expressive potential of electronic, telematic, and interactive digital media, how might the Collegium pursue developments in post-biological research, molecular engineering, neuroscience, and nanotechnology, while identifying artistic and spiritual strategies that optimize human capabilities and seed new visions of a planetary society. From its Hub at the University of Plymouth, England, the Planetary Collegium is currently expanding its network to include nodes worldwide. Z-Node opened in 2004 in Zurich at Hochschule für Gestaltungund Kunst. M-Node opened in 2005 at the Nuova Accademia di Belle Arte, Milan; P-Node in the School of Software, Peking University, in 2006. The Collegium is in negotiations to incorporate additional nodes in North America and Brazil over the next five years. The Collegium has a syncretic perspective which seeks the integration of art, science, technology, and consciousness research within a post-biological culture, and is involved in advancing the parameters of creative practice in consort with developments in telematics, Mixed Reality technology, Alife, hypermedia, agent technology, interactive systems, nanotechnology, transgenics, data imaging, music, intelligent environments, technoetics, Net art, performance and dance, installation, architecture, design and the techno-arts more generally come within the scope of our research. It is a community of closely connected doctoral candidates and graduates, post-doctoral researchers, advisors, associates and supervisors, professionals committed, through collaboration and shared discourse, to pushing the boundaries of art. We take a constructive and pro-active approach to the social, technological, and spiritual aspirations of the emerging planetary society, while sustaining a critical awareness of the retrograde forces and fields that inhibit social harmony and cultural transformation.

The current bifurcation of new media art away from its technoetic destiny towards a bland sociological materialism has been most marked. While both the aesthetic and the social can lead to the spiritual, the path is often blocked by the aesthete or the sociologue. We've seen a kind of ideological ping pong over the last century between these two poles of sensibility, between beauty and truth. Only if consciousness and contingency guide us are we likely to engage in the full potential of new media art. The online, networked, hypermediated, and mixed reality technologies and media of today constitute no more than a crude precursor to a biophysical reality that a fuller understanding of the mind-body in space-time will create. I'm referring to what can be called quantum consciousness, where cyberception is itself augmented by the quantum computer, and telematic networks elide seamlessly with our own organic biochemical/electronmagnetic networks. Then, distributed mind, collaborative thought, pervasive pereception, and integrated consciousness will take their place in our evolutionary adventure. Those who speak loudest of the necessity of maintaining a "critical distance" in networking or of networks usually do not seek the resolution promised by dialectical exchange, but already have a prior agenda. Critical self-awareness of the individual is something else; it has to do with seeking for coherence within the mind-body field and in its relationship to the world at large. This is to resolve any possible duality between the cyberself and its cyberception, on the one hand, and the "psiberself" and its psychic perception, on the other. The paradox of coherence in this conjunction is that the self and its presence can be de-centered and distributed: bifurcating, in a sense, to create multiple identities in a context of creative instability and uncertainty. This parallels the coherence of quantum states in which individual atoms pursue bifurcating pathways in a universe of uncertainty.

It is at the quantum level that we find parallelisms with telematic and post-biological art. The molecular structure of the body can be seen as constituting a network. Molecules emit biophotons, a quantum behaviour. Biophotonic research suggests that the coherence of living systems is due in large measure to the information network of photons emitted by DNA molecules. This can be seen as parallel to the telematic networks that inform the body of the planet. In the emergence of moistmedia and technoetic art, nanotechnology can play a significant role. Materialists may see working in the nano field as the endgame, but it is not necessary to embrace a radical transcendentalism to see that nano is located between the material density of our everyday world and the numinous spaces of subatomic immateriality.

The concept of immaterial connectedness confers a spiritual dimension on both telematic art and quantum mechanics. Field theory supports the contention that the material body may be a consequence rather than a cause of consciousness. I anticipate the convergence of esoteric knowledge and new media practice in a biotelematic field of networks, seen, for example, where the technology of psychointegrator plants in Amazonia and research in the chemistry of consciousness converge. It is my contention that a technoetic art may find its ground in the triangulation of connectivity, syncretism, and field theory. What is at stake is that all systems be coherent. Connectivity is at the root of cultural coherence, syncretism at the root of spiritual coherence, and field theory at the root of quantum coherence. Where there is dissatisfaction with materialist culture and reductionist thought, new paradigms are arising in science which may correlate to the emergence of new pathways to the spiritual in art.

### Conclusion
The computer is best understood as an immersive environment rather than simply a tool. Tools can be evaluated in terms of utility and function, but environments have ethical, social, spiritual, as well as cultural dimensions. We need perhaps to recognize that the classical high road to art has shifted to the five-fold path of connectivity, immersion, interaction, transformation, and emergence. To understand the implications for art of the (post) computational environment and to function creatively within it, a syncretic discourse has to be developed. The culture of connectivity means thinking out of the

box in a kind of hyperlinked, associative, mindfest. Telematic systems affect our relationship to time and space. The emergent faculty of cyberception affects our relationship with the perceived world. Technoetic inquiry is fundamental to artistic development: navigating consciousness may involve pharmacological as much as bionic technologies. There are many competing worldviews, esoteric as well as scientific, archaic as well as postmodern, and we ourselves are both transformable and permeable. Reality is ours to construct, and where ethical or cultural models conflict, a syncretic rather than homogenizing resolution should be sought. Young artists face the challenge of creating a syncretic art that can utilize: telematics (planetary connectivity); nanotechnology (bottom-up construction); quantum computing (augmented cyberception); cognitive science and pharmacology (field consciousness); esoterica (psychic instrumentality).

A syncretic process could hold together the current ferment of ideas, images, and models of reality that communities and cultures across the planet are generating. To recite the story of media art in its syncretic mode is not to advance its development, nor is it sufficient simply to outline the syncretic reality that is emerging. Strategies to strengthen this emergence are needed. Cultural habit is to be viewed as the enemy. The need to identify new knowledge fields and develop syncretic discourse must be confronted, along with the need to create syncretic, many stranded, organisms of exploration, inquiry, learning, and creativity. This requires a syncretic schedule of artistic, computational, psychic, biophysical, and nanotechnological projects in order to bring about new conditions for life and art. Field theories offer useful models in charting the relationship of consciousness to the material body. Scrutiny of the nano-field may lead not only to new tools of construction, but also to an understanding of the immaterial connectedness espoused by both quantum physics and Eastern metaphysics. More ancient cultures that retain a place on the margins of technological society have also something to tell us, both directly and metaphorically, about the perception of the numinous and our construction of reality. As it outgrows dialectical sociology, narration, and representation, new media art may play its part in the navigation of mind that will take us to new spaces and states of consciousness, while enhancing the technology of our connectedness. Finally, in order to identify new knowledge fields and develop syncretic discourse and practice, art education must in its teaching and research put its emphasis on subject before object; process before system; behavior before form; intuition before reason; mind before matter.

## Notes

1. www.brown.edu/Departments/MCM/nothing/index.php/ArtAndTechPgms.
2. mitpress2.mit.edu/e-journals/Leonardo/isast/spec.projects/LEFbiblio.html/.
3. www.media.uoa.gr/yasmin/.
4. www.his.atr.jp/~ray/.
5. "Synthetic organisms have been created based on a computer metaphor of organic life in which CPU time is the 'energy' resource and memory is the 'material' resource. Memory is organized into informational patterns that exploit CPU time for self-replication. Mutation

generates new forms, and evolution proceeds by natural selection as different genotypes compete for cpu time and memory space." (Ray 1991. "Tierra Announcement." *Ars Electronica Archive*) See also: www.his.atr.jp/~ray/tierra/index.html.

## Works Cited

Adonis 2005, *Sufism and Surrealism*. J. Cumberbatch (trans.). London: Saqi.

Ascott, R. 1994, "The Architecture of Cyberception." First presented at ISEA'94, The 5th International Symposium on Electronic Art, Helsinki, Finland.

See: http://pespmc1.vub.ac.be/Cybspasy.html.

Ascott, R. 1972, "Art as an Alternative to Art Education, or, The Rise of the Jam Factory." *Art* (Society of Canadian Artists) vol. 3, no. 1.

Ascott, R. 1964, *The Construction of Change*. Cambridge, U.K.: Cambridge Opinion.

Durr, H. p. 2002, "What Is Life? Scientific Approaches and Philosophical Positions." *World Scientific*.

Lippard, L. 1972, *Six Years: The Dematerialization of the Art Object*. London: Studio Vista.

Ray, T. 2004, "The Chemical Architecture of the Human Mind: Probing Receptor Space with Psychedelics." *Proceedings: Towards a Science of Consciousness Conference*, Tucson. See: www.corante.com/brainwaves/archives/2005/02/05/the_chemical_architecture_of_the_ human_min d_by_tom_ray.php.

Rorty, R. 1981, *Contingency, Irony and Solidarity*. Cambridge, U.K.: Cambridge University Press.

Wolfe, M. 2002, *OCA 1967–1972: Five Turbulent Years*. Toronto: Grub St. Books.

Youngblood, G. 1970, *Expanded Cinema*. New York: Dutton.

# SUSTAINING CREATIVITY AND LOSING THE WILD[1]

## Carol Gigliotti

This chapter explores the deep connections between the suppression and destruction of natural creativity – organic, ecological, and biological – and the corrosive effects of that destruction on sustained human creativity. This exploration will include discussion of various metaphoric approaches that are being used or might be used in new media art and design education to encourage creative solutions to both forms of destruction.

### Metaphors and Realities of Exchange

Through the open window, lined with honeysuckle, we can see the dark-haired graduate student as she sits, legs curled up under her laptop. The bed upon which she sits is strewn with programming books and course notes from classes she is taking at a large university in the United States. These courses have names like 'Theories of Media and New Media,' and 'Dynamic Media.' She is reading something on the laptop, however, and her look is one of disbelief mixed with both pity and anger.

She is reading a website that tells her the computer she is working on, which she bought a few years ago, more than likely contains a chemical element from a naturally occurring material called coltan. Coltan is an ore containing the element tantalum, used as extremely light, thin electrolytic capacitors in cell phones, videogame players, and laptops. The largest known reserves of coltan have been within Central Africa, particularly in what is now the Democratic Republic of the Congo. In the late 90s the price of coltan started to rise due to electronic technological demands. In early 2000, the release of Playstation 2 was delayed due to a scarcity in the supply of tantalum. Consequently, the market price of coltan shot up to US$400.00 per kilogram (Corporate Watch 2003: 1).

As Peterson (2003: 122) reports and various news agencies concur, peasant farmers and warring factions from the Congo, Rwanda, Uganda, and Burundi alike all began to overrun the Congo's national parks, clearing out large tracts of forests in order to mine for coltan. Animals living in and around these national park forests, including gorillas and elephants, chimpanzees, buffalo and antelope, fell victim to the illegal miners' need for food. The miners included poverty-stricken peasant farmers, run off their land by armed conflict and pillaging for resources, children of these families, and rebel prisoners.

The Kahuzi-Beiga National Park, a World Heritage Site, was one of these sites and there the numbers of gorillas, small and threatened to begin with, were cut in half from 258 to 130 (Delewala 2001). A number of the controversial UN Security Council reports from 2001 through 2003 outlined the existence of criminal groups linked to the armies of Rwanda, Uganda, Zimbabwe, and elite global networks of political, military, and business people that illegally exploit coltan and diamonds in the DRC, 'causing a dire humanitarian situation' (Kassem 2002: 28).

What is not controversial are the facts that armed conflicts in those areas included the death of 3 million people between 1998 and 2003, the rapes of tens of thousands of women and girls, and the widespread use of children as combatants by all parties. The DRC is currently one of the countries of the world with the largest number of child soldiers (Amnesty International 2005). More recent reports by Amnesty International and Human Rights Watch have concluded that the fighting and all its attendant ills will continue as long as no mechanism is set up to address the competition between rival militia – backed variously by Rwanda, Uganda, and the DRC government – to control and profit from the immense riches of the DRC's natural resources (Amnesty International 2003).

A large-scale international lobbying campaign by environmental and political organizations caused many corporations in the supply chain, Motorola, Kemet, and Cabot among them, to pledge not to import any material containing tantalum able to be traced from illegal mining in the DRC (Todd 2006: 13). The illicit trade in coltan, gold, tin, timber, diamonds, and other materials continues, however, according to a number of independent news sources as well as a well-publicized study by Human Rights Watch (Weymuller 2006).

The graduate student sits on her bed and wonders how it is that this information has not been more widely publicized. Suddenly her 'passionate commitment to innovative technology,' a phrase she has been using lately to cover a wide range of her interests seems suspect. With a growing sense of disquietude, she might ask herself: What is it specifically that I am contributing to: The decimation of African forest animals, the exploitation of children and women, the contribution to the increasing poverty in protracted battles over resources that do little to benefit the people of these areas or the land or non-humans with which they live? Her interest in both the sciences and the arts had led her to a graduate degree in new media, but much of her passion for this 'newer media' came out of the sheer love of creative approaches that seemed possible with a technology that was constantly being updated, shifted, and re-negotiated. How in the world, she thinks, is she ever again going to be able to immerse herself, her intellect, her soul, in the same way in digital media?

The paradox about all this, she thinks, is that the specific material responsible for digital media's responsiveness, its ability to be so open to collaboration, so conducive to the exchange of information, is itself the impetus for an extended global exchange in which, in the eyes of most, these atrocities play an inconsequential role. Once the coltan is dug up from the earth, it passes through the hands of the miners, to the rebel armies of Uganda or Zimbabwe, to the brokers in the cities who in turn sell the material to the electronic components manufacturers to be refined and made into components sold to computer companies. This series of exchanges is driven by both desire and need. What she realizes, however, is that even if the desire on her "end" of the cycle is sparked by a love of creativity, a commitment to what she likes to call "positive possibility," the need on the other end of the cycle, is one borne of poverty and hunger. In between, the engine of capital continues the cycle rotating back and forth across the globe.

This scenario, one based on fact and metaphor, may seem, to some, a bit misplaced in an essay on digital art education. It can be argued that including this kind of contextual information in a digital art or new media curriculum is useful for placing the medium in a critical cultural context, one in which the social and political implications of the digital medium are made transparent. That argument is valid and plays an important role in the composition of this essay's central thesis. Many current digital art curricula, however, include either a separate course focusing on critical and cultural contexts of media and/or new media or embed those ideas directly into studio classes. I would argue, as other authors have argued (Wilson 2002; Scholz 2005; Lister 2003), the benefits of including more courses on the social and political and cultural contexts of the digital realm in the reading of undergraduate and graduate students. In this essay, however, I want to focus on an interdependent but more obscured outcome of the global exchange outlined above.

This outcome concerns the deep connections between the suppression and destruction of non-human creativity – organic, ecological, and biological – and the corrosive effects of that destruction on sustained human creativity. The scenario above dramatizes a common symptom of these connections: a feeling of powerlessness in the face of global practices '...saturated with a particular kind of ethics which happens to be ecologically pathological' (Curry 2006: 6). In teaching both an ethics and ecology course, and currently an environmental ethics course for art, design, and media students at Emily Carr Institute, I have experienced firsthand the crippling effects of this feeling of powerlessness in students. In some cases it is something intuited by the student and not always understood for what it is. I have found, when offered a supportive and knowledgeable environment in which both the historical and contemporary worldviews upon which these systems of ecological pathology rest are clearly delineated, the student's intellectual, emotional, and psychic spaces are opened up for the investigation of decidedly different ethical systems.

These different ethical systems run along a continuum of those based on the recognition that nature, including humanity, is the conclusive source of all value. From the more anthropocentric (human-centered) to the more eco-centric (earth-centered) approaches to questions of values, options in ethical action begin to open up for students who previously felt at a dead end in their desire to embed meaning surrounding perceptions of nature and value in their work. All this being said, I am aware that many reading this essay may still question what kind of affect the destruction of non-human creativity might have on human creativity, if any. Specific answers to the reverse of that question lie all around us: in the 'extraordinary scale of animal killing conducted by human beings in recent years' (Animal Studies Group 2006: 1); in the global market conversion of 'million of acres of forests and farms into industrial monocultures, displacing and destroying both biodiversity and the cultural diversity of local communities' (Shiva 2000: 16); in the 'International scientific consensus (agreeing) that increasing levels of man-made greenhouse gases are leading to global climate change' (The Royal Society 2006). Whether or not the destruction of non-human nature is having an impact on human creativity in general is not something I can prove in this essay, but I am willing to make that argument in an area with which I am familiar, the education of new media artists and designers.

### The Interdependence of Human and Non-human Creativity

In one of the most profound discussions of creativity available, the physicist David Bohm (1998: 2) defines creativity as *'discovering* [original emphasis] oneness and totality in nature.' He explains that to be able to do this, both the scientist and the artist must create new overall structures of ideas in order to explain or communicate this oneness and harmony in nature. Bohm bases this understanding of creativity on a crucial outlook on the real task of creativity, which can

> never be to judge whether something is ordered or disordered, because *everything* is ordered, and because disorder in the sense of the absence of every conceivable kind of order is an impossibility. Rather, what one really has to do is *to observe and describe the kind of order that each thing actually has* [original emphasis]. (Bohm 1998: 8–9)

He suggests that structure is, in essence, a hierarchy of orders and this principle is universal (Bohm 1998: 9). The evolutionary process of nature, while similar to the extremely complex and seemingly 'chaotic' paths tracing the 'drunkard's walk' of Brownian motion used to describe random movements in a variety of areas, from sub-atomic physics to stock market fluctuations, also differs from this kind of potentially infinite order. Nature does not tend to approach a complete statistical regularity or symmetry. Evolutionary processes of order in nature can become the basis of a new higher order. He says: 'nature is a creative process, in which not merely new structures, but also new orders of structure are always emerging (though the process takes a long time by our standards)' (Bohm 1998: 10). For Bohm, neglecting or failing to understand that the conditions for the existence of creativity are 'unfolded from the whole earth' (1998: 112) leads to a failure in both human thought and practice.

Vandana Shiva, another physicist, also known as a world-renowned environmental thinker and activist, describes how 'the ecological web of life that species create in interaction' (Shiva 2000: 14) is expressed in biodiversity. For Shiva, biodiversity is a creative process involving all species, both human and non-human, and cannot be reduced to the genetic level. This kind of reduction is scientifically, ecologically, and creatively misguided. The creative value of biodiversity extends across three fundamental levels of biological organization: genetic, species, and ecosystem diversity. In this way, rather than being viewed in a fragmented or atomized context, the interdependence of all these levels across all species, including humans, means that the destruction at any level will negatively affect the others.

Shiva, in talking about her work in her home country, India, describes two root causes for the rapid destruction of biodiversity in Third World countries located in the tropics and similar ecosystems. Pointing out that these areas are cradles of biodiversity, she points to global trade and technology as creators of a new era of bio-imperialism. The current instances of this destruction, in Shiva's view, are caused by what she calls the 'empty-earth' paradigm of colonization and what she describes as the monoculture of the mind. The first cause 'assumes that ecosystems are empty if not taken over by Western industrial man or his clones' (Shiva 2000: 25) and the second, the idea that the world is or should be uniform and one-dimensional, is the scientific and technological reflection of the empty-earth worldview (Shiva 1993). These metaphors are rich descriptions of the thoughts and practices now dominating scientific and technological endeavor and share responsibility for much of the destruction of diverse species and diverse cultures.

These two complementary articulations of creativity, that of David Bohm and that of Vandana Shiva, are exceptionally instructive in an argument that envisions natural and human creativity as integrated components in a universal creative process, both of which need to be sustained to survive.

**Metaphors and Creativity**
This integration has profound implications for creativity in the arts and sciences as well as particular meanings for how we think about educating students in the digital arts and new media. In order to elaborate more explicitly on these ideas, I turn again to metaphor. Instead of a metaphorical narrative, however, I would like to look more closely at how metaphors might be used differently in discourse about new media. For this, I rely on Lakoff and Johnson's extensive work on the nature of metaphor and embodied thought based on research emerging from cognitive science. Contrary to accepted notions about reason being independent of perception, motion, emotion, and

other bodily capacities, often used to draw the line between us and other animals, Lakoff and Johnson insist reason grows out of such bodily capacities.

> Human reason is a form of animal reason, a reason inextricably tied to our bodies and the peculiarities of our brains...These results tell us that our bodies, brains and interactions with our environment provide the mostly unconscious basis for our everyday metaphysics, that is, our sense of what is real. (Lakoff and Johnson 1999: 17)

Without going into great detail about their theories of metaphor, what Lakoff and Johnson have to tell us about metaphor relates to this fundamental understanding of the connection between our bodies, our minds, and what we find to be true and, therefore, what we value. As we function normally in the world we automatically and unconsciously acquire and use a vast number of metaphors. Realized in our brains physically, they are a consequence of the nature of our brains, our bodies, and the world we inhabit (Johnson and Lakoff 1999: 59).

Lakoff and Johnson see conceptual metaphor as one of our greatest intellectual gifts. Their view of metaphor differs radically from traditional theories of language and truth, and challenge long-standing views of how science must be practiced, mathematical concepts are structured and, for that matter, how ethical decisions are made. Based on similar philosophies of the embodied mind, such as that of John Dewey and Maurice Merleau-Ponty, Lakoff and Johnson see metaphor as central to all of our thought and just as important in artistic thought, scientific thought, mathematical, economic, political, social, ethical, and spiritual thought. As artists we tend to rely heavily on the use of metaphor to stimulate our creativity. We know generally that metaphor is not merely a matter of language. When we use visual, aural, or kinesethic metaphors, we are using conceptual structures that are based on natural dimensions of our experience, including aspects of our sense experience: color, shape, texture, sound, feel, etc. Metaphors are not only expressed in language, but also visually, aurally, and as imaginative representations – sensed in the body and communicated through movement, gesture, tone of voice, and so on.

When we use metaphor, we are using our imaginations to map one aspect or set of aspects of an experience, an object, a person, an animal, an environment, whatever it is we are focusing on in the moment of creativity, onto another set of aspects of the target experience, object, person, animal, or environment. Metaphors operate as essential ways of understanding the world. They both create meaning and mediate or structure understanding of the world. They operate at the edge of our conscious awareness. Very often, however, metaphors are handed down to us with our 'blankies,' and we continue to use them without being aware at all that things might be different. Metaphorical frameworks function by highlighting certain aspects of experience and concealing other aspects – they construct our point of view.

Metaphor's fundamental location in our physical experience is immensely important in the following discussion. This discussion takes for granted the embodiment of the mind as inseparable from what David Abram (Abram 1996: x) calls the "more than human world." In other words, while we often engage in these metaphoric frameworks believing only our *human* bodily experiences inform the creative perceptions they offer, our engagement is actually due to our belonging to a somatic universe filled with non-human others with whom we share, in varying degrees and in varying ways, this physical universe. We have ceased to notice or believe that, but even our science, when practiced with an open mind, tells us that this is the case.

### Encouraging and Obstructing Metaphors of Creativity

Combining the discussion of embodied metaphor above and the views supported in the previous sections of this essay, it is possible to test various mandates in current metaphors circulating in digital art and new media for their encouragement or obstruction of understanding the importance of sustaining all forms of creativity – human, non-human, biological, organic, and ecological. One of the most useful metaphors with which to start is *innovation*, often used as a replacement word for creation. While working less as a metaphor, the term innovation has become a powerful command phrase in digital art and new media in the last decade. Leaking into these areas through research sponsored by product-oriented corporations, the term has lately even found its way into large digital art and new media conferences (ISEA 2006), as well as many university and art and design school program curricula. In many instances, the word often denotes a desire for a new product, tool, or idea that is an improvement on earlier developments.

Problems arise when innovation becomes the driving force of the creative impulse, rather than the reverse. Though related, innovation and creativity are not the same since creativity, as described above, is concerned, consciously or unconsciously, with uncovering underlying natural orders of the universe. Innovation, at its best, emerges as practical applications of these discoveries. Innovation, as it has been recently understood in diverse fields, may actualize in organizational, technological or economic outcomes. More often than not, in today's current global market environment, it builds upon corporate goals: increasing capital, increasing customers, and even, in what seems like a egalitarian reversal, innovation driven by customers' needs or customer innovation (von Hipple 2005). Even meeting customers 'needs,' however, does not insure the innovation comes from a truly creative impulse. It may, in fact, exist as the 'newest' example in a long line of uncreative designs, basing its existence on misplaced and destructive values – the "need" for more invasive military and political surveillance, for instance, or the patenting of life forms.

While the content of some digital artist's work is the critique of the values driving these innovations, the pressure to produce something new at any cost has begun to appear as a guiding principle in various new media and art and design educational settings. Specific reasons for this exist at the confluence of at least three current forces: western historical traditions of uniqueness in art; historical worldviews, still very much in play, that see the all of nature available for human intervention and use; and global corporate goals (Gigliotti 2006 22–34). As an overarching command phrase in current research and education models, this tendency needs to be noted, commented upon, and shifted (Gigliotti 1998: 89–92).

It is possible to rethink concepts and practices surrounding innovation based on entirely different metaphors. More fruitful investigations may come from a little remarked upon and relatively recent research finding, at least it seems to be recent for those not from indigenous cultures. The desire to improve upon tools or behaviors has been thought to be, until recently, an inherently human characteristic. This ability, however, is not ours alone. In fact, many animals invent new behavior patterns, adjust behaviors to a new context, or respond to changed or impoverished environments (Reader and Laland 2003). An interesting example, involving non-human use of human technology, has been documented in Japan, where crows have developed a unique feeding innovation. They perch at traffic intersections and patiently wait for the red light. When the vehicles come to a stop, the crows spring into action – they fly down to the cars and place walnuts under the tires, and then collect the open nuts to eat (Popple 2002). The impetus to innovate is not only an example of our common inheritance of cognition and consciousness, but, also, a vivid example of universal access to the creative impulse.

### Ecological Absence in New Media Metaphors

Metaphors abound in current new media and digital art: they range from open-ended (absence, community, networks, commons, mapping, social sustainability) to more prescriptive or medium-based approaches (urban space, tissue culture, locative media, container culture). What is evident in the use of these metaphors is the absence of any substantial reference to non-human nature and continuing assumptions about the centrality of human needs and desires. The absence of interest in non-human nature in much of digital art and new media greatly impoverishes the genre and limits its access to true creativity for reasons I have outlined above. In addition, and just as important, are the following two related reasons: the first involves the need for a serious moral consideration of the intrinsic worth of all species, and their right to their diverse, evolving creative capacities; the second is the immediate peril in which a great majority of species now find themselves along with the places in which they and fellow humans now live.

The IUCN Red List of Threatened Species (2006) brings into sharp focus the ongoing decline of the earth's biodiversity predominantly caused by mankind's impact:

> The total number of species declared officially Extinct is 784 and a further 65 are only found in captivity or cultivation. Of the 40,177 species assessed using the IUCN Red List criteria, 16,119 are now listed as threatened with extinction. This includes one in three amphibians and a quarter of the world's coniferous trees, on top of the one in eight birds and one in four mammals known to be in jeopardy. (IUCN 2006)

If that is not shocking enough, consider that the total number of species on the planet is unknown. Only 1.7 – 1.8 million species are known today out of the most accepted estimates of 15 million. The number of threatened species is increasing across almost all the major taxonomic groups and so the question becomes how many more unknown species are we causing to disappear.

Even in new media work that purports to use ecological metaphors, the preponderance of content is human-centered and seldom focuses on implications for non-humans. Heise (2002) makes the excellent point that one reason for this is a metaphorical "double transfer" of the concept of "media ecologies" from urban sociology, which in turn had been translated from categories in biological ecology. She says:

> Just as environmentalists need to address the ways in which recent technologies have altered our experience and conceptualizations of the natural, media theorists need to find ways of relating the global connectedness of virtual space back to the experiences of physical space that individuals and communities undergo. (Heise 2002: 168)

I agree with Heise, but I want to emphasize the importance of relating to and considering the impact those technologies and entailments of those technologies have had on non-human individuals and the ecosystems they inhabit, urban or non-urban.

Biotechnological metaphors appear to be an exception to the paucity of metaphors in new media emanating from non-human sources. I have written at length (Gigliotti 2006, 2005a, 2006b) about how some uses of these metaphors and connected artistic practice in new media circles confounds and clouds comprehension of the need for a shift from a reductionist to a relational approach necessary for both biological and cultural diversity. Deeper and more careful uses of these metaphors are instructive for reasons intricately connected to the discussion of innovation above. Biotechnological research and development has been heavily influenced by the desire for newness and the desire and assumption that humans must always be in control.

Thacker defines biological exchange within the context of globalization as:

> ...the circulation and distribution of biological information, be it in a material or immaterial instantiation, that is mediated by one or more value systems [original emphasis]. (Thacker 2005: 7)

This development of biological exchange has grown along with the ability of network technologies to archive and disperse the abstracted biological information. In this exchange the emphasis in on the network properties of exchange.

> If biology is considered to be an abstract pattern or form – not just a formation but an in-formation – then the material substrates through which this information is distributed are of secondary concern, and that which is seen to be at the core of biology (pattern, information, sequence) can be seen to exist apart from the material substrate (cell, test tube, computer). (Thacker 2005: 9)

This reductionist view allows for an unprecedented efficiency in exchanging biological information all the while retaining the ability to re-materialize it in other contexts. This has allowed for an enormous growth in the global biotech industry. The perceived ability to transfer 'life' at will encourages the dreams of human dominance and control, as well as allowing access to the seemingly endless supply of financial rewards owned by those who are or hope to be in control of this ability. These narrow misunderstandings of human potential limit true creativity, contribute to the destruction of biodiversity, and ignore the need for a serious moral consideration of non-human beings

Ignoring, even in critical contexts, the realities of the millions of non-human beings that actually make up that material substrate from which genetic information is abstracted stifles the use of metaphors able to unpack levels of assumptions about biotechnology. Clarity about biotechnology is becoming increasingly important as the industry grows at a pace difficult to keep up with, let alone question.

And yet, as early as the mid-70s, eminent geneticists were worried about the path biotechnological research was taking. Two quotes: the first from George Wald, a Nobel Prize–winning biologist and the second from Erwin Chargoff, sometimes called the father of modern microbiology:

> It is all too big and is happening too fast. So this, the central problem, remains almost unconsidered. It presents probably the largest ethical problem that science has ever had to face. Our morality up to now has been to go ahead without restriction to learn all that we can about nature. Restructuring nature was not part of the bargain...For going ahead in this direction may be not only unwise but also dangerous. Potentially, it could breed new animal and plant diseases, new sources of cancer, novel epidemics. (Wald 1976: 127–128)

> This world is given to us on loan. We come and we go; and after a time we leave earth and air and water to others who come after us. My generation, or perhaps the one preceding mine, has been the first to engage, under the leadership of the exact sciences, in a destructive colonial warfare against nature. The future will curse us for it. (Chargoff 1978; 190)

### Power of the Non-human

Urged on by the drive for newness, for money, for fame, and even, perhaps, for a mistaken idea that in the long run these experiments will help *mankind*, practitioners of reductive science and technology completely miss the point that the cosmos is an open system, and as such cannot be diminished to fit our human control by the manipulation of genes or any other integral ingredient of a complex and mysterious universe.

Every form of reductionism is mistaken and misguided. Nature cannot be reduced to culture, nor culture reduced to nature. But they are not opposites of an inherent dualism. Nature and culture develop interactively in a complex adaptive system. The increasingly enormous role that technology has played in this adaptive system in Western European culture, and now among its antecedents in North America, was not at one time a given, but directly related to that decision long ago to use technology to beat back the power of nature. Now, finally, we are beginning to see that this has been to our peril.

With its stress on relational dynamics, relatedness, creativity, and differential fragility, ecology and the comprehension of the uniqueness of ecosystems have helped to inform the newer theories of complexity. Many consider ecology to be a "subversive science," "a resistance movement," and the founding thoughts of a radical change from entrenched ways. It may be amusing to many indigenous cultures, if it were not so sad, that Western European thought has taken so long to join the resistance.

Even as we begin to come to terms with the ideas and principles of ecological science, we find that knowledge of these principles does not insure a contiguous ethical practice. We still tend to metamorphose in human terms. It is extremely telling that the idea of non-human or animal culture is seldom if ever remarked upon. The notion of our dominance still plays covert roles in our conjectures of cultural ecologies, such as the urban, economic, demographic, architectural, anthropological, psychological and, of course, the biotechnological and nanotechnological.

Even as we attempt to break from our Cartesian past and perhaps feel less fear and loathing of the power of the non-human and those who have knowledge of this power, it may be suggested that in the current global market situation, it is much easier to dismiss that which is perceived as having little or no power and use the knowledge of ecology and traditional people to manipulate nature instead of defending and respecting it.

Knowing is not enough, doing is crucial. What this means for us as new media artists, designers, and educators is that we may actually contribute to the destruction of our own creativity if we fail to see the connection of that creativity within the natural world. New media is not new if the ideas guiding it are just the old ones of control and dominance. Our job as educators, above all else, is to protect and encourage that sustained creativity, not only for our kind, but also in the world at large, not only for human needs, but also for that creative need that fuels the world.

## Note
1. The use of the phrase "the wild" here refers to the sense of that phrase as suggested by David Wiggins: "not as that which is free of all trace of our interventions...but as that which has not been entirely instrumentalized by human artifice, and as something to be cherished...in ways that outrun all considerations of profit.' (2000: 10)

## Works Cited
Amnesty International (2003), 'Democratic Republic of Congo: Children at War.' Amnesty International. http: //web.amnesty.org/library/index/engafr620342003. Accessed June 25, 2005.

Amnesty International (2005), 'Child soldiers,' Amnesty International. http://t2web.amnesty.r3h.net/pages/childsoldiers-index-eng. Accessed June 25, 2005.

Anon (2006), 'Zero One San Jose: 13th International Symposium of Electronic Arts', *ISEA 2006*. San Jose; California, Leonardo. http://www.01sj.org/ Accessed June 4, 2006.

Bohm, D. (1998), *On Creativity*, London: Routledge.

Chargoff, E. (1978), *Heraclitean Fire: Sketches from a Life before Nature*, New York: Rockefeller University Press.

Curry, p. (2006) *Ecological Ethics*, Cambridge, U.K.: Polity Press.

Delawala, I. (2001), 'What is Coltan?' *Security Council*. Global Policy Forum. http://www.globalpolicy.org/security/natres/generaldebate/2001/0907cobalt.htm. Accessed June 30 2005.

Gigliotti, C. (1998), 'Bridge To, Bridge From: the arts, technology and education,' *Leonardo*, 31: 2, pp. 89–92. http://mitpress2.mit.edu/ejournals/Leonardo/isast/spec.projects/planetcollegium/gigliotti.html.

Gigliotti, C. (2005a), 'Artificial Life and the Lives of the Non-human' *Parachute* 119: 06 (05).

Gigliotti, C. (2005b), "Shifting Vision: the importance of metaphor in the recent work of M. Simon Levin." In *C.H.A.R.T.*, catalogue for the exhibition. Surrey Art Gallery, Surrey, BC, Canada.

Gigliotti, C. (2006), 'Leonardo's Choice: the ethics of artists working with genetic technologies,' in Special Issue: Genetic Technologies and Animals (ed. C. Gigliotti), *AI and Society*, 20: 1, pp. 22–34. http://www.springerlink.com/media/lp3hupmuwl7p69xrkc3u/contributions/f/9/0/7/f90734736x787q27_html/fulltext.html.

Heise, U. K. (2002), 'Unnatural Ecologies: the metaphor of the environment in media theory,' *Configurations*, 10: 1, pp. 149–168.

Hippel, E. V. (2005), *Democratizing Innovation*, Cambridge, Massachusetts: The MIT Press.

Kassem, M. (2002), 'Final report of the Panel of Experts on the Illegal Exploitation of Natural Resources and Other Forms of Wealth of the Democratic Republic of the Congo, (ed. Security Council), New York: United Nations. http://www.globalpolicy.org/security/issues/kongidx.htm. Accessed 30 June 2005.

Lakoff, G. and Johnson, M. (1999), *Philosophy of the Flesh*, New York: Basic Books.

Reader, S. M. and Laland K. M. (ed.) (2003), *Animal Innovation*, Oxford: Oxford University Press.

Lister, M., Dovey, J., et. al. (2003), *New Media: A Critical Introduction*, London, U.K.: Routledge.

Peterson, D. (2003), *Eating Apes*, Berkeley: University of California Press.

Popple, I. (2002), '(A not so) bird-brained idea', *McGill Reporter*, 35: 5 Nov. 7.

Scholz, T. (2005), 'New-Media Art Education and its Discontents', *art journal*, 64: 1 spring, pp. 95–108.

Shiva, V. (2000), *Tomorrow's Biodiversity*, London: Thames & Hudson.

The Royal Society (2006), 'Climate Change,' London: The Royal Society. http://www.royalsoc.ac.uk/landing.asp?id=1278. Accessed May 25 2006.

Thacker, E. (2005), *The Global Genome: biotechnology, politics and culture*, Cambridge, Massachusetts: The MIT Press.

The Animal Studies Group (2006), 'Introduction', (ed. The Animal Studies Group) *Killing Animals*. Urbana and Chicago: University of Illinois Press.

Todd, B. (2006), 'Congo, Coltan and Conflict,' *Heinz School Review*, spring, pp. 1–13. http://journal.heinz.cmu.edu/Current/CongoPages/congo.html. Accessed 15 May 2005.

Vilwar, E. (2003), 'The Lost World War,' *Corporate Watch*, 13: spring, pp. 1–2. http: //archive.corporatewatch.org/newsletter/issue13/issue13_part3.htm. Accessed June 25 2005.

Wald, G. (1976), 'The Case Against Genetic Engineering,' *The Recombinant DNA Debate*, (eds. Jackson and Stich), pp. 127–128. (Reprinted from *The Sciences*, Sept./Oct. 1976 issue.)

Weymuller, E. (2006), 'Congolese Mineral Wealth as Coveted As Ever,' Inter Press Service News Agency. http: //www.ipsnews.net/news.asp?idnews=31665. Accessed 5 June 2006.

Wiggins, D. (2000), 'Nature, Respect for Nature, and the Human Scale of Values,' Proceedings of the Aristotelian Society XCX: pp. 1–32.

Wilson, S. (2002), *Information Arts: Intersections of art, science and technology*, Cambridge, Massachusetts, The MIT Press.

World Conservation Union (2006), 'Release of the 2006 IUCN Red List of Threatened Species reveals ongoing decline of the status of plants and animals,' Geneva, Switzerland: IUCN. http: //www.iucn.org/en/news/archive/ 2006/05/02_pr_red_list_en.htm. Accessed 1 June 2006.

# MAKING SPACE FOR THE ARTIST

## Mark Amerika

During the latter half of 2005, I was a Visiting Professor and Artist-In-Residence at the University of Technology at Sydney, and, while I was there, in addition to finishing my collection of artist writings called META/DATA, I was invited to give a total of five lectures, and in every lecture I gave, whether it was on new media writing and publishing, multi-media performance, digital cinema, net art, or even experimental pedagogy in the arts and humanities, I started my remarks by referring to something Vito Acconci once said in his essay "Steps Into Performance (And Out)," which I'll share with you here too. Acconci said:

> "...if I specialize in a medium, then I would be fixing a ground for myself, a ground I would have to be digging myself out of, constantly, as one medium was substituted for another – so, then instead of turning toward 'ground' I would shift my attention and turn to 'instrument,' I would focus on myself as the instrument that acted on whatever ground was available."

What he is saying, I believe, is quite simple yet something that tends to get forgotten in the mad rush to always keep up with the latest developments in technology as well as spending incredible amounts of time reading and writing out theoretical justifications for the practice-based research agendas of contemporary new media art, namely: that it's *the artist* that is the medium or instrument that is most capable of conducting radical experiments in subjective thought and experience, and that the tools we use, the theories that justify it all, and the outcomes that play into the preconceived agendas and methods of the academic research community as well as the corporate R&D divisions, should have very little to do with the way an artist or collaborative network of artists bring their creative compositions into society. This doesn't mean that artists are outcasts or meant to live on the outer edges of the mainstream economy, but that – like professional athletes – they are meant to play out their *performances-to-be* on whatever compositional playing field they happen to be on at any given time. That playing field would be the ground of the moment, not one they would have to dig themselves out of continuously, but one that they would *act* on as part of their constructed persona(s) as they move through time – what Manuel Castells calls a "timeless time" on the "edge of forever" – one that takes place in the networked "space of flows".

Now, when I talk about constructing personas that distribute themselves in the networked "space of flows," it immediately reminds me of something the artist Eleanor Antin said recently while a visiting artist at the University of Colorado at Boulder. Antin, the interdisciplinary artist now in her 60s, said that when she started making visual art, she began constructing new personas to step into and out of as a way to develop new work. These personas helped her produce what, in another context, she called "an art-making machine."

It's like what my colleague Paul Miller refers to in his book *Rhythm Science*, where the "also known as" – DJ Spooky aka That Subliminal Kid – is contextualized as part of a larger performance artwork where the artist fictionalizes their presence in the contemporary art scene as a brand-name meme or viral force in an "information overload" economy. As Miller says, "[c]reating this identity allowed me to spin narratives on several fronts at the same time and produce persona as shareware."

Persona as shareware. Spinning narratives from the perspective of the Meta-Muse so as to create an architectonically structured personal mythology that feeds into an ever-evolving interdisciplinary practice that uses whatever new media technologies are available at given moment in time. Think of it as fluid or flux identity intersubjectively jamming with other constructed personas in asynchronous realtime.

OK, but *how do we teach that?*

The thing is, we cannot really teach a student how to become Acconci's "instrument" nor Antin's "art-making machine" nor Miller's "persona as shareware." *That* fiction has to be generated by the student-artist who trains themselves to tap into their unconscious creative potential, one who is deftly aware of the fact that these constructed personas need not be construed as alien alter egos to the "normal" creative self. Quite the contrary, the best students I have worked with over the last ten years are attuned to the fact that they are inventing their creative art personas in a world where political fictions are constantly being written in a style of "truthiness" so sure of itself that even when it's dead wrong, it's still convinced that it's somehow dead right; a world where Reality TV is super-scripted in wild contrast to the unscripted behavior of, say, improvisational artists circulating in the aesthetic field of compositional play the best work oftentimes manifests itself in. Taking calculated risks and potentially opening up great opportunities for themselves, the best students are always compositing new role models to feed off of, borrowing from their professors, their fellow students, as well as the artists whose work they see in museums, galleries, and online. With source material everywhere, these top students turn into "remixologists" – performance artists who manipulate all of the useful data they have sampled from so that they can then reconfigure their own stories into a pseudoautobiographical narrative that spins the media attention right their way.

As all of the best students soon find out, the constructed artist persona has no choice but to realize that there is no "outside" the system anymore. At the very least, one could say *we are all in this together*, even if some of us like to role-play the "artist outlaw" living on the edge of forever. As Ron Sukenick has said in his *Down and In: Life in the Underground*: "...a renewed underground would have the courage of its contradictions, knowing how to manage the impulse to succeed in terms of the commercial culture without betraying its deepest political and artistic convictions." Our work, our practice, is not outside of the system. There is no such place as "away". We are in it and of it like everyone else, and this is what gives us the power to try and change what we don't like. In fact, some would say that this is the mission of the artist.

Now, as I tell my students, I think each artist has to figure out their own unique creative path for themselves. There is no surefire way of constructing the "right" set of digital personas so that you can build your own one-person "art-making machine." My own path is full of aimless drifting, a multi-linear narrative of free-form nomadic excursions into what I call the Unreal. This technomadic journey is full of writing, performing, hacking, and directing. It "takes place" in a networked "space of flows" littered with the remains of my collective failures and – much to my total surprise – a few successes that confound me to the point that when I look back and see what has happened over the last 15 to 20 years, all of the work produced across various media in both art and non-art contexts, I think to myself: that's NOT ME.

In fact, that's one subject-area of research I've been glomming on to for most of my active working life, the so-called NOT-ME. I thought I had invented that idea myself as I wrote it out of my system and started improvising entire theoretical fictions out of it via novels, hypertexts, complex works of net art, VJ performances, major installations, and now feature-length movies too.

But there are others on to this as well.

Tors Norretranders, whose book, *The User Illusion: Cutting Consciousness Down To Size*, explores the recent history of scientific investigations into the role consciousness plays in our day-to-day actions, has a three-page riff in the middle of his book where he writes about "art and the expression of me," speaking mostly in terms of theatrical performance, saying that the difficulty of putting on a good play is that the "I" does not have access to the great quantity of information that is required to make the actor present with her entire personality during a performance, that because we all convert information in an *unconscious* way, the conscious "I" cannot automatically activate all the information required for a good performance. The "I" can repeat the text, he tells us, but that is not enough. The "I" must follow the Me to "live" the part. To feel it as it develops. In other words, theater involves setting the Me free, so it can unfold.

He also goes on to say when the performance is over and the audience begins to clap, the consciousness and the "I" return as if from a trance and wake amidst the cheers, which is a shame, because it was not the "I" that gave the performance, but the Me.

Now, I know what he's talking about, not because I have been closely studying and running experiments in the field of behavioral and brain studies out of my digital art lab at the University of Colorado at Boulder, but because of my real world experiences over the last 15 to 20 years as an activist artist creating free-form metafictions featuring my various flux personas across a wide range of interdisciplinary works. But Norretranders and I see things differently. Whereas I can see that he is arguing there is something that exists inside all of us that precedes every conscious act we make, and that this something else exists somewhere inside the brain, I think he and most others who do this kind of research get it wrong in assuming that if it's not the "I" who is performing, then it must be Me. The way Norretranders describes it is like this: he says, "we must distinguish between the I and the Me. I am not identical with Me. Me is more than my I. It is Me who decides when I do not. The I is the conscious player. The Me is the person in general..."

But I would say that it's the NOT-ME who is performing when I engage in these hyper-intuitive acts of creative composition that enable my creative self to not only live my life here on Planet Oblivion, but that somehow leave very specific traces of my existence behind. Sukenick calls these traces *Form*, "like footprints in the sand." But there's a crucial difference to be taken into account when we try to separate the general person Me, who Norretranders would like to give the credit to, and the NOT-ME I feel so indebted to for making this creative life possible. Henri Michaux, the French writer who conducted his R&D writing practice heavily under the influence of mescaline, put it nicely when he said: "There isn't one me. There aren't ten mes. There is no me. ME is only a position of equilibrium. An average of "mes", a movement in the crowd."

The NOT-ME, I figure, is a shorthand way to coalesce my various flux personas (nowadays digital flux personas) streaming throughout the fictionally generated network space of flows I am constantly teleporting my creativity through.

But try and walk into a seminar or studio art setting and teach students, grads or undergrads, how to coalesce their various flux personas into an art-making machine that operates under the direct command of the unconsciously generated NOT-ME, and you might find the glazed-over looks impossible to ignore. *Why is that?*

The difficulties arise both because of the politically correct straitjackets as well as the prison houses of language that permeate contemporary university culture. The problem with much higher arts education today, is that we have become hog-tied by specific identity and cultural politics that encourage students to tap into what is perceived as their cultural identity, as if that referred only to ethnicity, sexual orientation, or gender-bending. All of that is fine, and useful, but what about the shared media culture that so many students, no matter their ethnicity or what kind of humanoid they prefer to sleep with, rely on for information, source material, and ideas on how to expand the emerging languages of new media?

Over time, though, the best students, whether they are of Native American, European, Asian, or African background, find a way to use the emerging language of new media to create constructed personas that challenge mainstream cultural values from whatever cultural perspective they happen to be coming from. *Why is that?*

Is it because they have successfully begun training themselves to embody the *digital-artist-to-be*?

We are still struggling to make space for this political fiction we might want to call the *digital-artist-to-be*.

Rosi Bradiotti, in the introduction to her book, "Nomadic Subjects," says:

> The nomadic subject is a myth, that is to say a political fiction that allows me to think through and move across established categories and levels of experience: blurring boundaries without burning bridges. Implicit in my choice is the belief in the potency and relevance of the imagination, of myth-making, as a way to step out of the political and intellectual stasis of these postmodern times. Political fictions may be more effective, here and now, than theoretical systems.

To which I might add, more effective than the innovative product development coming out of the corporate sector and the by now predictable forms of research methodology suffocating much of academia.

Locating spaces for the political fictions of the NOT-ME whose many flux personas nomadically drift through the networked space of flows is getting harder and harder as we see the viral effects of a rampant techno-capitalism infiltrate the academy, the museum culture, the publishing business, the traditional media outlets, and oftentimes, unfortunately, the minds of the artists themselves. Where is this imaginary *artist-to-be* to go, to go and play, the way any great athlete would play when they say, as Joe Montana, the former quarterback of the San Francisco 49ers did: "I am not conscious when I am playing."

That is to say, how can we encourage more research methodologies that essentially support the artist not being conscious while playing? Is that even possible in the corporate and academic spheres so obsessed with bottom-line profit-making and standard modes of assessment?

When people not familiar with my background ask me, "what do you do for a living?" I always have a problem answering that question, because there are so many different roles one plays in their daily life that it's never easy to quantify that question with a definitive answer, especially when considered in light of Acconci's quote. For example, I would most likely not say, "what do I do? I'm an instrument that acts on whatever ground is available." I also wouldn't answer by saying, "what do I do for a living? Well, I'm making space for the artist, the NOT-ME that distributes all of my flux personas into the networked space of flows." I just wouldn't say that.

Depending on my audience, I might say, "I am a writer."

But already, for me, that's just the beginning of a slippery slope into a long aside about how when writing my creative metafictions I am, like the quarterback Joe Montana, never really conscious of what it is I am doing, that these unconscious acts of creative composition infect an array of contemporary media, and that when I am really out on the fringe of my unconscious experience, and everything is totally "clicking" (to use the novelist David Foster Wallace's term), I am no longer even a writer but some kind of automated teller machine dishing out totally manipulated memory cache cashing in on the sediment of experience that has been slowly accumulating in the databanks of my imagination, not unlike the way Marcel Duchamp watched the dirt accumulate on his window sill and saw THAT as a kind of work-in-progress.

This manipulated memory cache of the player I am calling the NOT-ME is loaded with readiness potential, a readiness potential that can spontaneously generate an internetwork of flux personas, what in the old days we used to call characters. But characters are too composed for me, like scripted Reality TV characters and, as characters, always destined for plots, which (after all) is just another code word for gravesites.

The *artist-to-be* is always a fiction in the making, creatively visualizing the next persona's eventual becoming. My own constructed fictional personas actually teach me how to invent what I have come to call my Life Style Practice. LSP is what I call it, as opposed to LSD. Something that gets activated in what cyberpunk novelist William Gibson called the "consensual hallucination of cyberspace" when he wrote his book *Neuromancer* way back in 1984, that is, when he first introduced us to the term *cyberspace* which we all use now, the way electronic superhighway was used for a long time, a term that I believe was brought into the collective vocabulary by video artist Nam June Paik.

Actually, when you come to think of it, Paik himself was *all over* this unconscious NOT-ME persona tapping into their aesthetic potential. In March 2006, when I flew over to Germany for a series of live events as part of my on-again off-again *Professor Everywhere Tour*, I landed in Bremen, my first stop on the journey and, consequently, with major jet lag. Waiting for me at the airport was the early computer art pioneer Frieder Nake, whose 1965 computer art show in Stuttgart is generally considered the first computer art show ever. Frieder picked me up and speeded us to the Kunsthalle Bremen where the curators had put up a big show as part of the five-city simultaneous exhibition called *40 Years of German Video Art*. Think about that: 40 YEARS. Each of the participating venues devoted their exhibition to a decade of video art, including one on contemporary video art, and Bremen was featuring the 1960s. As soon as you walked into the exhibition, the first gallery presented an amazing scene. It was the original work from Paik's now legendary 1963 "Exhibition of Music – Electronic Television" exhibition in the small German town of Wuppertal. The room was filled with Paik's inventive playfulness as he, the interdisciplinary artist turning himself into an instrument that was now porting his creative potential through electric TV, triggered new modes of art with his loops, delays, distortions, and what he called "Participatory TV" work as well. These days we call it interactive art.

In addition to the various artworks filling the gallery, there was a long glass case that contained the loose, handwritten notes from an essay Paik wrote around that time called "Experimental Television" – that's what they must have called video art in those days – and I was struck by how he too really found it important to write down, to poeticize, what he felt was happening to him as he became this electronically infused, experimental persona "out of nowhere" – as when he says, referring to the word (in quotes), "ecstasy"

- to go out of oneself...
- completely filled time
- the presence of eternal presence
- unconscious, or super-conscious
-  – some mystic forgets himself (go out of oneself)
- abnormal
- the world stops for three minutes!

This last phrase of Paik's, "the world stops for three minutes!", seems to come out of nowhere too, but also anticipates Carlos Castaneda's "Journey to Ixtlan" where the impersonal "I" of the narrator is being guided through his philosophical life journey by the teachings of Don Juan, the shaman-trickster. Don Juan says to Castaneda's persona:

> "I am teaching you how to *see* as opposed to merely *looking*, and *stopping the world* is the first step to *seeing*.

> *Stopping the world* is not a cryptic metaphor that really doesn't mean anything. And its scope and importance as one of the main propositions of my knowledge should not be misjudged.

> I am teaching you how to *stop the world*. Nothing will work, however, if you are very stubborn. Be less stubborn, and you will probably *stop the world* with any of the techniques I teach you. Everything I will tell you to do is a technique for *stopping the world*.

The sorcerer's description of the world is perceivable. But our insistence on holding on to our standard version of reality renders us almost deaf and blind to it. I'm going to give you what I call "techniques for stopping the world."

Is this what Paik means by "to go out of oneself..." the way "some mystic forgets himself"? This is my state of mind too while I automatically generate my fictional personas as shareware. I like to think of it as experientially tagging the data that always floats throughout the docuverse. This unique style of experientially tagging the data is what an evolving digital poetics is all about and, although it can't be taught as a particular disciplinary field of expertise *per se*, it *can* still be modeled in the classroom through storytelling, intersubjective philosophical inquiry, and collaboratively generated improvisational exercises. It's by far the most powerful way to give emerging artists the techniques they need for "stopping the world" – for locating new forms of knowledge in the autopoietic environment being conducted by the artificial intelligentsia our work depends on for its life force. It's teaching through example how to enter a space of mind where the *artist-as-medium* improvisationally composes their work on and in the open playing fields of potential artistic development, while pointing to the radical, intersubjective experiences we are always filtering, tracing, remixing, and otherwise conjuring into multiple and hybridized works of art when tapping into our unconscious readiness potential. Whereas we may never be able to truly teach our students to "stop the world for three minutes (!)" nor create the perfect learning environment for them to experience what Michaux described as his mind running "at full speed, in all directions, into the memory, into the future, into the data of the present, to grasp the unexpected, the luminous, stupefying, connections," we must continually reinvent the collaborative performance space the best students are always desiring so that they can *train themselves* to become the digital artists of tomorrow, artists who are looking to transfer their creative and critical skills-set into the new media society they find themselves growing up in. These students are there to learn what it takes to participate in a highly technologized, social process of self-motivated personal discovery, social networking, and artistic invention, so that they can step into the fold and "play themselves" – even if that means having to reinvent their artistic personas over and over again.

## Works Cited

Antin, Eleanor. *Art in the Twenty-first Century* (Season Two). PBS documentary website accessed at http://www.pbs.org/art21/artists/antin/clip2.html.

Bradiotti, Rosi (1994), *Nomadic Subjects: Embodiment and Sexual Difference in Contemporary Feminist Theory* (New York: Columbia University Press).

Castells, Manuel (1996), *The Rise of the Network Society* (Malden: Blackwell Publishers).

Castaneda, Carlos (1991), *Journey to Ixtlan* (New York: Washington Square Press).

Gibson, William (1986), *Neuromancer* (New York: Ace).

Miller, Paul D. (2004), *Rhythm Science* (Cambridge and London: The MIT Press).

Norretranders, Tor (1999), *The User Illusion: Cutting Consciousness Down to Size* (New York: Penguin).

Plant, Sadie (1999), *Writing on Drugs* (London: Faber and Faber).

Rush, Michael (2005), *New Media in Art* (London: Thames and Hudson).

# NETWORKED TIMES

# Unthinkable Complexity: Art Education in Networked Times

*Robert Sweeny*

This chapter outlines the challenges and possibilities for art education in a networked society, looking to connections between complexity theory and contemporary art history and practice. The author draws examples from popular culture as well as current art educational and new media research, proposing a form of networked pedagogy that is informed by and responsive to decentralized networks such as the Internet.

> Cyberspace. A consensual hallucination experienced daily by billions of legitimate operators, in every nation, by children being taught mathematical concepts...A graphic representation of data abstracted from the banks of every computer in the human system. Unthinkable complexity. Lines of light ranged in the nonspace of the mind, clusters and constellations of data. Like city lights, receding...(Gibson 1984: 51)

The concept of cyberspace developed by William Gibson (1984) in his science-fiction classic *Neuromancer* has been influential in the conceptualization of contemporary spaces of digital interaction. *Neuromancer* helped to introduce a new form of science fiction – cyberpunk – which is just as its linguistic components suggest: a hybrid of slick, shiny digital technologies and gritty, raw, 'human' emotion. Gibson's texts turn upon this dichotomy, causing friction between the smoothness of virtual interactions and an abrasive dysfunctional near-future, placing characters in the ill-defined border between the two worlds.

One of the most resonant aspects of Gibson's writing can be seen in the theorization of the contemporary 'constellations of data' known as the Internet: specifically, in regard to the relationship between the virtual and the actual, the simulated and the experienced. In the disembodied interactions that take place in Gibson's cyberspace, there is always an impact upon physical space, experienced socially, in networked urban spaces or, intimately, in the body of the computer operator. And, while the operators of the present-day Internet make up only a small percentage of the Earth's population, these networks are expanding nonetheless at a remarkable pace, changing the lives of many. The Internet links individuals, fuses physical and simulated space, and blurs past and present experience, creating complex networks of 'unthinkable complexity.'

The relationship between cyberspace and the Internet is not only interesting on this general social level; it also raises interesting questions for contemporary educational practice. Students being taught 'mathematical concepts' certainly help to contribute to this global system; yet, might there be room for other forms of learning within these interconnections? What are the possibilities for artistic creation and critique in cyberspace? Are these spaces really 'unthinkable,' or might they bring about new forms of thought, perhaps those that could be described as *networked*?

This term has many connotations: to be networked can involve expanded communication and increased understanding, or it can place constraints on individual movement, if one is caught within the meshwork of the net. Educational settings are intricately woven through with networks of all types: material, social, and ideological, to name but a few. Those who benefit from the creation and maintenance of these networks can maneuver through multiple connections; they can work the net, communicating with a number of individuals, sharing information, and partaking in forms of commercial or social exchange. Exchange seems to be the key to networking; if this balance works in your favor, you can both provide and retrieve information. If you are weakly connected you might be able to participate at a disadvantage, or simply watch from the periphery. So, do you work the net or does it work you? That is the question for education in a network society.

'It' might not be the best way to describe the 'network society' as proposed by Castells (1996). He uses this term to describe a variety of economic, social, and educational connections that overlap, intersect, and intertwine. 'It' suggests that these connections take place somewhere beyond our grasp, somewhere beyond ourselves, which is simply not the case. If, in fact, we *are* the network, this situation would require a rephrasing of the initial question: Do you have a choice in regard to working the net, or being worked? In order to better understand the possibilities for working the network in educational settings, for actively negotiating this hybrid terrain, I will first break apart the term to explore the possibilities of its constituent parts.

### 'net_work_ed
Fragmented in this manner, the term takes on a new significance. First, a *net* could be used to capture that which is elusive, or could stand for one of the most relevant contemporary networks: the Internet. Next, how does the net *work*? Are there relevant aspects of the Internet that might be used to better understand everyday life in a network

society? And what of art *work* produced within a network society? Are there fundamental properties that can be used to describe and better understand networked artworks? The last fragment to be considered is *ed*: Education. How does education function within the networks of global exchange that proliferate in the twenty-first century? Are educators in or out of the network? Are the connected technologies that are increasingly found in higher education, public schools, homes, and community centers being used to their full advantage, or are art educators simply using a screen instead of a chalkboard, an easel, a pedestal? What are the possibilities and problems for art educators in networked times?

These fragments will be used to structure this exploration of networks in art education. Each section will take on one portion of the term, pushing into a variety of territories to later recombine them at the conclusion, to see what has been formed in the process of reterritorialization. To pursue questions relevant to art education in networked times, I will first explore the structure of contemporary networks in order to see how they function and how they might be useful in trying to understand our present interconnectedness, or lack thereof.

### 'net

The Internet is one of the most relevant contemporary models for networked interaction, both as a theoretical space involving virtual experiences and a practiced social place. The U.S. government DARPANet, designed to link distant military locations in decentralized configurations that could withstand a nuclear attack from the Soviet Union, provided the structure for what would become the Internet. Developing into a research network for U.S. universities, and then later opened into the public sphere, the Internet in its current state is a highly decentralized network, allowing for individualized modification and adaptation and prohibiting the possibilities for centralized control.

The social impact of the Internet has been influenced by these institutional actions, along with various popular culture productions. The cyberspace of William Gibson, as previously discussed, has contributed to notions of radicality associated with the contemporary spaces of the Internet, best identified through the activities of the 'hacker.' Another influential example of digital networks in the popular media comes from the Disney motion picture *Tron* (1982). *Tron* takes us inside the machine, allowing us to see the battle between the clever computer programmer that has been uploaded into the rigid geometries of computer chips and circuitry. Both examples from 1980s popular visual culture rely upon ideological beliefs that separate machines from humans. Computers are inert. Humans are active. Computers function only as they are programmed. Humans function according to their own will. While these fictional works bring the two diametrically opposed ideologies into contact, imbuing the machine with a measure of consciousness that leads to conflict, the two never meet. More than that, human ingenuity inevitably wins out over machine rigidity.

What is the relationship between these fictional worlds and the interactions that take place within contemporary educational networks? Do art educators reinforce similar dichotomies, favoring traditional, 'natural' notions of creativity and creation – making and doing – over the use of cold, inert digital technologies? What are the possibilities for educational practices that blur these binary relationships, that acknowledge the mechanical within the natural, and that see the potential for new forms of creativity related to computer operations? Is it possible that actual practices are far more complex than these rigid fictions? In order to explore these questions, we must first explore the networks of interaction that connect cyberspace and education, so that we might form new thoughts, and, perhaps, begin to work the net.

As I have mentioned earlier, the Internet is certainly not the only example of a relevant contemporary network. Currently, networks of global capital are redefining boundaries between nations, as in the case of the negotiations that threaten the stability of the European Union, and the recently passed Central American Free Trade Agreement. Communication networks allow American jobs to be outsourced to geographically-distant lands, rendering useless previous notions of 'first' and 'third' world, 'developing' and 'industrialized' nation (Friedman, 2005). Terrorist organizations composed of autonomous 'cells' carry out synchronized attacks such as the bombings of the London transportation system in July 2005, and the attacks on New York City and Washington DC on September 11th, which introduced many to the language of networks, framing them in rather sinister terms.

All of these examples have helped to contribute to the 'network society,' although not all inhabitants of Planet Earth are connected through the use of the *same* technologies, or have equal access to these connections. As Castells (1996) proposes, global models of networked interaction and exchange are prominent as both materiality and metaphor; the network society complicates modernist binaries such as Capitalist/Communist, foe/friend, to which Lunenfeld (2000) would add producer/consumer. The technologies that compose these global networks have also blurred the boundaries between public and private. Network forms of organization were once typical in private life, seen in the form of decentralized friendships and family interactions, while businesses and governments had previously been organized according to centralized hierarchies (Castells 2000). The Internet is only one of the most visible examples of these global connections that have blurred boundaries and changed public life in numerous ways. It is the most relevant network model for discussing both direct application as well as theoretical implications for art education. We live and learn in and through networks.

Networks are currently being studied in diverse fields. The mathematical theory known as complexity theory describes many of the attributes of complex networks. It ties together many of the previously-mentioned strands, and should therefore be discussed, in order to develop a greater understanding of there potential for networks in art educational systems.

## complexity

Complexity theory has become one of the most influential mathematical theories of the twenty-first century, developed from catastrophe theory in the 1950s and chaos theory in the 1980s (Taylor 2003). This study of complex systems that exhibits self-organizational properties has been applied with great success in fields as diverse as physics (Nicolis and Prigogine 1989), sociology (Barabási 2003), mathematics (Wolfram 2002), and historiography (Gattis 2002). While stopping short of declaring the discovery of a unified field theory, many theorists engaged in various applications of complexity theory believe that it describes characteristics of systems previously beyond comprehension.

The primary model used in complexity theory is the network. While networks take many forms, from simple unidirectional connections between nodes to intricate, yet rigid, hierarchical forms of communication, complex systems typically involve interactions that take place within decentralized network structures, linking nodes that develop into powerful routing centers known as hubs (Barabási 2002). Complex networks develop and evolve through feedback loops, which lead to *autopoetic*, or self-organizing, systems.

Taylor (2001) presents an interesting analysis of the relationship between complexity theory, art, and education in *The Moment of Complexity: Emerging Network Culture*. While his analysis is informative, his analysis fails to probe into that which makes contemporary networked art practices unique. If the properties of complex systems were to be compared with the practices of contemporary artists, might art educators have a better understanding of developing forms of creation, distribution, and collaboration currently in practice? If art educators were to then structure pedagogical approaches accordingly, what might these forms of networked art education look like? In order to pursue these questions, I will now look at the central fragment in this discussion of education in a networked age: art *work* in the network society.

## work

Works of art have always existed within complex personal, social, cultural, economic, spiritual, and philosophical networks. Therefore, it is not enough to simply state that artworks have always been networked, or that these networks are fully understood, and do not require further analysis. I suggest that a component of life in a networked age, an age of global interconnectedness, is the creation of works of art that follow entirely new principles. In order to pursue this line of thought, I will return to the characteristics of complex systems, analyzing specific works of art that exhibit these characteristics.

The first characteristic of complex systems is differentiation. This could easily be applied to the material aspect of any number of works of art; however, the process of making connections is unique in networked artworks. More specifically, who is able to make the connections, whether it be reconfiguring physical materials, reworking images on a screen, or influencing various forms of interaction.

The differentiation of the material structure of networked artworks leads to the second characteristic of complex systems: interaction. Discussing the process of interaction places the work of art into a larger social context, where it is viewed, bought, sold, stolen, and generally re-worked. In this process the viewer must become part of the system, in order to allow for self-organization to occur. Once again, this is not a new concept in the history of art. Viewership has always been at least a minor requirement for an object to be considered art, which has become increasingly important with the acceptance of forms such as performance art, installation art, and new media art. However, I suggest that certain artists in a network society make work that interconnects with a variety of nodes, "generating sequential as well as serial effects" (Taylor 2001: 142). Not only can the viewer physically reorganize the material; a networked artwork opens up possibilities for multiple forms of ownership, through reproduction, replication, and remixing, actions with particular cultural relevance, as Miller (2004) has argued.

The third property is self-organization. As this process complicates interiority and exteriority, it is hard to determine aspects of artmaking that are self-organized. Does this mean that the artist carries out a series of actions that she or he determines without direct instruction? If so, this would not bode well for the discussion of art education that will follow this section. If this means that the artwork assembles itself, it would limit the discussion to works of art that are composed of biological matter, or that integrate Artificial Intelligence programs, such as generative software art. I will suggest that self-organization in networked artworks consists of a process that the artist sets into motion, much like the biological systems or computational processes discussed earlier. Self-organizing artworks begin in a certain predetermined state, presenting the possibility for development that is outside of the control of the artist. This process places limitations on authorial control; the networked artwork can be said to have numerous authors, or creators.

The fourth property is emergent behavior, related to the structures that form from the processes of self-organization. One requirement of a complex system is that it evolves, is both open and adaptive. This implies that a complex system can shift to a simple structure, or branch into multiple derivatives. The self-organization discussed earlier allows the artwork to evolve into any number of structures, often simultaneously, involving aspects that may be quite far from the initial design. The ability for networked artworks to display emergent behavior is perhaps the most perplexing of these characteristics, as complex networks can potentially shift to simple structures.

These four characteristics of networked artworks – Differentiation, interaction, self-organization, and emergence – will be instructive for art educators looking to respond to contemporary network structures. These are by no means exhaustive; as more is added to the theories regarding complex systems, and as new technologies develop, so too might new practices be identified. Though the practices of artists who use the Internet are quite relevant, the scope of this project extends beyond the boundaries of net art to include work that operates according to the dynamic principles of the complex network system regardless of media or technique: *networked practices*.

In order to explore these practices further, I will now discuss specific examples of works of art that might be categorized as networked artworks. This discussion will be brief, as the space necessary for an extensive mapping of these practices extends beyond the parameters of this chapter, though they may be explored in further writings. The first are works of art that display differentiation. While it has been stated that most works of art are composed of various materials, therefore limiting the discussion of differentiation as a unique artistic practice, it might be instructive to look to one artistic movement that sought to resist such diversity: Minimalism. Influenced by the Bauhaus educational theories of Lazlo Moholy-Nagy and Joseph Albers, minimalist works of art from the mid-twentieth-century American and European art were created to reduce form and material to its most simple, pure state. These theories also informed much of the art instruction in post-WWII universities and colleges in the U.S., a point that I will return to later in this chapter.

Artists such as Ad Reinhard, Agnes Martin, Frank Stella, Donald Judd, and Robert Morris reduced the number of parts that composed the work of art, working with monochromatic color schemes, flat planes, and muted surfaces. There were many responses to this minimalist aesthetic; critical responses can be seen in Conceptualism and Pop Art, while artists such as Peter Halley revisited the theories in the Neo-Geo style. Robert Smithson's experiments with the idea of the non-site in the 1960s were seen as a critique of both the minimalist aesthetic and the gallery structure that allowed for its support. His work provides a relevant point of departure for this discussion of differentiation, though his non-sites establish a rather simple series of related binary nodes: site/non-site, organic/man-made, gallery/nature.

A complex example of differentiation can be seen in *Parasite* (1993) by Australian performance artist Stelarc. In this performance piece, Stelarc relinquished partial control of his body to both viewers in the gallery space and distanced Internet users, using electrodes attached to muscle groups (Figure 1).

The boundaries of Stelarc's body as performative material becomes blurred, multiplied, and manipulated through many conceivable forms of interaction, integrating distance in the critical manner that Benjamin (1968) famously attributed to mechanically reproduced works of art. Destroying the 'aura' of the original – original work of art, originator (artist), original body – the differentiated materials in Stelarc's networked performances open up possibilities for augmentation and intervention, which also relates to the second example of networked practice: interaction

Interaction relates to a networked form of ownership where the ability to participate and collaborate in the construction of both form and meaning becomes the central operating principle in the work of art. The role of technology is perhaps most relevant in the discussion of this practice, as the mechanical reproduction to which Benjamin (1968) referred was to inspire new forms of participation, both with the work of art and with the masses that were allowed the status of viewership. Interactivity is also one of

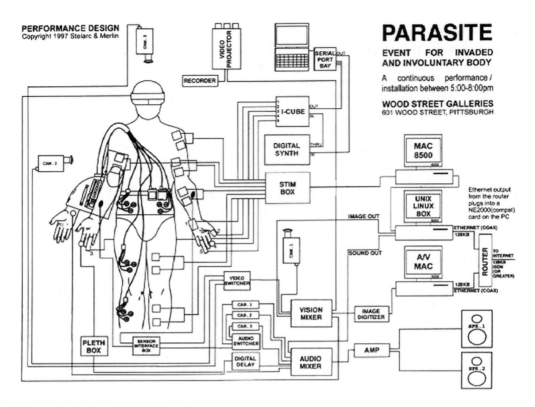

**Figure 1.** Stelarc (1993) *Parasite*.

the 'buzzwords' associated with new media technologies, which, as theorist Lev Manovich (2000) has shown, is actually far from what happens when engaging with a digital work of art. As Manovich suggests, the role of the viewer is reduced to following predetermined pathways established by the programmer, resulting in an experience that is far from self-determined.

Therefore, in order for a work of art to be interactive in the sense of the term used in complexity theory, the viewer must have the ability to substantially manipulate the work, potentially creating a new work in the process. This form of interactivity should be central to the operations of the work, as previously mentioned, and not simply added on as an afterthought. New media work should not be thought of as being interactive by default, just as art made with traditional media is not automatically limited to centralized control. In terms of artistic production, Internet-based collectives such as ®™ark take part in this form of networked practice. Their collective structure allows for diverse forms of interaction, based upon a market capital system where 'investors' buy shares of stock in public actions that respond to issues such as anti-corporate activism, civil liberties, and ecological devastation. 'Investors' can buy into previously existing projects, or suggest their own, augmenting the initial structure established by the ®™ark collective.

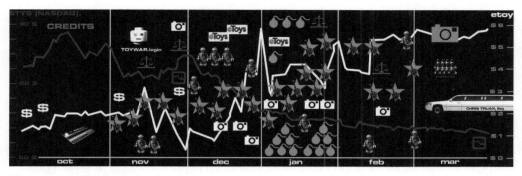

**Figure 2.** TOYWAR timeline.

The 'TOYWAR' project, which helped the artist group *etoy* disrupt and terminate the lawsuit of online toy distributor Etoy, stands as a potent example of artistic practice that effectively utilizes the structure of complex social, legal, and technological networks. The actions of 'ETOY SOLDIERS' who flooded the Etoy website with requests for content, effectively shutting it down for an extended period of time, was just one component of the legal victory that reaffirmed artistic expression over capitalist exchange (Grether 2000) (Figure 2).

Collectivity is an important aspect of networked interaction, where, as in decentralized networks, localized individual input has the potential to register at a global level, as in the *etoy* example. Crucial to this collectivity are legal structures that allow for interaction, such as Creative Commons and Copyleft movements. These contracts allow for the legal appropriation and reuse of images, words, and ideas, resulting in the continued free exchange of information, including the proliferation of networked artworks. If this type of collectivity is seen as a contemporary form of artistic creation, where individuals are linked with one another through the shared use of ideas and images, then educators might recognize the potential for complex interactive artistic approaches.

The third aspect of networked practice relates to the ability for differentiated, interacting components to self-organize. As previously discussed, the notion of self-organization is challenging to determine when discussing works of art, unless the larger context that surrounds the work of art is taken into consideration. The development of what Rheingold (2002) terms 'Smart Mobs' stands as one example of self-organization, as participants, contacted through various technologies, converge in a location, carry out a specific action, and then disperse, usually avoiding contact with law enforcement authorities.

Smart Mobs exist in a space between performance art and large-scale game. Whether considered art or not, they nonetheless point to actions that build from complex networks, in many cases adapting developing technologies in ways never intended by their designers. As complex systems develop, they eventually push beyond their initial boundaries, into new conceptual and physical territories. An earlier example of self-organization can be seen in the *dérives* of Situationist International. The *dérive*, or drift, was a way for the Situationists to explore the psychogeographic space of the city, where predetermined markers and boundaries limited the ability for individuals to develop individual meaning (Sadler 1998).

Self-organization as an artistic approach would require not only the possibility of interaction, but also an acknowledgement of the space that the work inhabits. Just as the Situationists saw the potential for the city as art, contemporary artists are engaging with spaces that allow for unpredictable, open-ended actions to occur. A recent project by the Graffiti Research Labs, in collaboration with Eyebeam, allowed participants to create 'L.E.D. Throwies,' small bundles of LED lights, magnets, and batteries that adhere to magnetic surfaces and emit light. The video of the project (available at http://graffitiresearchlab.com) shows the openness of the project, as passersby interact with the light mural being created on a large metal surface, grabbing them from the wall and throwing them back to change the overall pattern, or running off with the 'throwies.' Artists working in the field known as 'locative media' are also pushing the theories of the Situationists into the twenty-first century, mapping urban spaces and marking new territories with advanced networked technologies. When a work of art extends beyond the boundaries established by its creator(s), the general level of complexity increases, allowing for new forms to emerge.

Emergence is the fourth property of networked artworks. In emergence, the self-organization previously discussed reaches a point where new forms develop, forms that may bear little resemblance to the initial material or formal structures. Because of this concern, it is challenging to discuss emergence as an artistic property, as networked artworks have the potential to evolve into new sociocultural forms. Emergence can be seen in each of the previously discussed examples. In Stelarc's *Parasite* (1993), emergent behavior might take the form of new forms of interaction with the related technologies, or a different understanding of the connections between the body and these technologies. In the example of ®™ark, the legal decisions made create a precedence for both artists and online corporations to follow. The work of the Graffiti Research Lab extends into various communities, with the possibility that the urban space is rethought, as well as shifting the notion and function of graffiti in these spaces. However, one recent example that entwined artistic activity and post-9/11 legal issues might serve as an example of emergent behavior as complex, contemporary, and contentious.

The recent arrest of Steve Kurtz, professor of art at the University of Buffalo and member of the Critical Art Ensemble art collective, illustrates the interconnectedness of critical artistic practice, civil liberties, and contemporary legal structures. Kurtz was arrested following the death of his wife, when police found biochemical equipment in his house used in his artwork. Eventually charged under the bioterrorism section of the Patriot Act, Kurtz is currently awaiting trial for the reduced charge of mail fraud, along with University of Pittsburgh biologist Robert Ferrell (Pentecost 2005).

The initial work by Kurtz and the Critical Art Ensemble regarding bioethics and genetic engineering has evolved into a public service campaign aimed at raising awareness, and legal funds, for Kurtz's trial. It has also led to the publication of *Marching Plague: Germ Warfare and Global Public Health* (2006), which has also spawned a film that was included in the 2006 Whitney Biennial. While not his initial intent, Kurtz's work will continue to influence artistic, legal, and social practices in a post-9/11 era. Artworks that access and challenge networks of power will inevitably change in the process, just as the works have the opportunity to change the sociocultural environment in which they are produced, allowing for new critical practices to emerge, or for laws limiting such practices.

Each of these networked practices – differentiation, interactivity, self-organization, and emergence – are relevant within the spaces of art education, as the connection between artistic production and reception is common to both. What will follow is a discussion of the possibilities for networked practices in art educational practice.

## ed

What should education in a networked age look like? Most educators would agree that it is generally beneficial for educational systems to reflect and respond to their particular context. It is all the more important for art educators to demonstrate such an awareness, as artistic styles shift and evolve over time, traditional materials are rediscovered as new ones are developed, and art theory borrows from numerous fields. As such, it is important for art educators to be aware of the relevance and impact of complexity theory as it relates to the development of complex networks.

The history of art education in the United States includes moments when pedagogy and practice are closely linked with artistic theory. As previously mentioned, the establishment of the Bauhaus in Chicago in 1937, after its founders fled Nazi Germany, created a model of modernist artistic and cultural influence that is still felt in design practice and art schools around the world (Singerman 1999). The Bauhaus educational model, although it placed the visual arts in a central position in general educational programs, was typically delivered in a rigid manner that did not allow for augmentation or differentiation.

The response to modernist art educational practices espoused and reinforced through the Bauhaus took many forms at various educational levels. Many elementary and secondary level art educators saw potential in the child-centered movement, pioneered by Viktor Lowenfeld and influenced by Piaget and Cizek. In child-centered approaches, students were seen as innately creative and were given few limitations regarding materials or subject matter. Art educators at the university level became interested in programs such as those developed at Black Mountain College, which grew from the teachings of Bauhaus teacher Joseph Albers, but with greater interest in interdisciplinary practice. One of the most interesting fusions of art theory and pedagogy following modernism can be found in the work of Allan Kaprow, best known for the development of the 'happening' in New York in the 1950s. Kaprow, working in conjunction with Wichita Public Schools and Wichita State University, Kansas, organized a number of workshops with school children that explored collaborative, performative approaches to artmaking, in the vein of his happenings. These activities also included experiments with abstract expressionist painting and the incorporation of sound and language with visual art (Kaprow 1979).

These examples point to instances when the interests of contemporary artists and art educators merged, creating relevant sociocultural pedagogical forms. What are the possibilities for art educators in the twenty-first century, in networked times? I propose a networked art education based upon the network strategies discussed earlier. I will return to the network strategies for these possibilities to be explored. In order to carry this out, to propose a networked art education, I will look to a model of teaching that was, in many ways, a response to the regimentation and centralization of which the Bauhaus was part: the open classroom movement.

Initially conceived of as a comprehensive approach towards teaching influenced by 'informal education' theories in 1960s Britain, the open classroom movement sought to reconstruct both the physical environment of education along with the activities that took place within the public school (Silberman 1970). Typically, open schools were designed to have large spaces unencumbered by walls that would allow students to move about freely, from station to station, depending on their interest level and mastery of content. Teachers would refrain from group lecture, and would facilitate small group interactions, clusters that would shift depending on the participants and the topic being discussed.

The open schools movement was quickly adopted by many school systems in the United States, and was dismantled just as quickly, due to a number of reasons. First, the changes in the teaching environment were, for both teacher and student, too abrupt. Noise levels in open schools were unmanageable, making inaudible the traditional lecture of the teacher (Wee 1998). Even those who adapted their teaching style to accommodate the practice of 'clustering' found that the sustained shift necessary for adaptation to the open classroom was impractical at best. Many open classrooms were later walled in, creating unsightly spaces that allowed for containment and control, returning to the traditions of compartmentalization of both knowledge and physical space.

The open classroom also failed due to the lack of support from the federal government, accompanied by an increased reliance on standardized testing called for by President Richard Nixon in 1970 (Cuban 1993). By 1975, the movement was, by and large, outdated. The open classroom theories failed to influence education at the university level, beyond minor adaptations in teacher education programs. It is relevant for art educators teaching in a networked age at all levels to return to the philosophies of the open classroom, as many of these structures resemble aspects of complexity theory. Perhaps the theories were developed too soon and can only now be implemented in an age of networks.

Open classrooms provided students with the opportunity to access an abundance of *differentiated* materials. They also allowed for a variety of *interactions* between individual students and teachers. Students could cluster in small groups and work individually or gather as a collective whole. Teachers could choose to lecture, but the structures were better served by small group instruction, or team-teaching approaches. Open schools presented the opportunity for students to *self-organize*, although this was the primary difference between the informal school plans in the U.K. and the open schools in the U.S.: U.S. schools often constructed open school plans and arranged schedules accordingly, without a deep understanding of the important organizational role required of the teacher (Cuban 1993). Last, open classroom plans were developed with the intent that the boundaries between the school and the community were physically and conceptually blurred, evolving in the same way that complex systems often develop into numerous *emergent* forms, involving varied related systems, and blurring the boundaries between them.

It is now apparent to those who taught and learned in open classrooms that, though the ideas were pedagogically sound, the general culture was not open to such change. This may not be the case in an age of networked education. With the spread of the World Wide Web in the early 1990s, most schools and universities in the United States made it a priority to open connections to the 'information superhighway.' In the fall of 2002, 99 percent of schools in the U.S. were connected to the Internet, with an average of 4.8 students having access to one computer (Greene et al. 2003). However, the ability for students to access the Internet in educational settings does not automatically insure that networked learning is taking place, though the ubiquity of Internet connections reinforces the claims of relevance of the network society for public school children in the U.S. The open classroom in networked times might be considered a hybrid of real and virtual spaces, if linked with appropriate, networked pedagogies.

A connection to the Internet does not instantly bring with it infinite knowledge or immediate compatibility, and should not be seen as a panacea for struggling schools, as Oppenheimer (2003) has clearly shown. However, a carefully designed curriculum that includes inventive Internet applications and that takes into account the networked strategies described earlier, might provide appropriate learning options for education in a networked age. I will conclude with a discussion of these strategies that art educators at all levels might find appropriate for art education in networked times.

## A Networked Future?
In his theorization of the network society, Castells (1996) states that educational systems are the most resistant to change: in particular, the entrenched hierarchies of higher education. With the success of online courses, distance education programs, and universities that are primarily online, such as the University of Phoenix, many in higher education are debating the future of networked forms of education, while others rush to develop online course content (Trend 2001).

Art educators at all levels who wish to structure relevant practices should scrutinize the distance inherent to both traditional and networked forms of art education, and problematize these false binaries. Art educators might find the notion of distance discussed by Benjamin (1968) particularly instructive, as his theories of mechanical reproduction have been applied to various aspects of digital technologies (Gumbrecht and Marrinan 2003). As Benjamin famously proposed, the ability to mechanically reproduce a work of art eliminates the distance associated with ownership of a 'unique' object or image. For Benjamin, the reproduced work of art destroys the 'aura' of the original work of art or artifact, allowing it to be seen by a wider audience. In the process, the copy becomes more valuable than the original. Another shift takes place; the copy is valued according to new criteria, emphasizing issues of ownership and authority, moving from aesthetics to politics.

Similar challenges might be seen in the resistance to distance education, where traditional, 'authentic' instruction is subverted through technological mediation. The interactions that take place through electronic circuits are not 'real,' they lack the physicality of immediate presence. However, as Benjamin (1968) suggests, the distance associated with mechanical reproduction is both physical and ideological. The reproduction eliminates the physical separation of the object that is only to be viewed by those in power, undermining the power of those controlling the object. Mechanical reproduction allows for new social forms to develop, opening artistic traditions to new forms of critique.

Distance education might therefore be seen as an inversion of the reproduction described by Benjamin, if read with some flexibility. Distance education creates a physical distance between the student and the teacher, undermining traditional notions of authority that are reinforced in most classroom spaces. These physical gaps might diffuse the power of the educator, much in the same way the reproduced object allows individuals the opportunity to not only see, but to own. Conversely, these technologies might allow for greater control, as the power of the educator becomes diffused within the network, allowing for greater monitoring to take place. Art educators interested in creating open environments that access contemporary networks should pay heed to the decentralized structure of the Internet, and not reinforce what Lyon (1994) calls the 'Electronic Panopticon.' If structured according to the previously discussed networked properties, art education in a networked age might lead to not only new forms of creation, but also to new forms of ownership of knowledge.

In order for this to happen, art educators should take advantage of the flexibility that is part of the Internet and use it to inform pedagogical practices in general. This hybrid structure of the Internet, composed of research tool, interactive social space, communication channel, and art gallery, points towards the possibilities suggested by proponents of the open classroom. For instance, the ability for students to access not only a variety of forms of information, but also take part in social exchanges that the Internet enables, allows for differentiation in both physical space and virtual space, much like *Parasite* (1993) exists in multiple forms, simultaneously. As Patton (2004) has shown, the ability for students to participate in the exchange of visual images on websites such as www.whyproject.org demonstrates the ability for geographically distant spaces to connect and share thoughts on tragic events; in this case the terror attacks of 9/11. The project allows for numerous forms of response, with students sharing their varied viewpoints on a potentially global scale.

A networked classroom can allow for various forms of interaction to occur, if instruction is carried out in a thoughtful manner. Students accustomed to socializing via instant messenger or e-mail might see few options for expanding these forms of interaction. However, as the ®™ark example shows, these networks can be used as both art and political activism. Facilitating these types of interaction in the art classroom – whether in the form of exchange influenced by 'mail art,' the Surrealist parlor game Exquisite Corpse, or direct political activism – can fuse artistic expression and social issues in a meaningful way, especially for those too young to voice their opinion through political channels.

The networked classroom can also allow for self-organization, though in this case the challenge for the educator is to direct such activity in a productive, artistic direction. Young people inherently take part in self-organization as they learn to negotiate social space, often through actions that resist or subvert centralized authority. A recent example of this can be seen in the case of students in the U.K. using cell phone ringtones typically inaudible to those over 30, in order to send text messages during classes (Block 2006). The networked classroom could benefit from a redirection of this urge to subvert towards artistic actions, such as those seen in the activities of the Graffiti Research Labs, who take social behavior generally considered unacceptable – graffiti – and repurpose it using new technologies and social forms of interaction.

Finally, the networked classroom might be seen as consisting of emergent behavior if the products and processes within the art class are not predetermined. Much of the history of art education is based in the creation of objects and images that demonstrate understanding and mastery of concepts and techniques. What would happen if different criteria were to be applied to this process? What would be the result if students produced work that was *differentiated*, made of various materials that allowed for multiple combinatory arrangements? If students addressed various forms of interactivity, might these participatory networks create new opportunities for networked creativity? If collectivity were emphasized over individuality, might the end result be a form of self-organized authorship more closely related to everyday networked practices such as file sharing and open-source software exchange? And, if student practices were to be considered emergent, if the boundaries between student, teacher, administrator, parent, community, and artist were blurred through networked practices, might educational spaces engage with the political power of the multitude, as Hardt and Negri (2004) theorize?

Networked art education might offer the potential to open classrooms at the university, secondary, and primary levels, though, as the demise of the open classroom movement proved, theory must match materiality. One relevant example of this fusion can be found in the work of architectural firm Fielding/Nair International, who acknowledge the potential for contemporary open classrooms that accommodate both environmental responsibility and advanced technologies such as wireless network connections (Fielding 2002). Networked art education must be approached from the large scale as well as the small, just as complex networks are formed from both global and local interactions.

Teaching in the network society, through hybrid networks consisting of traditional physical spaces and cyberspaces offers art educators the opportunity to address the potential for complex networks to not only be identified, but for them to form and flourish. This is only possible if the technologies are used fully and critically, in the service of developing new forms of pedagogy and art, and not simply reinforcing the traditions of the past. As differentiated networks and artworks interact, self-organize, and emerge, educators have the opportunity to think the unthinkable, working the 'net through educational practices that are creative, critical, and complex.

## Works Cited

Barabási, A. L. (2002), *Linked: The new science of networks*. New York: Perseus.

Benjamin, W. (1968), *The Work of Art in the Age of Mechanical Reproduction*. In *Illuminations* (H. Arendt, ed.) New York: Schocken (originally published 1958).

Block, M. (2006), *Teens turn 'repeller' into adult-proof ringtone*. Available online at: http://www.npr.org/templates/story/story.php?storyId=5434687. Accessed 6/06.

Castells, M. (1993), *Life in the Network Society*. Boston, MA: Blackwell Press.

Castells, M. (2001), *the internet galaxy: reflections on the internet, business, and society*. London, U.K.: Oxford.

Cuban, L. (1993), *How teachers taught: Constancy and change in American classrooms 1880–1990*. New York: Teachers College Press.

Fielding. R. (2004), *What can $3.6 billion buy? Los angeles school construction has a choice.* Online at: http://www.designshare.com/Research/Fielding/LosAngeles_School_Design.asp. Accessed 5/06.

Friedman, T. (2005), *The World is Flat: A Brief History of the Twentieth Century*. New York: Farrar, Strauss, and Giroux.

Gumbrecht, H. U. and Marrinan, M (2003), *Mapping Benjamin: The work of art in a digital age*. Stanford, CA: Stanford University Press.

Gattis, J. (2001), *The landscape of history: How historians map the past*. Oxford and New York: Oxford University Press.

Gibson, W. (1984), *Neuromancer*. New York: Ace Paperbacks

Greene, B. (2003), *Internet Access in U.S. Public Schools and Classrooms: 1994–2002*. Available at http://nces.ed.gov/pubs2004/2004011.pdf . Accessed 6/06.

Grether, R. (2000), How the etoy campaign was won: An agents report. In p. Weibel & T. Druckery (eds.) *Net condition: Art and global media* (p. 280–284). Cambridge, MA: MIT Press.

Hardt, M. and Negri, A. (2004), *Multitude: War and Democracy in the Age of Empire*. New York: Penguin Putnam.

Kaprow, A. (1979), *Blindsight*. Wichita, KS: Wichita State University Press.

Lunenfeld, p. (2000), *Snap to grid. A user's guide to digital arts, media, and culture*. Cambridge, MA: MIT Press.

Lyon, D. (1994), *The Electronic Eye: The Rise of Surveillance Society*. Minneapolis: University of Minnesota Press.

Manovich, L. (2001), *The Language of New Media*. Cambridge, MA: MIT Press.

Miller, p. (2004), *Rhythm science*. Cambridge, MA: MIT Press.

Nicolis, G. and Prigogine, I. (1989), *Exploring complexity: An introduction*. New York: W. H. Freeman and Co.

Oppenheimer, T. (2003), *The flickering mind: The false promise of technology in the classroom and how learning can be saved*. New York: Random House.

Patton, R. (2004), "Why" project: Art in the aftermath. *Visual Arts Research*. 31 (1). 2005. School of Art and Design, University of Illinois at Urbana-Champaign, pp. 76–88.

Pentecost, C. (2005), *Reflections on the case by the u.s. justice department against steven kurtz and robert ferrell*. Available online at http: //www.caedefensefund.org/reflections.html. Accessed 6/06.

Sadler, S. (1998), *The situationist city*. Cambridge, MA: MIT Press.

Silberman, C. (1970), *Crisis in the classroom: The remaking of American education*. Random House: New York.

Singerman, H. (1999), *Art subjects: Making artists in the American university*. Berkeley, CA: California University Press.

Spring, J. (2000), *The American School, 1642–2000*. New York: McGraw-Hill.

Taylor, M. ( 2003), *The Moment of Complexity: Emerging Network Culture*. Chicago, IL: University of Chicago Press.

Trend, D. (2001), *Welcome to cyberschool. Education at the crossroads of the information age*. New York: Rowman and Littlefield.

*Tron* (1982), Walt Disney, (motion picture).

Wee, E. (1998), "Washington, DC's Open Classrooms are Noisy Failures." *The Washington Post*. January 25, 1998.

Wolfram, S. (2003), *A new kind of science*. Champaign, IL: Wolfram Media.

# ART/SCIENCE & EDUCATION

## Stefan Sonvilla-Weiss

**we have to know what we want to know before we can start looking for it.**

There has been an ongoing discussion for several years now on the relationship of art and science in educational and professional contexts. Is this just another attempt to put an old fashion into new clothes? I do not think so, because this time the arguments do not constitute an attempt to make a qualitative distinction between universities or higher institutions of art, design, and media. Nor is there a fundamental dispute involved whether the artistic singularity of an artifact or scientific objectivity claims to have more epistemic value. In search of significant sources nourishing the current discourse, paradigmatic changes in the process of renewing and preserving the conditions of cultural self-organization are key to a major shift in how we construct knowledge, technology, and cultural memory. It concerns institutional forms as well as the individual.

One of the standpoints is to consider a revival of the "Leonardo Principle." A second standpoint might close the chapter on the relationship between art and science for the benefit of scientific-economic prosperity, whereas a third engages with the question of how cultural, intellectual and spiritual fields are prerequisite to evolutions in art, science, and technology. My affinity is with the third, although some of the issues relating to this area are similar to other positions.

Many questions derive from the context of audiovisual restructuring of knowledge and communication areas in interrelated and cooperative fields molding into novel forms of interdisciplinary design, such as BANG design, whose acronym stands for the basic modules of our world (B=Bits, A=Atoms, N=Neurons, G=Genes).[1] This field will be extended by neurophysiological research into cognition and perception, not to be confused with the ontological and philosophical terminology of cognition and perception. In conjunction with media and biotechnological industrialization of codes, concepts, and design in the educational context of art and science have been renewed.

Can both art and science learn from each other and, if so, at what and for what? Do both act in the same framework of design and conceptualization, as some of the new generation of media artists suggest in their explorative approach? Would it make sense to exchange curricular modules between specific study programmes?

Narrowing down the thematic frame, one crucial question remains: Which of the teaching and learning fields between art (in terms of audiovisual media design and media use) and science (in terms of research of audiovisual cognition, development of formalized models containing complex mediality and prototyping of media structures) can be formulated? The paradigmatic closeness of art, science, the economy, and politics might suggest a consistent media evolution based on media convergence, yet this does not give us a satisfying answer.

The point is if, and if so, to what extent does it become meaningful to reformulate the very densely organized media evolutionary areas to make plausible and distinct the differences between artistic and scientific education. In that respect it will not make sense to reactivate old habits to distinguish between art and sciences. Current developments in media and biotechnology, neuroscience and cognition research, but also in humanity and cultural science, demonstrate the interrelatedness of knowledge creation and knowledge representation. These developments cope with the complexity of design and research, thus, being of a transferable structure. This principle similarly applies to art and science.

In fact, novel theoretical delineations of model, game, and communication knowledge in different contexts have changed the theoretical architecture if we consider the impact of second-order cybernetic and radical constructivism (von Foerster), positions in Endophysics (Rössler),[2] concepts of neuronal networks, and *fuzzy logic* and *boundary management* concepts mediating between disciplines and product developments. However, these radical changes in cognition and design architecture have had less impact on learning and knowledge organization thus far. A conceptual lag can be identified in both teaching and research.

We know, for example, that not only knowledge and media technology is changing rapidly, but learning attitudes and styles are also changing fluidly across different technologies, interfaces and modes of interaction. As a consequence institutions react with a stronger emphasis on project and praxis orientation. It is not so much about how specific themes relate to a subject or university-specific didactics. The crucial issue concerns to what extent the changing organization of perception and cognition, designing, processing, and selection is teachable, and, if it is teachable, how it can be conducted.

## "Education" – One of Three Leitmotifs of Documenta 12

If we accept one of the prevailing concepts in twentieth-century theory, art would predominantly be created by its viewer and users; based on the economy of attentiveness and the market, a serious discussion on curricular changes would be useless. In other words art cannot be taught if it is taught to "potential" art producers. Would education then solely be a privilege for curators, patrons, visitors of museums and galleries, cultural managers who create, reflect, and provide affirmative market behavior? Obviously there is still a dichotomy between institutional education and self-education.

In his introduction on "Education," one of the three leitmotifs of the forthcoming documenta, Roger M. Buergel's statement "What is to be done" appears rather apodictic.[3] Buergel stresses the importance of self-education through research and analysis that should be part of discursive practice.

> The global complex of cultural translation that seems to be somehow embedded in art and its mediation sets the stage for a potentially all-inclusive public debate. Today, education seems to offer one viable alternative to the devil (didacticism, academia) and the deep blue sea (commodity fetishism). (Ibid., p. 1)

Rather than specializing and emphasizing the boundaries between discrete areas of thought, Buergel wants to erase these boundaries. He thinks that the system of higher education in Europe is more or less bankrupt since the Bologna Process (promoting a common European area of higher education)[4] governs people too strongly. In this respect, Buergel excoriates the instrumental approach to education predicated on market economics. His critique points to tendencies in education based on commercialized access to high-quality information. The individual will no longer be the knowledge owner; rather it will be the enterprise in which he/she is employed.[5] In sharp contrast to the changing higher education policy in Europe, which is drifting away from free access (tuition fees have recently been introduced in several European countries) and fundamental, applied research that would blur and eradicate academic tradition and institutional uniqueness, Buergel stresses the need for autonomous education and development of one's personality. The educational concept with which he operates has a bold notion of an all-encompassing education, a concept going back to Wilhelm von Humboldt, that drastically differs from instruction and knowledge transfer.

The educational concept Buergel suggests, however, conveys a rather simplified antagonism between idealism and commodification, between a politically responsible and seemingly non-responsible audience and between low and high culture.

> Opinions differ on education: the ethos of education reveals the difference between an attitude of mere consumption and an emancipatory ambition. Here is where the exhibition differs from Disneyland, from a seminar at the university, from a discotheque, from the Louis Vuitton shop. Or not.[6]

In fact, the educational landscape and discourse relating to art has long since evolved to cover a much wider range of important issues to be explored such as media and popular culture. "Takeover – who is doing the art of tomorrow," the topics of *Ars Electronica* 2001,[7] strove for a much broader discussion on new manifestations of art and fluid learning arrangements driven by the dynamics of digital revolution. I do not agree with Buergel's postulate on such an idealistic approach of self-education, because the dynamism of "Takeover" does not originate from traditional art practice and mediation, but rather from largely heterogeneous, rhizome-like structures and networks of remotely connected individuals and online communities. The common goal of these activities pertaining to evolving culture is not merely a distant-reflective kind of reaction to techno-social changes; in fact, they constitute and develop further this genuine field.

Digital network culture has not only been changing the modes of media production and distribution: it coevally conveys emerging models of cooperation, communication, and interaction by accumulating various ideas, talents, and capabilities. Hence, the task of tomorrow's artist is that of an intermediary, a catalyst between diverse fields of knowledge, ways of thinking, social models, and solution strategies. The protagonists of this development, hackers, software artists, media and knowledge designers, who are irrespectively showing strong commitment in the face of considerable risk, are opening up new territories in which their role and their scope of action have not yet been fully explored. This alludes to critical inquiry, research, and development in sociopolitical and scientific (biotechnology and genetic engineering) contexts.

Interestingly, yet not surprisingly, the conventional artistic discourse has been cultivating and maintaining a self-referential and affirmative practice among galleries, magazines, investors, dealers, and critics. The corporate image of the artwork has long since replaced the artwork itself. A good example is the "Institutional Critique," an art practice in which often only advanced artists, theorists, historians, and critics can participate. Due to its highly sophisticated understanding of modern art and society, as part of a privileged discourse like that of any other specialized form of knowledge, it has predominantly yielded alienated and marginalized viewers. Net art in contrast has explored the field in a much broader context by exemplifying the work of art as a process, as opposed to a conception of art as object-making. Since net art is "immaterial," commodity value is replaced by utility value: i.e., the principles of the net economy are based on an economy of scale where there is no scarcity of goods. Thus, the added value is not generated by a thousand copies of the same "product" but instead by the "exchange value" that is based on each different source of information and not on each individual copy (cf. Ghosh 1998).[8]

In his lecture, "Science as an Open Source Process," Friedrich Kittler[9] argues that the liberty of science rises and falls in parallel with source code liberation. Only now will science become a university. In that sense, the definition of university implies, differently from in closed or secret research centers, that the knowledge must circulate and be accessible without the protection of patents and copyright issues. Media convergence gives us the opportunity to dissolve the media-technical boundaries between natural scientific, technical, and cultural knowledge.

**Transitory Processes**
In my reflection on transitory processes in art, science, and education, I will refer to Roger Fidler's Mediamorphosis, which describes the material, logical, and cultural practical use and developments of media. Art and science are dependent on these morphic surroundings by inventing, developing, and generating new ones. Relating to this dimension of mediamorphic events, I would like to add the following quotation:

> Cyberspace...enables its audience not merely to observe a reality, but to enter it and experience it as if it were real...Whereas film is used to show a reality to an audience, cyberspace is used to give a virtual body, and a role, to everyone in the audience. Print and radio tell; stage and film show; cyberspace embodies.[10]

Questions arising in this specific context relate to teachable contiguity in media production and design; the ratio between subject and media specific teachings; and how both can be applied in a dynamic, reciprocal mode.

Media evolution has been taking place over many centuries as specialization and fragmentation of sensual perception, communication, and concepts of truth. It has been a long history of segregation of multisensoric options in human self-organization. The effects of this process of specialization and disjuncture have generated particularly strong systems such as paintings, scripture, sciences, aesthetics, and so on. This has led to a material and mental disparity to which can be assigned the same texture and facture and distinctive canonic differences as with institutions, iconoclastic and iconophilic cultures. Some of the distinctive systems that arose out of this process, such as the privileged status of reading over vision, have come under pressure by multimodal and multicodal forms of production, perception, and reception. Alongside the media's evolutionary "agenda," postmodernist and post-structuralist concepts (Derrida, Foucault, Lévinas) and tendencies of individualization as for sociocultural changes and use of the new media are frequently being conceptualized as a dichotomy of unleashing ("deboundarization"). However, in the current media discourse there are tendencies to discover media practice from another perspective, which means that a connection between persistence and recombination of social structuring and social practices can be seen as a model for social change. This model is based on the hypothesis that the use of new media is based on given social structures and social practices. With respect to tendencies like individualization and globalization, the social potential of new media such as weblogs[11] offers distinct forms of media use within different social practices, including the strengthening of the latter as well as doing without them.

With regard to media-related functions and their proliferation, the extension of computer technology is irreversibly encoded in delocalized media and electronic networks as part of culture and society as distributed and diversified systems. A constituent factor in this process is media convergence or integration. Alongside the media synthetic approach to merge different media into one, we can identify another important attempt towards multisensory perception. The visual sense, the faculty of vision, gets back its vast cultural spectrum ("from *Lascaux* to the *Virtual Museum*") and in parallel the interface changes into a multisensory one. This epoch-making electronic and fiber-optic–based media convergence has ceased the history of media divergence. From now on, the point is how different media functions, whether in a *pure* or *crossover* mode, come into play.

Screenager, a term first coined by Douglas Rushkoff in his 1997 book Playing the Future, is a technologically savvy young person, living next door with audiovisual gadgets and interfaces, where he/she interacts in a mediated setting of learning, entertainment, peer bonding, and play. Is the interconnected "mediaspace a co-operative dream, made up of the combined projections of everyone who takes part,"[12] or do these trade-offs speak to a wider set of sociocultural implications and consequences in light of an education "close to reality"?

Taking into account the next generation of students there is now a way to cope with hybrid digital learning cultures. What was with all those demands for change in higher education institutional settings? Although several educational outreach activities have been undertaken since then, the mediation paradigm ("blended/hybrid modes of teaching and learning") often fails on the basics.

If we interpret art and science as two dimensions relating to (post)modernist and interface culture, the prerequisites in defining a new curriculum changes significantly. It would thus demand another structure of design capabilities corresponding with an all-encompassing model of knowledge design. Thus, many of the practices and alternative viewpoints these theories claim, as for adaptive, flexible, and transgressive forms of learning and developing new contextual abilities, would likewise change artistic and scientific educational processes. The most fundamental macro-question in communication, media theory, and cultural theory is the nature of mediation, which means that we have always been in language, in symbolic systems, and we know our lived-in world by language, discourse, and signs, not by immediate access to "things in themselves" (Kant). The primacy of mediation in any theoretical model is milieu, medium, structure, and system of mediation. Hence, artistic practice significantly changes into mediation between the viewer and the subject, between "art" and "life," media, technique and expression, art and institutions, copyright and artwork.

Over the last two decades, we have learned to know about dissipative structures in biology, fractal and chaos theory, network and self-organization theory, yet with little impact on academic institutional teaching and learning culture. With the notion of social technologies, the accompanying current transformation process from single authorship to co-authorship, public versus person-to-person communication, contributions versus display, has become virulent in the net activism of the 1990's that links in many ways with the social or socially critical processes of the 1960's and 70's (e.g., U. Eco's "open" works of art and J. Beuys's concept of "social sculpture" relating plastic creativity to socio-political activities, K. Galloway and S. Rabinowitz's "Hole-In-Space" regarding telematics and telepresence). Current social software developments are merging the socio-political and media-technological towards a democratizing and participatory media approach.

By applying this to learning processes in a digital age, one of the main questions is how the increased recognition of interconnections in differing fields of knowledge, systems, and ecology theories is perceived in light of learning tasks. Alternative theories deriving from chaos, self-organization, and social network theories suggest that we can no longer personally experience and acquire the learning that we need to act. We derive our competence from forming connections. Chaos, as a science, recognizes the connection of everything to everything.[13] The butterfly analogy highlights the challenge of how we deal with sensitive dependence on initial conditions that profoundly impact what we learn and how we act based on our learning. As for social-network theories, Albert-László Barabási states that "nodes always compete for connections because links represent survival in an interconnected world".[14] This competition is largely dulled within a personal learning network, but the placing of value on certain nodes over others is a reality. Connections between disparate ideas and fields can create new innovations. This amplification of learning, knowledge, and understanding through the extension of a personal network is the epitome of a new learning culture.

## Multiple Perspectives
The creation of multiperspective perception does not necessarily require interdisciplinarity, which sometimes disguises academic disciplinary thinking. Moreover it should be a process of reorientation and aggregation of subject-specific knowledge and coherences, yet under the premises of audiovisual introspection of our cultures through mediality. The reference system to which the process of knowledge creation adheres could be easily extended if we consider, e.g., the traditional panel not only as a technique of representation but also from the viewpoint of techniques of (self) observance, which means the cooperative integration of acoustics and optics, mathematics and epistemology, neurophysiology and communication theory, media evolution and visual sciences, Gutenberg and Turing, Disney and Almodóvar.

I think it is important to define (audio-) visual education no longer through either exposed or archived representativeness. There are neither economic arguments to make plausible a separation of text and image, generated and displayed in the same medium, nor other acceptable objections, whether they stem from platonic reasoning or similar epistemological coinage, to deny images the same intelligible and explanatory potential that has been ascribed to scripture and text over the centuries.

Computer-generated visibility applies to encoded data representations, which simultaneously show a typographic simulation and a visualization. The collapse of the classical semiotic reference system of "signification" (Pierce) has been superseded by the sober conclusion that "[i]mages do no more represent world but data", or, as Peter Galison puts it, "Images scatter into data, data scatter into images."[15]

*GoogleEarth* is a good example of how the cartography of the world increasingly flows into the cartography of the Internet. "World" becomes downloadable, navigable, and manipulable. Programming (technique), interface (aesthetic), and interactivity (human-machine, human-human interaction/social dimension) merge into new modes of production, perception, and reception. Since human cognition strongly relies on visual patterns, the enormous amount of data demands new visualization strategies. Simulation is an attempt to model a real-life situation on a computer so that it can be studied to see how the system works.

Another important aspect relates to communicative skills and competences as dialogical principles. Changing perspectives also means the communicative interdependency between the respective knowledge and skills in relation to social praxis. If we acknowledge the fact that knowledge, competences, and skills are circularly determined, long-term planned curricula would no longer work as for teaching in art or science. Courses of instruction claim to be flexible and adaptive, and, as a consequence, new dependencies emerge between institutions, processes of accreditation, and the actual course developments.

Another assumption pertains to the rhetorically well-trained relationship between ethics and aesthetics, or following Aristotle's formulation, phronesis (mitigation) and aesthesis (sense perception). Perhaps one should avoid making the mistake to constantly serve the purpose of complementary fulfillment of both, e.g., media-technological **and** artistic skills, mediality and aesthetics. It would be a fatal backslide into premodern concepts of harmonic principles, which are, in my point of view, from a media-theoretical standpoint, no longer applicable in contemporary contexts.

## Complexity
An all-encompassing thought relating to my final considerations is that of complexity, meaning an uncountable dimension of non-predictable events.[16] With regard to thinking critically and productively about media form, content, and context, it is difficult to say whether it will ever be possible to educate media competence that fulfils the demands of complexity. It seems to me that it is more appropriate to develop sensitivity in managing complex situations and demands. That is to say that neither artists nor scientists are able to predict if and how their ideas and concepts will be accepted, copied, evaluated, and varied upon. Artists by their nature seem to be more dependent on the selecting milieu of appreciation than might be said of scientists. In my opinion, thinking and doing are rather isolated qualities in artistic areas that need to be strategically developed for the competitive art and gallery business. This empowers artists, on the one hand, to display a sensibility for complex demands "just in time"; on the other hand, many promising artistic careers have failed to cope with those specific demands. Indeed, scientists have developed a certain kind of sensibility for complexity as well, but how they differ from artistic milieus is a peculiar attitude of prudence towards provenance, causation, and precondition that strongly relates to thinking in systematic order and theoretical boundaries.

Both of these current practices of sensibility for complexity in media arts and the sensibility for stringent reasoning in media, cognitive, and communication sciences, could, if flexibly applied in learning processes, stimulate the co-designing of novel hybrid forms in theory and practice.

## Practice

How can these expectations meet the challenges in learning and teaching contexts?

- *Modularization*: This is to increase the system's responsiveness to changing skill needs. Modules in audiovisual, media-technological, cognitive, and communicative areas are easier to revise and update than full courses. The pedagogical changes implied are to encourage more student-centered, self-regulated, participative, and active learning. Modules can be defined based on projects or tasks to encourage learning and to develop "transferable skills" such as personal autonomy, responsibility, decision-making, and the ability to exercise initiative. A modular structure is used to support independent study and individual student needs. This should be thought of and realized as a revocable, temporally limited structure within adaptive learning processes.
- *Projects*: Project work emphasizes explorative learning and research-based design in knowledge building communities and organizations[17] supported by socio-cognitive dynamics and technological dynamics. As for socio-cognitive dynamics, community knowledge, and collective responsibility equally foster individual achievements and contributions to shared, top-level goals of the organization.

Democratizing knowledge means that diversity and divisional differences represented in any organization do not lead to separations along knowledge have/have-not or innovator/non-innovator lines. In order to achieve symmetry in knowledge advancement, expertise is distributed within and between communities. To give knowledge is to get knowledge. Early acquaintance with such technological, theoretical, and communicative complexity advances thinking and acting in cooperative design processes.

- *Field Practice*: The dynamics of knowledge creation and distribution alongside the side effects of neoliberal labor policy requires critical and creative thinking more than ever before. Internships in diverse scientific, economic, artistic, public, and administrative working fields offer the possibility of learning and knowledge transfer in some of the professional areas with which teachers and learners are less familiar. In fact, new technologies require a much broader spectrum of competences, skills, and knowledge such as social communicative competences, contextual abilities, flexibility, and attendance to work and practice in collaborative environments, a disposition to challenge the ongoing paradigm shift in the knowledge society, an openness to sociocultural diversity, a wide range of ICT skills through work or study, practical and theoretical skills in media and visual literacy. The need for such experts is not confined to any of the cultural segments.

**Suggestive Curricular Topography**
I would firstly like to suggest three interrelated fields to which an integrated audiovisual curriculum should establish a clear reference. Secondly, I will deal with a more precise depiction of several interrelated layers in teachings.

I. Areas of sensual, mental, and reflexive media perception and usage that includes:

■ Visualization (image, text, text-image, three-dimensional, morphic, etc.);
■ Abstraction (scientific models, artistic modes of representation, virtual environments, abstract vis-à-vis such as avatars, e-agents, knowbots, etc.);
■ Imagination (poetic, literary, semiological, playful, fictional, etc.);
■ Operation (interaction, cooperation, synchronous communication, video-conferencing, collaborative work, etc.);

II. Spatio-temporal perception, contextualization, and reflexion in creative processes relating to;

■ Human-human interaction (face to face);
■ Human-machine interaction (based on division of labor);
■ Human-medium interaction (from face to interface);
■ Human-net-human interaction (endo-face);

III. Contextualization of present forms of knowledge and design containing:

■ Applied and systematic structures in scientific, technical, and vocational education;
■ Artistic knowledge areas;
■ Knowledge models (heuristics, theoretical architectures, communication media);
■ Prevalent artistic models from a historical perspective;
■ Differentiation between production, communication, and attendant media.

Finally, I would like to tackle some of the possible teaching and content layers, which I consider important in a variety of possible combinations. The following list suggests an open-ended and modifiable structure. You are invited to reshuffle, expand and to mingle new and existing areas of interest referring to an educational setting in scientific- and artistic-related media education.

Some of the knowledge areas are:

■ Data and information technology;
■ Digital media;
■ Network technologies;
■ Theories of perception from psychology, neurophysiology, brain research, and radical constructivism;
■ Prevalent communication theories;
■ Media (art) history, media evolution, and media anthropology;

- History of optical media and acoustics, theories and concepts of image processing and production (computer-generated images and non-optical images);
- Colour theory and optics;
- Acoustics;
- Artistic, cultural, scientific, spatial and temporal models;
- Cybernetics and second-order cybernetics, chaos, complexity theory;
- Media theory and media sciences;
- Cyberlaw;
- Network models and theories;
- History of aesthetic concepts of visibleness;
- Social research in usability and ergonomics.

It is obvious that the suggested list contains core areas where it is not yet defined how those areas of knowledge are purposefully mediated and how teachers establish pertinent ways of transfers relating to their competence and appropriate and media-adequate means and methods for modularization and project work. Apparently existing dilemmas relating to inappropriateness in bridging digital culture and traditional academic teaching and mediation concepts cannot be resolved only by acknowledging the preconditions of the various possibilities conveyed by a media-technologically generated reality. Hence, the challenges of curricular changes and re-orientation cannot be effectively implemented without respecting paradigmatic changes in non-formal and informal learning processes.

In search of an idea that could encompass all relevant thoughts, perhaps one can assume that the suggestions being made envisage stimulating a research-narrative and an explorative-narrative–based learning approach. However, there still remain differences between art and science. It is possible to educate to design the artificial, but it will not be possible to educate artistic design, concepts, and thinking. Although the purpose might be the same, at least from a media-technological standpoint, the objectives vary significantly. Artistic production is authorized by its percipients; the artificial by its immersed users. The previous sentence bears potential conflict, if both the artificial and the artistic happen to coexist in the same medium. Thus, the beholder changes into the position of the interactive user, and art transforms into full-body immersive spaces. But that is another story and would open up a new chapter, leaving behind an audience presumably evenly divided between curiousness and defense. How to decide.

That's another story...

**Notes**

1. Bolz, Norbert (2006): bang design – design manifesto of the 21st century. Hamburg: Trendbüro.
2. Interview with Otto E. Rössler (in German): Vom Chaos, der Virtuellen Realität und der Endophysik. http://www.heise.de/tp/r4/artikel/5/5004/1.html (15.11.2006).
3. Dcoumenta 12 – leitmotifs, http://www.documenta.de/english/leitmotifs.html (06.11.2006).
4. Education ministers from around 30 European countries had met in Bologna and undertaken in a joint declaration (the Bologna Declaration) to establish a European area of higher education by 2010. http://ec.europa.eu/education/policies/educ/bologna/bologna_en.html (16.11.2006).

5. Buergel, Roger M.: Correspondences. In: Circa Art Magazine. http://www.recirca.com/backissues/c113/p43_48.shtml (18.11.2006).
6. cf. Buergel, Roger M.: http://www.documenta12.de/english/news_a20.html (18.11.2006).
7. Stocker, G./ Schöpf, C. (ed.) 2001: Ars Electronica 2001. Wien, New York: Springer.
8. Ghosh, R. A.: "In an environment where it costs next to nothing to duplicate a product, exactly what is scarce? A Ferrari F40 would presumably be cheaper if it cost under a dollar to make a perfect copy." http://www.firstmonday.org/issues/issue3_3/ghosh/ (08.12.2006).
9. Kittler, F.: „Wissenschaft als Open-Source-Prozeß", http://www.mikro.org/Events/OS/reftexte/kittler.html (08.12.2006).
10. Walser, R: "Elements of a Cyberspace Playhouse" (1990), cited in Howard Rheingold, Virtual Reality (NY: Simon & Schuster, 1992), p. 192.
11. See also Herring, S. C., Scheidt, L. A., Wright, E., and Bonus, S. (2005) Weblogs as a Bridging Genre. Information, Technology, & People, 18 (22), pp. 142–171.
12. Rushkoff: 1999, p. 269.
13. cf. Gleick's "Butterfly Effect". In: Gleick, J., (1987). Chaos: The Making of a New Science. New York, NY, Penguin Books.
14. Barabási, A. L., (2002): p. 106.
15. cf. Peter Galison, In: Latour, B. P. Weibel (2002): Iconoclash: Beyond the Image Wars in Science, Religion and Art. p. 300, ZKM & MIT Press.
16. "Complexity" was an exciting new interdisciplinary area of inquiry that emerged in the 1980's (cf. M. Mitchell Waldrop, Complexity, Touchstone, 1992), in large part because computers made it possible for the first time to make observations on the behaviour of "iterative" systems.
17. Knowledge Building terminology stems from Scardamella & Bereiter, Ontario Institute for Studies in Education.

## Works Cited

Barabási, A.-L. (2003), Linked: How Everything Is Connected to Everything Else and What It Means for Business, Science, and Everyday Life. NY: Plume Books.
Bereiter, C. (2002), Education and Mind in the Knowledge Age. Mahwah, NY: Lawrence Erlbaum Associates.
Bolz, N. (2006), bang design. design manifest des 21. jahrhunderts. Hamburg: Trend Büro.
Fidler, R. (1997), Mediamorphosis: Understanding New Media. Thousand Oaks, CA: Pine Forge Press.
Galison, p. In: Latour, B., Weibel, p. (2002), Iconoclash: Beyond the Image Wars in Science, Religion and Art. Cambridge, MA: MIT Press.
Gleick, J. (1987), Chaos: The Making of a New Science. New York: Penguin Books.
Herring, S. C.; Scheidt, L. A.; Wright, E.; and Bonus, S. (2005), Weblogs as a Bridging Genre: Information, Technology, & People, 18 (22), pp. 142–171.
Rushkoff, D. (1999), Playing the Future: What We Can Learn from Digital Kids. New York: Riverhead Books.
Stocker, G./ Schöpf, C. (ed.) (2001), Ars Electronica 2001. Wien, New York: Springer.
Walser, R. (1990), Elements of a Cyberspace Playhouse, cited in Howard Rheingold, Virtual Reality. New York: Simon & Schuster.
Waldrop, M. (1992), Complexity: The Emerging Science at the Edge of Order and Chaos. New York: Touchstone.

# LEARNING, EDUCATION, AND THE ARTS IN A DIGITAL WORLD

## Ron Burnett

The cultural context for learning in the arts, particularly in art and design, has undergone a major transformation over the last decade. The changes have been profound with particular effect upon educators and curricula and upon the academic paradigms that have dominated art and design schools as well as art departments in universities. Part of what I would like to discuss in this chapter is the intersection of a number of crucial developments that have reshaped many of the assumptions that have governed art education. Numerous aspects of this change are being driven by digital technologies, but technology is not the sole reason.

In a general sense, the institutional infrastructure upon which so much of learning and education in art and design has depended – discipline-specific departments, specialized educational models, classroom lectures, studios as sites of teaching and practice, learning as training and vice versa, all of these elements no longer operate with the same authority as in the past. There are many reasons for this, not the least of which is that students no longer need to rely on teachers as they did over the course of the twentieth century. Certainly, as an example, the role of the artist as teacher does not carry the weight that it used to, both within art and design schools and within the community as a whole. This is largely because the legitimacy of the teacher/artist is now based on many more factors than just reputation, including the ability to translate their experience as artists into pedagogical practices that link creativity to community.

A student who plays videogames, connects to friends and others through MySpace.com, uses an iPod, does schoolwork on a computer, chats and surfs the Internet, takes photos with a cell phone, uses video to create Vlogs and then posts them at YouTube.com and also has a blog is already involved in a potentially creative space. This student may have edited video and created music on computers and may have developed a sophisticated set of ideas about aesthetics and storytelling. The role of instruction in this environment will not only be far more complex, but requires some connection to and understanding of these phenomena. At the same time, the challenge is to understand all of these activities and to analyze whether they open up critical discourses or shut down serious thinking. There is no question that the depth of involvement and commitment of students to these media has changed them and their views of the world. It is, however, essential that learning about these phenomena is framed by a self-reflexive understanding of their structure, function, and role as tools of communications and interaction (Nokes 2005).

In this environment, an argument can also be made that art education can no longer focus on one discipline or one practice, and teachers who were trained to work in one area cannot service the demands that students and our society have for a multidisciplinary education. Discussions of interdisciplinarity are not new. This is not the place to summarize the many debates that took place in the sixteenth, seventeenth, and eighteenth centuries and that were foundational to what we mean by the sciences and the arts in the twenty-first century. Suffice to say, that Western culture has been building disciplines and tearing them down on a regular basis for a long time and that there has been a non-stop effort on the part of many thinkers and practitioners to look for unity in difference, as well as to recognize how differences may have common foundations.

However, at the moment we have reached an important juncture and it is perhaps crucial to ask whether the cross fertilization of disciplines has become essential to the very future of disciplines as they are practiced in centers of learning. The challenges for art education are many, but none is more important than redefining the orientation of disciplines in art and design and to explore new disciplinary boundaries that reference history, but also deal with the future. The challenge is not to dilute some of the core strengths of disciplines, while at the same time recognizing the fluidity and permeability of their boundaries.

In order to narrow down the concerns of this chapter, I will focus more specifically on how networked forms of knowledge production and distribution are contributing to a reassessment of disciplines and their status. I will explore a number of intersecting issues: the role of digital technologies as change agents and their effect on the experiences of learning, the many ways in which networks alter the equation between different modes of learning and the synergistic relationship between technology, community, teaching, and art (Röhle 2005).

## Digital Technologies as Change Agents
Cultural claims about the various factors that produce change tend to be linear – the line being one that moves along a straight, if not narrow, trajectory from the less complex to the more complex. The approach that I will take looks at the *displacements* that are

created by the movement from one phase to another – movement in this instance being more like transportation framed by what Bruno Latour has described as "...connections, short circuits, translations, associations, and mediations that we encounter, daily." (Latour 1996: 183)

Digital technologies produce an intricate multi-dimensional media environment with many levels of mediation, connection, and disconnection. It may be the case, however, that digital societies are generating increasingly complex layers of human interaction and expression using already existing strategies of communications, and not recreating the terrain of cultural activity.

Although it is in wide usage, the term "digital technologies," has now become a trope for change itself. It is true that it is almost impossible to talk about culture without linking that discussion to the digital, and it is also true that we are in the midst of a context where many of the rules for cultural production and consumption are being rewritten. Nevertheless, the power of the metaphor – the strength of the term digital – far exceeds what digital culture itself actually produces. The key issue is not to make assumptions about the impact of a technology just because that technology exists. This in no way precludes thinking about the ramifications or the role of the iPod for example, but does require some methods for examining the phenomenon and linking that *research* to everyday use of the iPod by learners as well as to the creative potential that the technology makes possible.

In this context, there has been a growing recognition of the role of artists as producers *and* researchers – effectively bringing the creative arts in closer contact with the social sciences and natural sciences. This shift is an important one because it makes it possible for practitioner/teachers to explore the connections between audience and creativity in a more structured and less anecdotal fashion. It also values and recognizes the work of artists which to some degree always involves research whether it be of materials, space, objects, the process of interaction or cultural activity. Victoria Vesna says it well:

> One of the most important scientists to comment on the similarities between artists and scientists creative processes, physicist Werner Heisenberg, believed that artists creativity arose out of the interplay between the spirit of the time and the individual. For Marshall McLuhan, artistic inspiration was the process of subliminally sniffing out environmental change. In fact both artist and scientist are involved in the work of intuiting change in perception and materializing it for others to experience, see and ultimately change. (Vesna 2001: 121)

The materialization of intuition has always been an important part of work in the arts and is central to teaching and learning the skills and competencies needed to create objects and experiences. Often, far more weight is given to the outcomes of this process than is needed or deserved. This is largely because the object takes on a status removed from the activities of creating it. Learning in art and design is ultimately about practice, even when great weight is given to outcomes, but that practice is also circumscribed by the need to be self-aware and critical. So much depends on the strength and quality of the discourse used to reflect upon and articulate artistic work. The quality of the discourse cannot improve without a profound understanding of history, theory, and criticism. Often, a defense against these requirements is that creativity is based on inspiration and intuition. Some of this is true, but in the final analysis, materialization means that the work exists in the public sphere and, therefore, articulation and criticism become as important as the original impulses that went into the creative process. This is even more important when artists make claims about the impact of their work on society as a whole or during a time of intense change such as we are experiencing at the moment.

For example, when the first portable video machines became available in the late 1960s, many artists saw portapacks as liberating television from the control of corporations and governments. Portability and simplicity of operation combined to make it seem like artists could take control of at least part of the communications process (and many did). When the machines evolved into small cameras with the capacity to record images and sounds onto hard disks or DVDs and when the information could be moved onto computers and therefore distributed over the Internet, various groups made claims about grassroots power and made it possible for artists to seek a larger role in social change. Combine this one example with many others, from blogs to podcasts to peer-to-peer networks and there seems to be a flowering of individual and community-based cultural production. The difficulty is that the production and distribution of all of this material reveals very little about what users and audiences are doing and thinking – how they are translating these experiences into their personal agendas or points of view (Jain 2001).

In most cases, audiences for these cultural productions are small, but there are so many examples that the sum total of production, viewing, and interaction seems to suggest that a great deal is going on. Yet, the most important challenge is how to articulate *whether* there have been any effects and to situate the relationship between effect and intention in discourses that are both critical and historical. As people experiment with creative tools and as communities find ways of distributing their work, the networks become more and more layered with information and it becomes less and less clear how that information is being used. Claims are made for the impact simply because the sheer quantity of activity seems to suggest that some sort of change is underway. The challenge of how to evaluate whether a million blogs has made it easier for people to communicate (and produce rich content) is a major one. It is almost impossible to do a broad-based critical analysis (Hayles 2005).

In this context, one has to be wary indeed of claims that these technologies are transformative. Yet, artists can be, and often are, the arbiters of whether or not the technology facilitates change either through what they do with the technology or as a consequence of their own reflections on its influence and significance. And, as has often been the case with an artist like Jean-Luc Godard, for example, they produce a body of critical literature as powerful as their art (Godard, Ishaghpour 2005).

## Vantage Point

Juxtapose the following: The film *The Polar Express* by Robert Zemeckis, which bridges the gap between digital worlds and the human body and tries to humanize an entirely artificial world; The American election of 2004, which relied on the Internet both for information and misinformation; the spectacular growth of websites, like MySpace.com, which extend the way humans interact, communicate and develop relationships; the growth of blogs, which have pushed publishing from the corporate world to the individual; the growing importance of search engines and popular discussions of how to engage with a sea of information; and, finally, the spectacular growth of games, game consoles and online gaming. Together, these and many other elements constitute image-worlds, which, like a sheath, cover the planet, allowing and encouraging workers in India to become office employees of large companies in the West and Chinese workers to produce goods and manage inventories on an unimaginable scale. These image-worlds operate at micro and macro levels. They are all encompassing, a bath of sounds and pictures immersing users in the manipulation of information both for exchange and as tools of power (Johnson 2001).

Picture these image-worlds as millions of intersecting concentric circles built in pyramidal style, shaped into forms that turn metal into messages and machines into devices that operate at the nano-level. Then imagine using a cell phone/PDA to call up some information that locates humans on a particular street as was done during the crisis in Louisiana and you have processes that are difficult to understand, let alone see without a clear and specific choice of *vantage point*. It is one of the roles of the artist and of art to both choose and locate vantage point and, thus, to provide different ways of seeing not only works of art, but the world that surrounds and enframes them. One of the central roles of education is to provide students with the tools that they need to evaluate different vantage points and alternate ideas and practices.

Importantly, the key to the vantage points needed to understand all of these events and phenomena centers on how the history of technology and innovation is understood both by participants and by observers. There will always be greater dislocation if the networks, for example, are seen as simple connections among different nodes and not as multi-layered and often contradictory agglomerations of people's interests.

An argument can and should be made that we need a balance among competing interests and the ways in which technologies of communication translate human needs into different cultural and social activities. But, it seems clear that the responsibility of artists is as much to point out the impact of these phenomena as it is to create the necessary artifice to understand what is happening. And, education and learning in the arts are similarly implicated in this materialization of meaning and experience of accelerating technological and social change.

**Learning History**

The brilliant French philosopher Michel Serres proposes in recent publications that one of the best ways of understanding the type of history that I have been discussing in this paper is to think about human events and the narratives that accompany them as a series of interconnected folds, a network of networks in which events that may have taken place thousands of years ago are still connected to the present through human memory and human artifacts.

The folds of which Serres speaks can be visualized as a series of pleated pages in which different points touch, sometimes arbitrarily and other times by design. The metaphor that Serres has developed has another purpose. In order to understand the technologies, social movements, and cultural phenomena that humans have created, each point of contact among all these pleats needs to be drawn out in a detailed and narrative manner. Although Serres does not describe this method as stream of consciousness that is sometimes how his books read, to the point where the simplest of events becomes the premise for an expansive narrative.

For example, (adapting Serres's method) the notion of networks needs to be understood not only as a function of technology and communications systems, but also through the efforts by nearly every culture and every generation to develop a variety of bonds using any number of different means from language to art to music to political, religious, and economic institutions. This suggests that the Internet, for example, is merely a modern extension of already existing forms of communication among people. And, while that may seem obvious, many of the claims about the Internet suggest that it is a revolutionary tool with implications for the ways in which people see themselves and their surroundings. More often than not, its revolutionary character is related to obvious characteristics like speed of communications, which may in fact be no more than a supplement to profoundly traditional modes of information exchange. The intersection of the revolutionary with the traditional is essential to the success of new and innovative technologies and may be at the heart of how quickly any innovation is actually taken up by individuals or by society as a whole. But the question is to what degree can a series of vantage points be established to validate the process. What role can art play in this research?

My orientation in dealing with this issue is from a technology and communications point of view and is governed by what I will call an *aggregative approach*. For example, there are a large number of activities of dissent taking place within advanced societies that make use of various forms of media and new media. It is often difficult to see how all of these varied engagements are connected or whether they lead to genuine change. Nonetheless, the sum of all these parts adds up to something very important that is not as visible as one might like, but nevertheless may have an impact on mapping the process of dissent in Western countries.

Depending on the *vantage point* that one takes, and therefore depending on how broadly or narrowly one looks, claims can be made about levels and extent of dissent. The issue of vantage point is crucial. If the perspective I take is governed by a concern for the nature and quality of the public sphere, then my overview will of necessity be broad. If the approach I take is oriented towards communities and more specifically to micro-communities, then I will need to combine a broad understanding, let us say, of the *zeitgeist* and a more particular and specific understanding of grassroots forms of dissent.

The challenge is to combine a macro-view with a micro-view in a manner that does justice to both sides and at the same time elucidates the importance of both strategies. Of course, all of this is also dependent on the definitions and expectations that one has for dissent and for its impact. A macro-view can make many different claims, among the most important being that social change will not happen unless large numbers of people are involved and unless the changes have a transformative effect on the social whole. This is the democratic paradigm and is why our society continues to believe in a nineteenth-century model of political parties. Inevitably, the macro-view runs into problems when the outcomes to an election, for example, point toward a highly fragmented set of constituencies, more lack of knowledge than actual erudition in the choices that were made, and a clear lack of respect by the political parties for the kind of public discourse that would actually lead to new ideas and some measured growth in the learning process.

The overall aggregation of various forms of protest using a variety of different media in a large number of varied contexts generates outcomes that are not necessarily the product of any centralized planning. This means that it is also difficult to gage the results. Did the active use of cell phones during the demonstrations in Seattle against the WTO contribute to greater levels of organization and preparedness on the part of the protestors and therefore, on the messages they were communicating? Mobile technologies were also used to "broadcast" back to a central source that then sent out news releases to counter the mainstream media and their depiction of the protests and protestors. This proved to be minimally effective in the broader social sense, but very effective when it came to maintaining and sustaining the communities that had developed in opposition to the WTO and globalization. Inadvertently, the mainstream media allowed the images of protest to appear in any form because they were hungry for information and needed to make sense of what was going on. As with many other protests in public spaces, it is not always possible for the mainstream media to control what they depict. Ultimately, the most important outcome of the demonstrations was symbolic, which in our society added real value to the message of the protestors.

Another vantage point on this process is to think of various communities, which share common goals becoming nodes on a network that over time ends up creating and often sustaining a super-network of people pursuing political change and artistic projects. Their overall impact remains rather difficult to understand and assess, not because these nodes are in any way ineffective, but because they cannot be evaluated in isolation from each other. This notion of networks may allow us to think about communities in a different way. It is, as we know possible at one and the same time for the impulses that guide communities to be progressive and very conservative. There is nothing inherently positive with respect to politics within communities that are based on shared points of view. But, if the process is more important often than the content, then this raises other issues about critical discourses and the intersection of artistic innovation with community interaction.

The convergence of network connectivity and ideas leads to unpredictable outcomes. Take fan clubs on the Web, for example. They generally center on particular stars, films, or television shows. They are a form of popular participation in mainstream media and a way of affecting not so much the content of what is produced (although that is happening more and more, *Star Trek* has continued as a series on the Net) but the relationship of private and public discourse about media products and their impact. Over time, through accretion and sheer persistence, fan clubs have become very influential. They are nodes on a network that connects through shared interests, one of which is to mold the media into a reflection of their concerns with results that are often quite different from what the mainstream media would like to see. Similarly, new networks of artists are using both web-based and university-based networks to create grids that allow for simultaneous research and creation to take place among many groups and often the sheer productivity of contact far outweighs anything that is created.

All of these activities point toward the difficulty of making claims about change as a result of the introduction of new technologies. A claim could be made that digital technologies are *change agents*, but only if the connections between the digital and the analogue are placed into a context that links the history of their development to the social context in which they were created (Burnett 2004).

To me, this ambiguous and somewhat contradictory environment encourages new kinds of learning, which far exceed what learning institutions themselves can provide. In large measure, the way the old and the new intersect is a function of how knowledge and information are ascertained. At the same time, as Serres has suggested, the old and the new are never absent from each other and don't exist in separate silos. This is another reason that multi-disciplinary strategies are so essential because they facilitate clustering and joint efforts across many disciplines and the arts, for example. The social context for all of this has never been better which makes it all the more essential to transform the mission and organizational structure not only of education, but other institutions as well.

The important point here is that the macro and the micro are social phenomena and material for expression and creative output. Artists are inevitably involved with both sides; with the result that works of art are never just expressions of one individual or one community. The folds that link historical events from different epochs are integrated into the links between modes of representation and visualization from many periods. No work of art ever escapes its dependence upon history and no educational institution is ever outside the pressures that result from the intersection of the micro and the macro at the historical and community level. This puts further pressure on art and design education, because its specialized nature would suggest that the liberal arts (which provide many of the disciplines required to understand these issues) are somehow less important than the crafts and techniques that need to be learned. The tendency to equate technical practice with learning will only work if the very definition of practice is dramatically broadened.

## What are Medium-specific Disciplines?

The continuum that links real events with their transformation into images and media forms knows few limits. This is largely because of the power of digital mediation, which is a product of the capacity of digital cultures to aggregate large numbers of phenomena into sometimes quite specific entry portals. It is perhaps not an accident that terrorists, governments, and corporations all make use of the same mediated space. We call this the Internet, but that now seems a rather quaint way of describing the multi-leveled network that connects individuals and societies with often unpredictable outcomes.

Networks, to varying degrees, have always been a characteristic of most social contexts. But as I have mentioned, the activity of networking as an everyday experience and pursuit has never been as intense as what we have now, nor have the number of mediated experiences been so great. This may well be one of the cornerstones of what is being described as the new media environment. However, new media as a term, name, or metaphor is too vague to be that useful. There are many different ways of characterizing this process, and there should be many different methods available to talk about the evolution of networks and technologies and the ways in which information and artifacts are created and distributed. It is also important to talk about the extraordinarily intense way in which communities and individuals look for and create connections to each other, which among many effects actually transforms the locale and importance of disciplines both within educational institutions and outside of them.

The evolution of media studies as a discipline says a great deal about the response to this exceptionally fertile period of technological growth. Although humans have always used a variety of media forms to express themselves and although these forms have been an integral part of culture, and in some instances the foundation upon which certain economies have been built, the study of media only developed into a formal discipline in the twentieth century. There are many reasons for this, including, and perhaps most importantly, the growth of printing from a text-based activity to the mass reproduction of images (something that has been commented on by many different theorists and practitioners). The convergence of technology and reproduction has been the subject of intense artistic scrutiny for 150 years. Yet, aside from Museums like MOMA the disciplines that we now take for granted, like film, photography, television, and so on, came into being in universities, for example, only after an intense fight and the quarrel continues to this day (Austin, Kirby, Macmillan, Spence, Steele 2001).

The arguments weren't only around the value of works in these areas (photography, for example, was not bought by serious art collectors until the latter half of the twentieth century and was not taught in anything like a serious fashion until the 1960s), but around the legitimacy of studying various media forms given their designation as the antithesis of high culture. Film was studied in English departments. Photography was often a part of art history departments. Twenty years after television started to broadcast to mass audiences in the early 1950s there were only a handful of texts that had been written, and aside from extremely critical assertions about the negative effects of TV on an unsuspecting populace (the Postman-Chomsky phenomenon), most of the discourse was descriptive. The irony is that even Critical Theory in the 1930s that was very concerned with media didn't really break the scholarly iceberg that had been built around various media forms. It took the convergence of structuralism, semiotics, and linguistics in the late 1960s, a resurgence of phenomenology, and a reconceptualization of the social and political role of the state to provoke a new era of media study. In Canada, this was felt most fully through the work of Marshall McLuhan, Harold Innis, and Edmond Carpenter and was brought to a head by the powerful convergence of experimentation in cinema and video combined with the work of artists in Intermedia, performance, and music. Another way of thinking about this is to ask how many people were studying rock and roll in 1971? After all, rock and roll was disseminated through radio, another medium that was not studied seriously until well after its invention (sound-based media have always been the stepchildren of visual media).

The question is should all of these phenomena become disciplines in their own right? What makes a medium-specific discipline a discipline in any case? Is it the practice of the creators? Is it the fact that a heritage of production and circulation has built up enough to warrant analysis? I think not. Disciplines are produced through negotiation among a variety of players crossing the boundaries of industry, academia, and the state. The term new media, for example, has been built upon this detritus, and is a convenient way in which to develop a nomenclature that designates in a *part for whole kind of way*, that an entire field has been created. But, what is that field? Is it the sum total of the creative work within its rather fluid boundaries? Is it the sum total of the scholarly work that has been published? Is it the existence of a major journal that both celebrates and promotes not only its own existence but also the discipline itself?

These issues of boundary making are generally driven by political as well as cultural considerations. They are often governed by curatorial priorities developed through institutions that have very specific stakes in what they are promoting. None of these activities *per se* may define or even explain the rise, fall, and development of various disciplines. But, as a whole, once in place, disciplines close their doors both as a defensive measure, but also to preserve the history of the struggle to come into being.

It is within this context that interdisciplinary strategies of learning and teaching have become so central to pedagogical innovation in art schools. It is also within this context that new forms of collaboration between artists and scientists are developing. It is difficult to anticipate where all of this will lead, but it seems obvious that the silos that have for so long distinguished and prevented contact between disciplines are no longer functional.

## Conclusion

One of the greatest weaknesses of art education is the emphasis on output, projects, and objects. These can range from works of art to installations and from paintings to visualization and much more. The orientation always seems to be on outcome, as if creativity must have *practice* attached to it in order to legitimize *process*. The difficulty is that for the most part process is relatively private and internal to the practitioner and outcome is public. So, to resolve this, art schools have courses that attach a great deal of value to craft and the apprehension of technique(s). Presumably, as technique is learned over time through workshops and exercises, creative process and talent will reveal themselves. In addition, sharing studios, sharing classes, and sharing shows are all intended to unmask process and bring the private into the public sphere.

However, as I have mentioned throughout this piece, processes of creativity and learning are themselves mediated and, therefore, the various folds, connections, and disconnections that link creativity with outcomes are so multi-layered that a radically new interdisciplinary strategy is needed. Underlying the tensions here is another issue – and that is: How far can art-based learning environments go if the crafts, techniques, and technologies of creation are so fluid (in a kind of postmodern nightmare) that no boundary ever works? If distinctions between disciplines cease to have any meaning, then how can interdisciplinarity grow? The advent of sophisticated networks of communication and the speed with which artists and designers have made use of these networks has led to a broadening of all fields. It may be necessary for art and design schools and departments to radically alter not only their practices, but also the disciplinary structures that are at the core of their history.

## Works Cited

Austin, Simon, Kirby, Paul, Macmillan, Sebastian, Spence, Robin, Steele, John (2001), "Mapping the Conceptual Design Activity of Interdisciplinary Teams," *Design Studies* 22.

Burnett, Ron (2004) *How Images Think*, Cambridge: MIT Press.

Godard, Jean-Luc, Youssef Ishaghpour (2005), *Cinema: The Archeology of Film and the Memory of a Century*, trans. John Howe, Oxford: Berg Publishers.

Hayles, Katherine (2005), "Computing the Human," *Theory, Culture & Society*, vol. 22, no. 1.

Jain, Ramesh (2001), "Digital Experience," *Communications of the ACM*, vol. 44, no. 3.

Johnson, Christopher (2001), "A Survey of Current Research on online communities of practice," *Internet and Higher Education*, 4.

Latour, Bruno (1996), *Armais or the Love of Technology*, Cambridge: Harvard University Press.

Nokes, Christopher (2005), "Holistic Integrated Design Education: Art Education in a Complex and Uncertain World," *Journal of Aesthetic Education*, vol. 39, no. 1.

Röhle, Theo (2005), "Power, Reason, Closure: Critical perspectives on new media theory," *New Media & Society*, vol. 7, no. 3.

Vesna, Victoria (2001), "Toward a Third Culture: Being in Between," *Leonardo*, vol. 34, no. 2.

# Afference and Efference: Encouraging Social Impact through Art and Science Education

## Jill Scott

### 1. Introduction

Each one of our lives is but a brief moment in the vastly complicated networks of social relationships that comprise our shared worlds, but art and science are still largely separated cultures. This paper questions if a new form of social advocacy education can emerge from more sharing of knowledge between the arts and the sciences either in labs or in facilitated environments. In this light, four main topics will be discussed: potential metaphors and processes, knowledge-transfer, strategic discourses, and public understanding. These topics were chosen because through the adoption of scientific metaphors into artwork, the developing of new approaches to know-how transfer and the sharing of specific discourses between disciplines, it is hoped that more advanced research collaborations between the arts and the sciences can be encouraged. Furthermore, some strategies for educators may evolve which can spill into the public realm where facilitation can be seen as part of environmental advocacy.

#### 1.1. Potential Metaphors and the Educational Process

Before discussing these topics, the processes of *afference* and *efference* will be extracted from neuroscience in order to serve as appropriate metaphors for what the author calls *efferent education*. These are neurological processes, which cause the looped transmission of knowledge between humans and their immediate surrounding environments. The definition of these terms varies between the practical analysis of neuroscience and in its more theoretical partner, sensory psychology, the later discipline being the more controversial. In neuroscience, the terms *afferent* and *efferent* are used to describe the somatosensory perceptual process our bodies undergo in relation to the perception of our immediate environment. While *afferent* is the process of carrying information inward to a central organ or section, *efferent* processes are those which always proceed outward from the center, carrying sensation back to the peripheral parts of the body. For example, the human body has afferent nerves, organs, or blood vessels conducting impulses from the periphery of the body to the brain or spinal cord and brain. Efference is often seen as a different process, carrying impulses from the central nervous system to effectors, where reactions happen.

Creating facilities for the education of artists and scientists in responsive environments can be seen as an efferent process. One may consider the nerve centers to stand for society and the sense organs or filters as the artists, but this metaphor of a separate afferent process may no longer be appropriate. Alternatively, efference infers that the artists are the central sense organs and their interpretative response or the sending of impulses outwards are part of a whole system of essential feedback. Even in sensory psychology, controversies occur when these processes are either seen as disconnected from one another or when these behaviors of withdrawal or outgoing actions are believed to be compulsive or against one's wishes. In the first instance, science critics assume that when afference is rendered as separate from efference then actions are not seen as part of the same whole organism's environmental system. In the second instance, if these actions are compulsive then knowledge is acquired without any selection and digested before it is able to be re-delivered back into the environment. These scientists tend to believe that knowledge is cellular and explicitly obtained by or held in specialized organs.[1] Although afferent and efferent processes are mostly considered to be neural processes, sensory psychologists can also provide us with more conceptual definitions, which may be more appropriate for both the accumulation of and passing on of knowledge.

Some specialists in sensory psychology[2] suggest that afference and efference processes have dire consequences if they become separated in the body, while others claim that they can never be exclusive and must be seen as a one-system point of view, always involving the cognitive loop of both afferent and efferent elements. Sensory psychologist Timo Jarvilehto (1998), for example, affirms that this holistic loop is the essential behavioral process of the human environmental-organism and he coined one term, *efferent knowledge*, to describe information response. By this term he posits that the efferent or responsive process is an essential part of the nature and offers a broader conception of knowledge because it is "a switch that opens up vistas of knowledge and possibilities of impacting on the social level." In other words, *efferent knowledge* is always reactive while in parallel it is also a promoter of the cause of any social stimulation.

### 1.2. Efferent Education
Applying the term *efferent knowledge* to advocacy education would involve a response-driven methodology rather than offering students a predominately receptive role. A

range of educational theories exists, which can be applied to this type of feedback context called behaviorist approaches. For example, in *sensory stimulation theory* (Laird 1985) effective learning occurs when multi-senses are stimulated simultaneously including the potentials of cross-modal interaction. Another theory called *holistic experience* celebrates the individual personality and the intellect, in combination with emotions, the body impulse (or desire), intuition, and imagination. These methods often require the teacher or supervisor to be seen as a facilitator in any given educational context. This is a long way from the philosophy of Bertrand Russell (1912) who thought that knowledge gained by *acquaintance* and knowledge acquired by *description* should be seen as different processes. While knowledge by *acquaintance* was seen as direct sensory perception, knowledge by *description* was inferred through the use of symbols or language. Knowledge by acquaintance, infers that information can be depicted rather than interpreted causing the individual to be seen as separated from the world. In knowledge by description, one may draw a scene or evoke a mood with music or act out an event and this gives the individual experiential associations alongside interpretation.

However, these investigations did constitute knowledge as subject of study, and, today, Timo Jarvilehto (1998) still questions "what element in an abstract and general specification of being such as being–meaning–action or being–relationship–process corresponds to what is commonly taken for knowledge?" In other words, can the element of knowledge be actually identified as a knowledge-primitive and, if so, how can the elaboration of this knowledge be described? Furthermore, when he uses the terminology of "environment," he means not just the "physical" environment, but also the organism's surroundings in the context of their importance to other organisms who share it, as well as the efferent behavioral results. He argues that knowledge is not based on any direct action of the sensors but on the existence of a conductive system and any changes, which may widen and differentiate in this system. Therefore, the term "knowledge transfer" means that efferent influences can help students to discriminate between the new or the useful aspects in a given environment. *Efferent education* is a system in which levels of afferent and efferent processes not only contribute to a functional whole, but also deepen our understanding of information.

Ph.D. programs are currently being developed[3] by facilitators who believe that educational advocacy in art and science is related to the inseparable interaction between the organism and the environment. This means that long and intensive seminars, which require a whole group of student to be immersed on a daily basis, can evolve into a social knowledge pool, open for any type of behavioral results. If this one-system point of view is adopted for art and science, then the educational goals are neither *in* the environment (educational context) nor *in* the student's bodies, but distributed through the whole interactive learning-environment system. Perception is only a part of the jigsaw of the "situated" system of knowledge. While in neuroscience there is a tendency to see our perceptual senses as behavioral transmitters of information, *efferent education* suggests that knowledge is "situated," meaning that our immediate social and cultural environment is an integrated part of the loop between efferent transfer and uninformed outsiders.

Therefore, more appropriate metaphors need to be designed, which might bridge the gap instead of dry everyday metaphors currently used in scientific training. On the contrary, artists are trained in finding poetic metaphors, which they believe have more public impact. Instead of using metaphors only based on a language of generalizations, the contemporary poetic metaphor is created by conceptual associations. As Lakoff (1993) suggests, artists and writers learn that these consist of many conceptual types. There are 'structural' metaphors related to the concept of dimension, whose associations may change with differing cultures. Another can be based on 'propioception' and these are most appropriate when structures are experienced in terms of spatial orientation. Then there are 'ontological metaphors' when our experiences are structured in terms of abstract phenomena or in terms of concrete textures, forces, or objects. It would be interesting to see what would happen if science educators started to use poetic metaphors as educational cues for understanding. Perhaps how actual divisions between disciplines are seen from the outside may also be affected. In traditional science education facilities, one very problematic example of a language stereotype was the metaphor of 'soft' and 'hard.' As Swiss psychologist, Burton Melnick (1999), pointed out this caused physics, computer science, and mathematics to be labelled as 'hard' sciences, and psychology, sociology, and the arts as 'soft' or human sciences.

| COLD/HARD/SCIENCE | WARM/SOFT/ART |
|---|---|
| Reliable | Mutable |
| Well-defined | Ill-defined |
| Comprehensible | Illusive |
| Sharp | Flaccid or spongy |
| Precise | Imprecise |
| Difficult | Easy |

As can be seen from the table above, the division has very loaded connotations. *Efferent education* suggests that our current mediated learning institutions as well as our tele-literate public, particularly those majorities who live inside mediated environments, are more than ready to replace such language stereotypes. This may require artists to challenge themselves by finding new poetic metaphors for the public, which reflect scientific research. Thus, between the cultures of art and those of science a more common trans-disciplinary language might evolve, and, in turn, develop into a viable level of "situated" knowledge transfer.

## 2. "Situated" Knowledge
If knowledge is "situated" it connotes the inclusion of responses to the surrounding cultural environment, immersion in a particular contextual field, and considers the robust level of public dissemination and consequent understanding. Most of the

traditional educational institutions where science is taught have defined scientific investigation as a scientific method and process for evaluating empirical knowledge. However, today, in science labs, the specialist's concept of knowledge is becoming more controversial, as researchers need leaders who have a trans-disciplinary overview, in order to compare discoveries between labs and plan for the future. This implies that the discoveries of 'science' can be assessed in relation to the physical surroundings where the labs are situated. Could scientific knowledge be embedded in language, culture, or traditions as well as methods? Thus, the new efferent experimental approach to science education may be concerned with the search for firsthand information, or theory, the development of models to explain what is observed, but also include the influence of other research factors, which are dependent on place or economics or culture. In this light, *Efferent education* may also require that "situated" know-how transfer do away with problematic levels of snobbery!

In comparison, art is already heavily "culturally situated." But does art have an epistemology or a theory of knowledge, based upon any comparable evaluation of empirical knowledge? While traditionally, artworks are self-referential interpretations often made for an art public's appreciation, in contemporary art, mediums like documentary film or the Internet often involve critical studies by teams about issues like human behavior or the effect of technology on society. These studies may create efferent outcomes in the form of applications of research to human needs, but also cater to the basic gathering of empirical knowledge. For example, ethnographical studies and reactive data collection may be an important part of an interface design or interactive documentary that can reach out to a broader public. Programs like the Swiss artist-in-labs program[4] or Symbotica[5] at the University of Western Australia have proved that many artists are interested to learn more about empirical scientific research results by entering the houses of science. These "hands-on" lab experiences provide educational facilitators with the opportunity to observe a new type of "situated knowledge transfer" between the artists and the scientists involved. From prior residencies, scientists have often claimed that the artist's role inside science labs was to provide a 'new in-house social community environment' for their over-specialized scientific team members (Scott 2006). However, contextual immersion for artists inside the labs can facilitate a deeper level of learning for the scientists as well, and not merely see the artist's role as a social catalyst.

## 2.1. Contextual Immersion

As social scientist, Sandra Caravita states: "The science lab context is so fundamental for learning and for the exchange of information that education is problematic without it." (Caravita and Hallden 1995) By this she means that inside the lab, the scientist actively builds her/his knowledge through the personal interpretation of her/his experience, but must share this experience with both peers and also with "outsiders." *Efferent education* regards the artist not only as an important objective outsider, but as a key interpreter. If the artist is lucky enough to accompany a scientific researcher on any six- to nine-month specific experiment, then the operative involvement, the exploring of ideas and reality, even the placing of the hypothesis into practice will strongly influence the artist's resultant interpretation. Immersive knowledge accumulates over time, causing as Caravita further suggests, a receiving and a delivery of promotion from the cultural environment as well as the social interactions that accompany the learner's explorations (Caravita and Hallden 1995). Thus, the processes of immersive experience are both afferent and efferent. On the afferent level, psychologists like Susan Blackmore agree that compulsive mimetic reactions are unintentionally adopted in such an environment of learning, however, this process of learning by imitation has efferent qualities; for example, one has to make the decision to imitate a process, do what counts as the same or similar, make a complex transformation from one view to another, and, finally, match bodily actions promoted by memory (Blackmore 2000). In the lab context, it may seem that *knowledge by participation* is much more effective than knowledge by acquaintance. If more art and science Ph.D. collaborations were formed in educational institutions, then participatory knowledge could surely be increased. Furthermore, if more artists take part in the actual debates offered by scientists, their practical interpretations will become more scientifically robust.

### 2.2. *Robust Scientific Knowledge*
Through the everyday process of immersion in the lab, facilitators of residency programs have found that artists also want to learn about theoretical disputes and how they are resolved among peer groups (Scott 2006). More importantly, they want to "listen in" on the evaluation of the goals of the research and be involved in scientific debates. Many scientists seem to be open to give an artist the opportunity to participate in these discourses. As Elvin Fox Keller (2000) suggests, science in itself is an interesting process for the artist to observe, because the conventional accounts, which scientists discuss about their successes are far from value-free. She states that the very language, tacit presuppositions, expectations, and assumptions shared by natural scientific researchers are very value-laden. Reciprocally, scientists have been known to encourage artists to give lectures about the values and contexts of contemporary art. Some of the most beneficial exchanges in the artist-in-labs program came from resultant comments to exhibitions of artworks inspired by scientific research topics, especially if these artworks were shown right inside the facility of the science lab itself (Scott 2006). There seems to be a shared ethic in science, which demands respect for each other and values peer assessment, and the art world seems to fall into a similar category for them. While the scientific ethic mostly requires honest reporting of results, meticulous control and cementation of observations, as well as the formulation and avocation of ideas, each researcher like each artist has to leave a legacy for others to follow. The role of any *efferent educator team* may be to keep a diverse array of possible disciplinary ethics in respective art and science environments alive and, as well, maintain an equal inclusion in the concepts, theories, principles, and methods from both fields. This is a tall order, but the final aim would be to create shared reflective and critical educational environments where artists might produce artworks, which could inspire scientists, and scientists might gain respect for such artworks.

## 3. Strategic Discourses

It is also hoped that new discourses might emerge from this sharing of ideologies between art and science in the future, even though the prevailing controlled and guarded specialist attitudes of educational institutions often hinder fruitful exchanges. In this paper the author will mention only three of the many discourses, which might be relevant for *efferent education development*. These are relational creativity, ethical advocacy education, and collaborative innovation.

### 3.1. Discourse- Relational Creativity

*Relational creativity* is a term the author uses to describe an open-ended training process, which attempts to correlate many various definitions of creativity. As an example of this diversity, creativity is a very controversial and hotly debated topic in cognitive science whereas the meaning of the word in physics, engineering mathematics often infers a particular type of approach to solving problems. For contemporary art and design, creative thinking and communication skills are procedural and mediatory, whereas one cannot find similar courses in science education. One the one hand, creativity training in art schools often begins with a combination of abstract or controversial thematic topics and basic skill assignments, which may or may not evolve into dynamic results. On the other hand, scientific methodology often places art or design commissions only at the end of their processes, just before public presentation, thus deterring art collaborators from being involved.

In contrast, Jacob Bronowski (1965) once suggested that creativity in both art and science were very similar. He wrote that the "discoveries of science, the works of art, are explorations – more, are explosions of a hidden likeness. The discoverer or the artist presents them in two aspects of nature and fuses them into one. This is the act of creation, in which an original act is born, and it is the same act in original science and original art". Today, it seems that both similar and different attitudes towards creativity still need a great deal of further discussion, particularly if *efferent education* is to grow and any shared responsibility for originality can take place.

### 3.2. Discourse – Shared Innovation

One arena where shared innovation has already transpired is between the fields of media art and computer science or artificial intelligence, where teams have conducted innovative research together. This combination might indeed serve as a guideline for many other science disciplines, which have not been so open to collaborate. As an example of success, within the last 40 years, media artists together with software engineering groups have produced many innovative audio and visual tools (e.g. Photoshop), which are currently influencing research in efferent ways. These endeavors have required that facilitators team up and take on the role of trans-disciplinary assessment, assessing the skills of the artists and matching them with those of the scientists. This is not an easy task. It requires an efferent approach toward collaboration and integration as well as a juggling of the workload and the content evenly, and it requires the scientist to focus on creative concepts rather than the artist to simply illustrate scientific research results.

As Walter Benjamin (1963) predicted, scientists, like artists, are already being educated to invent or reinvent tools to see further, illustrate theories, or test the clarity of their inventions as an integrated part of their methodology. In *efferent education* these "ways of seeing" need further discussion. How does the use of the same tools by different disciplines affect how we interpret the results? In other words, will an artist make a visualization of water quality in a different way than a scientist, even if both are using the same tools? In this light, projects like the Institute for Distributed Creativity, an initiative of Trebor Scholz (2006), can encourage discussion through online blogging and the development of participatory open-source platforms for learning can further the potential for collaboration.

In this way, *Efferent processes* can support an old definition of innovation from the German philosopher Arnold Schopenhauer: "The task is not so much to see what no one has yet seen but to think what nobody has yet thought about that which everybody sees" (Schopenhauer 1844). In other words, *efferent education* might help to develop new ways of social participation between artists and scientists about very particular insights that have not been thought about before. Interestingly enough, one of the most beneficial ways to encourage team collaboration is to invite artists with scientists on field trips where empirical evidence is collected or request scientists to see art exhibitions. Here, in the respective social community-oriented environments, strategic debates are opened. Not only do the artists learn a great deal about data analysis but for scientists artistic process are revealed, and also perhaps at those late-night fireside talks or with a drink at the openings, scientists feel freer to give their true opinions, outside the walls of their institutions. This is one of the reasons why Dr. Lloyd Anderson, Director of Science at the National Endowment for Science, Technology and Art (NESTA)[6] in the U.K., currently recommends funding for collaborative thematic spaces or field trips and thematic journeys where artists and scientists can spend "quality time" together.

### 3.3. Discourse – Shared Ethics
*Efferent education* requires a substantial creation of time and space in which ethical discussions can take place and ideas can flow out to the general public. One can find 'critical resistance from within' in many environmental science labs, but the pressure to conform to the stoic methodologies of science often requires these resisters to dampen their radicalism. Today, scientists are required to "be seen" by the public (their greatest source of research funding) as standing in the middle of an informed debate. Take, for example, the values of Genetically Modified Organisms (GMOs), a subject that is often presented in a dualistic way: good or bad. Many laboratories like the Institute for Geobotanics at the ETH Zurich,[7] for example, not only cultivate test fields for genetically modified crops, but also conduct large international risk assessments of GMO adoptions in developing countries. Artists are often surprised to find out that so many conflicting viewpoints could simultaneously exist inside this field of research. How can

art help scientists bring such diverse and controversial debates into the public realm? While some artists might document and package their experience of immersion in the lab to explore how scientists construct their international and political debates, other artists might see themselves as informed activists and wish to help scientists conduct their critical enquiries or try to shift democratic decision-making.

One of the real motivations for a grounded and endogenous theory of *efferent education* is to promote trans-disciplinary training in the arena of environmental advocacy. In 1949, Aldo Leopold already suggested that "all ethics rest upon a single premise and that each individual is a member of a community of interdependent parts."[8] Unfortunately, environmental responses often tend to focus on outcomes and achievements of separated communities, rather than the educational processes by which combined achievements could be made. This requires facilitators to identify, implement, and evaluate a range of trans-disciplinary interventions, which can transfer robust scientific research into digestible packages for the general public. As Z-node member and artist, Tiffany Holmes (2006), posits artwork, which is informed by scientific research, might help to raise public awareness about energy conservation. In this light, *efferent educators* can help create the contexts where robust artistic interpretation is favored over pure scientific visualization as a means of communication.

In *efferent education* diversity of interpretation combined with poetic metaphor is the key to increasing levels of community response. Firstly, artists pride themselves on their own freedom of speech and they are not frightened to say what they think. Secondly, they are concerned with artistry. As artists-in-labs recipient Shirley Soh stated, "artistry in art comes not only in deciding what to say but also in how to say it. I am always searching for the 'one' image, which might have the power to make an ethical comment really clear" (Scott 2006). These skills of finding unique visual metaphors for the public are learned by trial and error with feedback from peers, art educators, and audiences. Thirdly, the corridor of communication from science to the public about ethics is often stifled by conformity or middle-of-the-road pressure from science peers. These three points are important factors to consider in relation to ethics and the public realm. Currently, in tertiary institutions there seems to be a conspicuous lack of professional development or support for educators who could be involved in facilitating and coordinating advocacy education programs. While generating texts for the public to read about ethics and science constitute one form of knowledge transfer, social strategies which encourage relationships between artists and experienced science educators may lead to more interesting methods of dissemination.

## 4. Conclusion

As suggested above, *efferent education* is a socially responsive facilitated type of education which can help an artist develop a unique voice about ethics and science in relation to public understanding. Pursuits in this direction may also constitute a new approach to adult advocacy education. As some educational psychologists like Simon Burns (1995) have said, "by adulthood people are self-directing, and prefer experience-based, problem-oriented themes and collaborative learning environments" to the older concepts of acquisition style learning. As Knowles (1990) has further revealed, these levels of social construction vary for different individuals and shift according to different cultures. Mature-age students not only vary in levels of knowledge but also in their life experiences. For adult participants, the efferent facilitator may need to consider that different themes are relevant at different times or that the participants might have subjective interpretations in different contexts. He or she is challenged to consider that individual approaches to the trans-disciplinary practice of art and science can be influenced by the formation of social liaisons in any experience. While artists may have already learned informally and unintentionally through participation in social activity or exhibitions, levels of public support for particular causes may require them to acquire more organizational skills from the social scientists, or more cognitive analysis from the sensory psychologists. Of great importance, immersive strategies, which situate learning in the context of action like the science lab or a trans-disciplinary seminar, can help scientists communicate in new ways with the public. More formal collaborations between public organizations, critics/curators and tertiary science institutions would help professionals further the discourses and create conferences around themes like know-how transfer, relational creativity, and shared-innovation teams.

In this paper, *efferent education* constitutes an attempt to confirm that these discourses cannot only be shared between the educational environments of art and science, but also filter through to the general public. *Efferent educators* attempt to establish conducive atmospheres between the two disciplines, one in which learners feel comfortable to consider new ideas and not be threatened by external factors or resistance or the unpleasant consequences of giving up what is currently held to be true. This requires a less protective construction and belief system that can encompass responses which fall in between positive and negative approaches and more informed debates as constructive insights for the evolution of thought and consequent advocacy behavior. Within advocacy education, evaluation and responses need ethical and social applications, which may even be able to be shown inside the immersive environment of the scientific lab itself.

The most important aim of *efferent education* is to generate a new level of respect and responsive social analysis between these two separated disciplines and associated cultures. What is central, indeed crucial, is that researchers in both art and science fields still retain a commitment towards the people they study and their respective subjects of study.

## Acknowledgements

The illustrations used in this text are from the following programs: Z-node of the Planetary Collegium based at the University of Plymouth, UK (http: //www.z-node.net) and Artists-in-labs (http: //www.artists-in-labs.ch). Z-node is a research program with a dedicated group of fifteen international Ph.D. candidates who meet regularly in the Institute of Cultural Studies, Academy of Art and Design, Zurich, Switzerland. The main aims of Z-node are to explore the collaborative potentials of design, art, science, and technology, to analyze methodologies as well as critical and ethical discourses in relation to sustainability and to focus on the impact of technology, communication, and electronic innovations on society. The artists-in-labs program provides artists with long-term opportunities to learn in scientific environments and create interpretations from their experiences. It is an ongoing residency program, which also perpetrates trans-disciplinary comparisons between art, science, and the general public.

## Notes

1. This paper will not explore further research in this direction, even though the concept of cellular memory does support the holistic afferent and efferent concept. For further information, see Hoffman, W. C.1998. "The Topology of Wholes, Parts and Their Perception-cognition." *Journal of Psychology:* 9(03) Part Whole Perception (4).
2. According to St. John, R., in moments of extreme stress these two states of mind can become separate functions and this he explains causes the characteristics diseases like Hypermetropia and Myopia. http: //metamorphosiscenter.com/rsj.affeff.html.
3. See the mission of The Planetary Collegium at http: //www.planetary-collegium.net/about/.
4. The artists-in-labs program can be found at http: //www.artistsinlabs.ch.
5. SymboticA. http: //www.symbiotica.uwa.edu.au/ The Art and Science Collaborative Research Laboratory at the University of Western Australia.
6. NESTA, Science, National Endowment for Science, Technology and Art: www.nesta.org.uk.
7. The Geobotanic Institute. http: //www.geobot.ethz.ch/index_EN.
8. *The Earth Charter* http: //www.earthcharter.org.

## Works Cited

Benjamin, W. (1963), *The Work of Art in the Age of Mechanical Reproduction*. Reprint. Continuum.

Blackmore, S. (2000), *The Meme Machine*. Oxford University Press. p. 52

Bronowski, J. (1965), *Science and Human Values*. Harper and Row, New York, 19. See also http//: www.drbronowski.com.

Burns, S. (1995), "The Adult Learner at work Business and Professional Publishing," *HRMonthly* June. Gulf Publishing Company, Book Division. Sydney. p. 203.

Caravita, S. Hallden O. (1995), "Reframing the Problem of Conceptual Change, Learning and Instruction," *Costruzione collaborativa di prodotti e tecnologia della comunicazione,* TD7. 4, p. 89.

Fox Keller, E. (2000), *The Century of the Gene*, Harvard University Press.

Holmes, T. (2006), *Environmental Awareness through Eco-visualization: Combining Art and Technology to Promote Sustainability*/http: //reconstruction.eserver.org/063/holmes.shtml.

Jarvilhto, T. (1998), "Theory of the Organism Environment: System 111.Role of efferent influences on receptors in the formation of Knowledge". *Journal of Integrative Behavioural and Psychological Sciences* 33.4.See also PSYCOLOQUY, http://www.cogsci.ecs.soton.ac.uk/cgi/psyc/ptopic?topic=Efference-knowledge.

Knowles, M. S. (1990), *The Adult Learner: a Neglected Species*. 4th edition, Gulf Publishing Company, Book Division, Houston Texas, USA.

Lakoff, G. (1993), *The Contemporary Theory of Metaphor*. Ortony, Andrew (ed.) Metaphor and Thought (2nd edition), Cambridge University Press. See also http: //www.ac.wwu.edu/ %7Emarket/semiotic/lkof_met.html.

Laird, D. (1985), *Approaches to Training and Development*. Addison-Wesley, Reading, Mass.

Melnick, B. "Cold Hard World \ Warm Soft Mommy-Metaphors of Hardness, Softness, Coldness, and Warmth in the humanities compared to the sciences." http: //www.clas.ufl.edu/ipsa/journal/1999_melnick01.shtml.

Russell, B. (1912), *The Problems of Philosophy*, "Knowledge by Acquaintance and Knowledge by Description" London: Williams and Norgate. Ch 5.

Scholz. T. (2006), *The Institute for Distributed Creativity*. http: //distributedcreativity.org/.

Schopenhauer, A. (1844), *The World as Will and Representation*. Dover, volume 11. See also http: //plato.stanford.edu/entries/schopenhauer/#2.

Scott. J. (2006), *Artists-in-labs. Processes of Inquiry*. Springer. Vienna /New York. See Ulrich Claessen, U. CSEM See p. 70, Case Studies-Artists reports. pp. 73–125, Exhibitions in Science Labs -Rohner, Soh, Bastianello pp. 73–125, Quote Shirley Soh p. 89.

# POLYCULTURAL PERSPECTIVES

# EXPRESSING WITH GREY CELLS: INDIAN PERSPECTIVES ON NEW MEDIA ARTS

## Vinod Vidwans

Artistic creativity flourishes along the contours of culture and the intentions of individual artists. Any artistic movement or ism is a combination of individual genius and collective consciousness. Historically, artistic genius has always explored possibilities of formal patterns of intentions and aesthetics. Prehistoric man documented struggle for survival in the cave paintings with a tone of magic and mystery. The early Egyptian, Mesopotamian, and Indus genius developed beautiful systems of pictograms and early scripts in response to the pressing needs of time. Early Indian artists revealed the majesty and tranquility of metaphysical experiences through meticulously developed canonical representations. Greek and Roman sculptors depicted sensuous muscular body rhythms and underlying grace. During the Gupta period, Indian art reached its golden epoch capturing the vibrant spirit of the life of Buddha by immortalizing it in the caves of Ajanta and Ellora. Renaissance in Europe was an era of enlightenment. Leonardo da Vinci, Michelangelo and Raphael gave new perspectives and standards of aesthetics. Impressionistic painters captured the creative moments in time and put them on the canvas as fresh as ever. Cezanne revealed solid and geometrical forms by means of juxtaposition of colors and patterns. Van Gogh heightened human emotions by violent and spontaneous expressive strokes in his paintings. The Cubists dissected the three-dimensional nature and depicted multiple facets of reality on the two-dimensional picture planes. Every artistic endeavor has attempted to achieve something that was previously untouched, novel, and out of the mind. Great works of art, from prehistory to postmodernism, depicted profound human concerns relevant to the epoch in a manner that took humanity forward.

Art has always been in close proximity with contemporary socio-techno-political developments. On numerous occasions, the entire art world was stirred up by technological developments. They questioned its content, function, and purpose in the society. At times the very existence of art was also questioned. Challenge put forth by photography during 1830 to 1840 was one such occasion. It was gracefully tackled by the art world leading to the emergence of Impressionism, one of the most profound art movements that changed the perception of artists about art itself. In the digital and information age, the art world is facing a similar challenge once again.

## Art, Science, and Technology: A Great Orchestration

The origin of various arts and crafts goes back to remote prehistoric era. Most of the earlier artistic and crafts expressions were restricted to household crafts till the Homeric period in Greece. The development of professional crafts and craftsmen was a later outgrowth in most of the early civilizations of the world. However, in India, classes of craftsmen had emerged by the pre-Buddha period (Buck 1965: 582–585). Gradually various arts and crafts were established without compartmentalization. Indian tradition believes in interrelation and interdependence among various arts and crafts. Knowledge of any one art or craft was considered incomplete without the knowledge of others. An ancient treatise, *Vishnudharmottar Purana*, gives elaborate descriptions of various arts. In the third volume of this treatise, there is an insightful dialogue between king Vajra and sage Markandeya, describing the coexistence and interdependence among various arts. King Vajra expresses his desire to learn the art of making images of deities to sage Markandeya. The sage says knowledge of this art makes it necessary to have the knowledge of other arts on which it is dependable. He says that the one who does not know canons of painting can never know canons of image-making or icon-making. He tells the king that it is very difficult to understand the canons of painting without the knowledge of canons of dance because painting is a two-dimensional imitation or representation of the world. Dance gives necessary understanding of three-dimensional spaces and dance is difficult to understand without the knowledge of instrumental music. The dialogue goes on as sage Markandeya explains to king Vajra the interdependence of various arts and takes him from learning sculpture, the art of image-making, step-by-step to painting, dance, instrumental music, vocal music, composing songs, prose and poetry, literature, languages, grammar, logic, figure of speech, aesthetic experience, theatrical arts, and even theatre-architecture. The interdependence of various arts and the consequent educational necessity of learning them together indicate a living pedagogy of arts in ancient civilization of India that believes in the convergence of arts (Shah 1961: 1–2). During ancient and medieval periods in India, various types of works demonstrating special skills were covered by the term *shilpa*.

> The term '*shilpa*' [original emphasis] designates any kind of arts and crafts in the Indian tradition and its antiquity is Vedic. It is a pervasive term to include within the ambit of its meaning anything creative, imaginative, ideational or skillful which in one sense or the other involves dexterity of hands or mind or both. *Shilpa* also implies a technique, a ceremonial act, an artifact of some craft – '*kratu*' [original emphasis] or – '*Maya*' [original emphasis] included. (Misra 1988: 145)

The Buddhist *Jatakas* (*Jatakas* are the stories related to Buddha's previous births) refer to eighteen arts or *sippas* or crafts. The *Majjhima Nikaaya* (from *Milinda Panho*, another Buddhist treatise) refers to seven of them namely counting, calculation, computation, trade, cow-herding, agriculture, king's service, and other crafts (Misra 1988: 157). Vatsayana's treatise, called *Kama Sutra*, mentions 64 types of arts which include, apart from well-established arts such as music, painting, etc., even archery, making garlands of flowers, wood-work, metalwork, and so on (Bhatt 1958: 332–333). The modern differentiation of arts and crafts is recent and still not rigorously defined.

The relationship between art, science, and technology is highly complex. Technology predates science. It is, broadly, a human endeavor to shape its physical environment. Technology is an act of making, shaping, applying, and solving problems. Historically, technology has a close affinity to art than science. Art is an act of beautifully making and shaping. Technology was always an inseparable part of artistic activity. At an earlier stage, artistic power of imagination used the available material resources and know-how to explore innovative applications. Creative genius treated emerging technology of those days with a magical touch that made it meaningful. The technology at their disposal may have been raw, but human genius gave it a definition, rule, and definite context. During the prehistoric era, some of the greatest accomplishments, like cave paintings, were earlier expressions of the fusion of artistic imagination, faith in magic, and technological know-how. Those were the first ever documentations in nonverbal form when humans were exploring material properties as well as expressive qualities of natural entities in their surroundings. There was no distinction between art, science, and technology. It was a human activity guided by awe, curiosity, primordial quest, magic, and mystery. The outcome was either tangible or intangible. Several years later, people realized the value of those expressions and timelessness of the work. With the industrial revolution, and due to the refinement in science, technology tilted towards science after the eighteenth century. In the twentieth century, scientific research became a major source of technological developments. Currently, science and technology work in tandem and borrow heavily from each other.

With the arrival of the digital age, once again the great orchestration of diverse disciplines of arts, science, and technology is taking place. The digital age is an age of convergence when art, science, and technology intersect. Convergence brought in by the digital age is of a special type. This convergence is not at conceptual or thematic level; but at the physical and virtual level, at the level of bits and bytes. Digital technology has provided a platform for art, science, technology, and culture to come together, to interface with each other and enrich each other. It has provided a language of synthesis, metamorphosis, transformation, and synergy. Digital language is acting as a catalyst for creative and scholarly experimentation and transformation across art, science, technology, and culture. It enables diverse cultural communities to explore common grounds. Digital technology provides platform, framework, and opportunity for cross-cultural connectivity. In this scenario, the art world seems to have lost its tradition, history, place, and identity.

**Art as Computation**

Art, broadly, is an act of creating, expressing, and making. Art is a presentation and representation of ideas, thoughts, feelings, and experiences through skillful, thoughtful, and imaginative use of tools, technology, and media. Artistic creations and expressions result from the artist's encounter with reality and environment. Normally, artists share their impressions and experiences of this encounter with the society at large through their artworks.

The word for art in Indian tradition is *kala*. It is a Sanskrit word which is etymologically derived from the root *kal* which means counting, calculating, or computation. It also means in a rather broader sense to do, to make, to accomplish, to observe, to perceive, to recognize, or to take notice. The word *kala* thus covers larger set of activities. Artists are doers and makers, and any artistic activity involves creative perception and calculation for visualization and articulation respectively. This etymological meaning of the word *kala* led to further exposition and development of mathematical and quantitative standards for artistic practices in India.

Especially in the field of plastic and performing arts, calculative and computational aspect of arts got elaborate exposition. Indian arts known for their spiritual and metaphysical content are very much quantitative in their material and physical manifestation. There is a substantial attempt by art theoreticians to quantify its content. Most of the Indian philosophical schools enumerate categories of existence and experience. In the same tone, art theoreticians attempted to quantify artistic activity and especially the process of manifesting or articulating creative experience. It is fascinating to see that all the theoretical concepts of Indian arts have quantitative or computational components. It is beyond the scope of this chapter to give elaborate exposition to all the concepts from a computational point of view, however, for clarification of the idea; the concepts of *Taala* and *Maana* (aesthetic measurement and proportions) are discussed in the following paragraphs. It is demonstrated that Indian arts and quantification go hand in hand. Artistic creations have profound computational and mathematical foundations in Indian arts. It does not destroy the quality of aesthetic experience, however; on the other hand, it enhances its quality. There exists a deeper level correlation between artistic quantification and the quality of aesthetic experience.

In Greece, when philosophers like Pythagoras and others were busy in finding correlation between musical scales and numbers as well as the mathematical canons of golden section as aesthetic standards for beauty in art and architecture (Stevens 1990: 49–55), their counterparts in India developed elaborate canons of aesthetic proportions for icons, images, sculpture, and architectural constructions. This tendency was universally prevalent in most of the ancient civilizations. These canons provide a perfect recipe for beautiful and aesthetic creations. Every culture has its set of norms for defining beauty based on the tradition, religious beliefs, as well as indigenously evolved notions of beauty. These norms have an impact on people's behavior and artistic expression. Traditional Indian artists have developed elaborate system of measurements and proportions. Once the conceptual framework for desired entity – an image, sculpture, or architectural monument – is designed or pre-visualized (of course, treatises lay down the process of visualization by emphasizing the importance of contemplation and meditation), artists were supposed to employ the *Taala* and *Maana* measurements for bringing the image into expected scale of proportion for actual manifestation. Since *Maana* is a system of proportions, there were several distinct sets of measurements. *Maana* is measurement along the vertical axes, *Pramana* is along the horizontal axes, *Parimaana* is around the circumference, *Unmaana* is along the transverse planes and depths, and *Upamaana* stands for proportions between negative spaces, i.e., space between the parts (Rowell 1992: 347).

These proportions are for the manifestation of physical form as well as content or specific aesthetic emotions to be evoked called '*Rasa*' – to be discussed in the next section. In the anthropometric parlance, hand span is normally treated as the unit of measurement. Thus, *Taala* unit is equivalent of a hand span (palm-spread), and all the other measurements of the body were decided in terms of *Taala*. In various treatises various scales of *Taala*, proportion for iconometry were established. For instance, heights of different entities were laid down as: ten *Taala* for a deity, eight *Taala* for men, seven *Taala* for women, five *Taala* or six *Taala* for Ganesha or Elephant, and four *Taala* for children. The system has units of measurements for common usage consisting of *Yava* (size of the barley grain); *Angula* (digit-width of a finger) equivalent to eight *Yava*; *Vitasti* is the standard *Taala* unit measuring a palm span equivalent to twelve *Angulas*; *Hasta* (cubit) equivalent to twenty-four *Angulas*; *Danda* (a stick) equivalent to four *Hastas*; *Rajju* (a rope) equivalent to four *Dandas*. The system has micro level units of measurements, *Anu* (atom), *Renu* (a speck of dust) equivalent to eight *Anus*, *Valagra* (tip of a hair) equivalent to eight *Renus*, *Liksha* (nit) equivalent to eight *Valagras*, and *Yuka* (louse) equivalent to eight *Likshas*. *Yava* is supposed to be equivalent to eight *Yuka*. The system also has macro level units for measuring long distances, *Krosh* equivalent to five hundred *Dandas*, *Goruta* equivalent to two thousand *Dandas*, and *Yojana* equivalent to eight thousand *Dandas* (Dagen 1992: 372). This systematic process of defining measurements proved to be a powerful tool for expression in visual arts apart from establishing consistent sets of correspondence among various images, intra-image proportions, and underlying emotions and vital rhythm that sculptor or architect seeks to express or communicate. The purpose of *Taala-Maana* system was to provide standardization that will eventually lead to harmonious creations.

The *Taala-Maana* measurements laid down in the treatises are supposed to be aesthetic proportions for visual composition. Indian tradition has evolved a unique calculus of aesthetic proportions applicable across plastic and performing arts. The *Taala-Maana* system is applicable to performing arts of music, dance, and theatre where units of measurements are interpreted in terms of time. The same *Taala* unit is interpreted in the context of dance as a relative proportion in terms of number of hand spans between the feet in a particular posture or the length of a step, and, with reference to music, it is the unit of a rhythmic cycle, a temporal unit (Rowell 1992: 348). The *Taala-Maana* system is in no sense a prescriptive system; in fact, it is a descriptive system, a calculus of aesthetics that lays down the canons of beauty allowing individual artists to freely explore the beauty of forms with all its possible variations. These canons were never a hindrance to artistic creativity. No two temples or sculptures are the replicas of each other, though they are based on these same canons. *Taala-Maana* system is a conceptual and perceptual standard of aesthetics, an essence of a long Indian tradition and collective wisdom. The system is sufficiently complex and evolved over a period of time. The idea of *Taala-Maana* stands for the integration and manifestation of inner structure, rhythm, and vital energy of the work of art. Artistic vision is scaled to human sense of proportion leading a way towards abstraction and idealized designs that reveal archetypical quest for form and meaning.

The ultimate objective of any artistic expression is to evoke a unique kind of aesthetic experience. To achieve this artists construct an imaginative world that is meaningful. A performing artist creates an imaginary world using the artistic devices of language, poetic phrases, dialogues, rhyming words, beautiful hand gestures, and body postures. In arts like painting, sculpture, and architecture, artists use the visual language of shapes, forms, colors, texture, positive and negative spaces to create meaningful reality. In both cases, the languages of creative expression require a grammar of aesthetics. Normally, this grammar is implicitly present and followed by artists intuitively. Otherwise artists have their own explicit grammar or canons for the language of artistic expression based on certain mathematical ratios or proportions. Any artistic creation has a definite structure in space and time. These canons or grammar provide mathematical foundations to create beautiful and meaningful structures. Mathematics is a study of quantifiable abstract concepts and their structure, order, and relations. Its results are applicable to the real world as well as imaginary worlds. Some times it is argued that there exists a significant similarity between mathematics and arts. Both indulge in dreaming about imaginary worlds or spaces without any reference to reality which have their own internal consistency, autonomous in themselves. These imaginary worlds are safe from mundane real-life connections, conventions, and compulsions; of course, they may have their own compulsions of consistency, soundness, parsimony, and elegance. Indian artists tried to create artistic worlds – images, sculptures, temples, and architectural monuments that are complete in themselves. Even a performance of Indian classical music, Indian classical dance or a play is supposed to be a complete world in itself.

Quest for beauty and aesthetics are the motivational factors for mathematical studies. Mathematicians seek beautiful structures, patterns, and the structural harmony of patterns (Hadamard 1945: 30–31). The search for symmetries and regularities in the structure of abstract patterns lies at the core of pure mathematics (Weinberg 1993: 113). Mathematics in tandem with digital technology is capable to develop a new aesthetics – digital aesthetics. The logical algorithms embedded in computers are designed for mundane – day-to-day operations. However, with some aptitude in mathematics, an artist can play with these algorithms and come up with innovative ones that can generate beautiful patterns. These patterns could be of images, sounds, or concepts. Digital technology has tremendous potential for such explorations. Artists are already trying their hands with them. There lies a tremendous opportunity for artists to create mathematically profound artistic worlds capable to evoke aesthetic experience. Indian canons of *Taala-Maana* could be the precursors in this regard.

## Art and Aesthetic Experience

Indian theories of aesthetics evolved independently along with various Indian philosophical schools. It appears that they borrowed moderately from them in terms of philosophical frameworks or core concepts and adopted them with certain modifications. A broad review of these theories suggests that there were two major trends in their overall thinking. Some of the theories have a close affinity with *Samkhya* philosophy (that propagates dualism) in their description, while most of the other schools show linkages with *Vedanta* school of philosophy (which propagates non-dualism) in their manifestation.

> According to pessimistic *Samkhya*, nature is not wholly beautiful but has in it phases of beauty as well as ugliness...It means that there is nothing in the nature which at all times is pleasurable to all...According to optimistic *Vedanta* philosophy on the other hand everything is beautiful and there is nothing in the universe to mar its inward harmony...The aim of art according to both the systems of philosophy is to induce a mood of detachment. But according to idealistic *Vedanta* the artistic attitude is characterized by forgetting, though temporary, of one's individuality; while according to the realistic *Samkhya*, it is due to an escape from the natural world. According to the former, art serves as a pathway to the Reality; but according to the latter, it is so to speak a `deflection' from the reality. The one reveals the best in the Nature, while the other fashions something better than the nature. (Hiriyanna 1954: 16–17)

Since the theories of aesthetics were evolving and the theoreticians did not have any philosophical compulsions, most of them developed their views independently or they tried to synthesize both the above-mentioned philosophical positions. As theories evolved, this synthesis took final shape. Barring differences of description, all theories agree about the universal and transcendental character of aesthetic experience that reflects the overtones of *Vedanta* school of philosophy.

Initially, the discussion on aesthetic experience was confined to performing arts of drama, dance, and music. Later on it was extended to poetics and literature since they were inseparable parts of performing arts. Then it also included arts of painting, sculpture, and architecture. Issues pertaining to the nature of aesthetic experience are specific to each art form. As the traditional wisdom believes in interdependence and interrelation among all the arts at core level, theoreticians succeeded in developing comprehensive theories of aesthetic experience applicable to all art forms. Art is either a realistic representation, imaginative representation or a representation of emotions. Indian theories of aesthetics consider the first category as the least aesthetic and do not give much attention to it. A work of art is a spontaneous and expressive response of a creative mind when it is under the spell of creative imagination or emotions. Indian theories of aesthetics deal with both the types of representations in depth; however, they give preference to the latter one in most of the theoretical discussions.

The first ever discussion about the nature of aesthetic experience appears in Bharata's *Natyashastra*, a repository of traditional wisdom on performing arts of drama, dance, and music. According to Bharata, aesthetic experience is the experience of immersing oneself in the act of experiencing artistic presentation or representation by excluding all else. This state can last for a few minutes or can last for a longer duration when the audience is completely absorbed into it. He mentions that there exist eight fundamental states of mind in every individual called *bhavas* or *sthayibhavas*. These are the natural dispositions of mind in the form of latent impressions and are always ready to appear in consciousness. Artists' encounter with life causes them to create works of art. It excites the *sthayibhavas* of the audience. Due to the impact of artistic work, these *sthayibhavas* are transformed, modified, and combined with each other in appropriate proportions to give rise to aesthetic emotions or aesthetic experience of a special kind called *Rasa*. Since there are eight *sthayibhavas*, Bharata mentions eight dominant types of aesthetic emotions, erotic, comic, pathos, furious, heroic, fear, disgust, and wonder. Later on, the ninth *rasa* called `peace' or serenity was added to it (Gnoli 1968: XV-XVII). These aesthetic emotions are not part of real life on the other hand; since they are caused by a work of art they have special ontological status. They are evoked in the consciousness of the audience and all the individual audience shares them with the rest of the audiences. In this sense they have a universal ontological status.

The above-mentioned theory of aesthetic experience is interpreted and re-interpreted by later theoreticians. Although they came up with multiple interpretations of the theory, there is an agreement among all the theoreticians about transcendental or un-worldly nature of aesthetic experience. In a narrower sense, the term *rasa* stands for an aesthetic emotion generated in the consciousness of the audience. But in a comprehensive sense, it is not just a particular aesthetic emotion such as pathos or fear, rather it is the generalized or universal state of consciousness attained by the audience during aesthetic experience.

A work of art is a suggestive or metaphorical representation of an artist's encounter with reality. One of the most influential thinkers, Anandavardhana, developed a theory called *Dhwani*, i.e., suggestive meaning or imaginative aesthetic resonance. He argues that there is no difference between *rasa* and *dhwani* (Masson 1970: 24). Aesthetic experience is beyond worldly pain or pleasure. The kind of pleasure that arises out of it is of a different type. It is neither worldly nor spiritual. It is universalized in nature and, therefore, selfless. The selflessness signified by the aesthetic experience comprises of disinterested or detached contemplation of beauty. It yields a pleasure which is not contaminated by even the least pain. This is the transcendental characteristic of aesthetic experience which is of higher order as compared to the ordinary phenomenological experience.

A noted thinker, Bhatta Nayaka, argues that aesthetic state of mind or consciousness is completely independent from individual interests. It is so because the aesthetic experience is a unique experience that has a universal quality. Bhatta Nayaka says:

> Rasa, the aesthetic experience revealed by the power of revelation (bhavana), is not noetic in character, is not a perception, but an experience, a fruition (bhoga). This fruition is characterized by a state of lysis (laya), of rest into our own consciousness, the pervasion of consciousness by bliss and light: it belongs to the same order as the enjoyment of the supreme Brahman. (Gnoli 1968: XXIII-XXIV)

The state of universality assumed by Nayaka implies that the audience is completely immersed into the experience, eliminating the awareness of space and time as well as eliminating the self-awareness. Abhinavgupta, who synthesized all the earlier theories and was exceptionally successful in bridging the most diverse theories of aesthetic experience, argues that during aesthetic experience, feelings and facts of everyday life, even if they are transfigured, are always present. Art is not an absence of life – every element of life appears in aesthetic experience – but it is pacified and detached from all the passions (Gnoli 1968: XL). Aesthetic experience is accompanied by a sense of wonder. He says:

> In literature the aesthetic relish (of the suggested sense) through the verbal paraphernalia (of drama) is like (the blossoming) of a magic flower: it is essentially a thing of the present moment which does not depend on past or future time. (Masson 1970: 17–18)

A poet or artist creates a world according to his wish. A poet is at once he who sees and he who is capable of expressing it. He is endowed with a special power of creating manifold, extra-ordinary reality due to power called Pratibha, the creative imagination (Gnoli 1968: XLVIII). In the same tone, another noted theoretician, Hemachandra, describes the nature of Pratibha in a vivid manner. He says poets have a vision. Vision is the power of disclosing intuitively the reality underlying the manifold materials in the world and their aspects. Rasa belongs to poet alone; it is nothing but his generalized consciousness. The audience and spectator during aesthetic experience are enchanted by this generalized consciousness, cognition, or perception. Therefore, all is pervaded by rasa: the poet, audience, artwork (Gnoli 1968: XLVIII–XLIX).

In the most dominant school of Indian philosophy called Vedanta, Brahman – the absolute truth – represents the inner harmony of the universe. Realization of Brahman is nothing but the realization of universal harmony. A metaphysical goal of every self-actualized individual is to attain this state of mind which is direct and not mediated. As per Vedanta, the aim of art is to create an ideal work of art by inducing an attitude of complete detachment and try to be as close as possible to the state of Brahman. Therefore, the work of art should lead the artist as well as the audience to that restful bliss, realization of that harmony. Universal harmony is realized in one's own experience and not merely intellectually apprehended (Hiriyanna 1954: 6–10). The artist is endowed with creative imagination and the required artistic skills. He or she can use various devices of art such as rhythm, balance, aesthetic proportions, *Taala-Maana*, symmetry, figure of speech, etc. to help the audience to contemplate or get immersed into the aesthetic experience and realize this harmony. It is confined to art alone. It helps the audience to get close to the absolute truth and get a glimpse of it. An artist's objective is to create a work of art that accelerates this process by taking the audience into the realm of a sort of unworldly, virtual experience.

Virtual reality and the augmented reality paradigm can be of great help in facilitating the process of simulating aesthetic experience. The augmented reality paradigm works on the actual physical reality augmented by additional information into the physical spaces as opposed to virtual reality (Manowich 2003: 79). In this case the audience resides in the physical space and at one level is always aware of it but is immersed into the simulated environment (a perfect situation to implement Abhinavgupta's idea of aesthetic experience). Therefore, it is possible to design augmented experiences of multiple kinds and quality. Virtual reality takes the audience into an entirely unreal situation, a virtual situation. Augmented Reality opens up possibilities for variety in the degree of immersion as well as the quality of immersion and overall experience. Both the paradigms are worth exploring in the context of simulating aesthetic experience as discussed in previous paragraphs.

## Pedagogy of Arts in the Digital Age
The digital age is a post-postmodern reality. The postmodern era is either on the verge of its conclusion or it has almost concluded. The current era is waiting for its definition while partially carrying the residues of the previous. Contemporary critical theory has not overcome the hangover of postmodern analysis and discourse yet. The art world has to move on either with or without postmodernism or deconstruction and spell out its own stance in the emerging digital age. New media, as one of the alternatives, can replace the theoretical vacuum created by the absence of postmodernism. In the changing context new media can be defined as a convergence of all existing and possible media. It is not restricted to the Internet and multimedia. New media may be understood from the Indian perspective as discussed in previous sections but may not confine to it. Particular facets of Indian perspective on arts such as convergence and interdependence of various art forms, art as computation, and transcendental character of aesthetic experience provide the necessary lead to position new media in proper perspective. In a sense new media is no different in its essence from Indian perspective on arts. Using new media technologies with all its diversity and possibilities of convergence, interaction flows, and ubiquitous connectivity, the world of art can expound new structures, architectures, and forms of cultural significance. In this emergence, the artists can see new orders of art practices, new aesthetics, new forms of presentations and representations, and a whole new cultural idiom. Convergence, computation, and calculus of aesthetics are the key themes for new age artistic

expressions. Art education needs to redefine and reposition itself in the new context and prepare itself to take up a historical challenge.

Individual artists have the liberty and privilege to choose their theoretical position and propositions. Artists who work with new media technology have a wide range of stances available to them. They can carry the historical legacy of realism, impressionism, expressionism, cubism, abstraction, surrealism, or others through their art expressions; or take forward the amorphous stance of postmodernism and deconstruction. They can innovate on prevalent new media technologies and extend the realm to explore endless possibilities offered by emerging new media aesthetics of pattern language and virtual spaces. They can interweave and synergize all the above and move forward. Digital era is a technology-dominated era. It will have unpredictable impact on thoughts and actions of people and art audience. However, the core quest for art and humane values will continue. History has shown that core cultural values always survive and humanity never dies. Artists who will keep working on current concerns and those who keep renewing themselves continuously will use new media as a tool to address issues and connect with reality and culture in a novel way. Such artists will see themselves as change-agents and seek to nurture revolutionary expressive capabilities of new media for the cause of art.

A curriculum and methodology that focuses on above-mentioned factors should be developed to educate artists in the digital age. Art has always been a profession of generalists. However, various specializations, fine arts, applied arts, design, or industrial art are established and even art institutions follow the same compartmentalization. There might be a certain advantage in being a specialist in a particular domain of arts. Various specialized domains of art are converging due to the emergence of new media. Fine artists are already designing websites and software-user interfaces. Electronic art and installation art require knowledge of multiple domains ranging from electronics, music, sculpture, and architecture. Artistic expressions do not follow the boundaries of specialization and super-specialization. There is an emergence of great orchestration of arts, science, and technology. Pedagogy of arts should address this issue and adopt a multi-disciplinary and multi-sensory approach in education. Art curriculum needs to include at least one course on comparative study of various art forms, such as dance, drama, music, painting, sculpture, architecture, poetry, and literature.

As already discussed, there is an important dimension of art that is not been given due consideration so far – 'art as computation'. On the contrary, there is a tendency among artists to treat art as anti-analytical and anti-computational domain. Art education should re-look at it in the changing scenario. Traditional Indian artists have made some valuable advances in this direction as already discussed and have demonstrated that computation and quantification can be an integral part of artistic practices. New media opens up a possibility of developing a calculus of aesthetics which is relevant to contemporary practices. Teaching science and technology to art students is a challenging task. However; at least few relevant topics from science, technology, and mathematics can be introduced in the syllabus to enrich art education. Artists and mathematicians are fond of creating abstract mental constructs. The digital tools provide enormous possibilities in this regard. Artists need to be taught how abstract constructs and spaces are created in the virtual reality environments. Moreover, the abstract spaces can be still elusive as they aught to be and need not be manifested literally. The new media artwork can indicate or connote the existence of such spaces and their patterns with beauty leading to a unique kind of aesthetic experience. As a part of training, masterpieces or great works of art may be deconstructed and freshly analyzed from a new media point of view. Few case studies will help art students to become more comfortable with the technology.

New media artists use technology either as a tool or supplementary device for their artistic expressions or they use its core strengths for a more profound expression. In the first case, they use application packages or software languages that provide readily available utilities and tools. In the second case, artists use core strengths of digital technologies, algorithms, generative programming, artificial intelligence strategies, genetic algorithms, fractals, cellular automata, so on and so forth. It is an advanced stage of creativity where an artist has more freedom to play with core strengths of new media technologies. In the first case, the artist is bound by the limitations of application software packages or languages. Currently, these applications and languages are at their primary stage of development and do not offer the necessary flexibility, ease of use to match with artistic spontaneity and expectations. Software packages and languages are designed and developed by software professionals. They may not have the insights to address the genuine needs of artists. It is suggested that art institutes should take a lead in the development of artist-friendly software and languages. In the second case, the scenario is much more complex. Artists will need to make extra efforts to master core techniques of digital technologies such as generative programming. Artists need to understand the underlying process of programming; they can very effectively apply their creative imagination for exploring the process of generating new algorithms. Computer algorithms are currently taught in the context of computer science. It is necessary to teach how to develop algorithms in the context of specific art, painting, music, sculpture, and so on. This is more difficult since artists will have to reorient their thinking styles. Most artists are intuitive and emotional in nature. Algorithmic thinking requires analytical bent of mind. The toughest task in front of artists in this case is to strike a balance. Such reorientation will open up unlimited worlds of creative expressions. The expressions will be more profound; aspiring towards heightened sensitivity. It will allow artists to deconstruct the essential geometry of the universal order of existence and experience.

New media technology offers enormous potentials in terms of self-generating and self-modifying images, texts, sounds, and so on. The multi-modal, multi-tasking capabilities provide scope for free, boundless, creative wanderings across domains that are otherwise impossible in a traditional way of working. The formal logic of algorithms offers infinite possibilities of informal creative spaces, serendipity, ineffable corollaries of timelessness, and the unfolding of hidden metaphors in the unfathomable depths of structures of space and time. It facilitates the artistic quest for pure form, beauty, and aesthetic experience at a deeper level that transcends sensation and emotions and attains resonance with the absolute truth. The concept of aesthetic experience described by *Vedanta* school of Indian philosophy expounds similar kinds of experience. During the creative process of generative programming and developing algorithms, concepts and digits are mapped onto each other leading to formation of abstract constructs, and if artists apply their sense of aesthetics, they can build a completely novel and beautiful reality. Irrespective of the final output, the whole process of developing algorithms itself is highly imaginative. The reality constructed out of this process echoes this beauty and the audience are privileged to share the same aesthetic experience.

## Expressing with Grey Cells
Learning at the cross section of arts, science, technology, and culture in a digital age insinuates the emergence of a new pedagogy for artists. Although the scenario is nascent, there are certain indications of future developments. The emergent pedagogy of arts will involve, at a broader level, a reasonable combination of intuition and analytical thinking. In specific cases due to the influence of new media, convergence of multiple media and computation will dominate the realm of artistic expressions. Art without losing its sensitivity will become more cerebral in its manifestations. Creative genius will use their brain cells – 'Grey Cells' for expression. Art has always been a presentation, representation, or reflection of contemporary ethos. With the arrival of a digital age, followed by information ecology and knowledge economy, the mind-set of the intelligentsia as well as the audience, critic, connoisseur, and consumer has changed. Intelligent and promising creative expressions from artists are expected by these cerebral and knowledge-seeking communities. There are indications that artists have sensed it. This certainly is a positive sign.

## Works Cited
Bhatt, M. (1958), *Roopaprada Kalaa* (Gujarati), Vadodara: Markanda Bhatt, Faculty Residence, University Road.

Buck, C. (1965), *A Dictionary of Selected Synonyms in the Principle Indo-European Languages*, Chicago: The University of Chicago Press.

Dagen, B. (1992), *Kalatattvakosha: A Lexicon of Fundamental Concepts of Indian Arts*, vol. 2, (vol. ed. Baumer, B.), New Delhi: Indira Gandhi National Centre for Arts, pp. 367–384.

Gnoli, R. (1968), *Aesthetic Experience According to Abhinavagupta,* Varanasi: The Chowkhamba Sanskrit Series Office.

Hadamard, J. (1945), *An Essay on the Psychology of Invention in the Mathematical Field*, Princeton: Princeton University Press.

Hiriyanna, M. (1954), *Art Experience*, Mysore: Kavyalaya Publishers.

Manovich, L. (2003), 'The poetics of augmented space,' *New Media: Theories and Practices of Digitextuality*. (ed. Everett, A.), New York: Routledge.

Masson, J. (1970), *Aesthetic Rapture*, vol. 1 (text), Pune: Deccan College.

Misra, R. (1988), 'Shilpa', *Kalatattvakosha: A Lexicon of Fundamental Concepts of Indian Arts*, (ed. Baumer, B.), New Delhi: Indira Gandhi National Centre for Arts.

Rowell, L. (1992), *Kalatattvakosha: A Lexicon of Fundamental Concepts of Indian Arts*, vol. 2, (vol. ed. Baumer, B.), New Delhi: Indira Gandhi National Centre for Arts, pp. 333–353.

Shah, p. (1961), *Vishnudharmottar Purana*, vol. 3: 2, Baroda: Oriental Institute.

Stevens, G. (1990), *The Reasoning Architect*, New York: McGraw-Hill Pub. Co.

Wardrip-fruin, N. (2003), *The New Media Reader* (ed.), Cambridge: The MIT Press.

Weinberg, S. (1993), *Dream of a Final Theory*, London: Vintage.

Wilson, S. (2002), *Information Arts: Intersection of art, science and technology*, Cambridge: The MIT Press.

# New Media Art as Embodiment of the Tao

## Wengao Huang

Western culture, rooted in Hellenism, must be radically revised to deal with the complexity of our digital age. The resonance between natural sciences and Eastern mystical traditions can contribute to the formation of a new worldview that is a holistic and ecological one with enhanced spirituality. New visions of reality demonstrate what the ancient Chinese perceived as the Tao – dynamic monism in which matter is not concrete and the self not centered and unified.

New media arts have been sensitive to and have actively catalyzed this paradigm shift. With their emphasis on connections, transformations, and emergence, new media arts are closely related to complexity science that parallels the traditional Chinese spirit. Generative and interactive art utilizing emerging technologies have great potential to vividly demonstrate the transforming spirit of the Tao and give new meanings to the well-known saying within the traditional Chinese art world: "Art is the embodiment of the Tao."

New media art is at the center of the cultivation of a new consciousness with a full understanding of the ongoing paradigm shift and the adaptation of human action to tapping the creative potential of complexity while avoiding its dangerous tendencies.

### Change of Paradigm

In our increasingly complex and interconnected world, with the growing understanding of nature brought about by experimental sciences, and faced with the pressing problems of post-industrial society, a necessary change of paradigm is reshaping ideologies that express a shift from Western to Eastern consciousness.

Mainstream Western culture originates in Hellenism. Rationalism based on conceptualization and logic, dualism between spirit and matter, reductionism in finding the fundamental "atom," and science and technology that seeks the domination of nature by man, are all found to be inadequate in dealing with today's complex world. Sciences in the last century have greatly changed our vision of reality. Matter is no longer concrete, the self no longer centered and unified, and fundamental entities have not been found. What remains is a dynamic monism, a web of interrelated events. This new vision of reality appears as parallel to the Eastern mystical tradition, understood by the ancient Chinese as the Tao.

Western culture can no longer ignore ancient Eastern wisdom. "The philosophy of mystical tradition provides a consistent philosophical background to the new science paradigm." (Capra 2000: 327) "The rediscovery of Asian philosophy...is a second renaissance in the cultural history of the West." (Varela 1995: 22) This merging of East and West, together with other parallel cultural movements, leads to a holistic and ecological worldview. In the new paradigm, sciences become more spiritual evolving towards wisdom, not just knowledge, but harmony, not dominance. This tendency also brings science closer to art.

Artists enjoy this spiritual aspect of new paradigms in science. Art in its intuitive mode has never cut off its deep roots in ancient magic. It has been spiritual in seeking creativity and harmony and in being sensitive to new technologies. New media arts inherit prevalent modernistic confidence by catalyzing cultural transformation through renewed media, pushing the technological sensitivity of modernism to the extreme. With increasing technological and social complexity, connectivity and interactivity become distinct features of new media arts, giving rise to the emergence of new meanings, new thoughts, and new experiences.

New media arts relate to new scientific paradigms as they draw closer to the traditional Chinese spirit. Art today, exploring aesthetic facets of connection, interaction, and emergence, can well be seen as a resonance of the age-old saying within the traditional Chinese art world: "Art is the embodiment of the Tao." In my chapter, I explore the embodiment of the Tao in the context of both its original meaning and its significance in our digital age.

### Chinese Arts and Philosophy
Chinese culture has a five thousand year history. Ch'i is the deepest root of Chinese thinking. The ancient Chinese perceived the cosmos as a flowing and ever-changing reality that includes everything within its process and called it Ch'i, or Tao. The theory of Ch'i-Yin/Yang-Five Elements is at the heart of Chinese culture, including religion, philosophy, and the arts.

Ch'i is the origin of all phenomena. It contains three in one: Yin, Yang, and mind symbolized by the middle curve that differentiates Yin and Yang (Zou 1988). Ch'i contains heaven/earth/ human, without distinct separation between subject and object. This is a unique character of Chinese thought.

Interaction of Yin and Yang gives rise to the Five Elements: wood, fire, earth, gold, and water. Yin and Yang interact as the Five Elements generate and inhibit each other. This is the basis upon which the universe operates. Yin, Yang, and the Five Elements can be regarded as images of motion with distinct characteristics. The meanings of these images are abundant, multiple, and correlative, forming a theory system that has rich implications and continually brings about new ideas. There are constant patterns in the change of Ch'i. The Chinese capture them in the hexagon with its variety of combinations of Yin and Yang, adapting its patterns in human actions.

Chinese thought, based on intuition and imagination, has an inherently aesthetic nature. It captures the secret rhythm of the universe in the image of Ch'i. "Art is the embodiment of the Tao" is a well-known saying within the traditional Chinese art world. The vitality of Ch'i is emphasized in Chinese arts. In aesthetics, Ch'i has three levels of meaning: Ch'i of the universe and Ch'i of the artist intersect each other and are embodied in Ch'i of the artwork, its inner living force, its rhythm.

Creating art is sensing the Tao in a meditative state and following the movement of Ch'i, like the spontaneous movement of the hand in calligraphy. This spontaneity, or *wu-wei* as Lao Tzu' put it, is the Tao's principle of action. "By non-action everything can be done." (Zhang 1988: 47) The Tao is not far from everyday life. It can be experienced in any activity. Chinese martial arts, especially inner martial arts such as T'ai-Chi, Xing-Yi, all emphasize Ch'i. Chinese poems often point to some deep Taoist meaning beyond the superficial words.

**Taoist Charms, Martial Arts, and Body Consciousness**
Art as embodiment of the Tao obtains its deepest meaning through primitive magic, which is the origin of culture. Taoism, inherited from primitive magic, is the native religion of China. The charm (magic diagram) is one of the most important elements of Taoism. It originates in ancient magic and symbolizes the divine world. There are thousands of charm diagrams in the Taoist canon, such as Heaven script, Cloud script, Dragon script, etc. These beautiful secret scripts look very different from ordinary Chinese characters, but use a similar pictographic method. They designate the inner reality of meditation that lies beyond the concepts of ordinary language. Their shapes coil or angle as they are combined into powerful designs. They provide a vast repertoire of forms for artistic development frequently appearing in paintings, in pottery, and on furniture. Some of these diagrams are ancient. They are said to be the origin of Chinese culture, including the Chinese characters. They even include musical and smell notations (Rawson 1984: 116).

The three *ling-bao* diagrams are among the most important charms. According to Taoist legend, they were created by Tianzhen Huangren (a Taoist ancestor) and then passed to Huang Di (the emperor of China, also a Taoist ancestor who lived more than four thousand years ago) in Mount Ermei. These three diagrams symbolize the processes of the creation and evolution of heaven, earth, and man respectively. The first one is the diagram of change. According to Taoist legend, this diagram, continually changing, appeared in the sky to Tianzhen Huangren. It recorded experience of cosmic creation as the interplay of Yin and Yang. It represents the penetrating force of the Ch'i and the transcendental action of the Tao. These diagrams have aesthetic power. Today, however, so long after their first appearance, their original meaning is difficult to comprehend.

I think these charms can be better appreciated in their original dynamic rather than static form. Digital technologies facilitate experiencing this dynamic form. In my digital video, *Dragon at Grass at Large*, I use the diagram of change throughout it, bringing the dynamic form to life through animation. I use it to symbolize the ancient Chinese spirit. The video finds fault with the materialist atmosphere of the modern world. The charm is a silent language spoken to the invisible spirit and a means of communication between heaven, earth, and man.

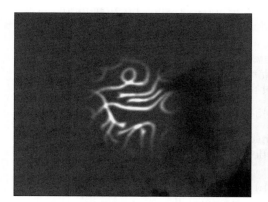

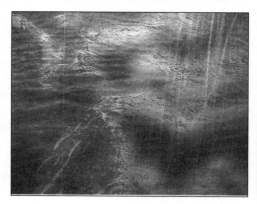

**Figure 1.** Images from digital video *Dragon at Grass at Large*

Figure 1 shows three images from this video. In the first one, the magic diagram appears in the center of the circle of the moving stance, a basic practice of the inner martial arts. It gives an introduction to the Chinese inner martial arts. The practitioner of the inner martial arts enters into a vast inner continuum of moving energies, in which he gradually develops "body consciousness." The ancient Chinese thought that organs of consciousness are not only the brain cortex, but also the thalamencephalon, heart, liver, gallbladder, kidney, etc. Mind and emotion are based on interaction between brain and viscera.

One inner martial arts, Xingyi, is based on the Five Fists, which correspond to the Five Elements, and also correspond to Heart set, Liver set, Spleen set, Lung set, and Kidney set. "Xingyi" literally means "shape and mind." The Five Fists enhance "body consciousness" while preserving the health of viscera. The Kungfu consists of three processes: transforming Ching to Ch'i, transforming Ch'i to Shen, and transforming Shen to the Void. Ching is the energy that is the essence of life. Shen is mind or consciousness, and Ch'i mediates between Ching and Shen. The Kungfu is to transform personal Ching-Ch'i-Shen into its original cosmic version. When the inner and the outer are united, the practitioner experiences the complete and unbroken Whole, encompassing all variations within its transcendent tranquility, and this is the Void, the Tao. Ch'i as mediation between Ching and Shen, is neither totally material nor totally spiritual. Its movement brings about coherence of the brain and body and gives rise to "body consciousness."

The second image shows a frightened and distorted face on which the magic diagram appears like burned scars. In a world far from the Tao, the charm acquires more complex meaning, even turns into a curse. In the third image, the character dives into the water. After a struggle, he adapts himself to the current and merges into the Void, symbolized by the same magic diagram which first hides and eventually emerges from the water wave.

Creating a video artwork is like meditation or practicing the stance of the inner martial arts. It is to foster and communicate Ch'i, to let it flow fluently and rhythmically between every element making the work into a living whole. Eventually the video creates an atmospheric field of artistic Ch'i. The Ch'i of this video is a vibrating one. It vibrates between two extremes of Chinese life: the gloomy and dangerous outer reality and the inner reality with profound insight and unsurpassed poetry. I realize that this viewpoint is not specifically Chinese, for it can found in the work of Franz Kafka and Francis Bacon.

### Rediscover the Tao in the Light of New Sciences
Western science used to be far removed from Chinese thinking and in opposition to art in its objective indifferent attitude. Interestingly, it has now come to something similar to ancient Chinese intuition, mainly owing to the growing understanding of nature brought about by the new sciences of the last century.

Relativity and quantum mechanics have changed our worldview profoundly. Matter disappears into the void, as Chinese sages declared long ago. Subatomic particles are nothing but bundles of energy. In quantum field theory, fields are primary physical entities from which the physical world emerges. They are a vacuum, or zero point fields, at ground energy level, and they become particles when activated. Vacuum is not empty, within it virtual particles spontaneously come into being from the void and disappear endlessly. This picture reminds us of Ch'i, which is matter when condensing and is void when dispersing. The void is not nothingness. "In it are things; In it there is form and an essence." (Zhang 1988: 25)

According to the Copenhagen interpretation of quantum mechanics, consciousness is necessary to establish physical reality by collapsing the wave packet to generate particles. This field-particle-mind relation seems to parallel the trinity of Ch'i. "The Tao of the Taoist, can be seen, perhaps, as the ultimate unified field from which spring not only the phenomena studied in physics, but all other phenomena as well including consciousness." (Capra 2000: 211) The Chinese may rightly call this ultimate unified field "the Tao field."

Consciousness remains the greatest mystery, which can no longer be ignored by science. Can Western science resolve this mystery by itself? Western philosophy and science has mainly been seeking to find truth through abstract and objective methods. This position is no longer adequate when we make our own consciousness subject of our scientific study. Any serious exploration of consciousness reveals limitations in the worldview of mainstream Western science. Though quantum theory seems compatible with philosophical idealism, "the implication is not that we may expect to learn more about consciousness by studying theoretical physics. Rather, it would seem to be that we must now seriously consider augmenting or replacing the dominant epistemology by...an epistemology of subjectivity." (Harman 1996: 746)

Consciousness research must give an explicit and central role to first-person accounts and to the irreducible nature of experience. As Western culture has no tradition of first-person methods for inner exploration, consciousness research explicitly draws from Asian traditions as living manifestation of an active, disciplined phenomenology. Traditional Chinese philosophy is never separate from subjective experience. Taoism consists of theories and disciplined methods based on these experiences. Its character is a balance between mind and body, and its inner alchemy reveals extended consciousness. It is only in such a state of consciousness that the meridians and Ch'i are to be sensed. Much like the inner martial arts, Taoist inner alchemy also consists of the three transforming processes with more explicit emphasis on mind's guidance of circulation of Ch'i through meridians, while in the case of martial arts Ch'i is mainly guided by correct stance and motion of body.

Taoism claims that there are three levels of consciousness: Shi Shen, Yin Shen, and Yang Shen. Shi Shen is conventional mind, including ordinary perception, judgment, reasoning, etc. Yin Shen is personalized subconsciousness, which is able to leave the body and has some paranormal qualities. Yang Shen is personalized original cosmic consciousness, which is the ultimate achievement of Taoist inner alchemy.

Many people consider that Taoism and Buddhism arrive at the same place on their higher level. Taoists in their initial processes are more concerned with body-mind unity and the preservation of health, while Buddhists directly work on the mind to more explicitly deal with phenomenological psychology. When Taoism and Buddhism met in China, they combined into Zen. What is uniquely Chinese in Taoism may be that which I have previously called "body consciousness," which lies between brain consciousness and original cosmic consciousness. Through meditation this consciousness extends beyond the physical body and merges with the Void. There are many legends about Taoists or martial arts masters who had super-perception and could avoid imminent danger even in their sleep.

These mystical traditions tell us much about our mind that is being verified by science. One important result is the breakdown of our naive concept of self. Cognitive subject is nonunified or decentered. The human mind has more than one center of control for our thoughts and emotions, and we have no absolute control over what happens in our mind. This is most explicitly expressed in Buddhist texts on the emergent structure of mental factors within a single moment of experience and the emergence of the karmic causal patterning of experience over time (Barendregt 1996). Within cognitive science, especially in the connectist model, the phenomenon usually attributed to self arises through self-organization without an actual self.

I think consciousness research will take a great leap forward if science eventually understands what Yang Shen, or Nirvana, is. Here is a point where Western science and Eastern wisdom can be most tangibly combined to benefit from one another. The naive belief in fundamental entities, the concrete nature of matter or the unification of self, has gone. The universe is understood to be a dynamic web of interrelated events with ever-changing emergent patterns. These emergent patterns are the essence of both complexity science and Ch'i theory.

## Complexity and Change

Complexity science studies emergence in varied complex systems – physical, biological, ecological, and social systems. It is a field researching global emergence from local interactions. There are still no unified formal theories of emergent property. The study of living self-organizing systems and artificial life is based upon this new paradigm (Longton 1995).

Emergence is a self-organizing process from non-linear interactions that cannot be predicted by reductive methods, namely, by analyzing separate elements of low levels. Emergence used to be difficult for science to understand. Now complexity science and artificial life are addressing this issue and are leading science toward holistic thinking.

They provide a new understanding of the dynamic process of interrelation and interaction and shed new light on ancient Chinese philosophy.

In the terminology of complexity science, Ch'i is a dynamic model of non-linear self-organization from the circulation and interchange of material, energy, and information within a system, and between a system and its environment. Yin can be considered as a tendency of self-organization towards stabilization, and Yang can be considered as a tendency towards adaptation. The Five Elements form a self-regulating network, achieving homeostasis through relationships of generating and restricting each other. For the human body, this homeostasis means being healthy.

Essentially, Yin-Yang and the Five Elements constitute a scheme of system analysis. They are subjective and qualitative functional models with a dark-box method. Yin-Yang represents minimum system analysis: all systems must have at least two sides that oppose each other but also complement each other. The Five Elements theory represents minimum relation analysis, including quality and direction of relation, as Figure 2 shows. When representing the Five Elements with Yin and Yang, we get the Eight Trigrams (Dong 2002).

Ch'i-Yin/Yang-Five Elements is a simple model with three levels, but it can contain unlimited inner levels. For example, each Yin and Yang can contain Yin and Yang, and each of the Five Elements can contain Five Elements. So it can model true complex systems such as the human body. In the body, the Five Elements correspond to Heart set, Liver set, Spleen set, Lung set, Kidney set, and some dozens of Ch'i circulate within the body, which closely relate to the environment including earth, sun, moon, and their periodicity. The human is a microcosm within the macrocosm.

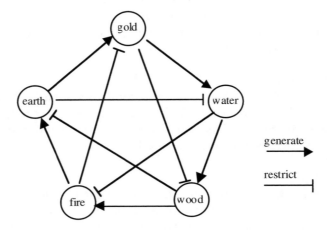

**Figure 2.** Relationships among the Five Elements.

## Creativity of New Media

"The Tao produces one, one produces two. The two produce the three and the three produce all things" (Zhang 1988: 56). This is an interactive and generative model of cosmic creation. "The two produce the three" is the key to understanding this process. Interaction of Yin and Yang is a non-linear, self-organizing process, giving emergence to a new thing, "the three." Through this process everything comes into being, and the complexity of the world increases.

While Ch'i is the basis of traditional Chinese arts, complexity science has become a main intellectual resource of new media arts. Complexity science, together with Ch'i Theory, constitutes an aesthetics of interaction and emergence in new media art and serves to construct models with rich emergence possibility. Emergence relates to cognitively interesting, unexpected, and novel happenings. While art engages in emergence processes in intuitive ways, complexity science gives us new understandings through working with modern emergence technology. Artists are interested in generating forms and behaviors that are beyond design and we are delighted to loose control in favor of emergence. Generative art and interactive art exemplify this new working mode with emergence technology that can be transcended to achieve spirituality.

Generative art is seeding as well as designing. It starts from a hypothesis about a possible world and transforming rules which lead to an increase in complexity. It is about designing and manipulating genotype and media within which genotype transforms into phenotype. It is about designing species where the individuals are unexpected emergences but not random events. Every individual process is unique and unforeseeable, a varied expression of the conception of an artist. It goes beyond the limits of tools by simulating the dynamics of nature.

Biological evolution and development are frequently simulated in media arts. Evolutionary computation is often used in exploring functional and aesthetic forms as emergent in living systems and artificial life. It has borne much fruit. A problem related to traditional evolutionary computation, however, is its ignorance of self-organizing development while relying heavily on the Darwinian theory of evolution. This has limited the complexity and evolvability of the system, which is why recent works put more emphasis on self-organizing development than on evolution.

Biological development is a miraculous process in which complexity continually increases while a zygote grows into a multi-cell organism. It has inspired many generative models, from early simple models such as L-system, artificial embryogeny, cellular automata, to more biologically based developments. With indirect, developmental genotype to phenotype mapping, evolvability will increase and more complex tasks can be addressed. Evolutionary developmental biology gives us a deeper understanding of the interaction between biological evolution and development. Genetic Regulatory Network (GRN), which lies at the heart of biological development, displays self-organizing behavior, the origin of much biological order. For example, cell type and cell cycle may relate to attractors of GRN and emerge spontaneously as "free orders" through dynamics of GRN near a parameter region called the edge of chaos (Kauffman 1993). Natural selection may be the mechanism by which GRN evolves towards the edge of chaos.

Many recent artworks are inspired by detailed scientific knowledge accumulated in the fields of genetics and developmental biology. Although bio-art holds great potential for artistic creation, the artist needs to resist becoming submerged in technical details. A balance between art and science must be maintained. One method to achieve this balance is to make art more interactive and, therefore, more psychoactive. Interactive art is a cybernetic system that addresses aesthetic issues. It generates artistic expressions in response to users' real-time inputs by automatic and intelligent processing of sensor signals. Interactive art aims to discover the sensation and formal character of interactive dynamics while merging it with images, sounds, and objects to form an aesthetic whole. Its basic structure expresses the principle of automatic intelligent control related to complexity science and emergent technologies.

I have been working on a project on interactive morphogenesis. Basically, it is an artificial evolutionary developmental system with a biologically plausible developmental model. Development is guided by interaction between genes and a morphogenetic field of protein gradients. An initial zygote contains a genome and some proteins. Through cell-splitting and differentiation, it grows into a multi-cellular creature with sensors, joints, and a neural network. Through evolution the creature develops successful patterns of motion in a 3-D physical simulated environment. The creature's morphology and behavior can change during interaction with the user and the environment. This interaction is implemented through sound reception and processing. Figure 3 shows this environmental simulation.

One important issue relative to this work is the interaction between body and brain. The dogma of traditional AI, seeing intelligence solely as symbolic processing, is outdated. Embodied AI emphasizes that intelligence must be embodied and environmentally situated. An agent's morphology, its body shape, its material, sensory, and motor properties form an integral aspect of intelligent behavior. An agent's morphology and neural network must shape and adapt in relation to others if it is to survive through evolution. Embodied AI is applied to robotic as well as virtual creatures as in Sims' work on coevolving of brain and body (Sims 1994).

Morphogenetic fields have been adopted by biologists as an account of developing organisms since the 1920s. No one really knows what these fields are or how they work. They may include not only chemical gradient but also other fields. I believe Ch'i is well qualified as the morphogenetic field. Of course, much remains to be done if this relation between Ch'i and morphogenetic field is to be taken seriously. I have worked on a smaller project beforehand making the 3-D graphic world more like some empty

**Figure 3.** A virtual creature in an artificial evolutionary developmental system.

mountains with some generative sound echoing in the forest. That is the poetry of ancient China, the paradise of Taoist hermits.

Morphogenesis is a multilevel, circular, generative process at different time and space scales. The higher level behavior is determined by the lower level processes, and vice versa. This circular causality or entanglement of levels lies at the heart of self-organizing pattern formation, which has just begun to be comprehended in complexity science. New media art is the alchemy of our time, bringing technology, consciousness, and culture into its global crucible, and leading to the only reality – the Tao, transforming diversity within coherence.

### Toward the Tao, the Artless Art
New media arts are based on but not predetermined by technology. While every tool brings with it an ideology and shapes its users, it also merges with the vast sea of human consciousness and history resonating with the old. This mixed consciousness, in turn, shapes the tool, bringing to it a more complex spiritual dimension. This interplay becomes more significant in our high-tech digital age of new media arts. Modern society

has reached such a complexity that a phase transition may occur sometime, and its direction more or less depends on the behavior of each individual. The human is not safe. Any social turbulence, even changes for the good, may destroy some individuals for no reason. This ridiculous human condition is largely due to our incomplete human nature and social system and is the current in which we have to swim.

Besides the brilliant inner wisdom and the unsurpassed poetry permeating their arts, the Chinese have repeatedly drifted into bloody turbulence throughout their long history, except for perhaps that preliterate age which Taoists often depicted as a paradise that we can only imagine through magic diagrams. Chinese sages and hermits found personal paradises through inner alchemy and the arts. It is not easy. More often than not, life is a vibration between these two realities, one inner, another outer. This is what my video artwork mirrors.

Creativity has two facets – from simplicity to complexity and from complexity to simplicity. This is the cycle of the Tao. The second process may be more relevant to the modern world. This is the creativity of lifestyle. At its highest level, one achieves the state of wu-wei when "by non-action everything can be done." I believe that art in an intuitive way can help us achieving this state, and it is this very life that constitutes the supreme art – artless art.

### Art Education in a Digital Age

Art, science, and technology are converging in new media. Artistic expression in new media does not fit within boundaries of areas of conventional specialization. New media art calls for generalists rather than specialists. Art pedagogy in a digital age should address this issue. Traditional Chinese education has aimed to produce generalists. Various art talents, including painting, calligraphy, music, chess playing, and literature, have been considered necessary for an intellectual to cultivate himself toward the Tao. Underlying various art forms there is a unifying aesthetics based on Ch'i, which links the arts, humanity, and the universe in a great whole that promotes artistic creativity.

The Bauhaus, that vital model of twentieth-century art and design education, adopted Taoist philosophy as a method for freeing creative potential locked deep inside students and stimulating a creative blend of art and technology. Johannes Itten, who was responsible for the half-year initial course, introduced Taoist philosophy into his course, including meditation and Chinese painting. He asked students to observe the model and the world from the view of Taoism, and to understand space and architecture in Taoist terms of being and non-being.

New media artists must choose their attitude toward technology. They can use it as a tool for artistic creation as in using application packages or software languages as ready-made tools. On the other hand, they can more actively explore the aesthetic potential of the technology itself by creating it. They can also adopt deconstructive schemes to question technology. To use strengths of new media to the fullest, artists need to master core techniques of digital technology such as cellular automata, genetic algorithm, artificial life, fractals, and chaos theory. Artists should learn how emerging technologies can give marvelous outcomes following simple rules, as gracefully exemplified by Conway's Game of Life or Craig Reynold's *Boids*. The process of algorithm development is in itself a highly creative and imaginative enterprise. Mathematics, in its quest for universal harmony in an imaginary space that is consistent and autonomous, is at its heart an art form. Ancient Chinese philosophy has intricate inner mathematical structures. *Hetu* and *Luoshu* are enigmatic mathematical systems even from our present-day perspective.

In addition to programming and algorithm design, other mathematical, scientific, and technological processes may need to be mastered for creating significant artistic work in new media. Electronic detection and control technologies, for example, can be used in installation art integrated with sculpture, architecture, painting, and music. There is no limit in an expanding art field in which any new technology may inspire artistic creativity. In fact, there is no explicit difference between art and technology in Chinese tradition. Art is a transcendental technology within which subjectivity and objectivity merge in the state of *wu-wei* when technology is fully mastered. This is the process of achieving the Tao through technology. Certainly technology in Taoists' terms always refers to simple tools used skillfully. Taoists did not like complex machines. In our world in which technology has become second nature, however, it is not difficult to see past the complexity of emerging technology and experience it as a humanized simple form.

Teaching technology to art students will remain a great challenge. The key is to achieve an aesthetic balance between art and technology. Chinese philosophy tells us much about this. Artists who in the past honored their intuitive and emotional sensibilities will have to develop their technological intuition without losing their aesthetic intuition.

## Works Cited

Barendregt, H. (1996), 'Mysticism and beyond Buddhist phenomenology, part II', *The Eastern Buddhist*, New Series, vol XXIX, 262–287.

Capra, F. (2000), *The Tao of Physics*, Boston: Shambhala Publications, Inc.

Dong, X. and Dai, R. (2002), 'Traditional Chinese Medicine as Viewed from System Science and Complexity Science,' *Journal of System Simulation*, 14: 11, pp. 1458–1464. (in Chinese)

Harman, W. W. (1996), 'Toward a Science of Consciousness: Address two Central Questions', *Toward a Science of Consciousness* (ed. Hameroff, S. R., Kaszniak, A. W., Scott, A. C.), Massachusetts: the MIT Press, pp. 743–751.

Kauffman, S. A. (1993), *The Origins of Order*, Oxford, U.K.: Oxford University Press.

Langton, C. G. (1992), Preface In: (Eds. Langton, C.G., Taylor, C.; Farmer, J. D., and Rasmussen, S.), *Artificial Life, Volume X of SFI Studies in the Sciences of Complexity*, Calif. Addison-Wesley, pp. xiii-xviii.

Rawson, p. & Legeza, L. (1984), *Tao: the Chinese Philosophy of Time and Change*, London: Thames and Hudson LTD.

Sims, K. (1994), 'Evolving Virtual Creatures'. In *Computer Graphics Proceedings, Annual Conference Series, ACM SIGGRAPH*, Orlando, Florida, 15–22.

Varela, F. J., Thompson, E., Rosch, E. (1995), *The Embodied Mind*, London: The MIT Press.

Zhang, M. (1988), *New Comment on Lao Tzu*, Chengdu: Chengdu bookstore of ancient books (in Chinese).

Zou, X. (1988), *Ten Lectures on the Theory of Change*, Chengdu: Sichuan publishing company of Science and technology (in Chinese).

# Between Hyper-Images and Aniconism: New Perspectives on Islamic Art in the Education of Artists

## Ismail Ozgur Soganci

My aim in the following pages is to raise some difficult, and, perhaps, at times unwelcome, problems concerning artist education in Turkey in relation to our world of hyper-images. The text consists of three sections: The first section includes my personal commentary on the context and current phase of Turkish artist education in relation to new media. The second is an initial attempt to address a fundamental problem with the history of artist education in Turkey which can give birth to a global approach toward taming our gazes against the inflation of images. The third section becomes, therefore, significant in its invitation to explore innovative directions for educating artists who live at a time when images are almost always preferred to essences.

### Artist Education in Turkey: Current Contexts

The council of Turkish higher education currently lists 48 artist education programs (37 for undergraduates, 11 for graduates) in Turkey. The list and the scope of this paper exclude art education programs whose aim, according to the same council, is to train art educators to work in teaching art in public schools. Apart from traditionally titled artist education programs such as "fine arts" or "visual arts," there are several programs, all in Istanbul, with the exclusion of one at Bilkent University, Ankara, that prefer to be called "communication technology" and "visual arts and visual communication design." Since all these programs comply with the centralized government authority represented by the council of higher education, their curricula and the general functioning rules are almost all identical. Several universities in Istanbul and Ankara supported by bourgeois foundations are the exceptions.

Public universities have visual art programs that have remained, in terms of their curriculum content, unchanged since the 1950s. The heavy influences of European styles and schools such as the Bauhaus, cubism, and abstract expressionism dominate the artist education curricula along with a strong emphasis on modernist hierarchies, criterion, and aesthetic attitudes. Calligraphy is considered to be a "minor art" in modern Turkish institutions, although it was for centuries considered to be the highest art by peoples of Turkey before the founding of the Turkish Republic in 1923. The blind adherence to modernist aesthetics is often a major obstacle to any kind of change in artist education curricula. Anything virtual, a conservative modernist would say, cannot be included in the sphere of art. The physicality of a work of art is a must. Another would claim that an artwork must be impossible to replicate and claim uniqueness as the main artistic quality. Such conservative points of view make new media unwelcome. New artistic tendencies that utilize new media technologies in most cases are located on one side of fruitless dichotomies of pigment versus pixel, canvas versus screen, rarity versus accessibility. Such binary perceptions, needless to say, limit the possibilities new technologies can bring to the visual culture of Turkey.

On the other hand, noteworthy efforts toward catching up with the demands of the globalized art world mainly reside in a couple of semi-private foundation-supported universities, most of which started their art programs in the last quarter of the twentieth century. These new institutions, such as Sabanci University in Istanbul and Bilkent University in Ankara, the nation's capitol, seem more eager to take on the responsibility of educating artists to understand and address the high-tech and postmodern conditions of our day. At Bilkent, for instance, the undergraduate course "Art and Technology" and the elective course "Computers in Graphic Design" provide an introduction to the graphic capabilities of sophisticated computer graphics systems that require students to learn "to create art on the computer." In most state-sponsored institutions, however, digital media, web art, computer graphics, and similar concepts are rarely mentioned for artistic purposes. Those who have the desire and facilities for teaching computer graphics do not focus on developments in the art world, but on a capitalist economy that is mainly interested in using new media for virtual advertisements. The focus in such institutions' instruction is neither on artistic creativity nor conceptual originality but almost solely on software literacy.

### *Mimesis* Versus Islamic Visual Traditions

Institutions of artist education in Turkey are not immune to some problematic tendencies in Turkey's political life such as the centralized organizational structure, modernist direction, and the erasure of pre-Republican era concepts. The modernist direction manifests itself in fine arts education in Turkey in a variety of ways, one of which is the dominance of Eurocentric aesthetics. Such dominance is the result of many deliberate choices that transformed the multi-ethnic, Islamic, Eastern monarchy, the Ottomans into a secularist nation state, the Turkish Republic. In attempts to ensure the success of such transformation, Turkey, beginning with the wake of the World War I, has undergone radical changes which spanned from traditional costumes to music, from civil code to the alphabet, from Koranic calligraphy to figure painting. The roots of such transformation planted in the previous centuries by the Ottoman aristocracy flourished during the Republican transformation managed by a military elite after the first quarter of the twentieth century. Although a replica of the French *École des Beaux Arts* for mainly male non-Muslim minorities was founded in Istanbul earlier during the Ottoman reign, it was the Republican era which gave crucial roles to this institution in shaping the artistic agenda of the new Republic. Institutions of nonrepresentational arts and crafts, calligraphy schools, the court workshop, and other traditional structures of artist education were replaced by Western style academies, which based their curricula almost totally on what can be called Aristotle's *mimesis*: The core theory of aesthetics that considers visual arts as the process and product of creating likenesses of real-world appearances. *Mimesis*, of course, constitutes the bulk of European aesthetics which was never preferred in the Muslim spheres. The Republic, however, equated mimesis-based figurative representation with Westernization. This equation was interesting since it entailed a religio-aesthetic switch. For instance, it was neither a tradition nor a formal rule in the Ottoman era to display portraits of administrators in state offices while the Republic used a considerable number of statues, paintings, and photographs to spread its new ideology. The calligraphic signs that symbolized the authority of sultans were replaced by figurative representations of the Republican administrators, and those paintings and photographs could be thought as the first naturalistic portraits most Turks had seen. The mimetic theory of art was, in an ideological sense, strongly recommended as a condition for becoming Westernized.

Today, almost eight decades after the Republican revolution, despite the difficulties of a developing economy, artist education in Turkey, as a field based on imported European ideals, is no different in its general characteristics than artist education in France, Belgium, Italy, and other European Union countries. Some in Turkey may call this similarity a story of success. And it is true that many positive contributions of the choices made in the Republican era undeniably deserve to be named successes. However, with all of them in mind, one might still ponder a fundamental question: Can a history of successful mimicry lead to a competent artist education system? When such mimicry remains at the bottom of an artist education mentality, does it matter much whether we are in the Digital or the Stone Age?

As Freedman (2003) clearly wrote, "connections between contemporary visual culture and the past are critically important if students are to develop an understanding of the complexity of their visual world" (p. 43). Ligtvoet (1987) argued that education in general must be a process of enculturation, "which provides students with cultural tools to explore their former and present cultures, to personally recreate them." The overly modernist-Eurocentric tone of artist education in Turkey, however, deprives students of their own cultural identity and history, leaving them with an alienated mind-set and ignorance of the visual traditions of their ancestors.

## Visual Tradition as a Possible Cure for Our Societies of Spectacle

The specific modes of visual culture in Islamic lands have potentials to help us configure ways and possible new dimensions for creating a critical visual literacy in our classes in the global context of artist education. This section is an attempt to construct initial steps toward using traditional wisdom in twenty-first-century artist education.

The artistic traditions that dominated the Turkish Peninsula after its Islamization in the eleventh century by Turkic peoples prior to the eighteenth-century-Westernization movements were dominantly Islamic. The visual traditions that the Republican cultural policy brought almost to extinction was Islamic in character with Abrahamian roots. Judaic and Byzantine artistic repertoires had strong ties to pre-Republican aesthetic choices.

Perhaps no other land bestowed more serious debates on representations of the divine than the Turkish Peninsula did. If one considers the Byzantium iconoclasm along with the already aniconic influence of Judaism, even without taking Islamic reluctance toward realistic figurative representation into account, one can conclude that the nature of images has been a permanent topic of discussion in the Turkish peninsula. What Islam brought into the already-confusing debates was not a totally fresh set of nonrepresentational temperaments, but a more widespread and popular approval of the ongoing reluctance toward the pictorial depiction of the human form.

When you enter a mosque in Iran, Turkey, Syria, Egypt, and in many other countries, the interior designs, unlike in churches, do not display representations of sacred personalities, figures of angels, or depictions of religious stories. The whole atmosphere of the Muslim temple speaks a non-figural visual language in which stylized flower gardens, geometric ornamentation, and Koranic calligraphy constitute an abstract harmony. The Muslim mosque in its tiniest details remains figuratively mute as if it suspects a potential danger in images of likeness (Soganci 2005, p. 140).

Grabar (1973) notes that when Islamic art is discussed, the one particular topic that will emerge as uniquely Islamic is the fascination with a form of nonrepresentational decoration which manifests itself especially in the case of religious art (p. 18). Scholars of Islamic art (Rice 1965; Arnold 1965; Ettinghausen 1977; Allen 1988) names Muslim reluctance or shyness with respect to representations *aniconism*. Flood (2002) refers to *aniconism* as "the eschewal of figural imagery," which can have a spiritually positive character while iconoclasm has only a negative sense (Burckhardt 1976, p. 38). Islamic art has chosen an artistic path that is distant from *mimesis* and, therefore, different from Western aesthetic philosophies. This choice, for the most part, determined its uniqueness in world art history.

Islamic prudence toward images that attract our gaze through constructing a likeness of phenomena, when thought over inquisitively, can lead prospective artists in Turkey to newer dimensions in visual culture. Almost all the museums in Turkey can serve as a laboratory of aniconic tendencies in Turco-Islamic culture. *Aniconism*, as a global concept of visual art, can be linked to philosophies that require a particular education of the human gaze. It is as if older generations of Islam had seen the unwanted and hyper effects of an overly visual culture centuries before the advancement of imaging technologies. By actually not providing specific images for mere consumption of the eye, the Muslims of past centuries, perhaps, foresaw and avoided the danger of becoming a culture of appearances, images, and icons. Although the Muslim reluctance toward mimetic figuration stemmed from religio-aesthetic origins, one can even find many resemblances between non-figurative modern art and Islamic painting. In a sense, both seek to surpass the immediate appearance of what is physical.

Today, the widespread advertising mentality in visual media is so strong that it often defines who we are and how we live our lives. Perhaps the contemporary philosopher Slovaj Zizek's (1997) question becomes relevant at this point: "Do we not find something similar in the new age cyberspace cult which attempts to ground the return to old pagan wisdom in the highest technology?" (p. 86) What Zizek, with a tone of satire, calls "pagan wisdom" is simply the idolatrous practices of our ancestors. And the one essential character of idolatry can be considered as the preference of image over reality or essence. Are we not becoming in many ways idolatrous like our ancestors by idolizing many things based on mere manufactured appearances? In addition to Zizek, there are others who concentrate on connections between contemporary difficulties regarding the inflation of images in contemporary life and the historical prudence of Islamic, Abrahamian, and Byzantine cultures toward images. Interestingly, contemporary authors such as Jacques Lacan (1973), Slavoj Zizek (2003), Jean Baudrillard (1995), Frederick Jameson (1992), Paul Virilio (1991), and Maurice Marleau-Ponty (1968) create arguments in their texts that are very relevant to aniconic and iconoclastic debates. Indeed, the relevance of aniconism and iconoclasm is increasing day by day as the bombardment of images on us through new visual technologies intensifies.

A critical visual literacy, I believe, must and can flourish if artist educators facilitate students toward developing their personal understandings of the old aniconic temperaments toward mimetic art. A theoretical course on facilitating students to think over the aniconic and iconoclastic traditions such as in the East Roman, Arabic, Turkish, East Asian, and Hebraic cultures can make meaningful contributions to artist education curricula in our postmodern era. The main crucial question to be investigated in such a course can be: Why has some older generations remained at a distance to art that copies reality? The relevance of this questions increases with the advancement of copying technologies. We need to direct our students' gazes toward the problems created by the blurring distinctions between real and virtual, original and copy, essence and appearance. The Islamic emphasis on mathematical beauty, geometric design, and abstract ornamentation sought an artistic climate beyond our immediate perceptions. Islamic art from its very beginning considered visual arts as a way of conveying essences and rejected manufacturing likenesses for the mere consumption of the eye. Today, at an age in which we discuss the ethics of manufacturing human clones, aniconic legacy of Islamic art becomes more and more relevant in its invitation to underline some question blurred by our quick answers. Zizek's question highlighted here is one among other possible ones.

*Aniconism* has untouched potentials for enlightening prospective artists about the negative, unwanted, and alienating consequences of hyper-images. Islamic prudence toward images can balance the overly iconic modes of representation in advertising, or the almost exhibitionist urges so common among the current generation. I invite every educator in visual arts education to think over the consensus reached by Abrahamic/Byzantine/Islamic visual traditions as possible cures for our "societies of spectacle."

## Works Cited

Allen, T. (1988), *Five Essays on Islamic Art: Aniconism and Figural Representation in Islamic Art.* Archnet Digital Library database. Retrieved November 20, 2002.

Arnold, T. W. (1965), *Painting in Islam: A Study of the Place of Pictorial Art in Muslim Culture.* New York, NY: Dover.

Baudrillard, J. O. (1995), *Simulacra and Simulation.* Ann Arbor: University of Michigan Press.

Burckhardt, I. T. (1976), *Art of Islam: Language and Meaning.* Westerham, U.K.: World of Islam Festival Publishing Company.

Ettinghausen, R. (1977), *Arab Painting.* New York: Rizzoli International Publications.

Freedman, K. (2003), *Teaching Visual Culture: Curriculum, Aesthetics, and the Social Life of Art.* New York: Teachers College Press.

Flood, F. B. (2002), Between cult and culture: Bamiyan, Islamic iconoclasm, and the museum. *Art Bulletin,* December 2002, 84 (4), 641-660. Retrieved October 13, 2004.

Grabar, O. (1973), *The Formation of Islamic Art.* New Haven: Yale University Press.

Jameson, F. (1992), *Signatures of the Visible.* New York: Routledge.

Lacan, J. (1973), *Seminar XI: The Four Fundamental Concepts of Psychoanalysis.* (D. Porter, Ed. and Trans.) New York: W.W. Norton & Company.

Ligtvoet, J. (1987), Arts education in a multicultural society. *Report of the International Association for Intercultural Education to the Council of Europe.* Strasbourg, France: The Council of Europe (The CDCC's Project No. 7: The education and cultural development of migrants). Croon Helm, New York: Methuen.

Merleau-Ponty, M. (1968), *The Visible and the Invisible.* Evanston: Northwestern University Press.

Rice, D. T. (1971), *Islamic Painting: A Survey.* Edinburgh: Edinburgh University Press.

Soganci, I. O. (2005), An Interdisciplinary Study of Problematizing a Curricular Muteness: Figurative Representation in Islam and Turkish Art Education. Unpublished doctoral dissertation, Arizona State University.

Virilio, P. (1991), *The Aesthetics of Disappearance* (trans. P. Beitchman). New York: Semiotext(e).

Zizek, S. (1997), *The Plague of Fantasies.* New York: Verso.

# TOUCHING LIGHT: POST-TRADITIONAL IMMERSION IN INTERACTIVE ARTISTIC ENVIRONMENTS

## Diane Gromala and Jinsil Seo

As the number of institutions that offer Ph.D.'s in art grow, the definitions of what constitutes art research is being explored, contested, invented. In an R1-ranked research university such as Simon Fraser University in Vancouver, what counts for knowledge and how one legitimizes that knowledge is well-scrutinized by the faculty within our School of Interactive Arts and Technology. The faculty range from disciplines as diverse as art, design, and dance to engineering, computer science, and cognitive science. In addition, the scrutiny of the new continues "up the hill" to the university's graduate school. While epistemologically challenging, we have graduated Ph.D.'s in Interactive Arts with relatively few problems.

What follows is one example of Jinsil Seo's exploration of artistic ideas of immersion in responsive or interactive spaces. Hers is the work of various cultures: the cultures of art and scientific research; interactive art's cultures of exhibition and dissemination (as interactive artists have taken on some of the former roles of critics and art historians); and her South Korean culture, displaced into a Canadian university with a Polish-American advisor.

This short, developmental phase of Jinsil Seo's academic and artistic research into immersion was comprised of a continual interplay of textual research with art-making. As in all dissertations, much time was spent in defining terms. The way Seo developed and delimited her definition of immersion was the result of traditional academic literature reviews. Her concurrent experimentations were important examinations of the idea in art-making methods and experiences that lie beyond textual inscription.

Within the concept of immersion, Seo explores four categories: ambient immersive natural space, body interaction, new forms of consciousness, and flow of energy (Qi or Chi). The paper presents examples of Seo's art-research work and offers detailed explorations of the quality of immersion, accompanied by the often tacit conversations that regularly occur between Seo and her advisor, Professor Gromala. Gromala's comments appear in italics.

*Henry Giroux (1991), Paolo Freire (2005) and Parker Palmer (1998) notwithstanding, few faculty like to admit what they don't know, the extent to which teaching is a form of constant learning and cultural indoctrination. In an interdisciplinary department full of radically differing knowledge bases, surrounded by emerging forms of technology, in a loose "culture" comprised of students from around the world, it is impossible to assume the stereotypical posture of an all-knowing professor. Rather, to articulate what one doesn't know is more productive than asserting a firm grasp of the Truth. My pedagogical orientation is a mix of early Montessori training with familial habits, a ruinous stint in a Catholic school and outsider suspicions evoked by the Ivy League. I simply try to create enough space for individual students to work independently, and stay out of the way until or unless students need advice. Advice in how to hunt for what they need, how to build intellectual frameworks and connections with their work, how academia works, and how to creatively navigate around the extra limitations that new forms of knowledge tend to provoke. Many students want the comfort of predictions of the future. Instead, I look to the interplays of future, present and past. It was the lesson I learned while teaching in New Zealand. Half of my colleague's Malaysian students were missing because an Imam was flown over to perform an exorcism, one which lasted two weeks. My South Asian students asked me why their work should always be new, and what they should do with their traditional forms of art and design – a distinction they did not hold.*

In this article, I outline a new framework for defining immersion in interactive art. This paper aims to define a certain quality of immersion that has emerged from artistic-research experiences. I focus on defining a certain quality of immersion that arises in the creation of immersive environmental installations, drawing on my cultural experiences that adopt the ideas of ambient natural spaces, physical interactions, new consciousness, and flow of energy. Overall, I define immersion is an integrated conscious state where mind, body, and environment are well-interrelated and interweaved. A review of previous research and results of my art installation experimentations will be described in detail.

In the literature review, I examined the history of Virtual Reality (VR) technology, interactive storytelling and videogame research. However, most researchers focus on the constraints of the hardware and software, and are less focused on the conceptual and philosophical implications of immersion and presence. Ideas in narrative forms seem obviously ill-suited for non-narrative work. Further, concepts from ancient traditions and marginalized cultures are generally absent. A paucity of academic research on the philosophical implications of immersion in the realm of artistic research was found. Artists do refer to immersion, but do not offer a definition of it that is beyond personal opinion.

I also draw on my experiences in South Korea, which has a strong sociocultural background of Buddhism and Eastern philosophy related to mind and body and the connectivity between them. One of the most interesting concepts is transmigration: the reincarnational cycle of birth, suffering, death, and rebirth. Formative experiences in the life of Korean children create a conceptual connectivity between consciousness and immersion related to space and time in human life.

*I spend less time advising than I do observing, ready to play midwife, hunting partner, or disciplinary alien. My context is that of a Polish-American who grew up in an extremely remote part of the U.S. I was raised by her grandfather, a "folk healer" in the tradition of isolated parts of the Carpathian Mountains. Though it is a tradition understudied in English-language anthropological studies, what is known is that this part of Europe clung longest to shamanistic practices, centuries after the introduction of Christianity. Closest perhaps to Curanderos of Mexico, my grandfather's way of life mixed shamanism and "homeopathic magic" with a mystical form of Catholicism. Decades of cult indoctrination in American academia were unable to wipe clean the un-American epistemological and ontological orientations I inculcated from my grandfather. Thus, I remain intensely curious about non-dominant and traditional cultures, much more so than a proper academic is generally allowed to admit.*

## Quality of Immersion

### Ambient Immersive Natural Space

In the *American Heritage Dictionary* (2000), immersion is described as placing of a body under water or in other liquids. Water is the most prevalent metaphor for environments used to create immersion. We are enveloped by surroundings, from natural space to air and water. We are most often enclosed by what we usually take for granted – air – and are not separated from nature. In Eastern philosophy, this concept is more stressed. The *I Ching,* the ancient Chinese classic text which describes an old system of cosmology and philosophy, is focused on the ideas of the dynamic balance within nature. This system is also in use in Korea. The *I Ching* uses symbolism: a vertical line '|' for yang and ': ' for yin to create an immersive matrix of possible meanings called Bagua. Through combinations of lines, it promotes a concept of balance between nature and people. Bagua has eight possible trigrams [Table 1]. Each possibility is connected to an element of nature. The *I Ching* emphasizes that humans are in the middle of nature and need to balance with nature.

| Trigram | Name | Nature | Direction |
|---------|------|--------|-----------|
| ☐ | Force | heaven | northwest |
| ☐ | Open | swamp | west |
| ☐ | Radiance | fire | south |
| ☐ | Shake | thunder | east |
| ☐ | Ground | wind | southeast |
| ☐ | Gorge | water | north |
| ☐ | Bound | mountain | northeast |
| ☐ | Field | earth | southwest |

**Table 1.** Bagua: Eight possible trigrams. [17]

So for the immersive quality which I would like to create, I will try to build natural environments using sky, water, land, wind, light, and so on, instead of building technological systems using "cold" machines such as current VR systems. Although I feel some VR work can be very immersive, it is a different kind of immersion I seek: one which engages as much of the human sensorium as possible, one closer to nature than to media.

*My VR artwork – in the nascent stages of VR Art (1990–1992) – was based on my experience with chronic pain and Sufism. Co-created with Yacov Sharir, the VR environment that users inhabited was based on an MRI of my body. The organic space of the VR body/environment that users inhabited, except for texture-mapping of poetry, was fairly literal initially. However, navigating into organs revealed much smaller, unexpected, surreal spaces that seemed infinite and ethereal. Sharir's and my experiences in the VR space were very similar to those of users, who commented that the organic aspect was part of the reason one could feel such a strong sense of immersion. We believe that this aspect, along with the spatial inversions, provoked a strong proprioceptive sense; that is, the sense of where one is in one's body. However, the limitatons of the technology, such as the small field of view of the cumbersome head-mounted displays and the entangling cords, were deemed detrimental to the experience by both creators. Subsequently, work by both artists evolved to the creation of larger, interactive "real space."*

*At exhibits around the world, Sharir and I took note of the users who did not want to use the head-mounted display or who immediately left. Most often, these users deemed the artwork "profane," especially several First Nations' people, Brazilians and a couple from the Middle East. This was, as far as I was able to discern in conversation, because we were using a body. I often wonder if the same would hold true with plastinated "real" bodies in Body Worlds.*

*Seo's desire to work with "natural space" spoke to the nature of my childhood. Clinging to the rim of the U.S. border with Canada, divided by the Great Lakes but connected by loons (in every sense of the word), it is the kind of place where people go to forget or to be forgotten. Our enclave of immigrants – multiple generations who came to avoid some war or another – was surrounded by a sadly disintegrating Native American reservation, an Amish community, small signs of abandonment by much earlier generations of French Canadians, miles and miles of national forest and, somewhere, a never visible military base. The population has steadily declined since the 1890s and is now so sparse that it is regularly considered for military experiments, like ultra low frequency grids that no other communities will have. My father died when I was very young, but left us a beautiful piece of land. Now usurped by an unscrupulous relative, it is stripped it of its minerals and filled in with toxic waste. Nature was both isolating and home, torn and bruised by the decaying detritus of human creation.*

*Seo's work is not some Romantic return to a pure nature that may be extraordinarily difficult to find without human damage, but belies experiences we all may have had and have forgotten. Artistically and technically sophisticated, it elicits for me a sense of awe, a bit akin to seeing the Aurora Borealis. Some users say it triggers for them a child-like awe. Could this simply refer to those times in our life when we are culturally "allowed" to feel the awe of the everyday? At times, within the cloud of haunting blue light, I feel lighter; most often, when the lab is deserted, I like to lie in this womb of light, the air of its inflation moving it gently as if a sea.*

## Bodily Interaction

People face and experience the external world by means of at least five senses (sight, smell, touch, taste, and hearing), kinesthetically and proprioceptively. Through these senses, they absorb the external world into their internal world. The internal world, the world of introception, introspection and of reverie is a world defined by the body. The immersive experience is sometimes interpreted as an out-of-body experience, and as such it perpetuates the persistent Christian-Cartesian split between mind and body (Penny 1995). However, human perception is often dominated by vision above all the other senses: ocularcentrism indicative of Western thinking. Even so, according to Juhani Pallasmaa (2005), eyes can touch; the gaze implies an unconscious touch, bodily mimesis, and identification.

In interactive, immersive environments, people's bodily movements are triggers to creating interaction and immersion. Merleau-Ponty's philosophy makes the human body the center of the experiential world and inextricable with the world. Inside of immersive environments, in spite of the dominance of vision, bodily motion and people's touch become very powerful means of communication and integration with that world.

When hands touch artworks, they make intimate connections. The tactile sense is significant for our experience and understanding of the world. Touch is one of the first senses we develop as infants to explore the world. We know that infants will wither or die if they themselves are not touched. Hands bring us direct knowledge of the world. Hands feel. They probe. They practice. They give us sense. Hands also discover: they grasp, they pinch, they press, they guide. They pick up experience (McCuillough 1996).

In *A Natural History of the Senses,* Diane Ackerman (1991) explains: in many ways, touch is difficult to research. Every other sense has a key organ to study; for touch that organ is the skin, and it stretches over the entire body. The skin is the oldest and the most sensitive of our organs, our first medium of communication, and our most efficient protector.

Although the sense of touching is the most intriguing sense for creating immersion, touch works using other senses create synthesized experiences. Also, there is an experiential quality that is not just a sum of visual, tactile, and audible senses. People perceive in a total way with their whole being. The sense of self, transformed by art, allows us to engage fully in the dimensions of dream, imagination, and desire (Vogelaar 2005).

> *My knowledge of bodily interaction stems in part from a lifetime of being poked, prodded and palpated by physicians; through working with choreographers and dancers; and by extensive travels to countries whose languages I do not know. It has always been apparent to me that in order to communicate and feel comfortable, I had to "attune" myself – the way I held and moved my body – to other cultures and places across America. This attunement extends to technologies as well, changing from clumsy frustration to the kind of prosthetic extension of an expert. Awareness of how people move was probably most intensely provoked by my grandfather's observation of his patients, and his uncanny way of interpreting what the movements meant. His self-curative of his arthritis had a profound effect on his own bodily movement. He began to hunch over and move obviously much slower because of the pain of his arthritis. One year, somewhere in his seventies, my grandfather got two guinea pigs (the proper animal was hard to come by in North America), and put them under his bed. Every morning and night, as he pet and fed these animals, he asked them, through a kind of singing, to take away the pain of his arthritis. Over time, one of the animals crippled up and died, and my grandfather remained free of arthritis, able to stand upright, grasp tightly, and walk quickly until his death at ninety-seven. It is a story few Americans believe, but one that is evident in photographs.*

> *Over the past two years, I have observed Seo experimenting with touch. It has become more expansive and multi-faceted. She has a keen facility of how different materials afford divergent ways of touching. Depending on how important the aspect of touch becomes in her work, academically, I would need to encourage Seo to find or build a taxonomy of the multitudinous aspects of touch and being touched, along with the meaningfulness of kinds of touch. Kinds of human touch are extensive, with shifting meanings across cultures and generations. Such a path would easily become an ever-*

*expanding study that could cover years of work. Thus, the interplay and relative importance of her four aspects of immersion in interactive art will need to be explored and delimited.*

## New Consciousness

When people experience compelling immersive art, they can fall into a dream-like state of consciousness quite different from normative cognitive processes. This state can be described as a transcendent state of consciousness, the Kantian sublime, or a hypnagogic or state of reverie.

Research on immersion is a part of exploring human spatial cognition and consciousness. The concept of immersion includes questions of how people continuously create and update their sense of the space that surrounds and engages them (McRobert 1999). Generally, art has used "virtual environments" such as painting, literature, music, and so on to conjure up other forms of consciousness, but recent technological developments have created unprecedented conditions that may open up new opportunities. Unlike the past, new digital virtuality permits three-dimensionality, interactivity, immersion, and multi-sensory phenomena. This invites us to wonder about the potential new forms of consciousness that may arise from these technological opportunities (Bermudez 1999).

*Opportunities for experiencing differing forms of consciousness are often one of the most dominant and intriguing aspects of new technologies. I find the interplay of traditions, explored through emergent forms of technologies as or more intriguing. In academia, it is difficult to account for traditional forms of knowledge, unless that knowledge has been strained through sieve of anthropology or similar disciplines. Artists have the freedom for this kind of exploration, but find it difficult to legitimize it in the systematic study entailed by the PhD. A particularly interesting method for doing so has been termed Post-Traditional Media theory. Unlike the limiting critique of PostColonialism, according to Naranjan Rajah, "Post-Tradition is, rather, the beginning of a free and fluid recognition of the persistence and plurality of traditions" in the context of the globalization made possible by technology. The promise of this theory is a productive one, a theory that does not automatically assign prior cultures as 'primitive' or less knowledgeable in a similar way that Europeans referred to indigenous cultures they found as "savage." By reintegrating the knowledges and values of traditional cultures, if this is possible without commodifying them, perhaps we can find transformative ways of working with technology that go beyond just being novel. The scores of books in the ancient library at Alexandria all went up in flames, but not all forms of knowledge were destroyed, as some forms of knowledge exceed textual inscription.*

## Flow of energy

Immersion is often described as a transition, a passage from one realm to another, from the immediate physical reality of tangible objects and direct sensory data to somewhere else. Experience of immersive environments includes a flow of energy from the external phenomena of the installation through the tactile surface of the artwork and the skin to the internal body. There are "flows" similar to rivers, veins, and oceans, which artists attempt to express or bring into consciousness through the artworks. An invisible force, like energy surrounding us, fills us up and gives us life (Suzuki 2002). Life is the organic expression of energy. To move, to breathe, to see, to grow, to metabolize, energy is needed.

Like the boundary where the sea meets the land, our life has boundaries between external elements and internal elements that co-exist and continuously share energy. Immersion can be considered as a phenomenologically balanced state between environment and human where the mental and physical merge like the seashore, a fluid energy between body and mind.

In Asian philosophy, 'qi' is a fundamental concept of traditional Chinese culture, most often translated as air or breath and, by extension, life force or spiritual energy that is part of everything that exists. People believe that qi circulates in channels within the body. Therefore qi experts cure patients by giving good qi and pulling out bad qi in traditional Chinese medicine.

Qi works like light. Light travels in waves (and sometimes particles). Light flows through electronic wires and luminescent materials. It enters the eye and is instantly gone, transmitted through a series of dynamics that in the eye begins with the vitamin A family and rhodopsin. "We can simplify things, here, by stating that mitochondria cells located between rods and cones in the eye are known emitters of photons within the body and, then, jump to the claim that cilium or microtubule-type structures probably transport endogenously created light throughout brain/body." (Simanonok 1997)

> *This is closely akin to the beliefs Gromala's grandfather held. In treating her frequent childhood illnesses, he would burn feathers and herbs under her nose, chant, and wave his hands over her body, holding his hands about three inches away. He was "redistributing energy" to balance it, but also to add energy to my body. Similar practices can be observed in Russian alternative and complementary medicine as well. Gromala dreaded the treatment, however, as it was a wretched, foul-smelling, otherworldly state of an immersion anyone would be eager to escape. Only after long hours of going through a seemingly hellish night of agony and nightmarish images did a deep sleep come. In the morning, the curatives were remarkably potent, the sickness and hell a distant memory, except for the bitterness that defied drinking, eating, toothpaste or gum.*

**Working Definition**
Based on the above-mentioned research, the authors redefine the idea of immersion in immersive installations. The characteristics of immersion can be summarized that 1) it is created in ambient, natural, immersive environments; 2) it is created by physical body

interaction with environment; 3) it involves ephemeral, transient conscious states; and 4) it offers a balanced state between environment and human physical and mental functions having flow of energy. Overall, it can be underscored that immersion is an integrated conscious state under the condition that mind, body, and environment are well-interrelated and interweaved.

**Creative Works**
The four aspects of immersion discussed above will be discussed in relation to the artistic immersive installation *Sky Reverie* and experiments with fiber optics.

**Sky Reverie**
*Sky Reverie* (www.skyreverie.com) is an immersive environmental installation created by artist-researcher Jinsil Seo in 2004. It is an inflated cloud-like translucent plastic structure that is large enough for human occupants. The shape represents an imaginary natural sky environment which people can easily identify with from their daily lives and dreams. In this piece, natural elements (sky, stars, and air) are used as the inspiration for an immersive interactive world. Inside of the cloud, an intimate zone is created by the play of LEDs and stars projected on the inflatable's inner surface.

The *Sky Reverie* immersive space invites visitors to explore contemplatively. People don't need to look for anything specific. It just gives people access to an organic

**Figure 1.** *Sky Reverie.*

experience. The space is intended to evoke memories and imagination through interacting with elements consisting of the space.

My definition of immersion includes physical interactivity; in *Sky Reverie* visitors are encouraged through subtle responsive cues to physically play with the swarm of stars projected on the interior of the huge inflated plastic cloud. When visitors stretch their hands up inside of the cloud, as if whispering their hopes to the sky, hundreds of star images fall into line to create a constellation triggered by fluctuations of viewers' shadows. Meanwhile a profusion of blue LEDs which react to visitors' movements facilitate people's immersion into an atmospheric celestial ambience. According to James B. Steeves (2004), 'experience' is received not only with the mind, but with the body as well. Traversing through physical space invites sensorial expectation and creates immersive and seductive states of tactile presence and connectedness. Based on the spatial cues, visitors can learn how to touch and experience the piece. The piece requires people's soft touches: caresses. This reinforced action (soft touch) drives people to explore reveries and mental material that are normally buried in the subconscious.

The piece's fluorescent-driven blue and purple haze serves as, in author Patricia Troyer's words, "primal substance, tangible but intangible at the same time, one that transforms the visitors experience into a kind of extension of self into the sphere of the greater

**Figure 2.** *Sky Reverie.*

universe." The translucent plastic used in its fabrication relates to the notion of the permeability of boundaries and space. Evoked in Miazaki's heartfelt film, *Kiki's Delivery Service*, when, with halcyon dreams for lush growth of their garden, kids and pets exuberantly lift hands from knees to air. Numerous rituals from earlier cultures involve gestures of reaching for the sky to solicit abundance and power beyond the indifferent vicissitudes of nature.

To symbolically represent 'flow of energy' in *Sky Reverie*, Seo utilized air and light. The structure is kept inflated using forced air; forced air paradoxically suggests a sense of openness and formlessness within a contained small space. In classical symbology, air and sky have significant meanings. Air is considered to be a space for rational human thought and imagination; sky is the immeasurable and endless; it has no substance and no surface (Steeves 2004).

In the installation, lights have life cycles. They are continuously turned on and off; this is their birth-death cycle; this is their story. The lights' activity resembles an archetypal interior human conception of life and death; the LED's life-death cycle similarity to the archetype of life-death is intended to elicit in the viewer an intimate encounter with the viewer's own story, life, dreams, and memories within themselves.

Through this piece, I offer a full-scale experience of immersion that includes the important factors in defining 'immersion' in a new, contemplative, yet embodied, and active way.

### Experiments with Fiber Optics
To explore the concept of immersion based on ambient immersive environments, bodily interaction, new consciousness, and flow of energy, four experiments were conducted. These experiments were started from four sketches of the ideas below. [See Figure 3.] The experiments were dealing with immersive spaces that had different styles and used fiber optics and LEDs for creating shimmering threads and luminous touching surfaces for deriving interaction and immersion. Since there were time and material limitations, scale models were created and the original ideas were re-examined to refine the models.

### Experiment #1
For the first experiments, an 8x11 ft. dome-like space filled with fiber optics created glowing blue light. Threads of fiber optics are stretched from the ceiling to people's knees. Therefore, participants can see the floating luminous lights around their knees. This creates an immersive feeling for the viewer, as if they are walking through a field of lights.

### Experiment #2
In experiment #2, a half-dome was created. The proposed idea was to create a big illuminated glass bead dome-chamber which people can enter. Inside the dome they interact with the thread of fiber optics on the surface of the shape. From the outside, it

**Figure 3.**

looks like the lights are animated and waving. The strength of the wave is dependent on the number of participants inside of the dome. Participants may find themselves experiencing an immersive experience induced by the undulant waving light pattern.

### Experiment #3
The third experiment is based on the third sketch. The proposed idea was that fiber optic threads cover one side of a wall diagonally. In this piece, the participant interacts with threads of moving light. It creates an experience of touching light that is analogous to touching water in a waterfall.

### Experiment #4
Experiment #4 focused on creating a delicate sense of touch. Lighting devices to realize a potentially immersive space were placed inside the dome. Fiber optics threads were used on the inside surface. It offers a sense of touching grass. When participants touch the fiber optic lights surrounding them, then it is anticipated that they will experience an immersive moment based on the visual illusion created by the fiber optic lights' motion.

The experiments bridge the four aspects of immersion. Especially, I explore immersive space with light: projection light, LED, and fiber optics. Touching and interacting with

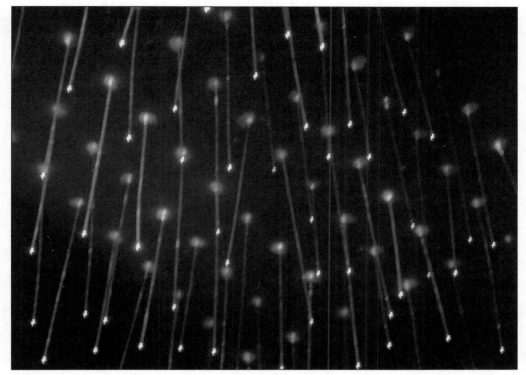

**Figure 4.** Experiment #1.

lights in the installations are perceived differently than in natural spaces under sunlight. Some configurations of artificial lighting can cause mysterious visual hallucinations and alterations in consciousness; this is what humans have known ever since the discovery of fire (McRobert 1999).

**Future Works and Conclusions**
This chapter presents a novel framework for a concept of immersion in artistic immersive environments. Immersion is defined based on four categories: ambient immersive natural space, body interaction, new consciousness, and flow of energy. Proprioceptive and tactile environments are pathways to immersion. Light can also be used as a tactile medium. It presents my early research stage of immersion study dealing with these concepts. To explore the creation of immersion that arises when touching light, deeper research into materials such as LEDs, fiber optics, projectors, and fabrics will be needed. In addition, a concrete conceptual framework for the ideas of immersion continues to be developed through in-depth theoretical and philosophical observations as well as experimental artworks. Through user research based on combining science, philosophy, and psychology with qualitative and quantitative methodologies, a new framework of immersion is emerging.

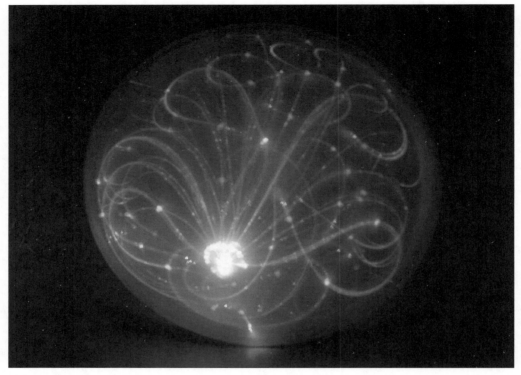

**Figure 5.** Experiment #2.

*My student projects often have a get-out-of-the-classroom component. One year, at the behest of then Texas Governor Anne Richards, my class became part of a so-called radical test in prison reform. The first thing we learned as outsiders in prison is that words are slippery, infrequent, and usually meaningless. Outsiders, after all, have no business there. What the prisoners – ages 16 to 20 – did was they "read us," our every movement. That is, they paid attention only to how we held our bodies, how we reacted to anything and everything, and discounted our words. The more flexible and low slung one's center of gravity was, the more trustworthy one was deemed to be.*

*According to ethnographer Paul Stoller, the Songhay of Mali and Niger consider the stomach to be the seat of personality, and learning is understood in bodily, gustatory terms. The histories of medicine and anthropological studies reveal a wide range of the meaning of body parts, usually visceral parts. Our contemporary Western culture is brain-centric; our science "proves" it to be the center of intelligence, the center of how the body works. Western scientists are trying to figure out how to understand qi, while some Chinese academics try to frame it and test it in scientific terms. Forms of knowledge and tradition are inextricable from their cultural contexts, so how can we know them at all? Histories show us it is usually a bloody business, and a long, complex*

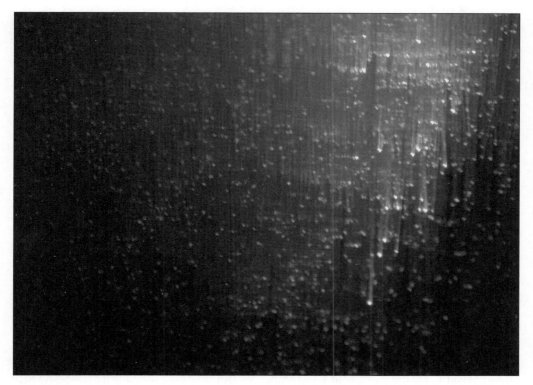

**Figure 6.** Experiment #3.

*process. While academia might be a snake pit of politics, it is more often than not at least not so bloody. Exceptions, of course, are abundant.*

*The question of what a PhD in art means will probably seem like an archaic, funny question some day. The struggle to find appropriate methodologies to legitimize artists' knowledges will undoubtedly be diverse. But as artists like Jinsil Seo struggle to find and redefine academic practices, they will respond to their cultures as they always have, whether it is to reject Modernism and PostModernism, embrace all-but-forgotten traditions, or to create radically different ones.*

### Acknowledgements
Thanks to Professor Thecla Schiphorst and Professor Maia Engeli for their pure and strong academic passion and encouragement. Thanks also go to David Jhave Johnston, Dr. Inhee Lee, and Dr. Joseph Nechvatal who have often helped with developing ideas and editing, locally and telepresently. We also would like to thank all Feral Computing members at SIAT (School of Interactive Arts and Technology) in Simon Fraser University.

## Works Cited

Ackerman D. (1991), *A Natural History of the Senses*. New York: Vintage Books.

Bermudez, Julio (1999), "Between Reality & Virtuality: Toward a New Consciousness?" in *Reframing Consciousness*.

Freire, p. (2005), *Education for Critical Consciousness*. New York: Continuum International.

Gander, Pierre, http://www.pierregander.com/research/publications.html.

Giroux, H. (1991), *Border Crossings*. 2nd ed. London: Routledge.

McCullough, Malcolm (1996), *Abstracting Craft: The Practiced Digital hand*, London: MIT Press.

McRobert, Laurie (1999), "Immersive Computer Art and the Making of Consciousness," in *Reframing Consciousness*.

Pallasmaa, Juhani (2005), *The Eyes of the Skin: Architecture and the Senses*. Chichester; Hoboken, NJ: Wiley-Academy; John Wiley & Sons.

Palmer, p. (1998), *The Courage to Teach: Exploring the Inner Landscape of a Teacher's Life*. New York: Wiley.

Penny, Simson (1995) ed., *Critical Issues in Electronic Media*. Albany: State University of New York Press.

Rajah, N. "Post-Traditional Media: Art Culture and Technology in the Wake of Postmodernism" http://artcamp. pbwiki.com/PostTraditionalDiscussion.

Simanonok, K. (1997), *A theory of physiologically functional Endogenous light and a Proposed Mechanism for Consciousness*, http://www.dcn.davis.ca.us/go/karl/consciousness.html.

Steeves, James B. (2004), Imagining Bodies: Merleau-Ponty's Philosophy of Imagination: Duquesne University Press.

Suzuki, David T., Amanda McConnell, and Maria DeCambra (2002), *The Sacred Balance: A Visual Celebration of our Place in Nature*. New York: Greystone Books.

Vogelaar, Frans (2005), *Hybrid Space*, Altered States.

# REFLECTIVE INQUIRY

# Media Golem: Between Prague and ZKM

## Michael Bielicky

My older brother and I were standing on the curbstone on the main street in my Prague neighborhood. I was seven years old at the end of April 1961, two weeks after the historical moment when the first human flew in space. An open limousine suddenly appeared with Cosmonaut Yuri Gagarin waving to the crowds. As a small-sized person in a dense crowd not knowing in which direction to look, I missed seeing this hero of all humanity. Although I missed seeing him, I felt the vibrant energies of the cheering crowds for a long time afterwards.

Four years later, cheering crowds standing along the curb greeted Pope Paul VI waving from an open limousine driving down Fifth Avenue. In the crowd was a Korean man who had recently arrived in New York. He was holding the first black-and-white portable video camera shooting the scene. This young man was destined to become the father of video art. His name was Nam June Paik. I had the good fortune to be his student twenty years later only because of my escape to the West in 1969 after the Soviet tanks invaded the former Czechoslovakia.

In 1981, I drove a horse and open carriage down Fifth Avenue into Central Park. After studying medicine for several years on graduating from high school in Germany, I realized that my future was not being a physician like my father and brother, but rather in the realm of visual media. I moved to New York and lived in the Westbeth art community on the Hudson River. In order to pay my rent, I earned a license as a horse-cab driver.

Perhaps, I should start somewhere else. We are in the year 1942 at my parents' wartime wedding. They are wearing yellow stars on their chests, kissing their parents goodbye on the run, not knowing that they would never see them again. As a small boy, I could not understand how my friends had grandparents and even great-grandparents. I had none. When I was twelve, I first learned about the Holocaust madness that had exterminated my parents' entire family because they were Jews. It was not surprising that my parents did not speak to me about this unspeakable horror until I was twelve, since we continued to live in the anti-Semitic environment of the former post-Stalinist Czechoslovakia where it was best not to be identified as a Jew.

In my home, the integration of art and science flowed naturally since my father was both a musician and scientist. He had survived the war years with my mother having acquired false identification papers which permitted him to work as a musician, often playing piano at parties where the Nazis were celebrating. After the war, he studied medicine and became a medical scientist. He would come home after a long day at work and play piano while I sat beside him listening. My father was also a composer who composed Czech tangos and rumbas which were released as recordings and played on the radio.

Ironically, my Jewish identity was awakened after arriving in West Germany. I changed overnight from a young Communist Pioneer to a Western hippie. I grew long hair, wore a goat-fur jacket embroidered with colorful flowers, started to socialize within the Jewish community of Dusseldorf, and joined a Zionist group. The true reason for joining this group had little to do with leaving for Israel. It gave me the opportunity to be accepted into a marijuana-smoking hippie circle of friends that helped transform the trauma of emigration into a positive experience isolating me from the brownshirt mentality of the older generation of Germans. It was even more difficult for my parents to relate to a generation with a Nazi past that included the murderers of their parents. I remember sitting with my parents in our new home in Germany watching the moon landing on our Czech black-and-white TV. This moment awaked in me the power of a real-time media experience.

However, there were earlier fascinating media experiences in my Prague childhood that had impact on my work as a media artist – frequenting the cinema, developing photographs in my neighbor's makeshift darkroom, immersion in a 360° panoramic film happening, seeing early time-base imagery in a technical museum, and creating an instant camera anticipating Polaroid. There were two movie theaters near where we lived and my friend and I would go there nearly every Sunday for the morning matinee. We saw Karel Zeman's fantastical films which are often shown today in university film schools and new media departments as early examples of compositing visualization. In contemporary terminology, it's called a "virtual set" in which technology allows the combination of actual actors with virtual reality creating a virtual setting and even individual characters. Zeman was a pioneer with this technology, and later I became interested in it as well.

I remember another early experience with film when my father took me to the panoramic cinema at the Holesovice amusement park. Inside a round building there was a circular screen on which was projected a 360° panoramic film from a Russian projection system. Spectators didn't sit as in a normal cinema but stood in the middle watching the changing view from an airplane. I remember that the plane began to bank making people lose their balance and fall to the ground. This was a powerful experience. In the same fair grounds in 1891, the artist Marold created a panorama, an image where reality and fiction were blurred, where three-dimensional objects emerged from a 360° panoramic painting. This interaction between reality and fiction later became one of the main features of my work. My friend and I made a make-believe "camera" from a cardboard box in which we placed pictures we had drawn in advance. We would go to the park and ask people walking by if we could photograph them. If someone agreed, we would click the "shutter release" and pull from the "camera" one of the pictures to give to the person we had "photographed." My childhood invention was the "precursor" to the Polaroid camera. A few years later, the son of my parents' friends from New York came for a visit with an actual Polaroid. I wasn't at all surprised.

When I was fifteen years old, I saw what appeared to be an action movie in the making hiking with my friend in the countryside not far from Prague. At the horizon, hundreds of tanks where rolling over the hills in the far distance. When we realized that what we were seeing on that summer morning in 1968 was not a movie, but the beginning of the invasion of the Russian army into Czechoslovakia, we ran down the road tearing down all the direction signs to make it difficult for the invading soldiers to find their way. This image will forever remain etched in my mind along with the horrible feeling of being helpless and powerless.

I was fortunate to have been born in Prague, a city permeated by the myth of the Golem, a pre-robotic being created by mystical algorithms four centuries ago invoked by Rabbi Judah Loew, the spiritual father of Norbert Weiner's cybernetic theory. Prague is the city in which the Czech word "robot" was conceived, the Golem was born, and Kafka told the tale of the metamorphosis of a young man into a giant cockroach. It is also the city in which the first interactive cinema, "Kinoautomat," and the phenomenon of "Laterna Magika," the fluid transition between the stage and projected film, were invented. Publishing the first illustrated book for children in 1658, the visionary Czech educator Comenius pioneered in developing a system of media pedagogy of great significance in new media studies.

I was fortunate once again to have immigrated to Dusseldorf where I studied in a high school not far from the illustrious Art Academy there. The Academy radiated out to the community at large, so I felt part of what was going on there. I couldn't help but notice the reverberations being sent out by the life pulsating there. Near the Academy were a number of cafés and bars where students and professors congregated. I spent a lot of time in one such local hangout that was named Creamcheese. Its interior was created by members of the ZERO group, Otto Piene, Günter Mack, Heinz Ücker, and was later installed in Dusseldorf's Museum Kunst Palast. This environment had a strong impact on me without my being entirely aware of everything that was going on there. In our neighborhood, I often saw Joseph Beuys. He was indeed larger-than-life, and not just because of his height and hat, but because he drove a Bentley. The strength of his personality and work wasn't clear to me until two years before I entered the Academy. I became aware of the significance of the art scene in Dusseldorf when I saw a video installation for the first time in my life in the city's Kunsthalle. Today, it's considered a seminal piece. It was created by Shigeko Kubota, Nam June Paik's wife, and was based on Marcel Duchamp's *Nude Descending a Staircase*. Although I appreciated the artistic energies in Dussledorf, I decided to study medicine that I enjoyed for three years and thought that this was going to be my profession. When I realized that the life of a physician was not what I really wanted for myself, I left medical school and left Dusseldorf for New York. I was always grateful for the ongoing support for my quest offered by my brother, Peter, himself a physician and collector of Czech avant-garde art.

When I first came to New York City in 1978, the cosmopolitan atmosphere of the city was liberating for me, even though my existence there was very tenuous. It was important to me that no one asked who I was or where I came from. It didn't matter. Being in New York gave me a burst of energy that dissipated when I relocated at the edge of a California redwood forest, in the beautiful mountains around Santa Cruz. In this perfect paradise where I did not have anything particular to do, I felt no motivation to do anything at all. I soon realized I needed the vibrant energy and existential challenge of a big city and returned to New York to begin intensive work in photography. A turning point came when I definitively decided to pursue photography as a profession. This came from meeting New York photographer Frederic Cantor, whose work I admired. He didn't know it, but for me at that time he was a real guru. I tried to imitate his work My New York photographs, created under Cantor's influence, helped me eventually get accepted to the Dusseldorf Academy of Fine Art.

I returned to Germany to work for *Monochrom* magazine, which offered me the freedom to create a wide variety of photographs that it published. The magazine was very progressive for its time, sometimes even provocative, both in content and design. I mostly did portraits of friends, people I was acquainted with, strong personalities for the most part. The photos were pseudo-staged in often-bizarre situations that were created without a lot of prior preparation. The magazine soon folded. I suppose it was too experimental for its time. During this period, however, I never really considered myself a professional photographer even though it paid my rent.

I first applied to the Dusseldorf Academy of Fine Arts in 1983. Although I was not accepted, something positive did come out of it as Joseph Beuys organized a special exhibition of those who were rejected. He was already so famous that he could invite the press. This exhibition of the rejected threw into doubt the very social status of the "Artist" and "Art." The following year, I was accepted into Bernd Becher's photography atelier at a time that photography was starting to become accepted on equal footing with the classical fine arts. My schoolmates, who continued with photography, Andreas Gursky, Thomas Struth, and Thomas Ruff, later became successful artists. For me, the work in Becher's atelier was boring. The conceptualism he encouraged did absolutely nothing for me although I appreciated it in Becher's work itself. However, I found the work his students were producing banal and foreign to me.

I met Nam June Paik by accident at the opening of an exhibition. I told him I'd like to study under him and he didn't ask for any further details about me. He just said, "You are my student." When someone came up to him, he introduced me as his new student. I was really lucky because it was not so easy to get into his atelier. He did not take everyone. When I began to study with Paik, a new period began for me. I felt like I had found my element working with video. Outwardly he was very humble. He was even skeptical about his own work. But looking back now, I realize that maybe this was a tactic of his. What impressed me about Paik though was his lack of pretension and his interest in just everyday things. I think that's why students liked him so much. He never played the star and you could speak to him about anything. Most people do not know this, but there would be situations when if he liked a student's work he would simply buy it. He didn't do this because he was collecting these objects but so that he could use it in his own installations. He considered it a form of partnership. He wasn't misusing his students' work. For me, of course, what was most important about Paik was his openness to his students. That was the greatest lesson for me, the one I identified with the most. I try to maintain this sort of openness with my own students. I consider them more as partners who I can learn from despite their age or limited experience.

At the Academy, Joseph Beuys had created a space he called Freie Internationale Universität (FIU). It was a gesture on his part to represent a clear alternative to academic seclusion, an open space within a closed space. Beuys, of course, always had his devotees around him. My friend the Bolivian painter Ricardo Peredo and I began to associate with Beuys and his group. He was such a charismatic personality that he attracted us to him. On the other hand, we felt uncomfortable with his students who acted like members of as difficult-to-define sect. When Beuys spoke, it was like they were listening to a sermon. Beuys's lectures themselves were incredibly inspirational and they forced us to think about the role of the artist and his work in a social context. He propagated a completely different type of artistic work. He thought the artist should create "social sculptures," that is, the artist's work should be focused on mending the world. I still mull this idea over today and always return to it and try to discuss it with my students as well.

My video installations evolved into video-sculptures at the end of my studies in Dusseldorf. The difference between the two is not exactly clear. The term "video-sculpture" didn't exist until it was used for the first time in 1986 (*Videoskulptur* in German) by the curator Wulf Herzogenrath for an exhibition at the Kölnischer Kunstverein. I guess one distinction is that video installations use monitors as the central element. In a video-sculpture, the object itself is so central that if the monitors are switched off, it still can be a meaningful artwork. I created *Menorah* at the end of my studies without having any idea what sort of response it eventually would have. It had small TV monitors at the ends of each of seven branches of a large steel candelabrum.

On the monitors' screens, video images of flickering flames danced. These virtual flames emanated from a hidden video transmitter sending spiritual messages to antennas topping each of the seven monitors.

Menorah directly referenced my Jewish identity in a German context. The first place in Germany that provided me some comfortable surroundings was the Dusseldorf Jewish community. However, it took me a long while before I was ready to openly and publicly acknowledge my Jewishness. The first time I publicly displayed Menorah at the Academy, I placed a ring around it made of defunct fire extinguishers. They weren't so easy to find because at the time everyone in Germany had the Baader-Meinhof Gang and other terrorist groups still fresh in their minds and their bombs were made out of old fire extinguishers. Nevertheless, I wanted to show the installation like this. I wanted to say that these old extinguishers were like old Nazis who no longer had the strength to snuff the flame of the menorah. This was the only time I used this literal interpretation when exhibiting Menorah. Actually, it was David Galloway, the noted curator and art critic, writing for the International Herald Tribune, who convinced me that the object was powerful enough on its own. The work was in great demand. I won a number of awards for it and it went from exhibition to exhibition. Actually, there exist two copies of Menorah. One was bought from me by ZKM [Zentrum für Kunst und Medientechnologie] in Karlsruhe as the very first work for the collection of its Museum of Media Arts (so it was given identification number 001). The second was commissioned in 2001 by the Jewish Museum in Berlin at the architect Daniel Libeskind's request.

Shortly after the fall of the Communist system in Eastern Europe in 1990, I was invited to return to Prague to found the first department of new media arts in the region. When I spoke to my mentor, Nam June Paik, about the offer of a professorship in new media at the Academy of Fine Arts in Prague, he told me, "Go for it! Good luck!" and spontaneously gave me 5,000 German Marks to get the new department started. With this money and some additional sponsorship, I purchased two video cameras and three video editing systems. This very basic video equipment was the basis for creating a lively and creative department in a cubistic villa next to the main Art Academy building. In the first years, I worked with my students on some early communications art projects like IPI (International Painting Interactive) in collaboration with students in many other countries who collectively created a virtual painting using a graphics tablet and modem. We were also involved in a pioneering interactive television project (Piazza Virtuale) which was presented at the 1992 Documenta IX in Kassel, Germany. The seminal philosopher of media, Vilem Flusser, inspired my students with his highly original lectures. After his tragic death, we organized a series of "Vilem Flusser Symposia" in collaboration with Prague's Goethe Institute.

During this period in Prague, I developed projects using locative media such as global positioning systems (GPS) that were presented at Ars Electronica in Linz, Austria. My Intelligent Mailman at Ars Electronica was the first GPS artwork ever. I integrated GPS and Internet technologies in a performance artwork that electronically transmitted my wandering through the Negev desert for four days retracing the steps of Moses in the Exodus from Egypt. I also created virtual environments at the Babeinsberg High-Tech Center in Berlin and at the ZKM Center for Art and Media in Karsruhe.

Living at the intersections of Czech and German cultures was and continues to be an amazing trigger for creative thought and action. Switching time-space while reflecting on one's encounter with changing environments is a great teacher for a creative person. I felt that the newfound freedom in Eastern Europe produced a level of energy and creative potential at the time that was much stronger than what was happening in Western Europe. I traveled extensively throughout the former Communist world between 1990 and 2000 as advisor to the Soros Centers for Contemporary Arts creating educational departments and centers for new media art from Bucharest, Odessa, and Moscow to Alma-Ata in Kazakhstan. I began the new millennium lecturing on new media arts in Thailand and founding with Francis Wittenberger the New Media Arts Festival in Bangkok. My experience in Asia led me to realize how much more dynamic this part of the world was in comparison to the more staid culture of Western Europe.

The challenge in educating future generations in the field of digital arts is the rapidly changing conditions that make today's media theory stale tomorrow. We know that ideas we taught a decade ago are irrelevant today. Perhaps, the most significant change is the democratization of video and computer technologies that makes everyone a potential digital artist. The aim to create Soros media centers in Eastern Europe modeled after the ZKM Center for Art and Media and MIT's Center for Advanced Visual Studies and Media Lab required heavy funding for sophisticated equipment and facilities. The concentration of digital art production in these centers has given way to powerful media tools that are cheap enough and compact enough for anyone to create serious digital artworks in their home. Prestigious media art festivals like Ars Electronica in Linz and Tranmediale in Berlin are having to reinvent themselves to claim to continue to be innovative, risky, and fresh.

The primary question is, What is the role of the artist in society in the twenty-first century? We need to completely rethink stereotypic images of the artist and the concept of the art school that are becoming obsolete. Perhaps art schools can be replaced by mobile educational units that adapt to alternative cultural environments. We need to acknowledge the hundreds of millions of pictures produced worldwide daily. This enormous inflation of images is radically changing our sensibilities. It is causing cultural pollution of our environment that may be as great a threat to our mind and souls as physical pollution is to our bodies. Does it make sense to educate our students to produce more and more images? Perhaps we need to encourage the practice of *cultural ecology* by creating an ecological movement against image pollution of our environment like those acting against chemical pollution. Students in a post-digital age are already creating new forms of dematerialized art – net art, locative media, data and information visualization, telematics – that reach into public spaces globally and even beyond our planet.

My impression is that most educational institutions are producing artists who are often swallowed by the media industry – television, advertising, and other large media corporations. Although I recognize that students coming out of art schools have to pay rent and other costs of living, they should not sell out to industry, but rather have the self-confidence to promote their unique qualifications as creative partners when negotiating projects with commercial enterprises. From the beginning, they should build a symbiotic relationship between themselves as media artists and commercial enterprises.

Although few art educators like to talk about it, I see many art schools around the world succumbing to financial pressures forcing them to often accept less talented young people just because they bring tuition money to the school. I am very much aware of the privilege I had in Prague where this was simply not an issue.

My sixteen years teaching at the Academy of Fine Arts in Prague convinced me that the key to educating future digital artists is less the quality of the school and the quality of the professor than the quality of the student who gets accepted. In Prague, I was fortunate to always be able to choose the best of the best. Consequently, those students were from the beginning more my partners than students. My students in Prague were invited and won awards in such new media art festivals as Ars Electronica in Linz or Transmediale in Berlin where they were not considered as students but as professional artists!

I guess I was lucky again to be appointed as a full-time professor and head of the Department of InfoArt/Digital Media at Hochschule fur Gestaltung, the university of arts and design in Karlsruhe, Germany. The fact that the school is situated at the same giant building as the ZKM Center for Art and Media is a great advantage for the students. They can see world-class media art shows, attend events with top international performers, and hear lectures by some of the most important artists and theoreticians in the world. After sixteen years in Prague, I am leaving the dreamy and poetic city to the more rational and functional Karlsruhe. This is my third emigration between Czech Republic and Germany.

Although primarily conceptual in orientation, my department at the Art Academy in Prague was also a technological laboratory in which there was a lot of freedom given to the students who, in turn, were expected to assume individual responsibility. Most students understood this challenge. Others misused it to their disadvantage. I believe that it is important to work with the students on highly innovative, challenging, and risky issues. My experience taught me that project-centered study motivates students more and is generally a more efficient educational methodology than more formal methods. It has also taught me the significance of being open to learning from teachers and colleagues through ongoing dialogue. My long-term dialogue and friendship with key thinkers and artists, such as Nam June Paik, Vilem Flusser, Woody and Steina Vasulka,

Mel Alexenberg, and Peter Weibel, have enriched me and facilitated my seeing alternative perspectives on life and art

Students should be encouraged to develop the need to break out of institutionalized frameworks. The young generation should learn to take risks rather than always follow their teachers. Often students exhibit fresh visions than exceed those of their professors. It is our duty to support their visions even when our egos are sometimes hurt. They should ask if the so-called art system (art school, gallery, museum, art critic, curator, art magazine, art fair, etc...) is the right framework for a digital artist at the beginning of the twenty-first century knowing very well how much this system is corrupted where often financial interests dominate and manipulate the art market independent of the quality of the artworks.

For the past two years, my wife, Kamila Bielicka Richter, and I have been collaborating on a project that we call "Falling Life." It operates completely outside of the art system. It is an ongoing project that was introduced for the first time in Berlin in August 2005. This urban screening project needs neither a curator nor a gallery. It does not need a fixed place or access to the electric power. We are equipped with a car, a laptop, a compact powerful projector, and a small power generator. With this very mobile equipment, we are able to create an instant presence in the urban landscape. We transform city architecture into dynamic and living organisms. Without any on-site preparation and without any permits, we operate a kind of guerilla theater-style projection. Within less than ten minutes, we can illuminate giant buildings with our artwork, reaching huge audiences that would probably never walk into a gallery or museum. We use a minimalist language of constantly appearing and disappearing pictograms. The moving icons often represent the collective reality of our interconnected globalized world. "Falling Life" has been projected during the Prague Berlin Festival, a subversive public interference in Ars Electronica in Linz, at ZKM in Karlsruhe, at the DOX Center for Contemporary Art in Prague, Interferencia Barcelona, MAF Bangkok, and will be shown in Jerusalem and Sevilla.

*Falling Life* has mutated into *Falling Times* www.fallingtimes.info, an everlasting and growing online real-time news translation machine representing permanently appearing and disappearing information about our times as we witness the fall of Western civilization. *Falling Times* refers to the heavy InfoPollution in which we live. It's estimated that 1.5 exabytes of unique new information will be generated worldwide this year. That's estimated to be more than in the previous 5,000 years. Half of what the students of technical colleges learn today in their first year of study will be outdated by their third year of study.

The InfoSociety has created a new kind of consumer – the InfoConsumer! The most consumed information is the news. The news has been turning more and more into entertainment creating Infotainment. The news producers are the biggest infopolluters of our time and thus are the biggest contributors to InfoEcological disaster.

In our *Falling Times* participatory artwork, the visualization of news content is reduced to headlines and key words that appear most often in Google news.  These news bits are translated into a dynamic pictogram language that aims to be universal and instantly understandable.  Online users have the opportunity to define collectively the meaning associated with each icon we created. In this way, the users decide which icon represents which news and which news is being searched for and displayed. This open platform permanently grows and transforms itself by learning from the collective contributions. Information does not transport meaning any more but rather creates a pattern decorating our daily life with the feeling that we are connected to reality.  It is urgently necessary to teach our students to deal with being inundated with massive amounts of information.

We projected on the façade of the grotesquely gigantic building built by the brutal Romanian dictator Nicholae Ceaucescu in Bucharest. With the fall of Communism and the execution of Ceaucescu, the building built by his dictatorial regime is being shared by the parliament of a democratic government and a museum of contemporary art. There was an exhibition in the museum of social realist paintings glorifying the dictator which after his fall looked absurd and preposterous. Boorish parliamentarians did not get the satire of these kitsch artworks and accused the curators of promoting Communist propaganda. Perhaps it is a sign of Isaiah's prophetic vision to beat swords into plowshares that the buildings of evil regimes are being transformed into centers for creative arts. The media department of the Dusseldorf Art Academy where I studied with Nam June Paik was housed in former Gestapo headquarters, and I currently teach in an enormous building shared by my art school and ZKM Center for Art and Media that was a Nazi munitions factory where slave laborers manufactured torpedoes.

# LIFE TRANSFORMATION – ART MUTATION

## Eduardo Kac

I introduced the concept and the phrase "transgenic art" in 1988 and proposed the creation (and social integration) of a real dog that glows with a green light. Transgenic art, a new art form based on the use of genetic engineering to create unique living beings, must be pursued with great care, with acknowledgement of the complex issues it raises and, above all, with a commitment to respect, nurture, and love the life it creates. I exhibited new transgenic artworks in 1999, 2000, 2001, and 2004. The implications of this ongoing work have aesthetic, social, and educational ramifications, crossing several disciplines and providing material for further reflection and dialogue. What follows is an overview of theses works, the issues they evoke, and the debates they have elicited.

For almost two decades my work has explored the boundaries between humans, animals, and robots.[1] Thus, transgenic art can be seen as a natural development of my previous work. In my telepresence art, developed since 1986, humans coexist with other humans and non-human animals through telerobotic bodies. In my biotelematic art, developed since 1994, biology and networking are no longer co-present but coupled so as to produce a hybrid of the living and the telematic. With transgenic art, developed since 1998, the animate and the technological can no longer be distinguished. The implications of this ongoing work have particular social ramifications, crossing several disciplines and providing material for further reflection and dialogue.

The presence of biotechnology will increasingly change from agricultural and pharmaceutical practices to a larger role in popular culture, just as the perception of the computer changed historically from an industrial device and military weapon to a communication, entertainment, and education tool. Terms formerly perceived as "technical," such as *megabytes* and *ram*, for example, have entered the vernacular. Likewise, jargon that today may seem out of place in ordinary discourse, such as *marker* and *protein*, for example, will simply be incorporated into the larger verbal landscape of everyday language. This is made clear by the fact that high school students in the United States already create transgenic bacteria routinely in school labs through affordable kits. The popularization of aspects of technical discourse inevitably brings with it the risk of dissemination of a reductive and instrumental ideological view of the world. Without ever relinquishing its right to formal experimentation and subjective inventiveness, art can, art should, contribute to the development of alternative views of the world that resist dominant ideologies. As both utopian and dystopian artists such as Moholy-Nagy and Tinguely have done before, in my work I appropriate and subvert contemporary technologies – not to make detached comments on social change, but to *enact* critical views, to make present in the physical world invented new entities (artworks that include transgenic organisms) which seek to open a new space for both emotional and intellectual aesthetic experience.

I have been employing the phrase "bio art" since 1997, in reference to my own works that involved biological agency (as opposed to biological objecthood), such as "Time Capsule"[2] and "A-positive",[3] both presented in 1997. The difference between biological agency and biological objecthood is that the first involves an active principle while the second implies material self-containment. In 1998 I introduced the phrase "transgenic art" in a paper-manifesto with the same title[4] and proposed the creation (and social integration) of a dog expressing green fluorescent protein. This protein is commonly used as a biomarker in genetic research. However, my goal was to use it primarily for its visual properties as a symbolic gesture, a social marker. The initial public response to the paper was curiosity laced with incredulity. The proposal is perfectly viable, but it seemed that few believed that the project could or would be realized. While I struggled to find venues that could assist me in creating the aforementioned project, entitled "GFP K-9," I too realized that canine reproductive technology was not developed enough at the time to enable me to create a dog expressing green fluorescent protein.[5] In the meantime, I started to develop a new transgenic art work, entitled "Genesis", which premiered at Ars Electronica '99.[6]

**Genesis**
Genesis is a transgenic artwork that explores the intricate relationship between biology, belief systems, information technology, dialogical interaction, ethics, and the Internet. The key element of the work is an "artist's gene," a synthetic gene that was created by translating a sentence from the biblical book of Genesis into Morse code, and converting the Morse code into DNA base pairs according to a conversion principle I specially developed for this work. The sentence reads: "Let man have dominion over the fish of the sea, and over the fowl of the air, and over every living thing that moves upon the earth." It was chosen for what it implies about the dubious notion – divinely sanctioned – of humanity's supremacy over nature. Morse code was chosen because, as the first example of the use of radiotelegraphy, it represents the dawn of the information age – the genesis of global communication. The Genesis gene was incorporated into bacteria, which were shown in the gallery. Participants on the Web

could turn on an ultraviolet light in the gallery, causing real, biological mutations in the bacteria. This changed the biblical sentence in the bacteria. After the show, the DNA of the bacteria was translated back into Morse code, and then back into English. The mutation that took place in the DNA had changed the original sentence from the Bible. The mutated sentence was posted on the Genesis website. In the context of the work, the ability to change the sentence is a symbolic gesture: it means that we do not accept its meaning in the form we inherited it, and that new meanings emerge as we seek to change it.

While presenting Genesis, I also gave a public lecture in the context of the symposium "Life Science", presented by Ars Electronica '99. My lecture focused on the "GFP K-9" proposal. To contextualize my presentation, I reviewed the long history of human-dog domestication and partnership, and pointed out the direct and strong human influence on the evolution of the dog up to the present day. Emphasizing that there are no packs of poodles and Chihuahuas running in the wild, and that the creation of the dog out of the wolf was a technology – a fact that we seemed to have lost conscience of – I proceeded to point out the complex relationship between dogs and humans throughout their long history together, going back to at least fourteen thousand years, according to archeological records. While some showed support and appreciation for the work, others reacted against the project and voiced their position. The stage was set for a very productive dialogue, which was one of my original intentions. As I see it, the debate must go beyond official policy-making and academic research to encompass the general public, including artists. "GFP K-9" was discussed in art magazines and books and science journals. Daily papers and general magazines also discussed the work in progress. While specialized publications showed greater appreciation for "GFP K-9," the response in the general media covered the whole gamut, from forthright rejection to consideration of multiple implications to unmistakable support. The shock generated by the proposal curiously caused one critic to declare "the end of art".[7] As I see it, there's no reason to see the beginning of a new art as the end of anything.

## GFP Bunny
This pattern of response repeated itself, at a truly global scale, when I announced in 2000 the realization of my second transgenic work. Entitled "GFP Bunny," the work comprises the creation of a green fluorescent rabbit ("Alba"), the public dialogue generated by the project, and the social integration of the rabbit. This work was realized with the assistance of Louis Bec and Louis-Marie Houdebine. Louis Bec worked as the producer, coordinating the activities in France. Bec and I met at Ars Electronica (September 1999) and soon afterwards he contacted Houdebine on my behalf, for the first time, to propose the project. Months later, in 2000, Alba was born, a gentle and healthy rabbit. As I stated in my paper entitled "GFP Bunny",[8] "transgenic art is a new art form based on the use of genetic engineering to create unique living beings. This must be done with great care, with acknowledgment of the complex issues thus raised and, above all, with a commitment to respect, nurture, and love the life thus created."

"GFP Bunny" attracted local media in the south of France in June 2000 when the former director of the French institute where Alba was born used his authority to overrule the scientists who worked on the project and refused to let Alba go to Avignon and then come to my family in Chicago. This arbitrary decision was made privately by one individual (the former director of the French institute where Alba was born). He never explained his reason for the refusal, so it remains unknown to this day. Bec and I denounced the censorship through the Internet and through interviews to the press.[9] If the objective was to silence the media, the result backfired. "GFP Bunny" became a global media scandal after a front-page article appeared in the *Boston Globe*,[10] sharing headlines with articles about the 2000 Olympics and US presidential debates. Articles about Alba were published in all major countries, with wire services further spreading the news worldwide.[11] Alba was also on the cover of *Le Monde*, *San Francisco Chronicle* and *L'Espresso*, among others. *Der Spiegel* and *Chicago Tribune* dedicated full pages to "GFP Bunny." She also appeared on the front page of the Arts section of the *New York Times*. Broadcasts by ABC TV, BBC Radio, and Radio France also took the Alba story to the whole planet. From mid-2000 to early 2003 the relentless response to "GFP Bunny" has been equally intense and fascinating, with fruitful debate and both strong opposition and support. Since October 15, 2000, the "Alba Guestbook" has been collecting general opinions about the work and expressions of support to bring Alba home.[12] Through lectures and symposia, Internet postings and e-mail correspondence, the debate intensified and became richer, more subtle and nuanced, as I had hoped. The response to "GFP Bunny" constitutes extremely rich material, which I hope to revisit in the near future.

As part of my intercontinental custody battle to obtain Alba's release, between December 3 and December 13, 2000, I staged a public campaign in Paris, which included lectures, broadcasts, public and private meetings, and the public placement of a series of seven posters. I placed individual posters in several neighborhoods, including: Le Marais, Quartier Latin, Saint Germain, Champs de Mars, Bastille, Montparnasse, and Montmartre. The posters reflect some of the readings afforded by "GFP Bunny." They show the same image of Alba and me together, each topped by a different French word: Art, Médias, Science, Éthique, Religion, Nature, Famille.[13] Between December 3 and December 13, 2000, parallel to radio (Radio France and Radio France Internationale), print (*Le Monde*, *Libération*, *Transfert*, *Ça M'intéresse*, *Nova*), and television (Canal+, Paris Première) interviews and debates, I posted these images on the streets in an effort to intervene in the context of French public opinion and gather support for my cause to bring Alba home. I also engaged the public directly through a series of lectures (Sorbonne, École Normale Superior, École Superior des Beaux Arts, Forum des Images) and through face-to-face conversations on the street sparked by the public's interest. In total, I reached approximately 1.5 million people (about half of the population of Paris). This was an important step, as it allowed me to address the Parisian public directly. In 2001, I created "The Alba Flag," a white flag with the green rabbit silhouette, and started to fly it in front of my Chicago-area house. The flag not only signals publicly the green bunny home, but most importantly stands as a social marker, a beacon of her absence.

Continuing my efforts to raise awareness about Alba's plight and to obtain her freedom, in 2002, I presented a solo exhibition entitled "Free Alba!"[14] at Julia Friedman Gallery, in Chicago (May 3–June 15, 2002). "Free Alba!" included a large body of new work comprised of large-scale color photographs, drawings, prints, Alba flags, and Alba T-shirts. Seen together for the first time were the posters from my public interventions in Paris (2000), an Alba flag flying outside the Gallery (2001), photographs that reclaim green bunny narratives circulated by global media (2001–02), drawings that reflect on our closeness to the "animal other" (2001–2002), and Alba T-shirts that extend Alba's cause beyond gallery's walls (2002). Through the leitmotif of the green bunny, this exhibition explored the poetics of life and evolution. The story of "GFP Bunny" was adapted and customized by news organizations worldwide, often generating new narratives that, both intentionally and unintentionally, reinstated or overlooked the facts. My "Free Alba!" exhibition featured photographs in which I reappropriated and recontextualized this vast coverage, exhibiting the productive tension that is generated when contemporary art enters the realm of daily news. The photographs in this series dramatize the fact that the reception of GFP Bunny was complex, taking place across cultures and in diverse locations. I will continue to develop new strategies to make Alba's case public and to pursue her liberation.

Parallel to this effort, transgenic art evolves. One new direction involves the creation of nanoscale three-dimensional structures built of amino acids. This "proteic art," or "protein art," can be experienced in many forms, including in vivo, in vitro, and expanded into other settings, such as rapid-prototype models and online navigational spaces. All of these forms, and many others, can be combined through new biointerfaces. A prominent aspect of this path is the fact that these three-dimensional structures are assembled according to combinatory rules that follow strict biological principles (otherwise it is not possible to produce them), even if one invents and synthesizes a new protein. This constraint imposes a biomorphology that offers a new and fascinating creative challenge. A second new direction involves complex interactive transgenic environments with multiple organisms and biobots, biological robots partially regulated by internal transgenic microorganisms. In what follows, I offer a discussion of these developments, both of which I explored in 2001.

## Sculpting New Proteins

While the first phase of "Genesis" focused on the creation and the mutation of a synthetic gene through Web participation, the second phase, carried out in 2000/2001, focused on the protein produced by the synthetic gene, the Genesis protein,[15] and on new works that examine the cultural implications of proteins as fetish objects. The Genesis protein is another step in the translation of the original biblical text, this time from the Genesis gene (itself encoding the English sentence) to a three-dimensional form made up of discrete parts (amino acids). The transmogrification of a verbal text into a sculptural form is laden with intersemiotic resonances that contribute to expand the historically rich intertextuality between word, image, and spatial form. The process of biological mutation extends it into time.

A critical stance is manifested throughout the Genesis project by following scientifically accurate methods in the real production and visualization of a gene and a protein that I have invented and which have absolutely no function or value in biology. Rather than explicating or illustrating scientific principles, the Genesis project complicates and obfuscates the extreme simplification and reduction of standard molecular biology descriptions of life processes, reinstating social and historical contextualization at the core of the debate. I appropriate the techniques of biotechnology to critique the language of science and its inherent ideologies, while developing transgenic art as an alternative means for individual expression. In its genomic and proteomic manifestations, the Genesis project continues to reveal new readings and possibilities.

Protein production is a fundamental aspect of life. Multiple research centers around the world are currently focusing their initiatives on sequencing, organizing, and analyzing the genomes of both simple and complex organisms, from bacteria to human beings. After genomics (the study of genes and their function) comes proteomics (the study of proteins and their function). Proteomics, the dominant research agenda in molecular biology in the post-genomic world, focuses on the visualization of the three-dimensional structure of proteins produced by sequenced genes.[16] It is also concerned with the study of the structure and functionality of these proteins, among many other important aspects, such as similarity among proteins found in different organisms. The second phase of "Genesis" critically investigates the logic, the methods, and the symbolism of proteomics, as well as its potential as a domain of artmaking.

In order to arrive at the visualization of the "Genesis" protein, I first explored aspects of its two-dimensional structure.[17] The next step was to compare the predicted folding pattern of the "Genesis" protein to another known protein to which it is similar: Chorion. With the goal of producing a tangible rendition of the nanostructure of the "Genesis" protein, I researched protein fold homology using the Protein Data Bank, operated by the Research Collaboratory for Structural Bioinformatics (RCSB). I then produced a digital visualization of the "Genesis" protein's three-dimensional structure.[18] This three-dimensional data set was used to produce both digital and physical versions of the protein. The digital version is a fully navigable web object rendered both as VRML (Virtual Reality Modeling Language) and PDB (Protein Data Bank) formats, to enable up-close inspection of its complex volumetric structure. The physical rendition is a small solid object produced via rapid-prototyping, to convey in tangible form the fragility of this molecular object.[19] This object was used as a mold for casting the final form of the protein used in the creation of the "Transcription Jewels."

"Transcription Jewels" is a set of two objects encased in a custom-made round wooden box. The word "transcription" is the term employed in biology to name the process during which the genetic information is "transcribed" from DNA into RNA.[20] One "jewel" is a 2-inch genie bottle in clear glass with gold ornaments and 65 mg of purified "Genesis" DNA inside. "Purified DNA" means that countless copies of the DNA have been isolated from the bacteria in which they were produced and accumulated and filtrated in a vial. The gene is seen here out of the context of the body, its meaning intentionally reduced to a formal entity to reveal that without acknowledgement of the vital roles played by organism and environment, the "priceless" gene can become "worthless." The other "jewel" is an equally small gold cast of the three-dimensional structure of the "Genesis" protein. By displaying the emblematic elements of the biotech revolution (the gene and the protein) as coveted valuables, "Transcription Jewels" makes an ironic commentary on the process of commodification of the minutest aspects of life. Both the purified gene in "Transcription Jewels" and its protein are not derived from a natural organism, but rather were created specifically for the artwork "Genesis." Instead of a "genie" inside the bottle one finds the new panacea, the gene. No wishes of immortality, beauty, or intelligence are granted by the inert and isolated gene sealed inside the miniature bottle. As a result, the irony gains a critical and humorous twist by the fact that the "precious commodity" is devoid of any real, practical application in biology.

All pieces described and discussed above, including the net installation with live bacteria, were presented together in my solo exhibition "Genesis", realized at Julia Friedman Gallery, in Chicago, between May 4 and June 2, 2001. The multiple mutations experienced biologically by the bacteria and graphically by the images, texts, and systems that compose the exhibition reveal that the alleged supremacy of the so-called "master molecule" must be questioned. The Genesis series (including the installation, "Transcription Jewels," and other works) challenges the genetic hype and opposes the dominant biodeterministic interpretation, stating that we must continue to consider life as a complex system at the crossroads between belief systems, economic principles, legal parameters, political directives, scientific laws, and cultural constructs.

### The Eighth Day: A Transgenic Net Installation
"The Eighth Day" is a transgenic artwork that investigates the new ecology of fluorescent creatures that is evolving worldwide. It was shown from October 25 to November 2, 2001, at the Institute for Studies in the Arts, Arizona State University, Tempe.[21] While fluorescent creatures are being developed in isolation in laboratories, seen collectively in this work for the first time they form the nucleus of a new and emerging synthetic bioluminescent ecosystem. The piece brings together living transgenic life forms and a biological robot (biobot) in an environment enclosed under a clear Plexiglas dome, thus making visible what it would be like if these creatures would, in fact, coexist in the world at large.

As the viewer walks into the gallery, she first sees a blue-glowing semisphere against a dark background. This semisphere is the 4-foot dome, aglow with its internal blue light. She also hears the recurring sounds of water washing ashore. This evokes the image of the Earth as seen from space. The water sounds both function as a metaphor for life on Earth (reinforced by the spherical blue image) and resonate with the video of moving water projected on the floor. In order to see "The Eighth Day" the viewer is invited to "walk on water."

In the gallery, visitors are able to see the terrarium with transgenic creatures both from inside and outside the dome. As they stand outside the dome looking in, someone online sees the space from the perspective of the biobot looking out, perceiving the transgenic environment as well as faces or bodies of local viewers. An online computer in the gallery also gives local visitors an exact sense of what the experience is like remotely on the Internet.

Local viewers may temporarily believe that their gaze is the only human gaze contemplating the organisms in the dome. However, once they navigate the Web interface they realize that remote viewers can also experience the environment from a bird's eye point of view, looking down through a camera mounted above the dome. They can pan, tilt, and zoom, seeing humans, mice, plants, fish and the biobot up close. Thus, from the point of view of the online participant, local viewers become part of the ecology of living creatures featured in the work, as if enclosed in a websphere.

"The Eighth Day" presents an expansion of biodiversity beyond wild-type life forms. As a self-contained artificial ecology it resonates with the words in the title, which add one day to the period of creation of the world as narrated in the Judeo-Christian Scriptures. All of the transgenic creatures in "The Eighth Day" are created with the same gene I used previously in "GFP Bunny" to create "Alba," a gene that allows all creatures to glow green under harmless blue light. The transgenic creatures in "The Eighth Day" are GFP plants, GFP amoebas, GFP fish, and GFP mice. Selective breeding and mutation are two key evolutionary forces. "The Eighth Day" literally raises the question of transgenic evolution, since all organisms in the piece are mutations of their respective wild-type species and all were selected and bred for their GFP mutations.

"The Eighth Day" also includes a biological robot. A biobot is a robot with an active biological element within its body which is responsible for aspects of its behavior. The biobot created for "The Eighth Day" has a colony of GFP amoeba called Dyctiostelium discoideum as its "brain cells." These "brain cells" form a network within a bioreactor that constitutes the "brain structure" of the biobot. When amoebas divide the biobot exhibits dynamic behavior inside the enclosed environment. Changes in the amoebal colony (the "brain cells") of the biobot are monitored by it, and cause it to move about, throughout the exhibition. The biobot also functions as the avatar of Web participants inside the environment. Independent of the ascent and descent of the biobot, Web participants are able to control its audiovisual system with a pan-tilt actuator. The autonomous motion, which often causes the biobot to lean forward in different directions, provides Web participants with new perspectives of the environment.

The biobot's "amoebal brain" is visible through the transparent bioreactor body. In the gallery, visitors are able to see the terrarium with transgenic creatures from outside and inside the dome, as a computer in the gallery gives local visitors an exact sense of what the experience is like on the Internet. By enabling participants to experience the environment inside the dome from the point of view of the biobot, "The Eighth Day" creates a context in which participants can reflect on the meaning of a transgenic ecology from a first-person perspective.

**Move 36**

"Move 36" makes reference to the dramatic move made by the computer called Deep Blue against chess world champion Gary Kasparov in 1997. This competition can be characterized as a match between the greatest chess player who ever lived against the greatest chess player who never lived. The installation – presented for the first time at the Exploratorium, in San Francisco, from February 26 to May 31, 2004 – sheds light on the limits of the human mind and the increasing capabilities developed by computers and robots, inanimate beings whose actions often acquire a force comparable to subjective human agency.

According to Kasparov, Deep Blue's quintessential moment in Game Two came at Move 36. Rather than making a move that was expected by viewers and commentators alike – a sound move that would have afforded immediate gratification – it made a move that was subtle and conceptual and, in the long run, better. Kasparov could not believe that a machine had made such a keen move. The game, in his mind, was lost.

The installation presents a chessboard made of earth (dark squares) and white sand (light squares) in the middle of the room. There are no chess pieces on the board. Positioned exactly where Deep Blue made its Move 36 is a plant whose genome incorporates a new gene that I created specifically for this work. The gene uses ASCII (the universal computer code for representing binary numbers as roman characters, on- and off-line) to translate to the four bases of genetics Descartes' statement: "Cogito ergo sum" (I think therefore I am).

Through genetic modification, the leaves of the plants grow multiple plantlets. In the wild these leaves would be smooth. The "Cartesian gene" was coupled with a gene for the expression of the plantlets, so that the public can easily see with the naked eye that the "Cartesian gene" is expressed precisely where the plantlets grow.

The "Cartesian gene" was produced according to a new code I created especially for the work. In 8-bit ASCII, the letter C, for example, is: 01000011. Thus, the gene is created by the following association between genetic bases and binary digits:

A = 00
C = 01
G = 10
T = 11

The result is the following gene with 52 bases:

CAATCATTCACTCAGCCCCACATTCACCCCAGCACTCATTCCATCCCCCATC

The creation of this gene is a critical and ironic gesture, since Descartes considered the human mind a "ghost in the machine" (for him the body was a "machine"). His rationalist philosophy gave new impetus both to the mind-body split (Cartesian dualism) and to the mathematical foundations of current computer technology.

The presence of this "Cartesian gene" in the plant, rooted precisely where the human lost to the machine, reveals the tenuous border between humanity, inanimate objects endowed with lifelike qualities, and living organisms that encode digital information. A single, focused light shines in a delicate luminous cone over the plant. Silent square video projections on two opposing walls contextualize the work, evoking two chess opponents in absentia. Each video projection is composed of a grid of small squares, resembling a chessboard. Each square shows short, animated loops cycling at different intervals, thus creating a complex and carefully choreographed thread of movements. The cognitive engagement of the viewer with the multiple visual possibilities presented on both projected boards subtly emulates the mapping of multiple paths on the board involved in a chess match.

A game for phantasmic players, a philosophical statement uttered by a plant, a sculptural process that explores the poetics of real life and evolution. This installation gives continuity to my ongoing interventions at the boundaries between the living (human, non-human animals) and the non-living (machines, networks). Checkmating traditional notions, nature is revealed as an arena for the production of ideological conflict, and the physical sciences as a locus for the creation of science fictions.

**Conclusion**
Quite clearly, genetic engineering will continue to have profound consequences in art as well as in the social, medical, political, and economic spheres of life. As an artist I am interested in reflecting on the multiple social implications of genetics, from unacceptable abuse to its hopeful promises, from the notion of "code" to the question of translation, from the synthesis of genes to the process of mutation, from the metaphors employed by biotechnology to the fetishization of genes and proteins, from simple reductive narratives to complex views that account for environmental influences. The urgent task is to unpack the implicit meanings of the biotechnology revolution and contribute to the creation of alternative views, thus changing genetics into a critically aware new art medium.

The tangible and symbolic coexistence of the human and the transgenic, which I have developed in several of my works discussed above, shows that humans and other species are evolving in new ways. It dramatizes the urgent need to develop new models with which to understand this change and calls for the interrogation of difference taking into account clones, transgenics, and chimeras.

The Human Genome Project (HGP) has made it clear that all humans have in their genome sequences that came from viruses,[22] acquired through a long evolutionary history. This shows that we have in our bodies DNA from organisms other than human. Ultimately, this means that we too are transgenic. Before deciding that all transgenics are "monstrous," humans must look inside and come to terms with their own "monstrosity," i.e., with their own transgenic condition.

The common perception that transgenics are not "natural" is incorrect. It is important to understand that the process of moving genes from one species to another is part of wildlife (without human participation). The most common example is the bacterium called "agrobacterium," which enters the root of plants and communicates its genes to it. Agrobacterium has the ability to transfer DNA into plant cells and integrate the DNA into the plant chromosome.[23]

Transgenic art suggests that romantic notions of what is "natural" have to be questioned and the human role in the evolutionary history of other species (and vice versa) has to be acknowledged, while at the same time respectfully and humbly marveling at this amazing phenomenon we call "life."

## Notes

1. Peter Tomaz Dobrila and Aleksandra Kostic (eds.), Eduardo Kac: Telepresence, Biotelematics, Transgenic Art (Maribor, Slovenia: KIBLA, 2000). Texts by Annick Bureaud, Edward A. Shanken, Christiane Paul, Aleksandra Kostic, Suzana Milevska, Machiko Kusahara, Gerfried Stocker, Steve Tomasula, Eduardo Kac. See also: <http://www.ekac.org>.
2. Atkins, Robert. "State of the (On-Line) Art", Art in America, April 99, pp. 89–95; Carvalho, Mario Cesar. "Artista implanta hoje chip no corpo," Folha de São Paulo, Cotidiano, 11 November 1997, p. 3; Cohen, Michel. "The Artificial Horizon: Notes Towards a Digital Aesthetics," in: Wonil Rhee (editor). Luna's Flow. The Second International Media Art Biennale. media_city seoul 2002 (Seoul Museum of Art, Seoul, Korea, 2002), p. 20 and pp. 32–33; Decia, Patricia. "Bioarte: Eduardo Kac tem obra polêmica vetada no ICI", Folha de São Paulo, Ilustrada, 10 October 1997, p. 13; Dietz, Steve. "Memory_Archive_Database", Switch, vol. 5, n. 3, 2000. http://switch.sjsu.edu; Dietz, Steve. "Hotlist", Artforum, October 2000, p. 41; Esnal, Luis. "Un hombre llamado 026109532", La Nacion, Section 5, Buenos Aires, 15 December 1997, p. 8; Kac, Eduardo. "Time Capsule," InterCommunication, n. 26, Autumn 1998, Tokyo, pp. 13–15; "Time Capsule," in Database Aesthetics, Victoria Vesna, Karamjit S. Gill and David Smith, eds., special issue of AI & Society, vol. 14, n. 2, 2000, pp. 243–249; "Art at the Biological Frontier," in Roy Ascott, ed., Reframing Consciousness: Art, Mind and Technology (Exeter: Intellect, 1999), pp. 90–94; "Capsule Temporelle," in: O'Rourke, Karen (ed.). L'Archivage Comme Activité Artistique/Archiving as Art (Paris: University of Paris 1, 2000), n.p. n.; Machado, Arlindo. "A Microchip inside the Body," Performance Research, vol. 4, n. 2, "On Line" special issue, London, 1999, pp. 8–12; Paul, Christiane. "Time Capsule", Intelligent Agent, vol. 2, n. 2, (1998) pp. 4–13; Scheeres, Julia. "New Body Art: Chip Implants", Wired News, March 11, 2002; Sherlock, Maureen p. "Either/Or/Neither/Nor", in Grzinic, Marina (ed.), Gallery (Dante) Marino Cettina – Future Perspectives (Umag, Croatia: Marino Cettina Gallery, 2001), pp. 130–135; Stiles, Kristine. "Time Capsule," in Uncorrupted Joy: Art Actions, Art History, and Social Value (University of

California Press, 2003); Strickland, Stephanie, "Dalí Clocks: Time Dimensions of Hypermedia," Electronic Book Review, n. 11, 2000; Tomasula, Steve. "Time Capsule: Self-Capsule," CIRCA, n. 89, Autumn 1999. Ireland, pp. 23–25.

3. Beiguelman, Gisele. "Artista discute o pós-humano," Folha de São Paulo, October 10, 1997; Decia, Patricia. "Artista põe a vida em risco" e "Bioarte," Folha de São Paulo, October 10, 1997; Geary, James. The Body Electric An Anatomy Of The New Bionic Senses (New Brunswick, NJ: Rutgers, 2002), pp. 181–185; Kac, Eduardo. "A-positive." In: ISEA '97 – The Eighth International Symposium on Electronic Art, September 22 -27, 1997 (Chicago: The School of the Art Institute of Chicago, 1997), p. 62; Kac, Eduardo. "A-positive: Art at the Biobotic Frontier." Flyer distributed on the occasion of ISEA '97 – The Eighth International Symposium on Electronic Art, September 22 -27, 1997 (Chicago: The School of the Art Institute of Chicago, 1997); Kac, Eduardo. "Art at the Biologic Frontier," in: Roy Ascott, ed., Reframing Consciousness (Exeter: Intellect, 1999), pp. 90–94; Machado, Arlindo. "Expanded Bodies and Minds," in: Dobrila, Peter Tomaz and Kostic, Aleksandra (eds.) Eduardo Kac: Teleporting An Unkown State (Maribor, Slovenia: KIBLA, 1998), pp. 39–63; Mirapaul, Matthew. "An Electronic Artist and His Body of Work," The New York Times, October 02, 1997; Osthoff, Simone."From Stable Object to Participating Subject: content, meaning, and social context at ISEA97," New Art Examiner, February 1998, pp. 18–23.

4. Kac, E. "Transgenic Art", Leonardo Electronic Almanac, volume 6, number 11, 1998. Also: <http: //www.ekac.org/transgenic.html>. Republished in Gerfried Stocker and Christine Schopf (eds.), Ars Electronica '99 – Life Science (Vienna, New York: Springer, 1999), pp. 289–296.

5. At the time of writing, February 2003, canine reproductive technology is still not developed enough to enable the creation of a transgenic or cloned dog. However, research is underway to both map the dog genome and to develop canine IVF. Clearly, "GFP K-9" will be possible in the near future.

6. Kac, E. "Genesis," Gerfried Stocker and Christine Schopf (eds.), Ars Electronica '99 – Life Science (Vienna, New York: Springer, 1999), pp. 310–313. Also: <http: //www.ekac.org/geninfo.html>. "Genesis" was carried out with the assistance of Dr. Charles Strom, formerly Director of Medical Genetics, Illinois Masonic Medical Center, Chicago. Dr. Strom is now Medical Director, Biochemical and Molecular Genetics Laboratories Nichols Institute/Quest Diagnostics, San Juan Capistrano, CA. Original DNA music for Genesis was composed by Peter Gena.

7. Mudede, Charles. "The End of Art," The Stranger, volume 9, number 15, Dec. 30, 1999–Jan. 05, 2000, Seattle.

8. Kac, E. "GFP Bunny," in Dobrila, Peter T. and Kostic, Aleksandra (eds.), Eduardo Kac: Telepresence, Biotelematics, and Transgenic Art (Maribor, Slovenia: Kibla, 2000), pp. 101–131. Also: <http: //www.ekac.org/gfpbunny.html>.

9. I had proposed to live for one week with Alba in the Grenier à Sel, in Avignon, where Louis Bec directed the art festival "Avignon Numérique". In an e-mail broadcast in Europe on June 16, 2000, Bec wrote: "Contre notre volonté, le programme concernant «Artransgénique», qui devait se dérouler du 19 au 25 juin, se trouve modifié. Une décision injustifiable nous prive de la présence de Bunny GFP, le lapin transgénique fluorescent que nous comptions présenter aux Avignonnais et à l'ensemble des personnes intéressées par les évolutions

actuelles des pratiques artistiques. Malgré cette censure déguisée, l'artiste Brésilien Eduardo Kac, auteur de ce projet, sera parmi nous et présentera sa démarche ainsi que l'ensemble de ses travaux. Un débat public permettra d'ouvrir une large réflexion sur les transformations du vivant opérées par les biotechnologies, tant dans les domaines artistiques et juridiques, qu'éthiques et économiques. Nous nous élevons de toute évidence contre le fait qu'il soit interdit aux citoyens d avoir accès aux développements scientifiques et culturels qui les concernent si directement."

10. Cook, Gareth. "Cross hare: hop and glow," *Boston Globe*, 9/17/2000, p. A01.

11. For a bibliography on transgenic art, see: <http: //www.ekac.org/transartbiblio.html>.

12. http: //sprocket.telab.artic.edu/ekac/bunnybook.html.

13. These posters have also been shown in gallery exhibitions: Dystopia + Identity in the Age of Global Communications, curated by Cristine Wang, Tribes Gallery, New York, 2000; Under the Skin, curated by Söke Dinkla, Renate Heidt Heller and Cornelia Brueninghaus-Knubel, Wilhelm Lehmbruck Museum, Duisburg, 2001; "International Container Art Festival," Kaohsiung Museum of Fine Arts, Taiwan (from Dec. 8, 2001 to January 6, 2002); "Portão 2", Galeria Nara Roesler, São Paulo, Brazil (from March 21 to April 27, 2002); "Free Alba!", Julia Friedman Gallery, Chicago (from May 3 to June 15, 2002); "Eurovision – I Biennale d'Arte: DNArt; Transiti: Metamorfosi: Permanenze," Kunsthaus Merano Arte, Merano, Italy (from June 15 to August 15, 2002); "Gene(sis): Contemporary Art Explores Human Genomics," Henry Art Gallery, Seattle, from April 6 to August 25, 2002. See also the following catalogues: Under the Skin (Ostfilden-Ruit, Germany: Hatje Cantz Verlag, 2001), pp. 60–63; Eurovision – I Biennale d'Arte: DNArt; Transiti: Metamorfosi: Permanenze (Milano: Rizzoli, 2002), pp. 104–105; International Container Art Festival (Kaohsiung: Kaohsiung Museum of Fine Arts, 2002), pp. 86–87.

14. Stein, Lisa. "New Kac Show Takes a Look at Ethics, Rabbit," *Chicago Tribune*, May 10, 2002, p. 21.

15. In actuality, genes do not "produce" proteins. As Richard Lewontin clearly explains: "A DNA sequence does not specify protein, but only the amino acid sequence. The protein is one of a number of minimum free-energy foldings of the same amino acid chain, and the cellular milieu together with the translation process influences which of these foldings occurs." See: R. C. Lewontin, "In the Beginning Was the Word," *Science*, vol. 291, 16 February 2001, p. 1264.

16. In 1985, I purchased an issue of a magazine entitled *High Technology* whose cover headline read "Protein Engineering: Molecular Creations for Industry and Medicine." Clearly, the desire to "design" new molecular forms has been evolving for approximately two decades. See: Tucker, Jonathan B. "Proteins to Order. Computer graphics and gene splicing are helping researchers create new molecules for industry and medicine," *High Technology*, vol. 5, n.12, December 1985, pp. 26–34.

17. Special thanks to Dr. Murray Robinson, Head of Cancer Program, Amgen, Thousand Oaks, CA.

18. Protein visualization was carried out with the assistance of Charles Kazilek and Laura Eggink, BioImaging Laboratory, Arizona State University, Tempe.

19. Rapid prototyping was developed with the assistance of Dan Collins and James Stewart, Prism Lab, Arizona State University, Tempe.

20. Terms like "transcription," as well as "code," "translation," and many others commonly employed in molecular biology, betray an ideological stance, a conflation of linguistic metaphors and biological entities, whose rhetorical goal is to instrumentalize processes of life. In the words of Lily E. Kay, this merger integrates "the notion of the genetic code as relation with that of a DNA code as thing." See: Kay, Lily E., *Who Wrote the Book of Life: A History of the Genetic Code* (Stanford, Calif.: Stanford University Press, 2000), p. 309. For a thorough critique of the rhetorical strategies of molecular biology, see: Doyle, Richard, *On Beyond Living: Rhetorical Transformations of the Life Sciences* (Stanford, Calif.: Stanford University Press, 1997).

21. The "Eighth Day" team: Richard Loveless, Dan Collins, Sheilah Britton, Jeffery (Alan) Rawls, Jean Wilson-Rawls, Barbara Eschbach, Julia Friedman, Isa Gordon, Charles Kazilek, Ozzie Kidane, George Pawl, Kelly Phillips, David Lorig, Frances Salas, and James Stewart. Additional thanks to Andras Nagy, Samuel Lunenfeld Research Institute, Toronto; Richard Firtel, University of California, San Diego; Chi-Bin Chien, University of Utah, Salt Lake City; and Neal Stewart, University of North Carolina at Greensboro. I developed "The Eighth Day" through a two-year residency at the Institute of Studies in the Arts, Arizona State University, Tempe. The exhibition dates: October 25 to November 2, 2001. Exhibition location: Computer Commons Gallery, Arizona State University, Tempe (with the support of the Institute of Studies in the Arts). Documentation can be found at: <http://www.ekac.org/8thday.html>.

22. See Brown T. A. Genomes (Oxford, UK: Bios scientific publishers, 1999), p. 138; and Baltimore, David. "Our genome unveiled," *Nature* 409, 15 February 2001, pp. 814–816. In private e-mail correspondence (28 January 2002), and as a follow up to our previous conversation on the topic, Dr. Jens Reich, Division of Genomic Informatics of the Max Delbruck Center in Berlin-Buch, stated: "The explanation for these massive [viral] inserts into our genome (which, incidentally, looks like a garbage bin anyway) is usually that these elements were acquired into germ cells by retrovirus infection and subsequent dispersion over the genome some 10 to 40 millions ago (as we still were early apes)." The HGP also suggests that humans have hundreds of bacterial genes in the genome. See: International Human Genome Sequencing Consortium. "Initial sequencing and analysis of the human genome," 15 February 2001, volume 409, no. 6822, p. 860. Of the 223 genes coding for proteins that are also present in bacteria and in vertebrates, 113 cases are believed to be confirmed. See p. 903 of the same issue. In the same correspondence mentioned above, Dr. Reich concluded: "It appears that it is not man, but all vertebrates who are transgenic in the sense that they acquired a gene from a microorganism."

23. This natural ability has made a genetically engineered version of the agrobacterium a favorite tool of molecular biology. See: Herrera-Estrella L. (1983). Transfer and expression of foreign genes in plants. Ph.D. thesis. Laboratory of Genetics, Gent University, Belgium; Hooykaas p. J. J. and Shilperoort R. A. (1992). Agrobacterium and plant genetic engineering. Plant Molecular Biology 19: 15–38; Zupan J. R. and Zambryski p. C. (1995). Transfer of T-DNA from Agrobacterium to the plant cell. Plant Physiology 107: 1041–1047.

# LEARNING THROUGH THE RE-EMBODIMENT OF THE DIGITAL SELF

## Yacov Sharir

This chapter discusses technologically mediated interactive art and the complex ways by which it can be applied in educating artists. Its aim is to demonstrate how performance augmentation (as a practice) can serve as primary objective for implementing a viable learning process. It explores how the disembodied digital self is re-embodied in cyber-bodies occupying increasingly immersive cyber-worlds. Through interactive collaborative art that embodies the principles of team "deep" listening processes, the ability to converse and respect each other's ideas, conceive, and conceptualize, students ultimately learn to create artworks where art, science, technology, and culture intersect.

I draw upon my own lifelong quest as an artist to come to understand this complex multidisciplinary trans-cultural learning process and its implications for educating young artists. My artistic journey from creating ceramic sculpture to dance, from choreography to digital animation, from collaboration to interactivity, and from Israel to Texas, color my work as a teacher addressing the remarkable growth in experimental, interactive, technologically mediated art with research related to human and social issues. These experiences spring from a field with a multi-disciplinary and trans-disciplinary character based on the foundation of the last several decades of experiments, developments, and growth.

### Learning through Body (Dance) and Material (Clay)
My artistic quest had its origins in my violin lessons at age eleven in Israel in the late 1950s. My violin teacher immigrated to Israel from Rumania. His way of teaching and playing his instrument embodied the gypsy way of experiencing music, which is to say

– you are wearing the music over and on you as if it has become your second skin. Music was his way of life, all day, every day.

The uncompromising value related to my first art teacher's artistic way of teaching lies in his insistence on embodying in me/his students notions related to the overall mood, the atmosphere, the colors, and the appreciation of/for meaning. "Tell me your story," he would say. "This is not very interesting," he commented while all I was looking for is to survive, to clearly deliver my notes. Nothing was predetermined in the structure of his lessons. They had more to do with his workshop-like way of teaching, as if we were in a lab of sorts. Paying insufficient attention to his instructional messages with all of its multiple meanings was not the thing to do.

Looking for the mood, the atmosphere, the colors, the meaning, and the story deeply influenced my artistic development, my ways of working and teaching. Time and time again, I am finding myself instructing my students as to how they can mutually build content and meaning before they embark on the pursuit of their technologically mediated collaborative assignments.

Clearly, this invaluable experience was not exclusively about the music per se, it was as much about the aesthetics, unity, and coherence by way of demonstration and execution. The impact of my first encounter with the pursuit of my music/art studies was immeasurable.

At age thirteen, I joined Kibbutz Mesillot, a communal farming community in the northwest part of Israel. Initially, the break away from home was quite difficult. However, life in the kibbutz proved to be extremely stimulating, productive, well structured, and disciplined. Needless to say, I was grateful for this opportunity. I learned about contributing back to my community by way of working and learning and most importantly, I learned ways of sharing personal responsibilities and resources. However, unlike my violin lessons where the music, the concepts of aesthetic and emotional experience, could be personal and sometimes vague, no room for ambiguity and hesitation was allowed in this communal way of growing up.

Soon the sense of immediacy and appreciation struck me, without postponement. I joined the regional choir and the regional folk dance company where I picked up the skill of fast and diverse footwork and the rhythms that represented multiple cultural sensibilities from throughout the world simultaneously converging in Israel while attempting to co-exist in harmony. The versatility and skill of my newly acquired footwork and communal way of dancing proved to be important and useful for my later studies and professional work as a modern dance practitioner with the Bat-Sheva Dance Company of Israel. Interestingly, the clear sense of enjoyment and appreciation of meaning and value did not deny the opportunity for reflection and greater intensity needed for the pursuit of my tendencies for multi-tasking and varied interests.

By the time I completed my high school studies at age eighteen, I could play the violin, sing in a choir, and perform folkdances. Most importantly, I learned how to listen, which later on in my life was most valuable and instrumental in the creation of collaborative trans-disciplinary artworks. Although these various abilities may seem to belong to very different disciplines, for myself they were all situated in the body with all of its preliminary explicit kinesthetic understandings, increasingly occupying the space around me in more educated intelligent ways from sculpting the body to learning how to dance and sing. Emphasizing the body's expressive role allowed me to attend and listen to it, gradually figuring out what the body could say about itself.

Then the big change, on to military service. Like every other Israeli citizen, the pursuit of my art related studies was interrupted due to my service in the Israeli Navy. However, that did not constitute an interruption in my overall growth and learning process. Three years of service proved to be an invaluable asset, learning about responsibility, discipline, leadership, and most importantly perseverance. Once these assets and qualities were acquired they have been applied in all of my future endeavors.

Although military service was a profoundly valuable growing and learning experience, my heart, wishes, and aspirations were in continuing my pursuit of art studies and practice. Acceptance to the premier Israeli art school, Bezalel Academy of Arts and Design in Jerusalem, was at the time a life-changing experience and one of the happiest periods of my life. My major and concentration were in ceramics and sculpture. However, studio art studies at the academy included drawing, painting, and art history courses and occasional meetings/interactions with prominent visual artists from around the world who were visiting Jerusalem. Simultaneously, I entered as a part-time student at the Jerusalem Rubin Academy of Music and Dance and began a more formal modern dance training regiment.

Working with the body (dance) and with material (clay) imaginatively with all of the possible potential collaborative and creative potency helped me to pick up fruitful ideas related to my own creative process and art-making beyond what I have experienced prior to joining the academy. This time was central to my artistic development, relentlessly and rigorously expanding the pursuit of my primary objectives.

Interestingly, in my work it became clear that the "body" and "material" are two co-existing entities having two related purposes. The first was to explicate what the 'body" is in term of its potential expressiveness. This became a central and distinctive aspect of my live-art work. The second and main purpose is to argue that body, like material, when serving the same purpose, is an efficacious means in the development, understanding, and promotion of my artwork.

As I became increasingly more experienced with the technology of my dancing body, I entered the process of understanding the totality of its wisdom and its intelligence from within, consciously considering the fullness of bodily sensations governed by a greater kinesthetic acuteness – "propri-oception."

Meanwhile, armed with these new notions – collaborative working and learning across disciplines – I began to understand what was required in order to attend to new ideas primarily related to consensus formation. The opportunities to design for dance performances required developing new skills of inclusiveness (directors/performers), dancing and posing for drawing lessons, required unconquerable enjoyable self-assurance and exhibitionistic tendencies. In short, crossing the boundaries between the various disciplines was not enough, sharpening perceptions, mutual development of accepted language were preconditions and practices necessary to assure productivity.

My first sensation related to the use of my body in support and on behalf of my friends/students was in drawing lessons at the academy. Experiencing both, being the student and the model, questions arise as to how I can refigure (as one or the other) in order to juxtapose myself in the foreground of everyone else's drawing papers/canvases. Identity related issues emerged; images of the self without acquired memories of spoiled or fouled identity.

An additional significant activity while pursuing my studies in Jerusalem was my association with the Jerusalem Students Folk Dance Company, a very well machined and still fully active touring and performing organization. A serious regiment included weekly regular practice hours, performing and touring, and attending international folk dance festivals.

Following my graduation from Bezalel, I moved to Tel Aviv, opened my own private ceramics school, admitting individual independent artists. I practiced ceramics, sculpture, and set design for the next thirteen years. Simultaneously, I was asked to join the prestigious newly formed Bat-Sheva Dance Company, a professional modern dance troupe of the highest international level/quality and reputation. Being a member of the company while I was also practicing my ceramic/sculpture work, positioned me very well to also design sets and costumes for several of the shows where I was also acting as a performer. At this point in my professional career, considering the various and multiple disciplines I was passionately pursuing, I was not at all sure how to measure importance any more. Initially, I felt a need to sort out my confusion as to where my emphasis should be placed. But then more precisely, a major question arose – for what and in which context?

Reflection on artistic and aesthetic experiences can form part of that experience itself. Whether I dance, choreograph, sculpt, or make pottery, I experience things from my own physical point of view. What I see is usually a function of what might be and the attitude I adapt that is relative to the subject at hand. Interestingly, at this point in my professional development I served as the "performer" – as a dancer – and as the "creator" – ceramicist/sculptor. Confusion? No. I enjoyed the immediacy, that creative moment to be treasured as it comes. Focusing exclusively on the artistic and aesthetic output lead to an embodied experience and a deeper sense of elevated self-worth in ways that made it more central in addressing concerns and anxieties related to how to handle it all.

Extensive dance performances and international touring schedule followed, simultaneously, museum and solo art gallery's commissions materialized, too. Needless to say multidisciplinary collaborative partnerships were integrated to the fullest in order for me to deliver the works. Also considering the increased experience about the technology of my dancing body, I had realized the process of understanding the totality of its wisdom and its intelligence from within, consciously considering the fullness of bodily sensations governed by a greater kinesthetic acuteness and the three-dimensionality of it all, both in the physical realm and as applied in my studio art work/output.

Twelve years of professional work followed, dictated by very stringent criteria to satisfy my personal needs as a creator and as a performer with the Bat-Sheva Dance Company of Israel. Ultimately this was an extremely rewarding experience reaching in practice at all levels, professional growth, acquired life images, visually rich, subtle with clear three-dimensional characteristics followed by appropriate praise and recognition.

However the boundaries of my cross-disciplinary experiences started to blur, my feeling was that I was beginning to rotate around my own axis, questions regarding the non-singularity of being and the sense of self as linked to time and place surfaced. What does that mean as this reflects upon my inter-dynamics of the work I was making? It appears appropriate now to consider where my dance performance and creative media art content platform are.

Before embarking on reviewing my past thirteen years as it applies to future projects, new options, practice, and conceptual concerns, I began to plan my future well into the next decade and beyond. It was evoked by a sense of "settled in familiarity" that began to cause mental and physical fatigue. Operating on muscle memory alone and responding with a great deal of familiarity was not a desired experience for continuing to provoke my creativity.

In 1979, I responded positively and enthusiastically to an offer from Texas to establish/form the first American Deaf Dance Company and the offer of a teaching position at the Department of Theatre and Dance of University of Texas at Austin. The opportunity to become a member of the faculty at a major research university facilitated new and exciting teaching, research, and professional work. Under my artistic directorship – shortly following its inception – the American Deaf Dance Company became the University of Texas College of Fine Arts "Company in Residence." It fostered new alliances with members of the fine arts faculty, architecture, engineering, and computer science that instantly lead to collaborative teaching, research, and performance. My important and unique program was supported by the National Endowment for the Arts, the Texas Commission on the Arts, the City of Austin and major local, regional, and national foundations and corporations.

The artistic works I have been exploring at that time led to analyzing the very initial implications of suggested use of digital technologies specifically as they related to artmaking, early ideas on interactivity, and some talks about the Internet that allow people to shift their visual experience of seeing what happens simultaneously together with everybody else.

## Art/Dance and Virtual Environments

Pioneering networking efforts among faculty at the University of Texas led to very fruitful collaborative and team teaching alliances not only locally but also through the formation of sister classes with other major universities in the USA and Canada (Seattle, Washington, Salt Lake City, Utah, Vancouver, British Columbia). These efforts soon became our learning grounds. Students and faculty alike conceived and made work locally and through distance by utilizing early means of visual communications (the first version of "see-you-see-me" software among other options). The aim was for both artists and technologists to collaborate across disciplines and across geographical borders. Anything we could find/make/invent at the time was put to use for the realization of this purpose. Distance learning was conceptualized and set in motion.

The electronic music faculty and graduate students had a much earlier head start over all other participants with the use of electronic and computerized technologies for researching and creating new sound-based material/works. Music technologists also were ahead in conceiving and making extensive use of gestural interfaces (instruments) for sonic production and processing. This was of huge importance for supporting our purpose at the time, specifically the interface idea being made tangible as mappings between performative input (gestural) and output (aural). These materials and related research were generously shared and put to use in our collaborative teaching and artmaking for the benefit of all participants.

The introduction of the personal computer (Mac +) revolutionized our ways of thinking and conceptualizing in relation to teaching and artmaking. Our initial intent in the introduction of computer technologies was to reinvent and explicate what collaborative and joint teaching could achieve as pedagogical practice and as an art form. It evolved, however, into a distinctive new field.

Some of the faculty and students involved argued that the introduction of technologically mediated studies might jeopardize the original pedagogical purpose. However, it created new terms in aesthetic theory, reconceptualized narrative structure, and employed new sound effects. Its very physical and virtual embodiment was too important to ignore. We recognized that the practice of technological augmentation in artmaking is not only an excellent vehicle for the promotion of transdisciplinary collaborations, but it created a new paradigm for what it is and what it could become.

In 1991, our collaborative team responded positively to a call for proposals from the Banff Centre for the Arts in Canada inviting artists or groups of artists to submit ideas for projects. This call initiated the first and only arts and virtual environments project to date. Its stated purpose was to provide opportunities for artists to work with emerging technologies as a means of forging new artistic options that facilitate the mutation of cultural practice. A new medium like virtual reality challenges traditional conventions. Douglas Macleod, the Virtual Environments project director, stated: "Artists no longer sit on the sidelines eventually to become grateful users of borrowed tools but have become active in development, creating a disturbance in the field with new contingencies."

My artwork, *Dancing with the Virtual Dervish: Virtual Bodies*, was conceived and set in motion. In the book, *Immersed in Technology: Art and Virtual Environments*, I wrote:

> As a choreographer and dancer, I create work kinesthetically, emphasizing movement, space, and the body. Through the Virtual Environments project, I questioned what worlds open when, as a dancer, I consider virtual environments in relation to the body. What artistic, intellectual, kinesthetic, and emotional issues could be addressed using this technology? How could these technologies affect the creation and experience by a dancer and by others? (Moser and MacLeod 1996: 283)

The opportunity to co-exist during performance – simultaneously – both grounded in physical space while at the same time being fully immersed in the virtual realm was the primary factor that stimulated my imagination and ultimately allowed the concept of the dervish-like experience/tradition to emerge. I continued to explain:

> Through the pursuit of this fantastical opportunity/project I begin to understand that virtual technologies allow us to manipulate, extend, distort, and deform information as well as our experience of the body. Furthermore, they serve as a vehicle that enables us to extend and color work in many ways, some of which are not possible in the physical realm and/or by traditional means. They offer a way to augment and extend possibilities creatively, experientially, spatially, visually, sonically, and cognitively. (Moser and MacLeod 1996: 283)

*Dancing with the Virtual Dervish: Virtual Bodies* is among the first virtual environment projects to synthesize immersive digitized new dance in a distributed performance environment that includes a head-mounted display, data-glove, three-dimensional sound, and interactive video projections. These technologies combined and set in sync and harmony, allowed me in performance to create multidimensional dance while interacting, navigating, and experiencing the environment virtually.

By the end of March 1994, visual artist Diane Gromala, architect Marcos Novak, and myself completed a two-year fellowship at the Banff Centre for the Arts, where we had collaborated on *Dancing with the Virtual Dervish: Virtual Bodies*, which was first performed at the Arts and Virtual Environment Symposium held in conjunction with the Fourth International Cyberspace Conference at Banff in May 1994.

Clearly the augmented level of knowledge, technological know-how, and experience gathered during the two-year fellowship working toward the realization of this project hugely impacted my personal, present, and future perceptions related to pedagogy, team teaching, and collaborative transdisciplinary work-making and consensus-building. Consequently, changes had to be considered and implemented in ways that positively and productively reflected the newness of what I had learned and accomplished.

Additionally, the magnitude, the scale, the attention, and efforts needed by each team of seven to bring these projects to a performative conclusion were beyond what we had originally anticipated. Participation in these projects contributed to our better

understanding of earlier perceptions related to the extravagant promises of technology. How will it make our students smarter and better artists? If we could place students in computer labs and smart classrooms, we would revolutionize the learning experience and see a miracle occur by real performative magic. We need only watch it to take place. A course, "Virtual Reality and Cyberspace in the Arts," was conceived and offered without interruption every spring semester since 1995. This course is preceded by a computer animation and 3-D modeling course offered every fall semester, thus allowing students from across the disciplines at the University of Texas to complete a sequence of two classes in new media arts. During the last three years, this sequence has been integrated in the "Bridging Disciplines Program: Digital Arts and Media" program at College of Fine Arts at the University of Texas at Austin. Teaching these courses has led to my doctoral dissertation at the Planetary Collegium, "Beyond the Electronic Connection," in which I explore theories related to convergence identities – the technologically manufactured cyber-human and its physical-human counterpart engaged in performance.

## Computer Animation, Virtual Reality, and the Immersive Body

How can a learning community begin to engage in a process of conceptualizing and making art in this emerging field that integrates art/dance with science/technology? What are the worlds that open up to us when we consider interactive technologies and the studies of virtual environments in education? What are the artistic, intellectual, visceral, and emotional issues which can be addressed using the opportunities of these technologies?

My pedagogical program focuses on the intersecting location of where science, art, and technology merge. It includes a sequence of two back-to-back courses that complement each other by means of their content and pedagogy. The first course, "Computer Animation and 3D Modeling," concentrates on concept-building techniques and on the creation of multiple projects. My theoretical focus is to develop the platform for class attendees to act as producers of meaning, employ strategies and develop skills that are essentially conversational in form.

This course includes a strong and fast turnaround of several small works that facilitate students acquiring technological knowledge, and, most importantly, the art of understanding how to engage in internal conversations and mutually arrive at a consensus about the creative process and the task at hand. Studies are supported by presentations and reading assignments (see bibliography) that are designed to provide students with opportunities to become familiar with cultural backgrounds, critical theories, and analytic tools. An additional strong component in this course includes discussions and critiques of mature finished works and related writings.

Course objectives include: the introduction to concepts of computerized, high-end, human character animation programs, the creation and understanding of 3-D virtual worlds, and how interactive technologies can support/augment many aspects of performance. Students learn how to explore the various software-editing programs as effective tools for the creation of human pedestrian movement, video games, and avatar personalities. Additional choreographic, theatrical, directorial, and or compositional tools are also explored.

The studies overall line of energy is motivated by the seductive powers and agency of interactive art and virtual reality that stimulate students' imagination as learners and researchers. As these options are explored, students notice that their disembodied self can be re-embodied in cyber-bodies occupying increasingly immersive cyber-worlds through the powerful sensations of wearable computers. The self-descriptive, self-reflexive, and recursive processes of consciousness reveal themselves as events that simultaneously express the real and virtual, flesh and re-configuration, sensory presence and re-presentation, cognition and re-cognition. In the ordinary flow of conscious experience, these pairs are not encountered as binary oppositions in conflict, but in continual events of transformation, one into the other. Students experience convergence with their own creations and learning utilizing various technological tools – giving birth to new ideas and new gestures of consciousness. Their interests, artistic learning, and practices eventually converge – literally and figuratively – in the zone of postures, gestures, gaming ideas, and communication between real, and virtual worlds, and the effects on consciousness of such cognitive spatial practices and learning.

Following the conclusion of the first technologically charged semester they are armed with augmented vision about making artworks and with technological knowledge. They are better able to conceptualize and see things from places where they are not necessarily physically present. With time-shifting technologies, they can also see things flow into the future and understand times and places they may have never have visited before.

The second semester course, "Virtual Reality and Cyber Space in The Arts," represents a progression into studies that primarily require collaborative efforts leading toward the realization of a fully integrated interactive work. The course is an intensive general introduction to the theory, principles, and practice of performance augmentation through the construction and use of an original interactive system of choice. It initially facilitates a set of conversations, learning about the notion of deep listening and the art of conversation and collaborative thinking towards generating a narrative. It then provides an overview of leading theories related to interface design and opportunities to work with interactive equipment and multiple sensory devices that serve as the core elements for the production of an interactive work of their own. Students collaboratively seek to create an intensive, highly productive workshop/laboratory environment. Their hands-on artmaking is supplemented by lectures and presentations on such topics as art theory, communications, choreography, cyberspace philosophy, robotics, privacy, and electronic publications. The works created must demonstrate that they can exist in a virtual environment. At the conclusion of this semester, students demonstrate their understanding and use of sensorial devices, motion tracking systems, real-time video manipulation, and virtual reality immersive environments.

The technological exploration in the classroom is mediated through the use of computerized information and content that typically responds to our direct commands for well-formed actions, but not to our spontaneously evolving inner desires and emergent ideas.

A topic of discussion and theoretical exploration addresses issues that suggest the creation of alternative systems, such as gestural recombinant knowledge and the human body and space visualization systems as a mean for augmenting creative innovation. Further exploration in the classroom deals with ideas of complex layering of language, image, and communication between physical and virtual constructs. The intention is to bring to the forefront the shifting strata of memory, dreams, and conscious visualization of content and matter, as we/they know it at the current level of inquiry.

As students become immersed in the ongoing process of technological exploration, serious questions emerge suggesting topologies of temporality. Questions arise as to the role of the physical body, resisting what it could become and notions of embodiment as machines. Students flirt with the subversive qualities of suggested magnified understanding of representation. In other words, they begin to experience the intersections between the grounded human, their own physicality experienced in physical space, and the immersive/virtual experience occurring simultaneously – the duality of existence. No matter how deeply involved they become in this process, the major issues and questions remain, suggesting dramaturgy of performance content, internal and external time, and consciousness continually reframed.

## Works Cited

Andersen, p. B. and Callesen, J. (2001), "Agents as Actors." in Qvortrup, L. (ed.) *Virtual Interaction: Interaction in Virtual 3D Worlds*. Springer-Verlag.

Artaud, A. *The Theater and Its Double*. (1966), Richards, M. C. (trans.) New York: Grove Press.

Ascott, Roy, "Is There Love in the Telematic Embrace." *Art Journal* 49: 3 (Fall 1990), 241–247.

Ascott, R. (2003), *Telematic Embrace: Visionary Theories of Art Technology and Consciousness*. Shanken, E. A. (ed.) Berkeley: University of California Press.

Bataille, G. (1994), *On Nietzsche*. Boone, B. (trans.) New York: Paragon House.

Cage, J. (1966), *Silence*. Cambridge, MA: MIT Press.

Derida, J. (1970), *The Double Session: Dissemination*. Johnson, B. (trans.) Chicago: University of Chicago Press.

Dixon, S. "Absent Fiends: Internet theatre, Posthuman Bodies and the Interactive Void." *Performance Arts International*, Presence online issue. <http: //www.mdx.ac.uk/www/epai/presencesite/index.html>.

Heidegger, M. (1991), *Nietzsche: Vol.1, The Will to Power as Art*. San Francisco: Harper San Francisco.

Laban, R. (1974), *The Language of Movement: A Guidebook to Choreutics*. Ullmann, L. (ed.) Boston: Plays, Inc.

Laurel, B. (1993), *Computers as Theatre*. Reading, MA: Addison-Wesley.

Little, G. (1998), *A Manifesto for Avatars*. http: //art.bgsu.edu/-glittle/ava_text_1.html.

Manovich, L. (2002), *The Language of New Media*. Cambridge, MA: MIT Press.

Massumi, B. (2002), "The Evolutionary Alchemy of Reason." *Parables for the Virtual*. Durham and London (eds.) Durham, NC: Duke University Press.

Moser, M. A. and MacLeod, D. (1996), *Immersed in Technology: Art and Virtual Environments*, Cambridge, MA: Leonardo Books, MIT Press.

# My Journey: From Physics to Graphic Design to User-Interface/Information-Visualization Design

## Aaron Marcus

Who am I? Why am I here? What should I be doing? These are questions that consumed a fair amount of my time and energy as a younger person in his teens and twenties. Now that I am nearing the "sunset years" of my working career as a designer and artist involved with computer graphics and visual communication, it is a well-timed and delightful challenge to think about educating designers and artists for the future by considering some past issues and their resolution in my own career.

I hope that this reverie will be of interest to some designers/artists and may serve them, and their teachers, as a springboard for consideration of how to prepare students for an age of ubiquitous computing, virtual social networks, cross-national cultures, and access, from one's current location, to almost any text, image, sound, and experience from any time and place. To design for a worldwide sensorium, a world of unimaginable size, density, variety, intensity, and activity, in which much is changing rapidly even while powerful economic and political forces grind slowly, relentlessly onward, will challenge all that we have as human, corporeal, mental, cognitive, spiritual, and emotional beings.

**In the Beginning**
Like some people, and especially some designers and artists, I was always interested in both science/technology and visual communication. As a small child growing up in Omaha, Nebraska, in the 1950s (I was born in 1943), I was interested in astronomy and paleontology, and I enjoyed drawing cartoons. At the ages of four and seven, my younger, late brother Stephen and I would play-act conversations involving our teddy

bears Katzy and Baby before we would go to sleep on our bunk beds. I remember imagining that there was a Big Book of Knowledge in which one could look up the answer to any question (an early pre-Web fantasy, perhaps). I recall theorizing that babies grew on trees, like apples and oranges, and fell off when they were ripe (my knowledge of biology was apparently limited). At the age of about 10 to 13, I constructed a pretend rocket-ship control room in a corner of the basement, by means of which my brother and I would take trips to imaginary planets. Built out of old radio parts and other paraphernalia gleaned from local trash cans, the system featured blinking light bulbs to lend an aura of authenticity. During this period, around 10 to 15, I also taught myself to draw cartoons in the style of major professionals of the day: Walt Disney (the Disney characters), Al Cap (Li'l Abner), Walter Lance (Pogo and friends), etc. Later, in secondary school, I taught myself photography, painting, and calligraphy (e.g., chancery cursive and other well-known styles).

This left-brain, right-brain parallelism continued throughout college. At Princeton University, I majored in physics with a minor in philosophy and mathematics, but I also participated in painting, drawing, printmaking, and letterpress printing workshops informally, in addition to official art history classes. I often dreamed of leaving my seemingly pre-ordained path leading me to work as a research scientist in some corporate laboratory and fleeing, as an undergraduate transfer, to a school like the Rhode Island School of Design (RISD) in Providence, RI, USA, about which I had learned. By the time I graduated with a B.A. and completed my senior physics thesis involving using lasers to study the refraction of light by gallium phosphide crystals, I had come to the conclusion that I must try out at least one year in a career path through the uncharted (for me) fields of art and design. Being ambivalent and nervous about leaving a known career for an unknown one, I applied not only to graduate schools of physics (like the University of Michigan's, where I would have worked with the inventor of the maser, which led to the laser, and the University of Pennsylvania), but also art and design schools (like RISD, the Art Institute of Chicago, Cooper Union, Pratt Institute, and one graduate school, the Graphic Design Department in Yale University's School of Art and Architecture). Yale's program was the only one that offered me, at that time (1965), the opportunity to study for an extra initial year to "catch up" on a missing undergraduate education in art/design, and graduate in two more years with a master's degree. I was accepted at all of the schools at which I applied, but on the waiting list at Yale. What to do? Five days before I was graduated from Princeton, I received word that I had been accepted at Yale. Relieved and avoiding a nervous breakdown, I shifted my expectations of life and of myself.

During three years at Yale, I had full access to all the art and design courses I might want: painting, drawing, photography, filmmaking, printmaking, calligraphy, typography and printing, and corporate-oriented graphic design. I was so excited by all of the new experiences that I barely slept for three years, spending most of my time at my drawing table, in the photo darkroom, or in studios. I remember distinctly that, for the first six months at an art/design school, I had trouble understanding what people meant by what they were saying: what was it that "worked" or "didn't work"? Eventually meaning filled in behind the initially obscure terminology, and I realized that what I was doing was similar to what I had done in physics labs: using theories and conjectures to guide one's experiments. One looked for patterns of cause and effect, behaviors, procedures, and results. What had become odious to me in physics (the experimental lab; I preferred theoretical physics, the study of space-time and gravitation, etc.) seemed delightful, serious, acceptable play in graphic design.

At Yale, I also began the study of computer science, taking a course in basic functioning of computers, and I learned FORTRAN programming at the Yale Computer Center. At that time, all departments and graduate schools were encouraged to use the "new" mainframe computers with time-sharing and were granted free time as an inducement to become involved. I became, to my knowledge, the only student in the Art and Architecture School to take advantage of this offer in 1966. By the spring of 1967, when AT&T Bell Labs staff scientists came to the campus to interview potential engineers and scientists, I went to an interview session with Peter Denes and A. Michael Noll who were visiting from the Labs. I apologized for my peculiar background in design/art and computers and mentioned that I probably was wasting their time. They looked at each other and smiled knowingly; they were looking for someone with exactly my background. From that summer of 1967 spent at Murray Hill, my life changed direction again. During that year I had the opportunity to work with the most powerful computers in the world and met many strange, interesting people from the worlds of computer science, art, and design. Some of my first computer art was generated during that summer based on simple mathematical algorithms that would produce elaborate, intricate, startlingly complex, yet also simple, graceful graphics of vectors and points of light recorded on high-resolution microfilm.

I began thinking about how artists and designers could work with computers and wrote one of my first articles on this subject in 1968 published in a new art/design magazine at Yale called *Eye*.

### Starting My Professional Career
When I was graduated, I once again was uncertain about what I was going to do. The Vietnam War was being waged, and I was certain to be called up for the draft. Again, unexpected events occurred. In 1967, I suffered a partially collapsed lung in the medical pavilion of the Worlds Fair in Montréal while on a class design study trip. That condition kept me out of the draft. I applied for and won a Fulbright scholarship to do post-graduate study abroad at the Ulm School of Design, one of the most eminent in the world at the time. Unfortunately, the *New York Times* reported at the same time that the school had collapsed from student revolts and faculty-administration-government strife. Ulm had ceased to exist only a few weeks before I was scheduled to go to Europe to begin one year abroad at a non-existent institution. Again, uncertainty reigned. One day, at about this time, the communal student phone rang at the school, and Emilio Ambasz invited me to join the faculty of the Princeton University School of Architecture and

Urban Planning. An unusually bright, forceful Argentinian, he had begun as an undergraduate with me at Princeton, but by the time I had finished my undergraduate career, he had zoomed far ahead, quickly obtained a Ph.D., and immediately began teaching at Princeton. He was then also the Assistant Curator for Design at the Museum of Modern Art, New York. He invited me to take over his basic design course, which, with much trepidation, I did.

During my first, unexpected year back on the Princeton campus, I had to set up a complete graphic design facility modeled after my experience at Yale. I was trying to help undergraduate and graduate architecture and urban planning students learn how to communicate more effectively the essential ideas and accomplishments of their designs. I also discovered that my design education at Yale had been somewhat narrow. I was now learning about design theorists, systematic approaches to design and visual communication, semiotics/semiologie, scholars like Umberto Eco and Roland Barthes, etc., that I might have learned at Ulm, had that trip not been cancelled. In effect, I received my "post-graduate" year of education in my first year teaching at Princeton.

I also became the Director of the letterpress printing facility in the Visual Arts Program at Princeton, in which I had a joint appointment. It was a strange turn of events that I was now teaching the kind of people I had been as an undergraduate only three years earlier. What made it additionally unusual for me was that there were now female students (when I was an undergraduate, Princeton enrolled only male students). And to top it off, I was teaching in a building that was formerly a primary school. In fact, my printing presses and type were located in the former kindergarten room of that school, the very school and very room in which my first wife, who was born and raised in Princeton, had gone to school twenty years earlier.

Over a nine-year period, I taught many bright students as much as I could about typography, color, layout, publication design, exhibit design, computer graphics, concrete/visual poetry, environmental graphics, history/philosophy of design (systematic design, information design, information visualization, etc.), and history/philosophy of visual communication (semiotics, experimental forms, historical forms, other cultural forms). Among my most famous students was Ms. Lisa Hallaby, who became Queen Noor of Jordan, and who, thirty years later, invited me to give the first-ever workshop in user-interface design in the Kingdom of Jordan. During this period, I also created and taught my first computer graphics course for "the two cultures" (borrowing C. P. Snow's term), i.e., the world of the humanities and the world of science/engineering. I attempted to pair up students from the two cultures and have them work in teams on projects of visual communication using the computer graphics laboratories on campus at the time (about 1976).

During these years, I also became a consultant in computer graphics at Bell Labs, Murray Hill (1969–71). At that time, raster-scan displays had been connected to be driven by computers for the first time. Around the corner from my office, Brian Kernighan and

Dennis Ritchie were inventing Unix. Ken Knowlton was inventing computer animation. Max Mathews was inventing computer music (some of which, like the "Daisy, Daisy..." computer speech/song later would be used in the movie "2001"), and A. Michael Noll was inventing computer-generated dance display and computer simulations of art (e.g., Mondrian). In the corridors and in the cafeteria, I would bump into artists whom Bell Labs was inviting to visit to interact with technology people: the video artist Nam June Paik, the cinematographer Stan Brakhage, and others.

The project that I eventually completed was programming a desktop publishing system for the Picturephone.™ For my somewhat humble task, I had to think about what users would need to see on a screen in order to lay out Yellow Pages, how type would be displayed and manipulated, and how they would interact with images. I published a case study in *Visible Language* (Marcus 1971d). This experience moved me along in my understanding of user needs/wants and towards the concept of the user interface, although the term did not, to my knowledge, exist until the late 1970s.

In 1977, I left Princeton and moved my wife, Susan, son Joshua, and daughter Elisheva to Jerusalem, to begin a new life in Israel. I was teaching simultaneously at the Bezalel Academy of Art and Design (in the Graphic Design Department and in the Industrial Design Department) and at the Hebrew University (in the Geography Department and in the Communications Institute). Neither institution knew that I had another "full-time position." As a result of mis-matched academic schedules, at one point in February 1978 for about two weeks, I was teaching seven studio and lecture courses simultaneously, or about a 40-hour contact-time schedule. Eventually, I burned myself out, and I could not work out a permanent teaching position at either institution. I did not quite fit into either one as a combination artist, designer, researcher, teacher, and writer. I had hoped to take over a new computer graphics laboratory at Bezalel, but it had collapsed in political and pedagogic controversy just before I arrived. Once again, timing was everything, not only positively, but negatively. I did the best I could. Just when I did not know what to do, an unexpected letter arrived from Sheila deBretteville, now Chair of the Graphic Design Department, Yale, asking if I would like to substitute for her at the East-West Center, a research institute in Honolulu, for six months. I jumped at the opportunity to re-enter the USA academic/professional world. Just then, my ex-wife and I caught hepatitis, and we had to be kept in quarantine for a month in Princeton after we recovered enough strength to return to the USA.

Relocating to Hawaii was a challenge, but we did it successfully, and I had an opportunity to head a five-person team whose objective was to invent a new pictographic-ideographic storytelling system of signs, charts, maps, and diagrams to communicate a very complex subject: global energy interdependence. The target audience included heads of state, economists and other scientists, as well as teachers and the general public. The East-West Center had come to the realization that not everyone was interested in their 600-page reports about the key issues facing world civilization. For that project, I invited Yukio Ota, a friend and colleague, and one of

Japan's key sign designers, to join me. Our team designed more than 1000 icons and symbols and completed our project, showing the special presentation in many countries. This project convinced me to change my professional career to information design and visualization through computer graphics.

I relocated my family again to Berkeley, California, where I was able to secure a teaching position at the University of California, once again in an architecture department. Once again, I could not secure a permanent position because there were few places in the world where one could devote full attention to computer graphics, information design and visualization, and theory of communication. During this time, I published two monographs, Soft Where, Inc., Volume 1 and 2 [Marcus 1975, 1982], about my experimental computer graphics artwork and my conceptual artwork of the 1970s, which included documentation of making earth-scaled signs. In one project, I connected five public telephones in four cities in the USA. People walking by heard a phone ringing, picked up the handset out of force of habit and found themselves connected to four other people (including myself). We made an electronic X or "crossing out" sign 3000 miles wide; hence, the name of the work is "An X on America." In another project, I went to the basement of the United Nations in New York City and completed a call from one pay phone to another next to it. The call went, by previous arrangement, to Japan, Europe, and back to the USA, completing a circuit around the earth. I picked up both handsets and delivered a short address (to myself) about the meaning of this art/typography/sign work. The title of this work was "A Zero-Circle around the Earth."

Eventually leaving academia, I became a Staff Scientist at Lawrence Berkeley Laboratory's Computer Science and Mathematics Department (because they could not figure out what else to call me). There, surrounded by state-of-the-art computer technology, I realized that I had in some sense "come home." Colleagues at the National Endowment for the Arts' Design Arts Program invited me to lecture on 22 November 1979 at the National Gallery in Washington, D.C., about the future of computers and design. I felt nervous but excited by this opportunity. In an agitated state over several days a few weeks earlier, I fell into a kind of trance, and suddenly terms and concepts started to come into my head. I wrote them down as quickly as I could, not even understanding what the words I heard in my head might mean.

Suddenly, after fifteen years, things began to become crystal clear. I saw that graphic designers and other visual designers had to work with computer technology professionals to humanize technology and to accomplish together what neither engineers or designers could accomplish alone. I realized that all of my education and training in humanities, art, and design previously had pointed the way and could now serve me in the computer technology world. Almost immediately, I began consulting for computer companies like Tektronix, and later Apple and Atari. Everywhere I turned, people seemed receptive to ideas about improving the visual communication with computers and that computer graphics technology helped to produce.

It was at this time that I joined Ron Baecker, now Professor of Computer Science at the University of Toronto, to apply for a US Defense Department Advanced Research Projects Agency (DARPA) research grant to study the typography of the C programming language and how it could be improved in hard copy and screen display. We were successful in obtaining the award, which allowed us during 1982–85 to conduct ethnographic studies of the interesting "tribe" of C programmers, design and test hundreds of variations of typographic design of pages, and, eventually, co-write a book, *Human Factors and Typography for More Readable Programs* (1990), that presented our research and showcased the results.

This project was also the catalyst to setting up in August of 1982 my design firm, Aaron Marcus and Associates (AM+A), one of the first, if not the very first, independent, computer-based graphic design studios in the world. Our office technology was strangely two-tiered. Thanks to the DARPA grant, we had one state-of-the-art, high-resolution graphic display, powerful workstation, and laser printer. At that time, the Three Rivers 300 dpi black-and-white display screen and workstation with Intran Metaform graphics-editing software cost about $80,000. The Xerox laser printer cost about $20,000, with limited fonts, and was about the size of a small refrigerator. That equipment was required for us to do our design studies. For the rest of our firm's work, we relied on an Atari 650, and later Atari 1200, game machines that came with a primitive word processing program, which enabled us to drive a simple dot-matrix printer, a Brother typewriter, and a simple video display terminal. Thus was born AM+A. Soon we converted to a networked Macintosh office in January 1985, perhaps one of the first such graphic design studios. Starting with just one other employee, Michael Arent, by 2002, we had grown to 25 people with an office in Emeryville, CA, and in lower Manhattan, in New York City. With the recession of 2003, we downsized and converted to a single office of a virtual company headquartered in Berkeley, CA.

At this point in time, 2007, I have been able to carve out a niche in the design world and in the world of computer technology. AM+A is a quarter-century young, and an established entity in the world of user-interface and information-visualization development. We combine expertise and experience in planning, research, analysis, design, evaluation, implementation, documentation, and training. The challenges concern the development of usable, useful, and appealing metaphors, mental models, navigation, interaction, and appearance for products and services across most communities of users and on most equipment or devices in most contexts of home, business, travel, play, and learning.[1]

It was not always so easy to describe what we do. It took years of trying to think out how best to explain the verbs and nouns of my professional life. I minted and tried to circulate many expressions:

■ The three faces of computing: outerfaces, interfaces, and innerfaces
■ Industrial-strength graphic design

- Knowledge visualization
- Baby-face design (for user interfaces of mobile devices like telephones and PDAs).

Along the way, we have been fortunate to work on many challenging projects, some of which left me gasping because of the number of things that were hard to imagine or issues that seemed impossible to solve simultaneously. Gradually, upon patient analysis, most became more tractable and eventually solvable.

All through these past 25 years I have spent much time and energy lecturing, tutoring, mentoring, training, writing, and helping further the education of people who wanted to learn about the subjects in which I had acquired some small amount of expertise. Since 1993, when I first co-wrote with Professor Andries van Dam an article in *Communications of the ACM* about the future of graphical user interfaces, I became interested in and designed, with my staff, prototypes of user interfaces designed for specific cultural/demographic target markets of users. Perhaps this interest came out of my experience growing up in the Midwest of the USA, living on both coasts for many years, living in Germany during two summers, living in Israel off and on for two years, and traveling worldwide as much as I have in the past four decades. Imagining user interfaces for different kinds of people was prompted specifically in the late 1980s or early 90s by a suggestion of my current wife, Leslie Becker. Since then, thinking about how other people view the world is a subject in which I have had great interest and to which have devoted time to study. With the rise of India and China, besides Japan and Korea, as non-Western consumers and producers of computer-based communication and interaction, this topic seems more relevant and important than ever before.

### Beyond Practice: Theoretical Studies and R&D Prototypes
In the first decade of my firm, user interfaces and computer technology in general were quite new to most people, whether consumers or specialists. Most of AM+A's work centered around R+D projects carried out for DARPA, NCR, Apple, etc. By the early 90s, many of these kinds of corporate projects became less frequent as attention shifted to commercial product/service development, and by the end of the decade, to innovative start-ups that became, in effect, giant R+D "farms" for larger corporations. As our project shifted, I learned to expect the unexpected.

**Expect the unexpected**. As a child and teenager, I thought I would become a scientist and live my life in a research laboratory. In my twenties and thirties I thought I would be a college professor. I had no idea I would start a design firm focused on user interfaces and information visualization that would require me to learn how to run a small business. Consequently, art/design education must expose students to new ideas, new technology, new circumstances, and new audience/user needs/wants, as well as some practical techniques to survive in a real-world context.

**Help may arrive when you most need it and from unexpected sources**. By cultivating many interests and connections to people, something will turn up, just when one needs it, to solve the seemingly unsolvable dilemmas posed by complex contexts. This approach to problem solving does *not* absolve one from hard work trying to think out solutions; it prepares one for what may, unexpectedly, arrive, and how to take action with the new situation.

**One primary objectives: Helping people to make smarter decisions faster**. This became a slogan for our firm. We could all use such help. Carrying out this objective well means being able to understand situations well enough to explain and convince others. Effective verbi-visual storytelling becomes a key technique, which is the essence of the challenge in good user-interface design.

**Think about other cultures, other times**. How have other people understood these circumstances? How have other civilizations dealt with the challenges we face now, or will face shortly? How would other people in other countries and cultures understand them? Professionals will benefit from a varied exposure to many kinds of people and societies.

**Think about things as a system of related parts**. Try to find the pattern in things and events. It will be almost impossible to understand and predict all structures and processes. Nevertheless, the more we know, the better our own decision making can be.

**Scan the horizon, scan the future**. We can hardly imagine the future. Many stories and predictions have proven erroneous. I never can predict where the next bit of important news will come from. For that reason, I read (quickly) through four newspapers per day, about forty professional publications per month. I am scanning the future, like a trail tracker in the jungle, eyes darting about, looking for signs of change.

**Know your fundamentals well**. Be grounded in your expertise. Even though I have had to learn many new techniques, tools, subjects, disciplines, and technologies, I continually return to fundamentals of typography, color, design, analysis that I learned in graphic design graduate school, as well as fundamental reading, writing, and researching techniques that I learned in grade school, with refreshers in secondary, undergraduate, and graduate education.

**Cultivate a terminology that can quickly, efficiently, and successfully describe your work**. You will not only use these terms to explain to others, but you will use these concepts as filters to understand the language and work of anyone else, and the phenomena you encounter..

**Do not neglect information-oriented, knowledge-oriented communication**. Alas, this kind of communication is in short supply worldwide. For example, in the United States, one-half of very young Hispanic children and one-third of very young African-American children, according to statistics quoted recently by Eric Schlosser, the author of *Fast Food Nation*, are already heading for obesity and later diabetes, with all of the attendant medical conditions and costs to them and society, because parents are not offered information about the dangers of fast food and how to prepare low-cost, more healthful, diets. Another way of looking at this design challenge: a beautiful, well-constructed website has a similar awesome grandeur of a spatial text just as powerful as any architectural monument.

## Conclusion

From my experience and the lessons learned, I think back to the curmudgeonly article about graphic design education that I wrote in 1970 for *Print* magazine [Marcus 1970]: "Why Design Training is Inadequate and What can Be Done About it." Even then I proposed that greater attention be given to systematic design, the design of a system of elements, not just a one-off design. I emphasized the importance of information-oriented design, and, of course, recommended that designers learn the fundamentals of computing.

Nowadays, it is too easy to become so immersed in tools and techniques that one forgets the larger issues of theory and practice related to user-interface design, ethics, visual communication, semiotics, culture studies and ethnography, information design and visualization, usability, universal access, and many other important topics. Study of these subjects refreshes and deepens the understanding and actions of professionals, teachers, and students.

I hope this traversal of my own path may shed some light on current and future teaching and learning.

## Note

1. The AM+A client list is an eclectic one, including both Fortune 500 clients and innovative startups. Some of our more than 100 clients worldwide are 3M, Adobe, Apple Computer, AT&T, Bank of America, Bose, Charles Schwab, Cisco Systems, Compuserve, Daimler Chrysler, DuPont, Epson, FedEx, Fujitsu, Kodak, General Motors, Hewlett-Packard, Honeywell, IBM, Intel, J. Paul Getty Trust, Kaiser Permanente, Microsoft, Motorola, NASA, National Institutes of Health, Nokia, Oracle, Pacific Bell, Random House, Reuters, Ricoh, Samsung, Siemens, Ford Foundation, The Learning Company, Tiscali, University of California, US Defense Department, US Federal Reserve Bank, US Treasury Department, Visa, Wells Fargo, Xerox.

## Works Cited

Baecker, Ron, and Marcus (1990), Aaron, *Human Factors and Typography for More Readable Programs*, Addison-Wesley, Reading MA, ISBN 0-201-10745-7.

Marcus, Aaron (2005a), "The Out-of-Box Home Experience: Remote from Reality." Fast Forward Column, Interactions, 12: 3, May/June 2005, pp. 54–56.

Marcus, Aaron (2005b), "User Interface Design's Return on Investment: Examples and Statistics." Chapter 2 in Bias, R. G., and Mayhew, D. J.., (eds.), *Cost-Justifying Usability*, 2nd edition. San Francisco: Elsevier, pp. 17–39.

Marcus, Aaron. (2005c), "User Interfaces of Wireless Mobile Devices." In Longoria, Roman, ed., *Designing Software for the Mobile Context: A Practitioner's Guide*, chapter 6. Berlin: Springer Verlag, pp. 135–150.

Marcus, Aaron (2005d), "User-Interface Design and Culture." In Aykin, Nuray, ed., *Usability and Internationalization of Information Technology*, chapter 3. New York: Lawrence Erlbaum Publishers, 51–78.

Marcus, Aaron [2004], "Vehicle User Interfaces," Fast Forward Column, *Interactions*, 11: 1, January-February 2004, pp. 40–47.

Marcus, Aaron [2003a], "The Emotion Commotion," Fast Forward Column, 10: 6, *Interactions*, November-December 2003, pp. 28–34.

Marcus, Aaron [2003b], "Universal, Ubiquitous, User-Interface Design for the Disabled and Elderly," Fast Forward Column, *Interactions*, 10: 2, March-April 2003, pp. 23–27.

Marcus, Aaron (2003c), "Vehicle User-Interface Design," *Proceedings*, Human-Computer Interface International, Crete, Greece, June 2003.

Marcus, Aaron [2003d], "12 myths of Mobile UI Design," *Software Development Magazine*, May 2003, pp. 38–40. See: http://milife.howardesign.com/jeff/12myths.html.

Marcus, Aaron. (2002a), "The Cult of Cute," Fast-Forward Column, *Interactions*, ACM Publisher, www.acm.org, 9: 6, November/December 2002, pp. 29–33.

Marcus, Aaron. (2002b). "Advanced Vehicle User-Interface and Information-Visualization Design." *Information Visualization Journal*, 1: 2, 9 Sep 2002, Palgrave Macmillan, United Kingdom, pp. 95–102.

Marcus, Aaron. (2002c), "Globalization, Localization, and Cross-Cultural Communication in User-Interface Design," in Jacko, J. and A. Spears, Chapter 23, *Handbook of Human-Computer Interaction*, Lawrence Erlbaum Publishers, New York, 2002, pp. 441–463.

Marcus, Aaron, (2001), "User-interface design for air-travel booking: A case study of Sabre." *Information Design Journal*, 10: 2, 186–206. Published for the International Institute for Information Design by John Benjamins Publishing Co., Amsterdam, The Netherlands, idj-office@io.tudelft.nl.

Marcus, Aaron (2000), "Designing the User Interface for a Vehicle Navigation System: A Case Study," chapter in Bergman, Eric, editor, *Information Appliances and Beyond: Interaction Design for Consumer Products*, Morgan Kaufmann, San Francisco, 2000, ISBN 1-55860-600-9, http: www.mkp. com, pp. 205–255.

Marcus, Aaron (1999), "Globalization of User-Interface Design for the Web," in *Proceedings*, 1st International Conference on Internationalization of Products and Systems (IWIPS), Girish Probhu and Elisa M. Delgaldo, eds., 22–22 May, 1999, Rochester, NY, Backhouse Press, Rochester, NY, USA, ISBN: 0-965691-2-2, pp. 165–172.

Marcus, Aaron (1998), "Metaphors in User-Interface Design," ACM SIGDOC (Special Interest Group on Documentation), vol, 22, no.2, May 1998, pp. 43–57, ISSN 0731-1001.

Marcus, Aaron (1997), "Graphical User Interfaces," chapter 19, in Helander, M. G., Landauer, T. K., and Prabhu, p. , eds., *Handbook of Human-Computer Interaction*, Elsevier Science, B. V., The Hague, Netherlands, 1997, ISBN 0-444-4828-626, pp. 423–44.

Marcus, Aaron (1995), "Principles of Effective Visual Communication for Graphical User-Interface Design," in *Readings in Human-Computer Interaction*, 2nd edition, ed. Baecker, Grudin, Buxton, and Greenberg, Morgan Kaufman, Palo Alto, 1995, pp. 425–441, ISBN: 1-55860-246-1.

Marcus, Aaron (1992), *Graphic Design for Electronic Documents and User Interfaces*, Addison-Wesley, Reading MA, 1992, ISBN: 0-201-54364-8 (also available in Japanese).

Marcus, Aaron (1982). *Soft Where, Inc.*, vol.2. Reno, NV: West Coast Poetry Review Press.

Marcus, Aaron (1975), *Soft Where, Inc.*, vol. 1. Reno, NV: West Coast Poetry Review Press.

Marcus, Aaron (1979a), "An Introduction to the Visual Syntax of Concrete Poetry," *Visible Language*, vol. 8, no. 4, Autumn 1974, pp. 333–360.

Marcus, Aaron (1979b), "Visual Rhetoric in a Pictographic-Ideographic Narrative." In *Proceedings of the Second Congress of the International Association for Semiotic Studies*, pp. 1501–1508. New York: Mouton Publishers.

Marcus, Aaron (1979c), "New Ways to View World Problems," *East-West Perspectives*, Journal of the East-West Center, Honolulu, vol. 1, no. 1, Summer 1979, pp. 15–22.

Marcus, Aaron (1973), "Symbolic Constructions," *Typographische Monatsblaetter*, St. Gallen, Switzerland, vol. 92, no. 10, October 1973, pp. 671–683.

Marcus, Aaron (1971a), "The Designer, the Computer, and Two-Way Communication," *Print*, vol. 25, no. 4, July-August 1971, pp. 34–39.

Marcus, Aaron (1971b), "New Directions for the AIGA," *Journal of the American Institute of Graphic Arts*, New York, no. 13, Spring 1970, pp. 3–4.

Marcus, Aaron (1971d), "A Prototype Interactive Page-Design System," *Visible Language*, vol. 5, no. 3, Summer 1971, pp. 197–220.

Marcus, Aaron (1970), "Why Design Training is Inadequate and What Can Be Done About It," *Print*, vol. 24, no. 2, March-April 1970, pp. 28–31.

Marcus, Aaron (1969), "Computer Art," *Princeton Alumni Weekly*, Princeton University, Princeton, 1969.

Marcus, Aaron (1968), "The Computer and the Artist," *Eye*, Magazine of the Yale School of Art, New Haven, no. 2, Spring 1968, pp. 36–39.

Marcus, Aaron, and Baumgartner, Valentina-Johanna. 2005, "A Practical Set of Culture Dimensions for Global User-Interface Development." In Masood Masoodian, Steve Jones, Bill Rogers , eds., Proc. of Computer Human Interaction: 6th Asia Pacific Conference, APCHI 2004, Rotorua, New Zealand, 29 June 29-2 July 2004, volume 3101 / 2004, p. 252–261. Berlin: Springer-Verlag GmbH, ISSN: 0302-9743, ISBN: 3-540-22312-6.

Marcus, Aaron, and Baumgartner,Valentina-Johanna (2004a), "Mapping User-Interface Design Components vs. Culture Dimensions in Corporate Websites," *Visible Language Journal*, MIT Press, 38: 1, 1–65, 2004.

Marcus, Aaron, and Baumgartner, Valentina-Johanna (2004b), "A Practical Set of Culture Dimension for Evaluating User-Interface Designs" in *Proceedings*, Sixth Asia-Pacific Marcus, Aaron (1979a). "An Introduction to the Visual Syntax of Concrete Poetry," *Visible Language*, vol. 8, no. 4, Autumn 1974, pp. 333–360.

Marcus, Aaron (1979b), "Visual Rhetoric in a Pictographic-Ideographic Narrative." In *Proceedings of the Second Congress of the International Association for Semiotic Studies*, pp. 1501–1508. New York: Mouton Publishers.

Marcus, Aaron (1979c), "New Ways to View World Problems," *East-West Perspectives*, Journal of the East-West Center, Honolulu, vol. 1, no. 1, Summer 1979, pp. 15–22.

Marcus, Aaron (1973), "Symbolic Constructions," *Typographische Monatsblaetter*, St. Gallen, Switzerland, vol. 92, no. 10, October 1973, pp. 671–683.

Marcus, Aaron (1971a), "The Designer, the Computer, and Two-Way Communication," *Print*, vol. 25, no. 4, July-August 1971, pp. 34–39.

Marcus, Aaron (1971b), "New Directions for the AIGA," *Journal of the American Institute of Graphic Arts,* New York, no. 13, Spring 1970, pp. 3–4.

Marcus, Aaron (1971d), "A Prototype Interactive Page-Design System," *Visible Language,* vol. 5, no. 3, Summer 1971, pp. 197–220.

Marcus, Aaron (1970), "Why Design Training is Inadequate and What Can Be Done About It," *Print,* vol. 24, no. 2, March-April 1970, pp. 28–31.

Marcus, Aaron (1969), "Computer Art," *Princeton Alumni Weekly,* Princeton University, Princeton, 1969.

Marcus, Aaron (1968), "The Computer and the Artist," *Eye,* magazine of the Yale School of Art, New Haven, no. 2, Spring 1968, pp. 36–39.

Marcus, Aaron, and Baumgartner, Valentina-Johanna (2005), "A Practical Set of Culture Dimensions for Global User-Interface Development." In Masood Masoodian, Steve Jones, Bill Rogers , ed., Proc. of Computer Human Interaction: 6th Asia Pacific Conference, APCHI 2004, Rotorua, New Zealand, 29 June 29–2 July 2004, volume 3101 / 2004 , p. 252–261. Berlin: Springer-Verlag GmbH, ISSN: 0302-9743, ISBN: 3-540-22312-6.

Marcus, Aaron, and Baumgartner,Valentina-Johanna (2004a), "Mapping User-Interface Design Components vs. Culture Dimensions in Corporate Websites," *Visible Language* Journal, MIT Press, 38: 1, 1–65, 2004.

Marcus, Aaron, and Baumgartner, Valentina-Johanna (2004b), "A Practical Set of Culture Dimension for Evaluating User-Interface Designs" in *Proceedings,* Sixth Asia-Pacific Conference on Computer-Human Interaction (APCHI 2004), Royal Lakeside Novotel Hotel, Rotorua, New Zealand, 30 June-2 July 2004, 252–261.

Marcus, Aaron, and Chen, Eugene (2002), "Designing the PDA of the Future." *Interactions,* ACM Publisher, www.acm.org, 9: 1, January/February 2002, 32–44.

Marcus, Aaron, and Gould, Emilie (2000), "Crosscurrents: Cultural Dimensions and Global Web User-Interface Design." Interactions, July-August 2000, 7: 4, pp. 32–46.

Marcus, Aaron, and Park, Seonghee (2005), "Wrist-Top User-Interface Design." *Proc. HCI International,* July 2005, Las Vegas, NV, CD-ROM Proceedings, unpaged.

Marcus, Aaron, Nick Smilonich, and Lynne Thompson (1994), *The Cross-GUI Handbook for Multiplatform User-Interface Design,* Addison-Wesley, Reading, 1994, ISBN 0-201-57592-2.

Marcus, Aaron, et al. "Shape Up Your Documents." Marketing brochure, Xerox Font Services, El Segundo, California, doc. no. 610P51268, October 1992.

Wildbur, Peter, and Michael Burke (1999), *Information Graphics: Innovative Solutions in Contemporary Design,* Thames and Hudson, London, ISBN 0-500-28077-0. Contains extensive AM+A project figures, including Sabre.

# EMERGENT PRAXIS

# Entwined Histories: Reflections on Teaching Art, Science, and Technological Media

## Edward A. Shanken

Relatively few art historians, particularly in the US, can claim research or teaching specializations in the historical entwinement of art, science, and technology (AST) or the more recent advent of New Media. As a result, very few courses on these topics are taught in US art history departments. At the same time, the greatest number of searches for fine art faculty in the US are for practitioners accomplished at using and teaching emerging technological media. Quite frequently these searches also specify that the successful candidate will be an adept theorist as well. This latter qualification is sought after because studio departments recognize that their students must have a strong grounding in the history and theory of art, science, and technological media in order to become effective practitioners. In the absence of faculty in art history departments to teach courses on these subjects, that responsibility falls on studio faculty.

The initial theorists of an emerging art-form typically are the artists who produced it. The practice and theorization of minimalism, performance, conceptual art, and various strains of art and technology exemplify this phenomenon, which accounts for and justifies the teaching of history/theory by new media practitioners. Studio courses involving conventional materials and techniques often incorporate a historical/ theoretical component; indeed, there may be benefits to classes that combine theory and practice. At the same time, it may be expecting too much of any one individual to be an expert theorist/historian and an expert practitioner and to teach in both areas. As the AST field matures, one can anticipate that more art historians will focus on it and the demands on practitioners to teach history and theory will diminish.[1]

Regardless of an instructor's background, obtaining access to digital media assets presents a common challenge to teaching the history of AST. Given the time-based and/or interactive nature of much work in the field, static images arguably do even less justice to their dynamic qualities than they do for the dynamic textures of paintings, the dimensionality of sculpture, or the immersive qualities of installation. Traditional slide collections rarely have significant holdings in this area anyway and visual resource collections are only just beginning to acquire substantial multimedia assets. This problem is becoming less pressing than in the past, as many artists are providing excellent online documentation of their work and other web-based resources offer extensive documentation, though frequently at relatively low resolution.[2] Many teachers dedicate a great deal of time, energy, and resources to developing their own personal libraries of media assets to use in the classroom, and we eagerly share and swap them with our colleagues. While this sort of ad-hoc community exchange helps address institutional deficiencies, a more centralized online collection would be a very valuable resource for teaching and learning.

The relative obscurity of AST in art historical literature combined with the complexity of its inherent interdisciplinarity present a further hurdle to teaching. The conceptual and technical richness of the best artworks in the field – what makes them so exciting and inspiring for scholars – also makes them extremely difficult to teach to students, particularly given the absence of canonical literature and media resources. AST engages multiple discourses and challenges or countermands established art practices and aesthetic orthodoxies in which students may have strong investments. Students (and critics) who do not have a firm grasp on the tremendous pluralism that characterizes contemporary art practice or on the concepts and histories of information theory, cybernetics, computing, networking, media, and so forth, cannot hope to have anything but a superficial understanding and appreciation of AST and its contributions to the discourses of art and visual culture. In addition to gaining an understanding of these diverse discourses, it is equally important that students develop an ability to think critically about the implicit ideologies and explicit rhetorics deployed in historical narratives.

* * *

I developed and taught my first AST course, "The Cultural Economy of Cybernetics," in spring 2001 as a graduate student at Duke University.[3] This 16-week course emphasized systemic thinking and conceived of the interdisciplinary science of cybernetics as part of a larger cultural economy that includes art, literature, and film and that is related to subsequent technocultural formations, including cyberspace and the World Wide Web. (Please see Appendix A for course description.)

The composition of the class ranged from first-year students to graduating seniors whose major fields included Computer Science, Economics, English, Engineering, and Political Science. Taught at the 100-level in the Markets and Management Studies (MMS) program, the course helped fulfill MMS certificate requirements for most of the 24 enrolled students, only one of whom had much background in art history. Even under the best of circumstances, it is challenging to teach the unfamiliar and as yet non-canonical history of art, science, and technological media to students who have a firm grasp of modern and contemporary art. How could I make the art historical material, which comprised a large part of my lectures, comprehensible and relevant to such a diverse and unknowledgeable group?

One of the "hooks" I used in the course was music. In my introductory lecture I used Jimi Hendrix performing the *Star Spangled Banner* at Woodstock as an object lesson. The amplified sound of his electric guitar cycling through his loud speaker and into the pickups on his instrument demonstrated feedback, a fundamental principle of cybernetics. The MP3 sound file itself, composed of binary data that had been digitized and compressed from analog recordings, then downloaded using peer-to-peer networking, demonstrated a range of technical and social systems characteristic of digital computing and cyberspace. The discussion of guitar feedback set the stage for exploring the use of feedback in artist's video and other forms of media art. By comparing negative and positive feedback loops, a valuable management lesson was learned. Students immediately understood that "yes-men" in a professional context provide only positive feedback, which ultimately can only lead to the destruction of the system.

I started each class with a musical interlude and encouraged students to bring in songs that were relevant to course material. The music we listened to ranged from Lejaren Hiller and John Cage to DJ Spooky and Marilyn Manson, whose song "Posthuman" includes the lyrics,

> God is a number you cannot count to
> You are posthuman and hardwired...
> This isn't god, this isn't god
> God is just a statistic
> God is just a statistic

It was illuminating to compare singer Manson's pop-culture notion of the posthuman as androgynous, statistical, and "hard-wired" with scholar Katherine Hayles' academic notion of the same term (disembodied, dematerialized, and flickering): "As you gaze at the flickering signifiers scrolling down the computer screens...you have already become posthuman."

Even if some of students did not have a great interest in the history of art, they all shared an interest in technology and its relationship to transformations in culture and society. I came to realize that the most effective pedagogical approach would be to teach the students strategies for thinking about systems and systemic behavior that would serve them well in the future and to illustrate those concepts with examples from art history that would function as visual markers of parallel cultural developments. In this way, I helped students learn how to think with their eyes and see with their minds. The class met for 80 minutes, twice weekly and was taught in lecture format, though with a great deal of class discussion. Students consistently reported that discussion was one of the most valuable parts of the course and that they learned a great deal from their peers and from participating in the debates that arose in class.

One effective exercise involved creating an awareness of, and facility in, metacritical thinking. After reading and discussing Gregory Bateson's Metalogues in *Steps to an Ecology of Mind*, students were set the task of writing a metalogue between a human and a computer. In order to do so, students not only had to understand the concept of a metalog but be able to actualize it – itself a metalogical process. While not all of them produced successful metalogues, the process resulted in an appreciation of the sort of thinking required to do so.

Key concepts the course addressed included:

- Core cybernetic principles of feedback, equilibrium/homeostasis, the "black box," and parallels between animals and machines
- The second law of thermodynamics (entropy)
- The difference between closed and open systems
- Network models: unidirectional/multidirectional; one-to-many/ many-to-many; centralized/decentralized/distributed
- Progress and evolution applied to science and technology
- The cyborgian condition: false dichotomy of human vs. technological; hybrid forms that combine both elements
- Reflexivity and the implications of observation
- Autopoiesis and emergent systemic behavior
- Artificial intelligence and artificial life
- Purposiveness, agency, free will
- Top-down, good old-fashioned AI, e.g. Moravec, versus bottom-up, embodied AI, e.g. Brooks
- The difference between information and meaning
- Deductive vs. inductive thinking and the limits of rationality
- Art as a "psychic dress rehearsal for the future"

These concepts were discussed in relation to art historical tendencies and genres including futurism and constructivism, the Bauhaus, kinetic art, robotic art, computer graphics, interactive art including closed-circuit video, VR, and other forms of installation, telematic art and net art. Prior to viewing *Blade Runner*, students read Turing's "Computing Machines and Intelligence," in preparation for a discussion of the Turing Test and the Voigt-Kampf test, the role of photography and visual memory as a foundation of identity, and the possibility of love between humans and non-humans. Likewise, *Count Zero* offered a fictional context for considering the possibility of AI robots producing art that humans would find meaningful, as exemplified by the objects, like Cornell boxes, generated in the novel by a machine harboring human memories. This discussion also brought into play artistic examples including Tinguely's *Metamatics* and Harold Cohen's *AARON*.

Given the diversity of student interests, I permitted the class great latitude with their final projects. They could address any topic related to the course, work collaboratively, and produce a standard research paper or an artwork, website, performance, or other non-traditional form. One particularly successful final project resulted from collaboration between majors in computer science, political science, and psychology.[4] The team devised a personality inventory that demanded subjective responses on the part of their classmates to questions pertaining to course concepts, including feedback, systems, and reflexivity. The answers to the questions established values for a set of parameters that altered a digital photograph with color, texture, and dimensionality. The group produced 24 different images, each corresponding to the response of a student in the class. The images were mounted and displayed in a row, resulting in a composite class self-portrait. As a gift, each student was given the portrait corresponding to his/her answers.

At the Savannah College of Art and Design, I developed "Digital Art and Culture" which I taught regularly between 2004 and 2007 for the Art History department.[5] This 10-week, 300-level elective helps students fulfill general art history requirements and is a required course for our New Media minor. Students' major fields range from graphic design, photography, and painting to sequential art, interaction design, and special effects. Prerequisites include Renaissance to the Present and either Twentieth-Century Art or Survey for the New Media. ARTH 356 examines parallels between the history of digital technology, including information theory, cybernetics, computing, and artificial intelligence, and the history of digital art. Students are expected to learn how to apply ideas from computer science and engineering to aesthetic discourses and to identify, analyze, and debate concepts associated with the intertwined histories of digital technology and art practice.

The main course text, Charlie Gere's *Digital Culture* (Reaktion 2002), offers a comprehensive yet comprehensible and succinct description of the emergence of cybernetics and computing in relation to digital art and culture. Gere's stance, summarized in his quotation of Deleuze, "the machine is always social before it is technical" (p. 13), provides an excellent platform for questioning technological determinism, the polarization of art and of technology as binary opposites, and the narrativization of the histories of art and technology in terms of continuity or radical rupture – all central tropes considered throughout the course. I have supplemented this text with either Christiane Paul's *Digital Art*, Margot Lovejoy's *Digital Currents*, or Mark Tribe and Reena Jana's *New Media Art*, all of which have more illustrations, provide a shared database of objects, and offer alternative theoretical positions for consideration.

Although designated as a lecture course, classes meet for $2^1/_2$ hours, twice weekly, a format that encourages approaches to teaching and learning beyond the lectern. In order to engage my classes in a more active style of learning, student-led discussion makes up approximately 30 to 40 percent of each meeting. The class is divided up into groups that are responsible for leading discussions about works related to particular artists addressed in the assigned readings. In connection with this regular responsibility, students draft a short statement (150 words) about a work related to the artist, including an image, links, and references, which is submitted as a pdf file to the course website in advance of class. These write-ups, downloaded and projected on the screen in class, serve as a stimulus for discussion, which often is very open-ended and spontaneous. We routinely use the WWW to explore and discover ideas and relationships that emerge serendipitously during discussion, with the added benefit of offering me an opportunity to demonstrate Boolean logic and effective strategies for using search engines. Students have, in a couple cases, taken the initiative to create a separate course website that compiles and archives the class's write-ups.[6]

One of the outstanding student projects for Digital Art and Culture in fall 2004 produced a model for paying parking meters using a mobile phone. It also demonstrated a variety of wireless communication technologies. The student, Andres Salgado, employed a webcam, wireless networking, his mobile phone, a laptop, iChat, and Apple Remote Desktop in his presentation. Beginning in the classroom, he walked with his laptop through the building and out onto the street while speaking with the class via iChat and controlling his PowerPoint presentation remotely. He used the webcam to show a car at a parking meter and a mock-up interface on his mobile phone to pay for parking using that device. Ideally, the student noted, one would be able to add money remotely via the mobile phone or have it withdrawn automatically from one's account if the meter ran out of time. Needless to say, the class was duly impressed both by this practical solution to a common problem as well as by the student's ability to combine and master a diverse range of technologies.

\* \* \*

As a researcher involved in producing critical and historical AST discourses, it is sometimes difficult for me to remember how complex this field is and how I struggled to gain an initial understanding of it as a student. I find that my classes best relate to this material when comparisons can be made with familiar monuments and themes, thus demonstrating continuities within the history of art.

In this respect, a media-archaeological approach has proven to be helpful, as historical attempts to create surrogates, simulations, and immersive environments can be mapped onto more recent artworks with related concerns involving technologies such as robotics, artificial life, and virtual reality. This approach benefits as well from emphasizing continuities in the histories of art and technology in a way that is not technologically deterministic. At the same time, it is important to emphasize the particular contexts in which historical and contemporary works emerge, for it is these conditions that make those works distinctive and significant statements about, and instantiations of, the epistemological and ontological circumstances of the cultures that produced them.

Students often struggle to grasp an understanding of AST that simultaneously embraces continuity and discontinuity. This is not surprising, since art historical narratives typically celebrate avant-gardism and novelty, using rhetoric that claims radical rupture with the past. Such rhetoric is also common in scientific and technological literature, so AST discourses – poised between the two – are especially prone to it. The tension between narratives of continuity and discontinuity itself provides a useful a tool for teaching. My students become mindful of terms such as "new," "radical," "unprecedented," and "progress" and interrogate what is at stake in their use. We debate to what extent such terms are useful for describing works of art and to what extent they reveal more about the cultural values, political ideologies, and/or personal agendas of those who use them. Most students are savvy that capitalism demands ongoing growth of production and consumption and that advertising creates desire that fuels that economic engine. But many of them feel demoralized when they must consider the insidiousness of this ideology in the discourses of art and art history. And they are further unsettled by the idea that to imagine oneself as part of something radically new and unprecedented gives one a (false) sense of historical importance.

Some of the liveliest debates have emerged from asking, "What is new in New Media?" Sometimes this discussion becomes a platform for metacritical reflections on the inseparability of interpretation from personal and cultural values. Sometimes this discussion leads to debates about form and content, e.g., New Media addresses the same ideas that artists always have addressed but does so using new materials and techniques; or New Media uses many of the same basic technologies originally invented decades ago but gives them a new meaning. While such paradoxical accounts are not easily reconciled, they do open up further discussion of the relationship between form and content and the limits of their conceptualization as binary opposites. If my students learn nothing else, I hope that they learn how to think critically about art and technology and the ideologies and rhetorics that inspire their production and shape their interpretation.

### Notes

1. Historian/theorist Erkki Huhtamo was one of the first hires made during Victoria Vesna's tenure as Chair of Design|Media Arts program at UCLA. Other emerging practice-based programs in the field are also considering searches for historian/theorists.
2. Artist Rafael Lozano-Hemmer, for example, provides excellent multimedia documentation of his work. See <http://www.lozano-hemmer.com/>. See also, Media Art Net <http://mediaartnet.org> and Multimedia: From Wagner to Virtual Reality <http: //www.artmuseum.net/ w2vr/> (November 28, 2006).

3. This opportunity to teach in my specialized field came not from my own department (Art History) but from the interdisciplinary Markets and Management Studies program (MMS), a pre-business certificate (similar to a minor degree) administered by the Department of Sociology. MMS was keen to offer courses that addressed the cultural implications of information technology in ways that would expand its students' intellectual horizons beyond conventional economic theory.

4. The students were Paul Keyerleber, Justin Marquez, and Michelle Rosengarten.

5. The course was conceived by the former chair of art history, Dr. Celina Jeffery, who gained administrative approval for it, though I developed the content for the course in consultation with Dr. Jeffery and colleague Dr. Timothy Jackson, who also teaches it.

6. I borrowed this idea from a blog produced by Michael Naimark's class, A Non-Linear History of New Media and the Arts, in the Interactive Telecommunications Program at NYU in spring 2004. See http: //stage.itp. nyu.edu/history/index.html (cited November 17, 2006). SCAD students Wilbert Cedeño, Phong Nguyen, and Jeff McNabb created websites for their sections of ART356. See, for example, http: //www.phongNguyen.net/DAC and http://www.tragicgeek.com/ dac/ (cited December 8, 2007).

## Appendix A

The Cultural Economy of Cybernetics (MMS 195, Duke University, Spring 2001).

### *Course Description*

This course explores the impact of cybernetics on the formation of culture. Students will learn the history of cybernetics and its relation to fields such as information theory, artificial intelligence, and artificial life. Cybernetics anticipated an intrinsically interdisciplinary systems aesthetics that the course will map onto parallel developments in art, film, and literature. Students will also examine the relationship between cybernetics, cyberspace, and web-based multimedia. Readings will include canonical texts on cybernetics and writings by artists and critics about the relationship of cybernetics to the economy of culture.

### *Required Texts*

Gregory Bateson. *Steps to an Ecology of Mind: Collected Essays in Anthropology, Psychiatry, Evolution, and Epistemology*. Chicago: University of Chicago Press, 2000, c. 1972.

William Gibson. *Count Zero*. New York: Ace, 1987.

N. Katherine Hayles. *How We Became Posthuman*. Chicago: University of Chicago Press, 1999.

Norbert Wiener. *Human Use of Human Beings: Cybernetics and Society*. New York: Da Capo, 1988, c. 1950–54.

Additional readings included Turing's "Computing Machine and Intelligence," Jack Burnham's "Systems Esthetics," essays by Roy Ascott on cybernetic and telematic art, and selections from the Cybernetic Serendipity catalog and Maturana and Varela's *Tree of Knowledge*.

# A GENERATIVE EMERGENT APPROACH TO GRADUATE EDUCATION

## Bill Seaman

I have sought to embody a series of potentials for graduate education – to define a program that enables one to explore and enfold elements of artistic practice, contemporary cultural relations, design pursuits, scientific research (and/or its abstraction) and technological inquiry, in varying degrees, relevant to each differing student. Such a program presents an exciting space for individual expression through contemporary forms of creative investigation. The Digital+Media department opened at Rhode Island School of Design in 2003.

I have been the graduate program director at four different major institutions in the US and in Australia. Thus, over the last fifteen years I have adopted and honed a series of approaches to enhance the personal development of the graduate student. My methodology is a generative, combinatoric one. Many different processes are enfolded contributing to the growth of the individual. In my own classes, a series of structured assignments function to help the student define their own particular practice. Along with my personal approach to education, I have developed the notion of interdisciplinary and transdisciplinary node classes that bridge to differing disciplines at RISD and Brown University. These node classes also embody current trends that in multiple ways explore contemporary approaches to creative technological practices that employ digital media. Each student articulates an appropriate selection of these classes (in conjunction with their advisor) and defines a unique trajectory through department curriculum, along with study in a core set of classes. The node classes balance theory and practice, provide technological background as well as hands-on learning experience.

Multiple readings inform and contextualize the student's study. Ongoing critique and discussion by lecturers and peers becomes central. The program culminates in a highly articulated written thesis process and final thesis exhibition. Thus, a broad range of potential studies are enfolded in a highly unique educational experience in a manner that becomes relevant to each different student. A rich field of emergent potentials is entertained as part of an ongoing mentoring process which is steeped in thought mapping, articulate self-reflection, process-oriented growth, hands-on technological experience, diverse textual input, articulate feedback and critique, as well as ongoing informed discussion. This study is augmented with multiple generative associative exercises.

## Introduction

Educating artists in the digital age is a great challenge. Exploring interdisciplinary and transdisciplinary education calls for a special commitment to learning and growth. In transdisciplinary study, a series of focused research areas are bridged. Because no singular discipline, pairing of disciplines, and/or history of those disciplines, can be used to elucidate the work that is arising, the term transdisciplinary is employed, suggesting that such study goes beyond any individual discipline or coupling of disciplines. Transdisciplinary research brings a set of fields of inquiry together in the service of emergent knowledge production. Education that explores this challenging knowledge domain mandates that the graduate mentor continue their own education (be it formally or informally) in an ongoing manner, be open to change, embrace collaboration and continuing communication with multiple colleagues functioning in differing domains. This can mean staying on top of updates of numerous digital programs; keeping abreast of the changes in multiple fields in terms of technology; maintaining their own research practice; reading across a range of research topics and domains; and in general keeping a broad scanning-type awareness open to this field of fields.

## Curriculum

I have worked at four different institutions as Graduate Director – The College of Fine Art, University of New South Wales (Sydney) in the department of *4D – Time Based Arts*; at the University of Maryland, Baltimore County in the department of *Imaging and Digital Arts*; at UCLA in the department of *Design/Media Arts*; and at Rhode Island School of Design where I am currently Graduate Program Director and Department Head in *Digital+Media*. Each institution has had its own particular qualities and educational demands. At RISD, I was hired to build a curriculum from the ground up with the brief of creating a department that could provide interdisciplinary education for a new department of approximately 30 students in a two-year program. Part of the mission was to design a program that could also bridge to the entire RISD graduate division representing sixteen departments, be open to advanced seniors and fifth-year students at RISD, as well as include students (and curriculum) from Brown University. The challenge was to design a curriculum for contemporary interdisciplinary/transdisciplinary artists and designers that is unique to the RISD setting. The institution has many existing facilities that might facilitate embodied/physical digital media practice. Thus, the task became to construct an emergent system exploring recombinant educational goals.

I created the concept of node classes, borrowing a navigational concept from the structure of the internet. A node class is a class that balances the study of technology and art (or design) with inquiry that is conceptual, social, and cultural. These classes are an extension of "studio related" study, although they tend to be shorter – lasting five hours. They bring core Digital+Media department students together with a broad range of students from other disciplines. Central is the multi-perspective approach to knowledge acquisition – where different students articulate particular relationships that are relevant to their own fields. The notion of defining a bridging language is essential – of communicating and coming to understand multiple approaches to contemporary creative technological practice.

Susan Leigh Star and Geoffrey C. Bowker in their text *Sorting Things Out: Classification and its Consequences* define the notion of the Boundary Object, relevant to this approach:

> Drawing from earlier studies of interdisciplinary scientific cooperation, we define boundary objects as those objects that both inhabit several communities of practice and satisfy the informational requirements of each of them. In working practice, they are objects that are able both to travel across borders and maintain some sort of constant identity. They can be tailored to meet the needs of any one community (they are plastic in this sense, or customizable). At the same time, they have common identities across settings. This is achieved by allowing the objects to be weakly structured in common use, imposing stronger structures in the individual-site tailored use.[1] (Star, S. and Bowker, G. 1999: 1)

Thus, node classes employ such a strategy. Node classes embody a "recombinant" methodology that is drawn from my artistic research[2] (Seaman 1999) into meaning production, where in this case differing educational modules are recombined to form an emergent educational practice. Students articulate particular trajectories through these courses that are specifically relevant to them.

**Beginnings**
Having had years of experience in graduate education, one comes to know that the first semester is a highly chaotic one – the student has just moved to a new place, has potentially taken up major loans, has shifted relationships with their friends and also possibly their significant others. Unlike undergraduate education, they must think primarily for themselves, forming their own particular approach to their practice. The notion is to form an initial grounding experience to enable them to establish a series of bonds with their fellow students. One of the most important elements of graduate education is the contribution the students give to each other through dialogue, technical collaboration, and collegiality.

The curriculum at the Digital+Media department begins with a class called the *Continuum Studio* – exploring the continuum from the physical to the digital. This is a "hit the ground running" course that covers many different introductions and approaches to software, while simultaneously building a space for conceptual exchange, critique, and articulate reflection. Central is the defining of a vocabulary of relevant processes to build upon for each student's practice. This class also helps students define their own working processes. The grads come to Digital+Media from multiple disciplines so they often have been informed by differing "histories," bodies of knowledge, and modes of critique. The commonality that forms a pre-requisite for the program is as follows: students must have four years of Digital Media study of some kind to come into the program. There are many different potential foci that could play into these four years – this may entail experience with authoring and/or programming for the Internet, experience with responsive environments, locative media, digital video, media-oriented programming, digital photography, digitally oriented performance art, rapid prototyping (digital sculpture), and/or digitally driven installation work (or others). Media computer scientists are also considered. One student had studied biology and artificial life and successfully applied. Thus, the department is highly eclectic and each graduate student comes to the department with a slightly different skill set. In the first year, along with the *Continuum Studio*, a history of digital media focusing on interactivity is presented – *Perspectives*, a second class – the *Lecture Series Seminar* presenting relevant visiting artists and/or theorists, and one node class are required. A *Seminar/Tutorial* class that I teach is also mandatory. I will speak in depth below about my approach to the *Seminar/Tutorial* class below.

My teaching method has been to articulate a core set of concepts and approaches by providing essential texts and central technological methodologies, augmented with a broad range of study related to more individual, eclectic practices and research potentials. Thus, I draw on texts from numerous research domains. If we are *Learning at the Intersections of Art, Science, Technology and Culture*, then it goes without saying that a student may be reading texts from a multiplicity of research contexts. This means that the Digital+Media student must pull from a plethora of readings exploring new ideas and methods surrounding digital media production. This potentially includes exploring digital media from one or more perspectives. Because digital media is used in almost every discipline, this means that each student will define their own particular approach to its creative, expressive potentials. One particular text that we have found helpful is the *New Media Reader*, edited by Noah Wardrip-Fruin and Nick Mountfort[3] (Wardrip-Fruin and Mountford 2003). This book brings together a set of readings that I had often drawn upon in the past, earlier providing the tests in Xerox form. A second book that we also recommend is Stephen Wilson's *Information Arts: Intersections of Art, Science, and Technology*[4] (Wilson 2002). In general, each class provides its own suggested reading list and/or reader. These lists are presented along with the focused lists that I provide for each individual. In terms of my own approach to reading, I suggest that along with the broad set of foci that one can study in the Digital+Media department, one can also draw on a more personal set of readings – poems, novels, interactive texts, magazines, textual forms originating from, or commenting on pop culture, and a vast range of URLs related to art and/or experimental design practice. In general, the above approach is quite inclusive – the course is emergent in nature and each individual, to some extent, drives the trajectory of the research through their individual interests as focused through directed mentoring.

Central to an education in the department of Digital+Media is a richly focused liberal arts/conceptual/social agenda that falls in relation to a digital practice. This form of education is presented in counter distinction to a set of common practices that are passed on to students in a "cookie-cutter" manner, characteristic of some digital media departments. Education at D+M becomes emergent as a general methodology where multiple foci are informing the student's practice. As students share their work and research a very broad education is fostered across multiple research frontiers. The graduating student explores and builds a broad knowledge base and develops a particular approach relevant to their own practice in concert with their advisors, their peers, lecturers, independent study mentors, and eventually through their thesis committee and thesis chair.

In the RISD Digital+Media department, the core conception is to take a series of node classes to become fluent in multiple aspects of digital media practice, where exploration via the computer falls somewhere in the loop of production. It is interesting to note that sometimes the fact that the work arises from computer-oriented practice does not preclude that the computer will be visually present in exhibitions of the work arising from the curriculum. Sometimes the computer falls entirely out of view later in the process, if the process leads to an artifact, like a 3-D model, a digital print, a particular form of installation or the articulation of new approach to digital/physical processes. This is why we have given the department the '+Media' designation, pointing toward creative production that is embodied, embraces physicality and explores digital/physical relationships.

A Digital+Media student will choose the set of node classes that best fit their particular needs. They work in conjunction with me and others to pull salient information from these differing classes and enfold that information and knowledge within the sphere of their individual practice. Mentoring in this instance helps them to define how these diverse studies can be brought together in their artwork or design practice. One comes to see how their practice might expand to take on board the new knowledge that has been gained through the multiple perspectives that the node classes offer. Mentoring also includes suggesting people to the student who might be actively sought out as mentors at RISD in other departments and Brown University (and in terms of the broader artistic community) to meet the needs of the student's research and practice. We have also undertaken a rich visiting artist and lecture program in the department and once the artist or designer has visited and critiqued the student's work, there is a potential for them to develop a continuing dialogue.

**Working in Concert with Individual Graduate Students to Develop Their "Voice"**
The most rewarding part of graduate education arises out of a series of deep creative relationships that are fostered with each individual student. In particular this has to do

with helping each student find their own voice – this includes discussing their conceptual methodology, outlining a set of viable working processes, articulating their field of interest, and honing their personal and/or collaborative research and practice in an ongoing manner.

## Associative Diagram

The first assignment given, as I am getting to know an incoming class, relates to the development of an elaborate *associative diagram* as a means to register relevant foci. In particular the 'thought flows' of each individual can potentially be brought to the surface, embodied through this exercise. The assignment goes as follows: I suggest that the student start with a very large piece of paper. They write one word in the upper left that is in some way central to their practice.[5] (Greene 2001). I then ask them to further associate and write a word next to and below this word. They are asked to continue this process as an iterative task until they fill up the page. This process often leads to an extraordinary textual diagram, providing a set of links and relationships that are relevant to each particular individual. The multiple forms that these diagrams take, as each student interprets the assignment in a subtly different manner, are as unique as the individuals partaking in the class.

Face-to-face meetings are facilitated with each person in the class. We work through these diagrams in depth, beginning with my own associative set of processes – what artists and/or designers would this person most benefit from looking at? What does the greater field of their work encompass? What is at operation in their work? What technologies might this person use to expand their work? What classes might be best for them to take from the school's offerings? What other professors should they meet in the local area? Who might they contact nationally or internationally? What books should they look at? What URLs might help to inform their practice? What other fields are relevant for them to study? In general this discussion begins a dialogue that continues throughout their entire graduate education. This relationship grows and can in some ways continue long after graduation as a lifelong dialogue that shifts from a perspective of lecturer/student, to a peer-to-peer relationship. Thus, these exercises and discussions foster the initial seeding of a dialogical process related to ongoing thesis development that expands over their entire graduate educational experience.

## Generative Bridging Diagram

Related to this initial associative diagram is a second diagram they develop. I call this the *Generative Bridging Diagram*. This diagram takes the individual modules of conceptual thought that each word or phrase represents in the initial associative diagram and seeks to build a *generative thought engine* that is relevant to the individual. I ask them to take their grid and, in this case, type or write out the words in a long list along the left edge of a page. I then ask them then to copy this list on the right-hand border. Subsequently they work to articulate a series of bridging words (or concepts) [this might include the development of an imagistic, sonic, textual, or technological relation] that bridge each word or concept on the right to each one on the left, articulating a relationship between the two. This potentially becomes a vast process. In general each individual finds a method of self-editing that enables them to pull out the most salient foci from this conceptual bridging process.

This generative procedure enables the student to make a much more complete registering of the field of ideas they have outlined in their associative diagram. The working through of this process actually suggests ways to approach and 'grow' new projects. Thus, it suggests entirely new potential works based on their articulated 'vocabulary' of ideas and processes. These ideas get further developed via discussion both with me and through class critique. Again, such a process is central in articulating each individual's unique 'voice'. Dialogue surrounding these lists and the processes that bring them to life are often deeply rewarding and "eye-opening" to the student. Much is revealed about their conceptual processes that in the past lived buried beneath the surface of their thought processes. Often these meetings are highly inspiring and open out a much more clear understanding for the individual of their oeuvre. Such exercises can be repeated at different stages of the matriculation as well. It is also stimulating to revisit these exercises some years later to see elements of ongoing interest as well as to articulate changes in the flow of their work processes.

### The *Book of Notice*
I have for many years asked students to keep what I call a *Book of Notice*. I suggest that students pay attention to the different things that they are "noticing" or that stand out to them across a series of differing domains. Often we pass by particular environmental relationships or aspects of media-related phenomena as we wing our way through the average day, without taking mindfully aware[6] (Varela, Thompson and Rosch 1996) notice of particular relationships, objects, situations, concepts, and/or unique aesthetic qualities. This kind of "collection" process makes people begin to take time and re-see the world and its complex relations. I also suggest they find a format that is pertinent to them as individuals, to collect and/or register their observations. For some, this becomes the standard artist sketchbook. Yet, I suggest that each person articulate a specific form to present their observations that is relevant to their own particular practice: This might become a catalogue of video clips, a series of photographs, a set of URLs, a list of words, a collection of images of every kind, an accumulation of objects, a compendium of quotes, a set of computer graphic animations, etc. Each *Book of Notice* should be unique to the person defining the collection process. One can use these compendiums to help them define elements and qualities of their oeuvre. One can also go mining in them to seed ideas for new projects or to articulate elements of nuanced artistic sensibility.

### Thinking Large
Another assignment I give to beginning graduates relates to 'thinking large.' I assign a major presentation that asks students to articulate a proposal for a major work, without the normal economic, technological, and/or space-related constraints. I discuss the potentials of this work with them at length. The student draws from their *associative diagrams* and past works as well as their *Book of Notice* to develop a major piece, or

suite of related works in proposal form. This assignment is highly pragmatic. Students working with digital media need to be able to articulate their ideas in order to apply for grants and funding – to define elements of their working processes. Large-scale digital works can take years and often draw on the expertise of an interdisciplinary team. Such an assignment gets them to visualize and lay out the salient aspects of a given work in a clear and cogent manner, from multiple perspectives. I later suggest ways the work could be developed given the current resources and restraints, once the student has completed the process of thinking large. Often a scaled-down version of this assignment becomes the thesis work. I always imagine the two years of graduate study as opening out a ten-year research agenda that is different for each student where such a project might later fully be developed, or grown, into a new, related project.

**Annotated URLs and Bibliography of Quotes**
Students are asked to collect a series of bibliographic references and URLs in an ongoing manner. When they are doing their collecting I ask them to annotate each entry – to write down some form of relation to their work. These text references and annotations become part of the fabric of the written thesis and can also inform in a meaningful manner aspects of the thesis project. The concept here is to break down the process of writing so it becomes less of a Herculean task and more process-oriented, direct, and effortless as an ongoing pursuit.

**Input/Functionality/Output**
I have more recently begun a new generative exercise related to interactive projects. This suggests mapping out a series of potential 'inputs,' 'functionalities,' and 'outputs' (both conceptual and technological). This exercise draws from my work *The Hybrid Invention Generator* (see below). This assignment enables students to register a series of different options to consider in terms of brainstorming surrounding the generation of new interactive works. "Inputs" would be related to different interface strategies; "functionality" relates to what processes the use of the system will set in motion; and "output" suggests both the outcome of the interaction as well as the technological platform that might be used to display this output.

**Generative System Texts**
Along with the above exercises, I have also (where needed) provided my own generative system texts for students to employ as creative tools. One text is entitled *Toward a Vocabulary of Image, Sound, Text Relations*. This text, generated initially two decades ago as a teaching tool for video classes (and subsequently honed over the years), provides a breakdown of video related processes such that an author can draw from them to think through new ideas in a combinatoric manner. Topic areas are elaborated in a set of lists within the text which include the following headings:

THE FRAME/SHOT
LIGHT
SOUND RELATIONS TO THE FRAME/SHOT

KINDS OF EDITS – VIDEO AND AUDIO
SOUND
KINDS OF STRUCTURES
TIME
FUNCTIONS
GENRES
INTERFACES
TEXT
COMBINATION OF THE ABOVE RELATIONS

Another generative text I authored to help students brainstorm, in this case virtual space authorship, is entitled: *VR/Variables – Periodic Table of VR*. This text was authored in the 90s to extend the thinking of students surrounding Virtual Reality production. It includes many variables to consider in the production of virtual reality works and again can be approached as a combinatoric tool.

**Current Processes**
As students take the multiple node classes at RISD described above, they begin to amass a broad vocabulary of potential technological processes and conceptual approaches to their work. It is my role as advisor to help each student pull out the particular salient aspects that are relevant to their practice. Thus, their work becomes informed by their associative writings and *Book of Notice* as well as other ongoing research. I see another of my roles as helping them see how they can enfold multiple observations in a single work, drawing from the breadth of their investigative experiences. Such an approach enables one to focus the complexity of their research foci. Alternately, some students explore simplicity in their approach. Even here one asks how they might enfold their ideas in the service of a 'minimal' work. I seek to be pluralistic in my support methodology, reflecting back the needs of each individual.

**Assigned Readings**
In terms of assigned readings that I provide, I tend to draw from a broad set of categories. Central to my role as advisor relates to providing a bibliography that will enable them to expand a core body of concepts relevant to their individual practice. I point out to them a series of pertinent artists and or experimental designers that they should come to know as well as discuss with them the work of artists they may have uncovered in their research. I often suggest for them to seek out the writings that the artists (or designers) themselves have undertaken. I also often draw from twentieth-century art history but my suggestions can encompass older traditions as well. Thus, this necessitates the development of an individual reading list for each student. Along with this selection of artists and historical texts, I also suggest critical texts, the writings of relevant theorists, as well as more popular texts – novels, poetry, magazines, etc. This broad set of texts enables them to build out their ideas in a clear manner. In many ways this is opposite to the notion of a "cannon" for digital media. Yet, in Digital+Media's curriculum we also provide a core set of readings that do function somewhat like a "cannon." My emphasis

is to have each person define a field of literature that contextualizes their work and establishes a broad focused context from which their work can be discussed and understood. In this way, each student graduating from the department brings with them a unique, articulate sphere of conceptual underpinnings they can draw upon in discussion, in artist talks and in future published texts that they author. In this way, the work does not spiral inward, being informed by a few central theorists, but expands outward in an articulate manner, broadening the scope of creative artistic and/or design-related thought and production.

## Growth
Perhaps the most difficult question for the graduates (and ourselves) is how do we go beyond what we know? This is actually a matter of personal courage. I have used the above methodology as a means to help students through this very process. I must also admit that the set of processes described above also continues to foster my own growth and learning. I often do my own research related to the student's inquiry to keep well informed about new development in the field. The exploration of such generative processes in the service of creative production is a lifelong concern. Working with top students is a deeply fulfilling way to live, continue to learn, and study multiple fields.

## Thesis
At the center of graduate education is the thesis process. The written thesis is pragmatic and enables the student to position themselves in terms of their work in relation many different kinds of digital practices, as well as art historical, social, conceptual and, alternately, more personal/eclectic relations.

At RISD the thesis process entails both the defining of a cogent and thoroughly researched document contextualizing the students work, as well as the development of a thesis show which presents a major culminating artwork – a 'proof of concept' technological/art presentation; a design-related project; and/or suite of relevant works. I have worked closely with my colleague Teri Rueb in the Digital+Media department to articulate a clear procedure and set of deadlines to streamline the thesis process, drawing on both of our extensive experiences in graduate education. Along with a set of prescribed deadlines, we work with each student individually to help them map out a timeline related to their own production schedule. Each student has a unique working process and early on in the graduate program we try to help each of the students discover their own functioning process methodology.

At the end of the first year, students write a preliminary thesis statement and are assigned a thesis chair. The chair works with the student to define a relevant thesis committee. This often means working with teachers from other departments at RISD, local artists, adjunct faculty, as well as other artists and theorists from around the world. In concert with the chair, the students begin doing a series of related readings over the summer. Often an extensive bibliography is researched in the period before starting the thesis process. In the fall semester of the thesis year, students take relevant node classes, further developing their ideas as well as key themes related to their thesis. The student undertakes a set of writing workshops. We have been working with Anne West at RISD, who has developed an interesting set of processes for 'mapping' the student's conceptual framework for the thesis. It is fascinating to note that Anne West and I both came to such "mapping" processes from study in quite different domains, although we share a deep interest in facilitating the thought of the individual, and we were drawn to working together based on this drive.

At midterm of the fall semester the student works up a "matrix map" related to their thesis, revealing their thought processes, along with their bibliography which is still 'in progress.' The students develop an outline and preliminary exhibition plan during the fall semester. Their work is ongoing in the studio and they begin to write a first draft of the thesis. This draft of the thesis is honed over the RISD winter session (January and early February). In the spring semester a first draft is turned in, approximately 30 pages, double spaced, as informed by the initial outline. In addition the student prepares an official title page, table of contents, endnotes/footnotes, and bibliography. The spring is a period for focused work on further honing the written thesis in concert with the student's committee and in particular via meeting regularly with their thesis chair. The graduate students develop an in-depth exhibition plan. A final written thesis class and thesis project class are undertaken along with one final node class in their culminating semester. The thesis exhibition is mounted and an exciting final critique takes place with top critics, peers, and theorists as well as members of the thesis committee.

The Department of Digital+Media's written thesis guidelines are flexible in order to support individual approaches. At RISD we have adopted what might be considered a "research university" -based approach to the written document. We articulate a series of different options or approaches in laying out the content of the thesis, where the chair works with each individual to define an appropriate methodology and format. We suggest that the thesis should reveal the conceptual and philosophical infrastructure of the student's practice, focusing on elucidating the thesis exhibition. A concise abstract states the central questions or problems that the work explores. We recommend that the thesis be an articulate research document, footnoted and correctly formatted. Alternately, on occasion, we also work with students to define more individual and experimental frameworks to present their ideas. Again, we see the document as being pragmatic – that is, students can later draw upon their research to inform future practice. The written work thus becomes source material for journal length publications, and can potentially provide the basis for a professional talk after graduation.

We expect that the written document critically examine and illuminate the individual's practice, positioning it historically and theoretically. Working with each student as an individual, we help them position their work in a relevant manner. Thus, a student may define for him/herself a particular approach to this articulation in concert with their chair while also getting additional focused advice from their thesis committee. Each committee member may bring a different area of expertise to the table, be it conceptual, technological, historical, etc. In general we suggest that the written thesis in the Digital+Media department should address the following: creative process, historical context, a wide variety of influences, conceptual/philosophical/theoretical foundations, and future directions. In terms of format the work may take on one of the following approaches: a critical approach; an anecdotal approach; a catalogue-oriented approach – commenting in a critical autobiographical manner on one's practice at RISD, culminating in the thesis exhibition; a formal research paper discussing philosophical and aesthetic issues as they relate to the student's work; and/or a manifesto approach – articulating ideas about new forms in the arts and/or design in a critical manner.

Along with critical reflection we ask that students present quality documentation – visual material that will be integrated into the text of the thesis to support its salient points. All visual materials are appropriately captioned and cross-referenced in the text. This may also take a digital form. Sometimes this means defining a secondary document that is specifically formatted in a relevant manner to extend the content of their thesis. There is also the potential to develop a hyperlinked document or interactive documentation environment, potentially publishable on the Internet. A hypertext on DVD or CD-ROM can be submitted to augment the written document. This might include related programs, video and audio materials.

An extensive dialogue is facilitated with the chair and committee. In all cases the form and content of the thesis is discussed and agreed upon with the thesis chair. Although there is often a deep interest to make this written document be a creative and poetic work, we stress that the thesis exhibition is the place for experimental practice and functions as the central arena for the student's inquiry and creative expression, where the written thesis functions in a scholarly manner. Thus, the document presents a clear examination of the issues that become operative through the work(s) of art and/or design practice presented in the thesis exhibition.

## Art, Science, and Technology

There is much educational potential that flows from the research that bridges art, science, and technology. Most recently, I team-taught a class entitled *Cognitive Science and Digital Media* with Dr. Barbara Von Eckardt, Dean of Liberal Arts at RISD, cognitive scientist and author. The course provided students with an introduction to important approaches and findings in cognitive science and contemporary analytic philosophy (especially, philosophy of mind, epistemology, and metaphysics) relevant to the field of digital media. It also explored a number of specific digital media works which connected with those approaches and findings. Some of the questions that were addressed in the class included: How has perception/sensing been modeled in cognitive science and within digital media works? What are current cognitive science theories related to language, meaning, and language acquisition? What is the relevance of empirical findings related to the mind/brain, to artistic practice and in particular to the field of digital media? What is the mind/body problem and how can it be solved? Can machines think or be persons? How do we come to know the world? What is the relevance of theoretical discussions in analytic philosophy to digital media?

Here is a list of strategies that came out of the class in relation to approaching a potential bridging between Cognitive Science and Digital Media:

- A work can function as a question.
- A work can function as a pointing mechanism.
- A work can embody a critique.
- A work can function as a documentary.
- A work can use the principles of one field to explore another, i.e. Artificial Intelligence.
- A work can make fun or be a parody of another field.
- A work can use the formal qualities derived from one field to approach another, i.e. cognitive experiments to inform the making of performance art.
- A work can employ abstracted terminology from one field as a poetic strategy.
- A work can function as a map of a potential approach in an alternate field.
- A work can explore related issues from an alternate set of perspectives.
- A work can poetically describe processes and research that CS explores via digital media.
- A work can explore the strategy – *displacement illuminates placement.*
- A work can explore a subject in a nonsensical manner.
- A work can employ a strategy from one arena and use it in another, i.e. telerobotics/telepistemology.
- A work can function as a database of ideas that enable differing people to access particular aspects of information from multiple fields.
- A work can try to present approaches to particular questions that science will not allow.

The class provided a space for reflection across the fields and fueled many interesting discussions pertaining to the above topics.

### Research Projects – Art/Science/Technology/Culture
Along with the formal aspect of holding a class, I have undertaken a number of research projects that have included students that explore art/science issues. I have also published a number of papers that explore art/science relations.[7]

*The Poly-sensing Environment* is one such project. The Principal Investigators include Dr. Ingrid Verbauwhede – UCLA Electrical Engineering, Mark Hansen – Statistical Computer Science, UCLA, and myself.

As a research team, we have been exploring the exciting potentials related to the development of new sensing technology. In particular in the research for the *Poly-sensing Environment* we were seeking to explore the creation of a poetic/informational interactive IT system that would be facilitated through the use of multi-modal sensory devices that could collaborate in a distributed fashion, linked to a dynamic virtual imaging environment and the Internet. Many researchers have seen the importance of parsing "sense" data within interactive environments. The biological model of the human body, parsing a series of sensory modalities in the service of knowledge acquisition and general functioning, became one focus for the development of our model. We came to understand that technologies might enable the appurtenant extension of the senses. Organism-like, self-organizing technological systems have in the past enabled new forms of poetic/informational interaction. Other organisms also provide sensory models that we could draw upon to inform the authorship of the system. Our goal was to create a "poly-sensing" environment. We were seeking to facilitate the integration of multiple heterogeneous sensors on one "system-on-a-chip. " The unique aspect of our technology was the collection of information from the parsing of an integrated "collaboration" between a diverse collection of micro-scale sensing devices. Such a system could be focused for multiple kinds of uses, be they artistic, scientific, and/or cultural.

While at UCLA we worked with two different student researchers, Shenglin Yang – Electrical Engineering (UCLA) and Fabian Winkler – Design | Media Arts (UCLA). Fabian went on to Teach at Carnegie Melon and more recently has taken on a post in the Department of Visual and Performing Arts at Purdue University. The research continues to this day yet the universality of the project has made it difficult to fund in an ongoing manner from 'scientific' funding sources. Ongoing funding becomes a central concern for research scientists and a deep challenge to Art/Science collaborations. The work was funded initially by a special interdisciplinary fund at UCLA. It was further funded for one year by the Langlois Foundation.

During my time at UCLA, I was also awarded an Intel Research gift over a period of three years. I worked on a project entitled *The Hybrid Invention Generator*. The work was a computer-based language system exploring hybrid invention generation. It was developed by me working in conjunction with the programmer Gideon May. Initial research was undertaken by a student team from UCLA including Daksh Sahni – Architecture; Gustavo Rincon –Architecture; Kalim Chan – Design | Media Arts; Grace Tsai – Architecture; Craig Chun – Design | Media Arts and consultant Kostas Terzidis, Ph.D. – Assistant professor in Architecture (Kostas now works at the Harvard GSD); with myself functioning as principle investigator. This work explored 3-D visualization with related generative texts and recombinant audio/music, as well as a series of textual descriptions. Computer-based environmental meaning was explored through the inter-authorship and operative experiential examination of a diverse set of media elements and media processes, focusing on the virtual construction of hybrid inventions. Varying combinations of individual inventions could be experienced through direct interaction with the system. Each participant potentially had a different experience with this open work, combining two differing inventions at a time to create a kind of "machinic" genetic process with related visualization. Thus, students gained direct experience with an exciting and challenging research process.

Along with continuing aspects of this earlier research, I have been most recently working with the theoretical biologist and physicist Otto Rössler. In this research the potential is to generate an intelligent, situated computer-driven robotic system. Two different initial approaches have been discussed: the creation of such a machine via the embodiment of a series of specific algorithms on a parallel computing platform working in conjunction with a specific situated machinic sensing environment and robot; and the development of a new paradigm for computing through the generation of an electrochemical computer, functioning in conjunction with a robot and related sensing system. Rössler's seminal concepts including *A Relational Approach to Brain function* and *An Artificial Cognitive-plus-motivational System* (among others) will be enfolded and form a top-down "relational" analogical/biologic perspective informing both projects. We will also employ a bottom-up inquiry exploring an approach for the development of an electrochemical device, abstracting and applying Rossler's "relational" approach via an electrochemical articulation. This will include the development of a *Poly-sensing Environment* as it might be used to inform the machinic senses for both "entities;" and the notion of *Pattern Flows* of sense perturbations as applied to potential learning, language acquisition, embodied navigation, and robotic behavior. The long-term goal of this part of the project includes mapping and abstracting specific neural processes into an electrochemical/sensing/situated robotic environment which I have entitled *The Thoughtbody Environment*. Many papers have been written related to this topic and these are shared with students. Along with the knowledge that papers provide, David Dao at the Digital+Media department at RISD has assisted in transcribing a complex research diagram that Rössler and I have been working on. The project is large in scope and has a long-term potential with the hope of including students in differing aspects of the research.

Currently, I am seeking to create a new form of multi-modal database to house the various research related to *The Thoughtbody Environment* with the computer scientist David Durand. I will be seeking student help with this project as well in the coming months. I also hope to facilitate an approach to the creation of the electrochemical computer. I have had a number of discussions with Peter Cariani, scientist, and participated in a major symposium entitled Finding Fluid Form[8] (Cariani 2006), at the University of Sussex in the fall of 2005 where a number of researchers working on related topics gathered.

I have been very active in writing papers over the last two decades. I also share these papers and research findings with students in an ongoing manner, where the research informs both my practice and teaching. These diverse papers can be found online at http: //www.billseaman.com.

Common to many of my research activities has been an emergent, combinatoric approach to meaning production. I have drawn on this set of processes to inform the larger sphere of my ongoing research, educational techniques, and artistic practice. Thus, a rich set of processes, teaching methodologies, projects, and concepts have become enfolded in the service of *Educating Artists for the Future*. It is clear that students are *Learning at the Intersections of Art, Science, Technology and Culture* via this *Generative Emergent Approach to Graduate Education*.

## Notes

1. Star, S. and Bowker, G. (1999), 'Sorting Things Out: Classification and its Consequences,' http://epl.scu.edu: 16080/~gbowker/classification/. Accessed 10 August 2006. "At this site, we present the introduction, first two chapters and concluding chapters of our book on classification systems published by MIT Press in 1999."
2. Seaman, B. (1999), 'Recombinant Poetics: Emergent Meaning as Examined and Explored Within a Specific Generative Virtual Environment' Ph.D. Dissertation, The Center for Advanced Inquiry in Interactive Art, University of Wales, http: //www.billseaman.com. Accessed 10 August 2006.
3. Wardrip-Fruin, N. and Mountford, N. (2003), *The New Media Reader*, Cambridge, MA and London: MIT Press.
4. Wilson, S. (2002), *Information Arts: Intersections of Art, Science, and Technology*, Cambridge, MA and London: MIT Press; related website http: //userwww.sfsu.edu/~swilson/. Accessed 10 August 2006.
5. For an elaborate approach to creative potentials see Greene, R. (2001), 'A Garbage Can Model of Creativity, the 4 Cycle Model', *Kwansei Gakuin Journal of Policy Studies*, 11: 9/2001, pp. 1–204. In this elaborate text he presents 42 differing models of creativity.
6. Varela, F., Thompson, E. and Rosch, E. (1996), *The Embodied Mind, Cognitive Science and Human Experience*, Cambridge, MA and London: MIT Press. "Speaking about Buddhist mindfulness/awareness in relation to Cognitive Science: Its purpose is to become mindful, to experience what one's mind is doing as it does it, to be present with one's mind. What relevance does this have to cognitive science? We believe that if cognitive science is to include human experience, it must have some method of exploring and knowing what human experience is."

## 2006

The Thoughtbody Interface (Poetic Text) & Toward The Creation of an Intelligent Situated Computer and Related Robotic System: An Intra-functional Network of Living Analogies, Seaman, B. and Rössler, O., *Catalogue for Emoçào Art.ficial*, Itau Cultural Center (forthcoming).

Pattern Flows: Notes Toward a Model for an Electrochemical Computer (forthcoming), Itau Cultural Center website.

## 2005

"Recombinant Poetics: The Thoughtbody Environment", *a Minima Magazine*, 13, New Media Actual Art -ISSN 1697-7777.

Interview with Professor Dr. Yvonne Spielmann in *Transcript Magazine*, Manchester University Press

"Pattern Flows | Hybrid Accretive Processes Informing Identity Construction," *Convergence Magazine*.

Cariani, p. (2005), 'Finding Fluid Form', http: //www.brighton.ac.uk/architecture/findingfluidform/. Accessed 10 August 2006.

## 2004

(RE)Sensing the Observer – Offering an Open Order Cybernetics. Gaugusch, A. and Seaman, B., *Technoetic Arts* vol.2.1.

Interview with Professor Dr. Yvonne Spielmann in *Transcript Magazine*, Manchester University Press (forthcoming).

Recombinant Poetics in New Media Poetics (expanded edition) (ed. E. Kac), Leonardo Press (forthcoming).

Toward the Production of Nano-computers and in Turn Nano-related EmotiveVirtual/Physical Environments, http: //www.billseaman.com. Presented at the Banff Centre.

## 2003

Recombinant Poetics – Media-Element Field Explorations published in the MIT press book: *First Person*: *New Media as Story, Performance, and Game*, (ed. N. Wardrip-Fruin and p. Harrigan). See also paper entitled: A response to Kate Hayles text "Metaphoric Networks in Lexia to Perplexia."

The Hybrid Invention Generator – Assorted Relations, *Technoetic Arts* 1: 2

## 2002

Recombinant Poetics: Emergent Explorations of Digital Video in Virtual Space in "Transluminations: New Screen Media Narratives" (ed. Zapp and Reiser), BFI Publishers.

## 2001

Exchange Fields: Embodied Positioning as Interface Strategy, *Convergence Magazine*, special Issue on Intelligent Environments, Summer 2001 issue of *Convergence* 7: 2.

OULIPO|vs|Recombinant Poetics, *Leonardo Digital Salon* 34: 5 (ed. C. Paul).

Recombinant Poetics: Emergent Explorations of Digital Video in Virtual Space in "Transluminations: New Screen Media Narratives" (ed. Zapp and Reiser), BFI Publishers.

## 2000

"Red Diice / Des Chiffrés", Adelaide Festival Catalogue.

"Motioning Toward the Emergent Definition of E-phany Physics," presented at Consciousness Reframed III, http: //www.billseaman.com.

## 1999

"Nonsense Logic" in the book Reframing Consciousness (ed. R. Ascott).

## 1998

"Emergent Constructions: Re-embodied Intelligence within Recombinant Poetic Networks" *Digital Creativity* (1998), 9: 3, pp. 153–160.

## 1994

"Hybrid Architectures/Media Information Environments"

"Intelligent Environments-Spatial Aspect of the Information Revolution," (ed. p. Droege), Amsterdam.

# MEDIA LITERACY: READING AND WRITING IMAGES IN A DIGITAL AGE

## Shlomo Lee Abrahmov

This chapter explores definitions of visual literacy which consist of the combined abilities of 'reading' and 'writing' images. It suggests a set of common categories for both activities based on observing and creating three levels of meaning in images: Factual, Interpretive, and Conceptual. An effective strategy for teaching visual literacy is a blended approach where the writing of images is through face-to-face teaching on campus and the reading of images is through e-Learning using a Web-based teaching platform. Such an approach creates synergy between theoretical and practical activities in a digital age when images become fluid and are used to convey messages and intentions with ease.

### Visual Literacy

Many interpretations of comprehending visuals exist, such as visual thinking, the act of looking and cognition, the skill of seeing and the way things physically appear. How we make sense of images is often believed to be the result of the ability to think in pictures (Moore 2003). Raney (1999) suggested that if we use cultural products to think and to communicate – 'speak' to one another, then visual systems of signs, such as film narratives, computer games, clothes, exhibitions, public monuments, and advertisements, as well as architecture and art, become our objects of study. If such systems of signs are like languages, 'read', and 'written' – then visual literacy, or media literacy, seems like the normal way to describe the skills involved in using and understanding such system of signs.

Avgerinou and Ericson (1997), basing their findings on an extensive research by Baca (1990), offered the following areas of focus for visual literacy:

- The use of visuals for communication, thinking, learning, constructing meaning, creative and aesthetic expression.
- A visual in the realm of visual literacy may be: man-made objects, natural objects, visual events, actions, pictorial representations, iconic representations and symbols, non-verbal symbols, digital symbols such as numbers or words when they are part of an iconic element.
- Visual literacy study includes: theory, research, implementation and the relationship among the activities of theory, research and implementation.

Kirrane (1992: 58) referred to the definitions of visual literacy developed by the International Visual Literacy Association (IVLA) at the Virginian Polytechnic University:

> Visual literacy refers to several visual competencies a person can develop by observing and at the same time having and integrating other cognitive experiences. The acquired aptitude to interpret images as communicative visual symbols and to create images that use such communicative visual symbols. The capability to interpret (translate) visual images using verbal language and the ability to transform verbal language into imagery. The ability to find and evaluate visual data in visual media.

### Three Levels of Meaning

The critical foundation for reading and writing of images is based on the understanding of the structure of levels of meanings in them. In this chapter, I suggest that one of the most effective ways of comprehending images is to look at three levels of meaning in them: Factual, Interpretive, and Conceptual. The following discussion uses photographs as examples, but it could be applied to other visual media as well.

Victor Burgin, in his essay, 'Looking at Photographs,' (1982: 148), provides an example for the analysis of the three levels of meaning in a photograph. The first level is a factual one. In a photograph of General Wavell and his gardener, one is wearing a uniform and the second a galabiya. At the interpretive level, we observe that the general represents the West while the gardener represents the East. There is an allusion to the dominance of one over the other. The third level is the conceptual level which is derived from assigning a universal theme to the reading of the relationships between the factual and the interpretive levels. In the case of this photograph, Burgin suggests that the conceptual level is the uneasy interaction between East and West or the division of capital and labor. We could add as a possible conceptual level, the interaction of the first world with the Third World, or the dominance of white man over black man and the complex relationships that develop as a result.

Following Burgin's example, we can look for the three levels of meaning – Factual, Interpretive, and Conceptual – in Barthes's second essay, 'Rhetoric of the Image' (1977). Barthes analyzes a photograph of a pasta advertisement. He explains that he chose an advertising image because in such an image, intentions are predetermined. Barthes finds three messages or meanings in the image (excluding the linguistic message in Panzani, the name of the pasta). Looking for a coherent analysis of this image, Barthes argues that if we can describe the structure of the image in a simple and coherent fashion and if such a description leads to a possible explanation of the role of the image within society then such a description is justified.

Adopting this intention, and offering a slight departure from Barthes's original reasoning, we can examine if three linked levels of meaning can be found in this image. What we need to do in order to find the conceptual level, is ask the question, what is the aim of this image? The immediate answer would be, to sell this particular manufacturer's pasta. The second question would be, then, how to achieve this goal. The answer is by the association of pasta with *Italianicity* (Barthes's term) and the concept of pasta as being a traditional fresh and healthy food. In addition, we can say that *Italianicity* also implies family, happiness, and sunshine, in short a set of positive associations. We have to remember that this positive association is aimed at offering a better image for this pasta, which otherwise could be associated with a cheap, mundane domestic product. If this is the conceptual level, let's see how the factual level is described by Barthes: "some packets of pasta, a tin, a sachet, some tomatoes, peppers, a mushroom, all emerging from a half-open string bag, in yellows, and greens on a red background."

Barthes continues to an analysis that belongs to the interpretive level. The half-opened bag which lets the products be spread over the table as just unpacked, implies a return from the market, which alludes to the freshness of the produce and a domestic scene where this food stuffs are to be prepared. Another interpretation in this level is the bringing together of the tomato, the pepper and the three colors (yellow, green, red) in the poster to read a reference to Italy or rather *Italianicity*. It must be noted that since the Italian tricolor is green, white, and red, we may assume that the yellow color in the poster is a symbol for the warm sun and light we commonly associate with Italy.

If we suppose that in a formation, where there are three levels of meaning, the interpretive level is the one that connects the factual level with the conceptual level, it can be observed that that our reading of this advertisement is coherent and fits well with the interpretations offered by Barthes. Here is a summary:

- Factual level:
  Pasta, sachet, tin, peppers, tomatoes, mushroom, half-opened bag, colors, and a certain composition of these objects in the photograph.
- Interpretive level:
  'Coming back from the market', freshness of produce, domestic scene, bringing together (interpreting) the meaning of the colors, a carefully balanced dish, a reference from the visual structure of the image to still life paintings of the past.
- Conceptual level:
  Italianicity, and its association with pasta, the positive association of the product with traditional values, culinary wholesomeness of the product as a dish.

Three levels of meaning can be found in Erwin Panofsky's (1955, 1983) exploration of signification in Renaissance art. As an example, he uses the levels of interpretation of an observer who is seeing a man in the street who tips his hat when he meets him. The first phase is a factual or natural meaning, like recognizing that the object one sees is a man and that the gesture perceived is that of a man raising his hand to his hat and lifting it slightly. Panofsky defines this phase as expressional and called this act of interpretation as Pre-Iconographical description.

The recognition of the man's gesture as a greeting belongs to a second level of interpretation and it is founded on a shared cultural context, in this case a custom belonging to modern Western culture. This according to Panofsky is a secondary or conventional meaning which he defines as Iconographical analysis of the image.

The third level of meaning is what Panofsky calls the intrinsic meaning of the image. It is the level that contains the philosophical aspects observed in a picture. As such, it aims to explain the essence of the situation, its general meaning, or expressed concepts. Panofsky terms this level as the Iconological level of interpretation.

We can observe, then, that Panofsky's Pre-Iconographic, Iconographic, and Iconological levels of meaning have similarities with the Factual, Interpretive, and Conceptual levels of meaning in a photograph. In a similar fashion to the progress from the Factual to the Conceptual levels of meaning, Panofsky's three levels are continuous and there is a progression of interpretation from one level to the next.

Similarly, the three levels of meaning proposed by the father of semiotic theory, Charles S. Pierce, are Index, Icon, and Symbol. Indexical relationships signify a direct existential link between sign and object. Iconic relationships relate to likeness or resemblance between the sign and its referent. Symbolic relationship requires convention, agreement within a community, since the relationship between sign and what it signifies is arbitrary (Morgan 2006). A handprint is an indexical sign, whereas the hand on a stop sign is an iconic sign. The hand on the stop sign as a traffic sign for stopping is a symbol, since only convention makes us relate to it as a signal to stop traffic.

### Three Levels of Meaning in Art Photography

We can examine how these three levels of meaning apply to art photography by studying a photograph, 'Cassidy Bayou, Sumner Mississippi 1969–1970,' by William Eggleston (http://www.artnet.com/Magazine/reviews/krygier/krygier1-22-2.asp). Eggleston is a photographer who creates photographs with a predetermined intent. Working in documentary environments, he looked for situations that would transmit his overriding concerns. This practice is in contrast to the more common situation, when photographers find a scene and only later discover whether it has expressive qualities that match their beliefs. The following is the analysis of his 'Cassidy Bayou' photograph:

■ Visual/Formal/Factual Aspects

In the photograph, a white man with a black jacket is in the front of a black man with a white jacket. Both have their hands in their pockets. A car with its door open is not parked in an ordinary parking lot. The background of the photograph consists of a carpet of dry leaves, cropped tree trunks, and in the depth appears the Cassidy Bayou.

■ Interpretive/ Connotational Aspects

The figures of the white American man and the African-American man draw our attention. The photograph shows an ambivalent relationship between them. The two men seem planted in their places, as if someone ordered them to be in these positions. On the one hand, connection (they are in the same place), on the other hand we see a contrast (one is white and other is black). The older white man in the front of the photograph stands for the white segment of society, while the man behind him represents the other segment of society in the South of the United States. Another clue to this social hierarchy is the white jacket worn by the man in the back, a jacket associated with waiters or other persons of service. The car in the photograph is of a typical model for those years, and it is possible to view the car as a metaphor to white society and as another element that gives service to the white man. Despite the fact that the men are in a natural environment, there is a sense of disconnection from it that makes this environment seem sterile.

■ Conceptual Aspects

The photograph examines a central social issue in Southern society of the United States, the unresolved relations between white and black society. Eggleston did not portray his opinion on the subject, but rather presented it and let the viewer ponder its social significance. He hinted that the South is stuck in its past because of this unresolved issue.

**Common Categories**
If we are to teach 'reading' and 'writing' of images it is important for us to use common categories, both for the activity of 'writing' of images concerned with practical activities and 'reading' of images concerned with theoretical activities. The defined categories for evaluation of images combine two axes, one relates to the progress across three levels of meaning, the second to the particular elements in photographic images. Table 1 shows the activity in each level of meaning as it applies to each of the categories.

| | Levels of meaning | | |
|---|---|---|---|
| *Elements of Images* | Description of activity in each level | | |
| Categories relating to elements of images | Factual Level Observing factual details. | Interpretive Level Assigning significance to factual details. | Conceptual Level Deciphering the intrinsic (deep) meaning. |

**Table 1.** Structure of categories for analysis of images.

## 1. Framing and Perspective

In addition to its basic first function of determining the boundaries of the photograph, the choice of subject and the fundamental decision influencing the structure of the image, it has critical influence on the reduction of details in the original scene. Such action removes documentary details and by doing so enhances the focus on a specific subject. It could also leave part of the referent outside the frame, causing the viewer to relate to something that is outside the frame, and to reconstruct the complete referent in his mind thus relating to a presence that is absent (Krauss 1986).

As we can see from the sequence of five frames that Dorothea Lange photographed while creating her famous 'Migrant Mother' (http: //www.loc.gov/rr/print/list/ 128_migm.html), the tight cropping of her last frame removed the documentary details of the scene and enhanced the essence of the subject. This action enabled the image to have its universal reference to Madonna and Child, or the development of its second level of meaning, its *interpretive* level. This attribute of framing, expands the scope of the content of image and its implications by removing details that are not essential for contextual representation, and it transforms the length of the quote into the quality of the quote (Berger 1995).

## 2. Quality of Light

Light is an essential aspect of all photographic production. It is involved in expressing the richness of the medium and creating intriguing visual effects. It could be used to enhance also the content of the image at its expressive/interpretive level and its conceptual level. Krauss (1999) discusses Cindy Sherman's use of backlighting as part or her visual strategy, where in her 'Untitled Film Stills' #95,#139, it is used to disrupt the viewer's direct gaze on the figure, transforming the figure into 'a kind of blind spot.' Krauss (1999) calls Sherman's use of lighting 'Gleams and Reflections' and describes at length how the use of lighting is directly related to the 'gaze' aspect of Cindy Sherman's work.

Philip-Lorca diCorcia had used the effects of lighting extensively in his work. As can be seen in 'Head No. 1, 2000' (http: //www.portfoliocatalogue.com/36/index.php), by placing professional strobe lighting on street locations, diCorcia is able to produce images that look like they are stills from a film or a theatrical production. This effect is directly connected to diCorcia's conceptual approach of showing the blurring between found (documentary) reality and the fabricated reality of movies. Princethal (2003: 44) describes this act as 'inserting a moment of theatre into the shapeless movement of pedestrian life.' Lighting among other photographic techniques could make the familiar strange and in doing so transform even the most mundane objects to appear as burdened with meaning (Savedoff 2000).

## 3. Composition, Depth of Field, Focal Points

These three categories are all interrelated as they are creating the basic visual structure of the image. Composition could be dynamic or static creating the sense of movement or stillness. In William Eggleston's untitled image (http: //www.hasselbladfoundation.org/

prize_1998_en.html), the symmetrical placing of the figure is meant to allude to the solidity of the environment in which the white woman is living. The 'straightness' of the suburban society is an issue which relates to the conceptual level of this image.

Focal points in a similar fashion to their use in painting could direct the viewer towards the most important details of the image and in doing so give these details an added significance. Sally Mann's 'Candy Cigarette,' (http: //www.artnet.com/artwork/424714198/424705927/sally-mann-candy-cigarette.html) demonstrates effective use of focal points, where the face of the girl and the candy cigarette are the main focal points of her composition and are also the focal points of the content of this image which deals with the adult-like posture and simulated habit by a young girl. In a similar fashion, in Jeff Wall's 'Woman with a covered tray' (http: //www.artnet.com/artwork/423987332/460/jeff-wall-a-woman-with-a-covered-tray.html), the main focal is the covered tray which signifies its central significance in the meaning of the photograph; here we see the progress of this category across the levels of meaning from factual (formal) to conceptual.

### 4. Color
The effect of color in the photograph. Color can convey feelings or emotions beyond its factual level. The color red, for example, can convey strong emotions. Color could be connected to other themes, for example, the red and green colors of Christmas in Eggleston's photograph of 'Christmas Bathroom 1996' (http: //www.artnet.com/artwork/424039696/william-eggleston-untitled-christmas-bathroom.html).

### 5. Figure and Background
The relationship between the figure or subject and the background in photographs is of critical importance. Its first significance involves the formal aesthetics of the photograph, its composition, the visual hierarchy between the figure and background and the assigning of roles between them. We could compare this relationship to a theatre where the figure is the actor and the background is the stage with its various backdrops. Where the actor is responsible for carrying the plot or narrative, the stage function is to create scenery that enhances the sense of drama and ambience where the act is taking place. In this manner we could relate to the relationship between figure and background, first in its formal importance to the structure of the photograph and, secondly, to its significance regarding the content of the photograph in general and the creation of second and third levels of meaning in particular.

As an example, look at Diane Arbus's 'A family on their lawn one Sunday in Westchester NY 1968' (http: //www.masters-of-photography.com/A/arbus/arbus_westchester_family.html). In this photograph, Clarke (1997) describes the lawn as portraying the sense of emptiness, sterility, and dislocation that engulfs the image. Equally, the trees in the back have a looming haunting presence, all contributing to an atmosphere that is gloomy, depressing, and empty. We can see that the relationship between figures and background in this photograph contribute to a connotative level of emotional and psychological tension and conflict, which overall create an image that is 'almost an iconic statement on the nature of suburban America' (Clarke 1997: 33).

## 6. Relationship between Figures or Objects

This category relates mostly to the content of the photograph and the influence the relationships between figures and objects can have on the second and third levels of meaning.

In figure 1, the relationship between man and doll creates the photograph's second and third levels of meaning. In the second level, we realize that this is an uncommon situation because the usual function of this doll is as a toy for children, whereas in this image an adult holds it. This setting causes us to associate the doll as representing a baby. The tight cropping of the man on the left also equalizes their sizes and, thus, their significance. We can see the doll as equal or even slightly dominating the man, which is not our common experience. The third level of this image relates to a pertinent contemporary

**Figure 1.** Shlomo Lee Abrahmov, Untitled (guy with doll) 2002.

**Figure 2.** Shlomo Lee Abrahmov, Row 2004 from the Eucalyptus Grove, Yakkum 2003–2004/

issue of our culture when we are approaching a time when it will be difficult to distinguish the original from its simulations (Batchen 2001). There are no hints of any clothes worn by the man in the photograph, a fact that enhances the feeling of 'flesh to flesh' between him and the doll.

In some photographs, these two categories of the relationship between objects in the photograph and the relationship between figures and backgrounds are combined to create the images' conceptual levels. In 'Row 2004' the relationship between the trees shows a straight line, which hints that this grove is not a natural forest but was planted by man. The relationship between the trees and the plants in the foreground shows that they are still in a natural environment, as these sorrels are wildflowers. In addition, the relationship of the first tree hints at its individuality, or a metaphor to a body of a standing man. The conceptual level in this photograph is of the relationship between manufactured order and natural order, between man-made environment and nature.

## 7. Description/Representation of the Referent
This category is unique to photography as the term referent implies. In a situation where there is a direct, clear, and non-transformative representation of the referent, one could see a photograph in which the concept of 'Transparency' is present. Such a photograph, in which there is a linear connection to the referent, does not usually depict a dramatic

visual transformation. This lack of difference between referent and photograph effects the *imaginative transfiguration* (Friday 2000), that is possible within the medium of photography. When a marked difference between the photograph and its referent is present, we have to relate to the photograph first and only then think about its referent and in a way reconstruct it for ourselves. This is the essence of the concept of *spacing*, which makes clear that 'we are not looking at reality, but at the world infested by interpretation or signification' (Krauss 1986: 107). Historically, this aspect of photography was closest to the Surrealist movement heart (Krauss 1986), as for the surrealists the logical distinction between what is imaginary and what is real tends to disappear in the production of an image that functions as 'a hallucination that is also a fact' (Bazin 1967).

The significance of this category is apparent when we have a photograph of a photograph or a representation of representation. A noted contemporary example is Richard Prince photographs of images from Marlboro cigarettes advertisements (http: //www.metmuseum.org/toah/hd/pcgn/ho_2000.272.htm). The conceptual level of these images is derived from the fact that they are reproductions of already existing images. The re-photographing of existing images in this case causes them to be recontextualized (Savedoff 1993). As such, we have a photograph with two levels referent, one is the original referent (cowboys and horses in Prince's case) and the second referent is the advertisement photograph of the original scene. In today's digital world, this category is also important because it challenges our relation to the photograph. Where in the past the contiguous referent was representing the factuality of the photograph; today we cannot be certain of it.

## 8. Title of the Photograph
Information gained from the title can influence our understanding and interpretation of a photograph. Often, with the combination of knowledge about the circumstances involved with the creation of the photograph we can decipher its conceptual level. Observing Christopher Williams's 'Kiev 88 4.6 lbs 2.1KG' (http: //www.secession.at/ art/2005_williams-r-r_e.html), Rimanelli (2003) explains that Williams's intention was to focus on the issue of originality and reproduction of an original. In Williams's photograph, we see an inexpensive Soviet imitation of the famous and expensive Hasselblad camera. We could get a hint for Williams's intention from the very detailed title, describing the manufacturer and place of production of the Soviet (now Ukrainian) camera. Williams intends us to relate to globalization and the transfer of products from one country to another. The photograph created in California, as we learn from the title, is a visual reproduction of a Soviet camera bearing a name of a specific Ukrainian city. The camera is also an imitation of a Swedish camera (Hasselblad). These circumstances create a chain of reproductions and simulations, which raise the question of the relationship between an original and its reproductions.

## 9. Context: Circumstantial Evidence about the Creation of the Photograph
In contemporary art photography, in many instances we need to know the circumstantial information leading to the creation of a particular photograph in order for

us to grasp its conceptual level. In Jeff Wall's 'Woman with a covered tray 2003' (http: //www.artnet.com/artwork/423987332/460/jeff-wall-a-woman-with-a-covered-tray.html) or 'Mimic 1982' (http: //www.tate.org.uk/modern/exhibitions/jeffwall/ rooms/room3.shtm), it is important for us to know that what look like a successful decisive moments are in fact carefully staged images. Wall's intention is to challenge the view of the factuality of the photograph, or the usual factual relationship between the photograph and its referent. Yes, Wall's photographs represent a reality, but it is a manufactured reality, which fits Wall's intention of representing the single frame from an imaginary film.

It is important for us to know that Rineke Dijkstra's 'Julie, Den Haag, Netherlands February 29, 1994' (http: //www.tate.org.uk) is from a series titled 'Young Mothers' and that the photograph depicts a young woman, holding her baby, immediately after giving birth. Dijkstra is interested in capturing the moment of transition from a young woman to young mother, and knowing the particular timing of this photograph, is crucial to comprehending its conceptual level. The circumstances leading to a creation of a contemporary photograph, for example, can include the particular visual or literary reference the artist had in mind when planning the production of the image.

These categories were developed while observing and creating photographs. They have been used extensively in teaching the reading and writing of images. As these categories originate from the perspective of the practitioner, they were useful in combining theoretical concerns with practical ones. Different categories could be added according to the practical experience and need of each practitioner. For example, one could add the category of materials or media used, while analyzing contemporary art.

### e-Learning Strategies for Teaching Reading of Images
One of the phenomena of the digital age is the ease of transfer of visual materials via communication technologies in general and the Internet in particular. It just follows that common practices in a professional field would be transferred to the disciplines of education and training of such a field. Yet it seems that the visual disciplines are late in adopting the advantages of using e-Learning strategies. The difficulties in using Web-based teaching by the visual disciplines could be explained by the necessity to transform the content of teaching in order to match the pedagogical strategies of e-Learning. Thus, a double challenge is encountered. The first is the mastery of e-Learning platforms and institutional development and support for them. The second is the adaptation of teaching approaches in order to utilize the added benefits of Web-based teaching.

For the past four years, we have been using a blended teaching and learning approach that combines Web-based teaching with face-to-face instruction to teach 'reading' and 'writing' of images. This approach demonstrated the effectiveness of using e-Learning strategies combined with practical teaching. The blended approach confirms that when the content (pedagogy) is carefully matched to Web-based platforms, teaching outcomes that could not be attained otherwise are achieved (Abrahmov & Ronen 2007).

Teaching 'writing' and 'reading' of images requires two kinds of activities. The first is practical, the second theoretical. In practical art courses, it is often difficult to combine these two activities because of class-time limitations, or the students' expectations from a practice-based course. The adoption of a blended teaching and learning approach is a possible solution for this difficulty. Blended models usually refer to hybrid approaches in which the online components replace part of the on-campus traditional activities (Dean et al. 2001; Murphy 2003; McDonald & McAteer 2003; Myint & Atputhasamy 2003; Voos 2003). In the case of using a blended model within a practical course, the teaching model actually is acting as a *double blend* as it combines practical activities with theoretical activities as well as on-campus instruction with online learning (Abrahmov & Ronen 2005).

In the suggested double-blended teaching approach, writing of images is taught in class while reading of images is done by using a Web-based teaching platform. What is common to both teaching activities is the use of *common categories* as described earlier. The use of common criteria is useful in creating a synergy between the theoretical activities and the practical activities, or narrowing the gap between theory and practice. It is also useful in introducing the same terminology and concepts while discussing creation and interpretations of images.

Using e-Learning strategy for teaching the 'reading' of images is particularly effective, as it allows each of the students on his time to engage with visual text. Class activities for reading images as suggested by Barrett (2003) are less effective as the instructor cannot ensure individual participation. The common categories in the case of visual 'reading' act as the scaffolding for the practice of such interpretation and analysis.

In the double-blend course structure, the online theoretical assignments are performed in tandem with the practical activities. All Web-based assignments are individual. The assignments are worded identically for all students but require individual students to perform their work independently. Some of the online assignments are openly submitted to the course website, to a group discussion board created specifically for that assignment. This open submission model allows the students to learn from peer examples (Ronen & Langley 2004). The Web platform used for these activities is the HighLearn system by Britannica. Other assignments are performed while using a 'post before viewing' approach (Duffy et al. 1998). The teaching platform used for these activities is the new CeLS platform (Ronen et al. 2006).

The double-blended approach for teaching of reading and writing of images has been applied successfully for the past four years in both art photography courses and visual literacy courses. We suggest that this double blending approach combining online theory with on-campus practice could be used to cope with similar instructional challenges in other visual domains (Abrahmov & Ronen 2005).

Table 2 illustrates a student's submission of a Web-based portrait analysis using the full set of categories.

**Your Name:** R Z

**Photograph link:**
http://www.castellodirivoli.it/ita/homepage/Press/Frame/Pag_Immagini/Beecroft.htm

**Title:** VB. Ponti
**Photographer:** Vanessa Beecroft
**Year:** 2001

**Analyze the photograph:** describe as many details in each category.

| | |
|---|---|
| Framing and Perspective | In the picture there is no emphasis on perspective except the bed the black stripes of the bed enhance the feeling of depth. |
| Quality of Light | Artificial light, sterile, increases the feeling of alienation and sterility in addition the hospital bed portrayed in the picture as reference to the sterility present in hospitals. |
| Composition Depth of Field Focal Points | No depth of field – same sharpness – horizontal composition – central |
| Color | Color photograph with strong contrast only black and white. |
| Figure Background Relationship | The relationship between figure and background is very strong; there is an attempt to create a continuation of the figure into the background and at the same time to completely isolate the figure by changing the direction on the stripes her body in an opposite direction to the stripes on the background. A creation of flatness of picture and in the same time depiction of three-dimensionality.<br><br>Relationships between Figures and Objects |
| Representation of the Referent | The figure in the picture is silent. There the freezing of the moment, but it is clearly possible to notice a movement in the picture – the movement of the eyes like an Op-Art Painting where the referent jumps out and gives a feeling of three-dimensionality. |
| Title | VB Ponti – The title does not give an additional layer to the picture. It does not hint at the intention of photographer in creating the picture. The picture speaks for itself. |
| Context – what is known about the photograph | I did not find material on the photograph but on other works by the photographer, who used many times human figures. Bodies torn from the environment. The |

| | intensification of anonymity by lighting and the blurring of the differences by the figures. The unity of hair color and shoes creates the feeling of equality and unity among the photographed figures. Mostly in full nudity and high-heeled shoes – a reference to the status of women. |
|---|---|
| Personal impressions from the photograph (what kinds of feelings or associations do you get from it?) | The photograph raises a lot of associations. A figure that is seen as half-human half-mannequin. Torn from her natural environment. The pale skin and the pale light in contrast to the black stripes are increasing the feelings of inhumanity and lack of empathy. At the same time a strong feeling of sexuality and eroticism. Nude without a nude, an emphasis on the high-heeled shoes as an inseparable part of the power and femininity of the woman. |
| Why did you choose this photograph? | The duality between the highlighting of the portrait and its connection to the background. |

**Table 2.** Use of categories as scaffolding in a Web-based portrait analysis assignment.

In the portrait analysis assignment, each of the categories is hyperlinked to a simple explanation and examples for the category as shown in table 3. Such hyperlinking demonstrates one of the advantages of e-Learning when study materials are immediately available for the students while performing the assignment.

**Color**

| What color could be connected to the overall intention behind the photograph | William Eggleston Untitled (Christmas Bathroom) 1996 |
|---|---|

**Photograph link:**
http://www.artnet.com/artwork/424039696/william-eggleston-untitled-christmas-bathroom.html

| William Eggleston Untitled (A. J. Kelley & Co) 1970 | Illuminated only by the solitary streetlight that appears as a starburst in the night sky, the J. A. Kelley & Co. building sits bathed in a saturated blue light like the glow from an enormous television. A vague foreboding hangs densely in the unpopulated scene. William Eggleston made the mundane mysterious, transforming an ordinary building by using color, light, and mood. (http://www.getty.edu/art/gettyguide/artObjectDetails?artobj=46264) |
|---|---|

**Table 3.** Sample of hyperlink Color category for the Portrait analysis assignment.

**Figure 3.** Self-Portrait next to a Synagogue Tel Aviv from a Portrait and Beyond practical assignment by Ravit 2005.

**Student Name:** Nora

Philip-Lorca diCorcia. Eddie Anderson 21 Years Old Houston Texas $20 1990–92

**Photograph Link:**
http://faculty.cua.edu/johnsong/hsct101/pages/dicorcia01.html

**Factual Level**
In the photograph we see a boy looking at a store window, where the view is from within the store outside – it appears to be a restaurant. There are different levels – a restaurant, a shop window, the text on the window, the boy, the city.

The boy seems to be a passerby, his gaze is focused but not on us. The light that highlights the body shows that the photograph was taken in the summer (also by the dress), and the time seems to be the hours before sunset. The background of the city is alluding to not a very developed city where also the kind of text on the window shows it is painted with a brush.

**Interpretive Level**
The photographs sends a message of 'cheapness' which is expressed in the layers of the photograph – the food is cheap – hamburger and disposable cup – they did not invest in a special sign for advertisement and of course the boy with his exposed body and rumpled hair – what encloses the viewers to connotation of return from the beach (or maybe the place is by the beach). There is something hazy about the boy, it is difficult to decide on what exactly he is looking at and he seems to be a little tired. The town seen from the window is not very developed, this can be surmised from the buildings, the phone booth, its marking and the bus station. There is in the photograph a combination of new and old, two different rhythms. Hamburger – apex of progress-technology – fast production in contrast to the place where progress has not reached which is expressed in the strange machine on the countertop, the town, the text and the boy.

**Conceptual Level**
The photograph shows a kind of reflection, the boy looks at the place he would like to enter, but he does not do it and it does not seem that he is about to do it, a sense of unavailability. The photograph itself is a kind of peeking on life outside, progress in contrast to its voids, where we are so placed on the good side, in the advanced section of hamburger and drink and maybe in the materialistic side, when from the outside we can only observe the will to enter, the seeking and maybe the spiritual – the boy is seen as returning from the beach – something ostensibly spiritual and he has no shirt that branded him with a certain population. He is a kind of a blank page.

**Personal Impressions**
For me the photograph is very interesting and the more I observed it I discovered wider and deeper meanings. There is something in our observation on the boy as something that we would like to help – but not to touch – he is always going to be behind the glass and we will continue to watch him and remain in the side that is more "worthy." There is something in the

boy that will frighten us more had he entered the restaurant – because then we would be "nauseated" by him. So it is good that we can see him behind the glass and even better that he does not see us – he is as if imprisoned in this dirty outside, but maybe it is actually us as well.

**Your Name:** Ron

**Factual Level**
A young man partially dressed outside the display window of an American diner in the late afternoon. There is no reference to a specific location (except the name of the place in the title but this is a big city). There is a frame-like effect by the soft white light within the cerulean blue. Additional light source comes from the right side of the picture. There is a focal point triangle created from the jukebox – the hamburger – the cup and the head of the man – Eddie. The writing on the wall cuts the frame into two segments and separates him from the inside, not only the glass window. A shallow depth of field in the photograph.

**Interpretive Level**
The lonely boy in search of something else (the look in his eyes) from what other young men are looking for – music (jukebox), food (hamburger), drink (the cup) and friends (the logo for the phone). There is dirt on the glass in the area of Eddie's lower body – a certain disease? Is there a connection with the sensual boy and the emphasis on the nipples marked by the circle of the letter O and the shadow on the other one?

Is there a connection between this issue and the sum of money in the title of the photograph? Is he for sale? Is he on display and not the objects on the counter?

**Conceptual Level**
The young man is certainly marked as a sexual object – is posing next to the electric pole – a very phallic objects which might be repeated by the columns of the Pantheon which is reproduced on the cup. A mundane electric pole, so is the hamburger, the drink, the public phone, the dollar jukebox. Things that are common and available – so is the young man – and he is disposable.

**Personal Impressions**
A very complex photograph and one which I find disturbing, from the kinds of subjects which are not discussed or known in our country. Definitely the perspective and the lighting are very influential. I would eliminate the strobe that comes from the left as it creates an unnecessary focal point. It is not clear to me if the number 7 button is purposely sticking out in the jukebox.

**Table 4.** Final Web-based analysis of art photographs.

In the case of the portrait analysis assignment, a practical assignment of creating a portrait with a predetermined focus is given in order to enhance the interaction between a 'reading' and 'writing' of a particular kind of image. An example is shown in figure 3.

In the end of the courses the students are asked to 'read' art photographs using the three levels of meaning structure. No other scaffoldings are given in this assignment. This assignment is performed in the CeLS platform and the results are posted for class review after the students had completed the task. Table 4 shows two students' responses as they were posted to the website. The responses demonstrate the advanced 'reading' skills gained by students during the course.

### Transformation in the Ontology of the Photographic Image

The use of photographs in the discussion regarding media literacy in contemporary society has immediate relevance since the digital age creates a transformation in the ontology of the photographic image (Fried 2005). This transformation has two aspects. The first is that with the advent of digitalization the adherence of the photograph to its referent dissolves (Fried 2005). This means that we have to view all photographs as non-transparent. However, according to Kellner and Share (2005), in a similar manner to our approach to photographs, we must observe now all images as non-transparent, as carriers of visual messages and intentions. In this fashion, past 'incomplete utterances' (Sekula 1982) become today's lucid visual statements.

The second transformation is that the digital photographic image becomes less physical and more fluid. We view most such photographs on screens and projectors and not as prints. This transformation applies not only to photographs but also to other images. Fluidity of images is directly tied to the way we visually communicate. E-mails, web blogs and photo-sharing sites such as Flickr, mean that we can share photographs or other images around the world in matter of minutes after their creation. The shift in the ontology of the photographic image in the digital age is bound to influence all contemporary images both in their production and the ease with which they can be used to visually communicate globally. If such an influence seems apparent, then the way meanings are constructed as described in this chapter has relevance beyond the singular discussion regarding photographs.

### Developing the Critical Skills of the Visual Practitioner

The approach described in this chapter develops visual literacy by presenting a theoretical framework and simple teaching approach to reading and writing of images at a time when traditional boundaries between different art media are dissipating. Teaching reading and writing of images is valuable, therefore, not only in teaching photography, but in teaching all areas of art, design, and visual communications with both traditional and new media. These critical skills are intended to be taught in tandem with the teaching and practice of special skills required to execute works in a particular medium.

In educating the *visual practitioner*, we adopt the approach that we first look at contents and concepts before we explore the visual means used to express them. The structured approach proposed here develops basic skills that help students better conceptualize when they are set free to be imaginative and intuitive in creating their own artworks. It is helpful when teaching structured reading and writing of images to promote student involvement, to welcome personal opinions and stances when reading images, and to encourage choice of subjects with personal relevance when writing images. I can testify, as a visual practitioner, that the critical sharpening of my visual reading and writing skills has not impeded my practice, but rather enriched it.

## Works Cited

Abrahmov, S. L. & Ronen, M. (2005), The Double Blend: Integrating an Online Theoretical Layer into Practical Photography Instruction, in Designs on eLearning, Proceedings of the International Conference on Teaching and Learning with Technology in Art Design and Communication 14–16 September, University of the Arts, London.

Abrahmov, S. L. & Ronen, M. (2007), Double blending: online theory with on-campus practice in photography instruction, *Innovations in Education and Teaching International*, in press.

Avgerinou, M. & Ericson, J. (1997), A Review of the Concept of Visual Literacy *British Journal of Educational Technology*, 28 (4) 280–291.

Baca, J. C. (1990), Identification by consensus of the critical constructs of visual literacy: a Delphi study Doctoral Thesis, East Texas State University.

Barrett, T. (2003), Interpreting Visual Culture, in: Villeneuve p. (ed.) Why Not Visual Culture? *Art Education*, 56 (2) 6–12.

Barthes, R. (1977), Rhetoric of the Image in Image, Music, Text. Ed. and trans. Stephen Heath. New York: Hill and Wang, 32–51.

Batchen, G. (2001), Ectoplasm in *Each Wild Idea*, Cambridge, MA: MIT Press.

Bazin, A. (1999), On The Ontology of the Photographic Image in *What is Cinema* 1967, reprinted in Baurdy L. and Cohen M. (ed.) Film Theory and Criticism, Oxford: Oxford University Press, 195–199.

Berger, J. (1995), *Another Way of Telling*, New York: Vintage Books.

Burgin, V. (1982), Looking at Photographs in *Thinking Photography* Burgin V. Ed. London: Macmillan Press.

Clarke, G. (1997), How Do We Read a Photograph? In *The Photograph* Oxford: Oxford University Press, 27–33.

Considine, D. M. (1986), Visual literacy and Children's Books: An Integrated Approach *School Library Journal*. Retrieved July 22, 2004 from Academic Search Premier Database.

Dean, p. , Stahl, M., Sylwester, D., & Pear, J. (2001), Effectiveness of Combined Delivery Modalities for Distance Learning and Resident Learning, *Quarterly Review of Distance Education*, 2 (3) 247–254.

Duffy, T. M., Dueber, B. & Hawley, C. L. (1998), Critical Thinking in a Distributed Environment: A Pedagogical Base for the Design of Conferencing Systems, in: Bonk, C. J. and K. S. King (eds.), *Electronic Collaborators: Learner-centered Technologies for Literacy, Apprenticeship and Discourse*, Mahawah, NJ: LEA associates, 73.

Friday, J. (2000), Demonic Curiosity and the Aesthetics of Documentary photography *The British Journal of Aesthetics*, 40 (3) 356–376.

Fried, M. (2005), Barthes's Punctum *Critical Inquiry*, 31 (3) 539–574.

Kellner, D. & Share, J. (2005), Toward Critical Media Literacy: Core concepts, debates, organizations, and policy discourse, *Studies in the cultural politics of education*, 26 (3) 369–386.

Kirrane, D. E. (1992), Visual learning *Training and Development*, 46 (9) 58–63.

Krauss, R. (1999) Cindy Sherman: Untitled in *Bachelors* Massachusetts: MIT Press Krauss R (1986) The Photographic Condition of Surrealism in *The Originality of the Avant-Garde and Other Modernist Myths*, Cambridge, MA: MIT Press.

McDonald, J. & McAteer, E. (2003), New approaches to supporting students; strategies for blended learning support in distance and campus based environments, *Journal of Educational Media*, 28 (2 & 3) 171–188.

Moore, R. (2004), Aesthetic Experience in the World of Visual Culture, *Arts Education Policy Review*, 105 (6) 15–27.

Panofsky, E. (1983), *Meaning in the Visual Arts* [1955] Chicago: University of Chicago Press, Reprint edition.

Morgan, D. (2006), Rethinking Bazin: Ontology and Realist Aesthetics *Critical Inquiry,* 32 (3) 443–481.

Myint, S. K. & Atputhasamy, L. (2003), Blended learning approach in teacher education: Combining face-to-face instruction, multimedia viewing and online discussion. *British Journal of Educational Technology*, 34, 671–675.

Murphy, p. (2003), The hybrid strategy: Blending face-to-face with virtual instruction to improve large section courses, Teaching, Learning, and Technology Center, University of California Regents. Retrieved Sept 10, 2005 from http: //www.uctltc.org/news/2002/12/feature.php.

Princethal, N. (2003), Forty Ways of Looking at a Stranger *Art in America*, 91 (12) 43–46.

Raney, K. (1999), Visual Literacy and the Art Curriculum, *Journal of Art & Design Education*, 18 (1) 42–47.

Rimanelli, D. (2003), Portfolio: Christopher Williams. *Artforum International* 41 (10) 165–170

Raney, K. (1999) Visual Literacy and the Art Curriculum, *Journal of Art & Design Education*, 18 (1) 42–47.

Ronen, M. & Langley, D. (2004), Scaffolding complex tasks by open online submission: Emerging patterns and profiles *Journal of Asynchronous Learning Networks*, 8 (4) 39–61.

Ronen, M., Kohen-Vacs, D. & Raz-Fogel, N. (2006), Adopt & Adapt: Structuring, Sharing and Reusing Asynchronous Collaborative Pedagogy ICLS International Conference on Learning Sciences Bloomington, IL June 27 – July 1, 599–605.

Savedoff, B. E. (2000), *Transforming Images: How Photography Complicates the Picture*, Ithaca: Cornell University Press.

Savedoff, B. E. (1993), Looking at art through photographs *Journal of Aesthetics & Art Criticism*, 51 (3) 455–463.

Sekula, A. (1982), On the Invention of Photographic Meaning in *Thinking Photography*, Burgin V. (Ed.) London: Macmillan Press.

Voos, R. (2003), Blended learning: What is it and where might it take us? *Sloan-C View*, 2 (1). Retrieved Sept 10, 2005, from http://www.aln.org/publications/view/v2n1/blended1.htm.

# THE CREATIVE SPIRIT IN THE AGE OF DIGITAL TECHNOLOGIES: SEVEN TACTICAL EXERCISES

## Lucia Leão

Writing about my pedagogical experiences is a challenge that evokes the questions: How to stimulate the creative spirit? How to propose a fertile situation that enhances the creative potential of students? As a professor of art and new media in Sao Paulo, Brazil, my classes have been a space of experimentation and research through which I seek answers to these questions.

I started teaching in 1989 at the Museum of Modern Art of Sao Paulo (MAM) where I developed a program called *Drawing and Painting: Poetic Relations* in which the main objective was to explore relationships between these two kinds of languages. In order to stimulate the production of unexpected images and expand creative possibilities, I proposed exercises that asked the students to draw and paint using their entire body. These exercises were based on my studies of Chinese calligraphy and watercolor techniques. My students were predominantly people who had had some experience in painting but, at the same time, were looking for a more holistic framework to conceive and understand creative process. They commented that they were tired of courses that only emphasize technical aspects. They were looking for something that could help them discover their own personal expression. Reflecting on this, I now realize that all my pedagogical practice has been associated with exercises of body consciousness and the concept of body as an essential medium of access to inner states. Moved by the necessity to better understand interrelationships between body, mind, and spirit, I studied different mythologies, semiotics of the sacred and esoteric theories. Later, I wrote an article that describes our multiple bodies and how these bodies are interwoven in our everyday activities (Leao 2005a).

Several years before, I had an interesting experience teaching poor children in the city's outskirts. We organized a workshop for creating toys using discarded plastic materials. At that time, in 1985, consciousness about the importance of recycling was only in its beginnings. The Saturday afternoon workshops were appreciated by the families, especially by the mothers, who loved to see their children creating their own toys. From my point of view, the contact with the culture of the periphery was a deeply spiritual experience. Different from the urban individualistic lifestyle, I discovered there a way of life based on cooperation. Because of their very poor living conditions, they have a code of participating in a group that values collective work. Although the importance of generosity and helping each other in their case is a matter of survival, it does not diminish the value of their acts. *Mutirão*, for example, is a very festive multimedia event. The main objective of *mutirão* is to build a habitation for someone from the group. The logic of *mutirão* is that everybody helps one another in a circuit in which all members benefit. This joyful meeting, much more then a mere working moment, celebrates the power of union with music, dance, and communal food.

Since this experience, I have been absolutely sure that there is a great power when people work together. Inspired by Deleuze's concept of multiplicity, I developed the concept of *Webmatilha* (Leão 2004). Perceiving that we are connected with other people is a fundamental fact to transform our consciousness. Everybody that has been touched by this collective enthusiasm is bound to discover new dimensions of values, feelings, and happiness. Further inspired by this feeling, I started research on Dionysus, the god of wine and ecstasy, and Umbanda, a syncretic Brazilian religion using popular circle dances and rituals as media to access mythic consciousness. *Corposcopio*, a collaborative performance with real-time image manipulation (VJs), is one of the results of this research (Leão 2006).

When I started teaching as a university lecturer in 1989, my interests in video as a new medium for artistic exploration led to my introducing it in my teaching. In order to experiment with computers, I created the Laboratory of Art and Technology at Faculdade Santa Marcelina (FASM). During this period, I discovered Roy Ascott's writings and artistic projects. His inspirational theories helped me recognize the validity of my intuitions.

During my master's project on communication and semiotics (1993–1997), I proposed an investigation on hypermedia and labyrinths in which ancient wisdom was related to the new language of hypermedia systems (Leão 1999). I continued my labyrinthine studies during my Ph.D. research by investigating the prevalence of the labyrinth in culture history. Through this research, I defined the concept of "Labyrinth Aesthetics" as a kind of sensibility connected with complexity, the sacred, and a holistic view of the world (Leão 2002).

These conceptual and artistic processes have guided me in questioning and re-creating my pedagogical practice. While I experimented with different software and systems, I witnessed my students' movements and advances in cyberspace while catalyzing their personal development and consciousness expansion.

**Departing Points**
There are four stimulating tasks that have accompanied my experience and direct my work as an educator in the field of arts and new technologies. The first task is to recognize that teaching technoetic arts requires a considerable investment of time and energy in research. A good teacher is a researcher with a tireless spirit who must love reading, participating in congresses, scientific meetings, and virtual communities, and enjoy surfing the Internet looking for new networks and connections. Dealing with new technologies is a constant exercise of discovery. This task is closely related to consciousness of the fact that teachers, like any other human beings, are neither fully accomplished nor definitive. Therefore, we must abandon the idea of an inexorable content plan and think about the pedagogical experience as a work-in-progress. Moreover, it is important that we deal with the unknown and the risks that emerge with an enthusiastic attitude. Even if we have exceptional knowledge or experience in a field of endeavor, dealing with cyberspaces and cyber enthusiastic people it is a great lesson in humility for the teacher. In the age of telematic networks, it is not rare that some of our students, who usually have more time than us to browse the Web and participate in forums, have more updated information. For this reason, the teacher must appreciate that the learning process is a triadic process that demands communication, collaborative process, and constant evaluation. In this process, students are not neutral receivers, but join their teachers as protagonists. "Teaching is not transmitting knowledge. Teaching is creating possibilities for its production or its construction" (Freire 1996: 28).

The teacher adopts the posture of critical mediator in the process of knowledge construction. Besides, each student learns how to collaborate actively with a group in which one helps the other. For this purpose, the main role of the teacher is to cultivate an atmosphere of solidarity in which there is cooperation between all members of the group that constitutes this small community that we call a class.

The second fundamental task is creating a system that simultaneously records the learning process and, through dialogue, stimulates the emergence of collective intelligence. Conversation and networking are absolutely essential skills to teach and learn in digital domains. There is no escaping the fact that recycling and updating are essential. Being part of a community, can give them a feeling of being anchored when then encounter the rushing flood of information and digital data. Developing the habit of sharing information with the group can transform the anxiety of excess of information into a collective data repository. In this context, I have developed a method of cooperation with the group and a communication system with the students. Dealing with the concept of social webs, I have been using different tools like social bookmarks (del.icio.us, technorati), web logs and cooperative writing software. Sites that serve as community-building Web spaces, where students can post narratives, thoughts, insights, images, drafts, dreams, quotations, ideas, plans, sounds, drawings, are essential tools to promote conversation and to create a repository of memories and trajectories. Conversation must be understood as a channel that enhances collaboration.

The third task is raising the consciousness that we, educators, are educating not only when we are talking and sharing information. All our actions have potential educational impact. The timbre of our voice, body language, feelings, and the happiness that we express unconsciously during the teaching process are much more than mere signs. This means that being a teacher requires permanent self-analysis that involves awareness expansion. Even our attitudes outside the classroom can be symbolic of our values. Parallel activities like visiting exhibitions and participating in seminars must be planned as vital elements to increase the connections with the students in a powerful and transforming way.

The forth task consists of constructing a value system together with the students without the professor imposing her/his values. The definition of what will be valued by the group must be created collectively, being the first creative exercise. Without it, the group lacks direction. The preparation of a visual representation of the concepts that will direct the learning journey will foster collective discovery as a process of acquiring knowledge. The map works like a vision in which everybody contributes to trace a collectively expectation. After designing the values map, the comprehension of the process of evaluation becomes natural and easy.

With these considerations in mind, I describe some tactical exercises. I am using the adjective tactical in the sense proposed by French scholar Michel de Certeau in *The Practice of Everyday Life*: "a tactic is a calculated action determined by the absence of a proper locus…The space of a tactic is the space of the other" (Certeau 1984: 36–37). In a world dominated by technological and materialistic views, these exercises may look like paradoxical. Nevertheless, I think that our mission as educators must be to promote a renewed meeting with the sacred. These tactical exercises intend to disturb the univocal discourse and create space for a landscape of spiritual dimensions.

**Seven Tactical Exercises**

*1. The Wisdom of the Labyrinth: The Importance of the Trajectory*
Although creativity is a very powerful characteristic present in every person, it has been neglected in our society and in our schools. It seems that our most important force is not valued as a vital element in our lives. A creative person is someone connected with the Eros instinct, a person with a lot of energy to look for new solutions. A person whose creativity is obstructed has lost this connection. This first exercise has the objective to renew the creative connection.

I think it is important to remember that when we talk about creative people we are not necessarily talking about artists. My premise is that the potentiality of creative expression is something inherent to every person. The creative act can only be understood in its global and contextual sense linked to a specific historic and cultural period. The creative spirit of the human being exists, develops, and flourishes in her/his relation with the cultural context. In other words, there is an intertwined knot integrating life and creativity.

In our inner world, there are two forces confronting each other: the power to create, to invent, to discover new solutions (Eros impulse), and the power to deny this capacity, to remain in the realm of repeated habits (Thanatos impulse). We do not have to decide which one is going to win. We just have to know they exist and learn how to deal with both. Each time we feel paralyzed with fear of trying a new way, we are being victims of Thanatos power. This fight is narrated in many myths such as the famous Egyptian story in which, everyday, in the morning, Night (Nut) gives birth to Sun (Rá). Nevertheless, the myth has another important part: every night Nut swallows Rá, in a cycle without end. What can we learn through this myth? Creative processes have the same cycle. They are composed by moments of light and moments of darkness. In order to deal with this, it is necessary that we create a ritual that helps us to perceive these two movements. In my experience, the ritual demonstrates a powerful system for understanding the nature of cyclic phenomena.

Moreover, I defend the idea that the path to creativity must be a path of self-discovering, a journey into the spirit realm. When I dedicated myself to the study of labyrinth wisdom, during my master's and Ph.D. researches, I discovered the importance of the trajectory. According to several different mythologies, the experience of labyrinth is an experience of walking. Through its different circumvolutions, different difficulties and challenges, the labyrinth is a great master in the process of knowledge acquisition. On that ground, I embrace and value the importance of the process, the importance of the pathway. The focus of the professor's activity should be to guide students to the sacred importance of the entire process of learning. Respecting the pathway is the first step in learning how to grow creatively.

The exercise to expand the natural creativity that exists as a potentiality aggregates elements of ritual and validates the process by registering inner experiences. Memory repository and cyclic habits enhance the creative spirit. To illustrate, I show images from the notebooks of Leonardo da Vinci and the contemporary artist Bracha Ettinger. While Leonardo's notebooks are tools that help him to organize his ideas, Ettinger's notebooks form an integral part of the exhibited work.

The exercise consists of creating systems of recording the process with certain regularity – everyday in the evenings or early in the morning. The student uses at least three types of recording media: handwriting (notebook, notepads, etc), blog, audio, photography; video, etc. The students are encouraged to take notes several times and preserve every draft. The memory bank should include thoughts, feelings, images, reports, and drawings.

### 2. The Mirror Lesson: A Nonsense Self-Portrait
This second exercise deals with dichotomies, questioning, and inner conflicts. As we know, every human being has her/his ambivalences. Part of the process of being creative is abandoning a Cartesian view and understanding that these oppositions are complementary pairs.

Lewis Carroll's *Alice in Wonderland* is the departure point to discuss non-sense and the contradictions that permeate each person's life. The story is full of examples that subvert classical logic. Some M. C. Escher's drawings and paintings are also introduced, as emblematic images that create paradoxical realities. One of the most amazing examples, *Möbius Strip II*, features ants crawling around the surface of a Möbius strip. Where are the ants? Inside or outside the ring? A Möbius strip is the first one-sided surface discovered. It has a great power of disestablishing certainties.

The exercise has three parts. First, I ask the students to read Carroll's book looking for paradoxes. In the second part, the idea is to think about the non-sense and discuss it with the group. To improve the conversations, I ask them to read some parts of Gilles Deleuze's book, *The Logic of Sense*. The third part is personal. The students are asked to reflect on non-sense aspects of their own lives and prepare a video piece.

Dealing with our polarities is something crucial to personal growth. This exercise is a preparatory step to discuss concepts like the crises of classical logic, the necessity to reframe dualistic presumptions, the complexity paradigm, yin-yang as an image that represents the interaction of polarities, and the structures of imagination proposed by Gilbert Durand (1989), especially his esquizoid system.

I show artists' projects that highlight contradictions and nonsense like the Dada manifesto (Hugo Ball 1916) and Manifesto of Surrealism (André Breton 1924). I also discuss contemporary art pieces, like the three-screen video installation, *The House*, from the Finland artist Eija-Liisa Ahtila that makes no clear distinction between outside and inside. Later, I ask the students to search other examples.

I intentionally make the exercise open-ended. The limitations are only about duration (between 60 to 180 seconds). Some of the most interesting projects deal with other people's opinion about themselves (parents, brothers, friends). One student shows images of everyday routine interwoven with a narrative collage of his parents' dialogues.

### 3. Webmatilha: We and Our Multiplicity
The third exercise is about visualization of complex systems. I start the class presenting Maciunas' map[1] of the concepts of the Fluxus group. Secondly, I introduce the concept of mapping as a process to acquire new understandings, as a cognitive tool. Later, I present the challenge to think about the *webmatilha* condition. Webmatilha is a concept that I proposed during research about digital communities. The term "Webmatilha" is formed by a hybridization of web (as networks) and wolf pack (*matilha*, in Portuguese).

The intention is to emphasize the rhizomatic nature that constitutes our beings (Leão 2004). Inspired by the idea of multiplicity as it has been discussed by Deleuze and Guattari (1987) in *A Thousand Plateaus*, when they analyzed *The Case of the Wolf-Man* by Sigmund Freud, I present some art projects that reveal this collective aspect.

The exercise consists of creating a visual representation of a personal network. I ask the students to think about three levels: their interests and values (rational), their feelings, preferences and relationships (emotional), and their dreams and spiritual aspirations. I then ask them to map all the groups to which they belong: family, faculty, sports, friends, musical preferences, hobbies, religion, and so on. The idea is to create an image of visual complexity, composed by several lines. I suggest they perceive the rhizomatic connections: persons who are situated in two or more nodes, lines that cross each other, etc. They are encouraged to use different colors and line thickness. The drawing can be made in the technique they prefer (pencil, pen, digital image, etc.).

### 4. *The Wisdom of the Fairy Tales*
The fourth exercise is devoted to the paradigms that are fundamental in our everyday life of which we are often not conscious. Paradigms, in the sense proposed by Thomas Kuhn (1962), are presuppositions that orient our way of thinking. This exercise aggregates three main goals: to get in touch with the collective unconscious and its archetypes through the careful and reflective reading of fairy tales, to explore the crises of the authorship concept in information society and hypermedia language by using digital systems for collective writing, and to instigate a reflection about relationships, polycentric structures, rhizomatic creative potential, and open-ended storytelling.

I propose an exercise of collective writing with particular characteristics. After reading short stories, the students organize themselves in groups to discuss universal archetypes. I ask them to observe their feelings and personal identification. Based on the seminal telematic art project of Roy Ascott (2005), *La plissure du texte*, the students are stimulated to personify one of *Dramatis Personae* proposed by Vladimir Propp (1985). I suggest they understand the archetype that they incorporate in creating a character driven by this primordial impulse. In this project, everybody is the author of her/his own character and the narrative evolves from inputs of each element of the group. In order to create an environment for this exercise to take place, I developed a system called *As mil e uma histórias* "one thousand stories".[2] It is based on Drupal,[3] a free software modular content management framework, and blogging engine, written in PHp. The story can be continued by anyone on the Internet.

### 5. *Lessons from the Body: From Lygia Clark to Corposcopio*
The body is the master of our fifth exercise. Not the body conceived as flesh and bones but the body as a multilayered and multidimensional organism (Leão 2005a). To start this discussion, I ask the students to think about their bodies (form, characteristics, power, weakness, feelings, sensations, etc), about the body of the class (invisible

connections, quantum level, etc), about the whole Earth as a unique body (Gaia Theory), and about the body of the Universe.

I present some of Lygia Clark's projects, especially her *Relational Objects* series. Following Suely Rolnik's idea, Clark was looking for the vibrational body, the body that has been forgotten by our *fat dominant health* (Rolnik 2002).

I introduce the *Corposcopio* project and ask the students to dance together. *Corposcopio* is a collaborative project that integrates two different worlds or territories – circle dances and new media technologies. Ancient circle dances are cultural manifestations present in different countries around the world. They have a great power of community integration and provide a unique experience of extended consciousness. In Brazil, there are many amazing circle dances. One of the most popular, ciranda, has movements inspired by sea waves. Ciranda is performed by hundreds of people and some participants fall into a trance. *Corposcopio* invites the participants to experience some circle dances and aggregates real time image manipulation, software art, VJ, and remix aesthetics. This exercise of dancing together provides the power to discover the collective body. Everybody in the group is also invited to participate in real-time image manipulation, to take pictures, and to compose a hybrid body image (Leão 2006b).

### 6. A Pregnant State
The idea of this exercise is to show that developing the ability to see inspiration everywhere is absolutely necessary to exercise the creative spirit. The basis of the discussion is Helio Oiticica's *Parangolés* (Osthoff 1997) project created after living into the *favelas* in Rio de Janeiro. Oiticica was contaminated by this experience. Favela culture penetrated his subjectivity and idea of *Parangolés* emerged naturally.

To develop our creative spirit we must adopt the attentive posture of a child, hungry to interiorize the world as it appears. We must assume the posture of outsider, of a person that is moved by great curiosity. It is necessary to value the feeling of a "state of grace." The attention is fundamental to evoke a state of suspension (*epoché*), the wonder of being there.

Sometimes this posture requires that we enhance our senses. As Rupert Sheldrake discusses, there is a morphic field in which all the knowledge reverberates. Each thing that a person discovers contributes to this vibrational field. A creative person is someone connected to this – a surfer and a collaborator (Sheldrake 1981 and 1989).

For this exercise, I propose some readings of Bachelard's studies of poetic language and daydreaming (Bachelard 1994). I divide the class into four groups, and each of them working with one of the four elements (fire, water, air, and earth). Being creative is a pregnant state. The main idea is to nourish the spirit with inspiring sources. We learn from Bachelard that poetic works are great stimulants of creativity because they offer us refreshed and unknown views. After these readings, I invite the students to collaborate in the Hermenetka[4] database. The idea is to stimulate the creation of an image bank and cartographic cyberspace landscape.

### 7. Learning from Umbanda

The last exercise is about the necessity to create a space of conversation and to stimulate a tolerant point of view. In the era of planetary networks, the mainstream discourse explores unification. But, as we know, bridges between differences must first be constructed.

Umbanda is a syncretic religion in Brazil. The wisdom of Umbanda comes from its capacity to absorb different influences: Indian traditions, African religions, Catholic elements, Spiritism, and more recently, Hinduism, Buddhism, and Kabbalah.

Umbanda's ritual is composed of music (*atabaques* – drumming percussion and songs), clapping hands, dance (*gira*), drawings (*pemba*, mandalic diagrams that represent divinities), special costumes and accessories. During the cult ritual some people incorporate spiritual entities. One part of the ritual is dedicated to help people from the audience with their problems. The spiritual assistance is based primarily on semi-private conversations in which the person can talk about her/his sufferings and necessities. The spiritual communication happens through the medium (a person who has the ability to receive the spirit). In general, the spirit gives advice in order to stimulate the person to change attitudes and recommends cleaning rituals (taking herbal baths) and meditation (lighting candles).

There are a lot of different kinds of Umbanda, each one with its particularity. The Cosmic Proto-Synthesis,[5] for example, is a type of Umbanda that postulates that there is a unity based on a universal principle. This group proposes Umbanda as a Knowledge System based on the synthetic understanding of Philosophy, Science, Art, and Religion (Rivas Neto 1988). For this presupposition, the word *umbanda* came from *aumbandan*, a sacred term from the Abanheenga language, spoken by members belonging to the Tupy lineage. This term means a set of divine laws. According Rivas Netto (2003: 85), there is an ancestral interconnection that permeates all ancient spiritual knowledge. His research is based on a triadic foundation: divine power, wisdom, and love. Mantra, Yantra, and Tantra, the three spiritual paths of Hinduism, are also important elements in this Umbanda School. Diagrammatic studies that demonstrate interrelations between hermetic traditions, planets, Hinduism (chakras), and *orixás* or *arashas* (spiritual guides with particular characteristics that have similarities with archetypes) are other demonstrations of deep syncretism. As we have seen, Umbanda reveals isomorphisms and similarities between so many different cultures that it can be seen as an exemplar of coexistence. In addition, the wisdom of Umbanda can also be seen in its capacity to help people through the mediunic[6] conversations.

There are some artistic projects that associate the construction of a tolerant way to live with dialogical propositions. In his book *Conversation Pieces*, Kester (2004) describes a group of art projects that focus their practices into the facilitation of dialogue among diverse communities. One of the projects analyzed, *Intervention in Drug Policy* (1994), proposed by the Austrian arts collective Wochenklausur,[7] is about the importance of creating a space for conversation in the process of looking for a solution to a social problem. In *West Meets East* (1992) proposed by Loraine Leeson,[8] we have collective expressions of the experience of living between two cultures. One of the strongest images of the project features a girl from Bengali, India, joining a sari with a denim jacket. The hands of the girl are painted with traditional Bengali patterns and she is using an industrial sewing machine. In the frame of the picture, a visual collage with icons like McDonald's logo and scenes from village life in India reveals the mix of different cultures.

The exercise I propose to the students is composed by three elements. The first is dedicated to thinking about problematic quotidian situations. I ask them to read newspapers, to walk in the streets, to observe people's movements, to talk with people they do not know, in short, to be open to the complexity of the urban scenery. Then, they are asked to choose a problem they are going to discuss. The idea is to create a website that catalyzes the discussions. I suggest they use video cameras and prepare interviews. As we know, hypermedia is a potent multivocal language. Their challenge is to exercise the art of listening

**Conclusions: Art, Teaching, and Collaboration**
Everything in our lives presents creative options. We choose and create all the time. My options as a teacher are based on the understanding that researching, learning, and teaching are inseparable in the process of expanding consciousness. The sacred dimension of education is a search for meaning. The exercises I had chosen resemble the mythic movements of the labyrinth path. 1) The student is invited to go inside her/himself. 2) She/he departs to discover her/his complexities. 3) There is a moment dedicated to recognizing her/his affiliations. 4) The student is invited to learn to work in groups, realizing archetypical structures. 5) The collective body, the relation between *one and wholeness* are experienced. 6) The exercise stimulates the encounter with the creative habits. 7) Going back to the world, sharing knowledge, exercising the art of listening, the art of tolerance and being an agent of integrative coexistence. The goal is that, after these pedagogical elements, the student discovers new transformations in her/himself. With this perception, the cycle re-starts and a new labyrinth path can be penetrated.

When I am with my students on the first day classes, I used to begin by saying that I am glad to be with them, at that moment, living my mission. I explain that I believe that nothing is by chance and if we are going to spend six months together, this should have some special meaning. After, I introduce myself saying that I am a teacher since 1989 and I am an apprentice since I was born. I say that I am absolutely sure I am going to learn a lot. Then I add, as an artist, I would value the aesthetics dimension of the learning process, in its transformative power. To illustrate, I quote Guattari (1995: 91): "I simply want to stress that the aesthetic para-digm – the creation and composition of mutant percepts and affects – has become the paradigm for every possible form of liberation."

To conclude, I propose that we reframe our concept of art. We should consider art as quality and intention in which subjectivity is an interconnected field in a continuum of changes that requires assuming responsibility for our actions. I ask my students to think about their lives as a masterpiece. I invite them to invest their spirits in the process of becoming and in facing the challenge of developing the aesthetic dimensions of human experience that makes the learning process a path to creative liberation.

## Notes

1. George Maciunas: Expanded Arts Diagram, 1966. In: Fluxfest Sale, 1966.; Happening & Fluxus. Hrsg. von H. Sohm. Koelnischer Kunstverein, Köln, 1970. o.n.; Lund Art Press, Vol. 1, No. 4, Summer/Autumn 1990. Melléklet.
2. The title was inspired by *The Book of One Thousand and One Nights*. http://www.lucialeao.pro.br/asmileumahistorias/index.php
3. Drupal is open source software licensed under the GPL, and is maintained and developed by a community of thousands of users and developers. http://drupal.org/about
4. http://www.lucialeao.pro.br/hermenetka/info_en.htm
5. Represented by The Iniciatic Order Of the Divine Cross (Master Arapiaga).
6. A mediunic conversation is a dialogue between a person and a spirit, or a disembodied being. The conversation happens through the body of a medium, a person with capacity to incorporate spirits and receive communications from the spiritual world.
7. http://www.wochenklausur.at/texte/arbeitsweise_en.htm
8. West Meets East (1992) was proposed by Loraine Leeson when she participated of The Art of Change. Now, Leeson is working on cSPACE. According the website: "cSPACE uses the visual arts, media and cyberspace to support local communities, children and young people in the expression of their visions, dreams and aspirations around issues of regeneration". http://www.cspace.org.uk/

## Works Cited

Ascott, Roy (2005), 'Plissando o texto: origens e desenvolvimento da arte telemática', in: Leão, Lucia (org.). *O chip e o caleidoscópio: reflexões sobre as novas mídias*. São Paulo: Ed. SENAC.

Bachelard, Gaston (1994), *The Poetics of Space*. Boston: Beacon Press.

Ball, Hugo (1916), 'Dada Manifesto', Zurich, http: //en.wikisource.org/wiki/Dada_Manifesto_%281916%2C_Hugo_Ball%29. Accessed 24 November 2006.

Breton, André (1924), 'Manifesto of Surrealism', http: //pers-www.wlv.ac.uk/~fa1871/surrext.html. Accessed 3 November 2006.

Carroll, Lewis (1996), 'Alice's Adventures in Wonderland,' in *Literature.org, The Online Literature Library*, http: //www.literature.org/authors/carroll-lewis/alices-adventures-in-wonderland/. Accessed 01 November 2006.

Da Vinci, Leonardo (2004), 'The Notebooks of Leonardo Da Vinci,' in *Gutenberg Project*, http: //www.gutenberg.org/etext/5000 Accessed 10 January 2007.

De Certeau, M. (1984), *The Practice of Everyday Life*. Berkeley: University of California Press.

Deleuze, Gilles (1990), *The Logic of Sense*. New York: Columbia University Press.

Deleuze, Gilles and Guattari, Felix (1987), *A Thousand Plateaus: Capitalism and Schizophrenia* (trans. Brain Massumi), Minneapolis: University of Minnesota Press.

Durand, Gilbert (1989), *As estruturas antropológicas do imaginário*, Lisboa: Presença.

Ettinger, Bracha (2006), 'Notebooks,' *Flickr*, http: //www.flickr.com/photos/bracha-ettinger/sets/1072024/. Accessed 15 January 2007.

Freire, Paulo (1996), Pedagogia da autonomia: Saberes necessários à prática educativa. São Paulo: Paz e Terra.

Guattari, Félix (1995), *Chaosmosis: An Ethico-aesthetic Paradigm*. Bloomington: Indiana University Press.

Kester, Grant H (2004), *Conversation Pieces: Community and Communication in Modern Art*. Berkeley and New York: University of California Press.

Kuhn, T. S. (1962), *The Structure of Scientific Revolutions*, Chicago: University of Chicago Press.

Leão, Lucia (1999), O labirinto da hipermídia. Arquitetura e navegação no ciberespaço. São Paulo, FAPESP – Iluminuras.

Leão, Lucia (2002), *A estética do labirinto*. São Paulo: Ed. Universidade Anhembi Morumbi.

Leão, Lucia (2004), 'O habitat da webmatilha', *Cibercultura*, São Paulo: Instituto Cultural Itaú. www.itaucultural.org.br/index.cfm?cd_pagina=2014&cd_materia=947. Accessed 18 January 2007.

Leão, Lucia (2005a), 'The mirror labyrinth: reflections on bodies and consciousness at cybertimes'. *Technoetic Arts*, Bristol, United Kingdom, v. 3, n. 1.

Leão, Lucia (2005b), 'Hermenetka'. http: //www.lucialeao.pro.br/hermenetka. Accessed 17 January 2007.

Leão, Lucia (2006a), 'Corposcopio: an interactive installation performance in the intersection of ritual, dance and new technologies'. In: *Consciousness Reframed 8, 2006*. Plymonth: University of Plymonth, pp. 25–29. http: //www.planetary-collegium.net/conferences/200607/Abstracts.pdf . Accessed 10 January 2007.

Leão, Lucia (2006b), 'Corposcopio project'. http: //www.lucialeao.pro.br/corposcopio. Accessed 10 January 2007.

Osthoff, Simone (1997), 'Lygia Clark and Hélio Oiticica: a Legacy of Interactivity and Participation for a Telematic Future', *Leonardo Journal*, vol. 30, n. 4. pp. 249–259.

Propp, V. (1985), *Theory and History of Folklore*, Minneapolis: University of Minnesota Press.

Rivas Neto, F. (1988), *Umbanda: A Proto-Síntese Cósmica*, Rio de Janeiro: Freitas Bastos.

Rivas Neto, F. (2003), *Sacerdote, Mago e Médico*. São Paulo: Ícone.

Rolnik, Suely (2002), 'Molda-se uma alma contemporânea: o vazio-pleno de Lygia Clark'. In: Leão, Lucia (org). InterLab: labirintos do pensamento contemporâneo. São Paulo: Editora Iluminuras – FAPESp.

Sheldrake, Rupert (1981), A New Science of Life: The Hypothesis of Formative Causation, London: Blond & Briggs.

Sheldrake, Rupert (1988), The Presence of the Past: Morphic Resonance and the Habits of Nature, London: Collins.

www.intellectbooks.co.uk/ppjournals.php?issn=1477965X. Accessed 19 January 2007.

# Epilogue: Realms of Learning

# FROM AWESOME IMMERSION TO HOLISTIC INTEGRATION

## Mel Alexenberg

This concluding section identifies realms of learning that weave together the complex issues of theory and practice in a post-digital Conceptual Age presented in my introduction and developed in the multifaceted chapters of this book.

The post-digital Conceptual Age is an age of creators and empathizers who activate the right hemisphere of their brains to complement the left-hemispheric dominance of the Information Age of knowledge workers and the Industrial Age of factory workers. In the Conceptual Age, well-developed high-tech abilities are no longer enough. They must be integrated with high-concept and high-touch abilities.

> High concept involves the ability to create artistic and emotional beauty, to detect patterns and opportunities, to craft a satisfying narrative, and to combine seemingly unrelated ideas into a novel invention. High touch involves the ability to empathize, to understand the subtleties of human interaction, to find joy in one's self and to elicit it in others, and to stretch beyond the quotidian, in pursuit of purpose and meaning. (Pink 2006: 51–52)

In keeping with the high-concept and high-touch character of the Conceptual Age, I identify realms of learning through an autoethnographic method of inquiry that creates a narrative highlighting episodes in my life that have particular significance for the education of artists at the intersections of art, science, technology, and culture. My autoethnographic inquiry begins in my childhood summers in the Catskill Mountains of upstate New York and leads six decades later to the creation of a new school of art and multimedia in Israel. It explores the dynamics of integrating multiple roles –

artist/researcher/teacher/writer, multiple fields – art/science/technology/culture, and multiple identities – a Jew, an Israeli, a third-generation American, and an artist working internationally in an era of globalization. It identifies interweaving realms that create a colorful fabric of lifelong learning: awesome immersion, playful exploration, aesthetic creativity, morphological analysis, interdisciplinary imagination, morphodynamic beauty, semiotic communication, cybersomatic interactivity, global connectivity, polycultural collaboration, ecological perspective, responsive compassion, spiritual emergence, moral courage, and holistic integration.

## Learning through Awesome Immersion

My integration of art and science had its origins in the summers of my childhood when I was set free among the sowbugs, salamanders, and swallows of the Catskill Mountains. My days were filled studying the behavior of the creatures of the forests and ponds and making drawings and paintings of them interacting in their natural habitats as well as in imaginary worlds of my creation. My intellectual curiosity and zealous observation coupled with my creative encounters and intimate friendships with these creatures made boundaries between science and art diaphanous. I had no clue that science and art were not one integrated human endeavor.

As I lifted a log beside a pond deep in the forest, I saw salamanders and centipedes scramble as sowbugs stopped in their tracks to roll up into compact balls. A barn swallow swooped down over the pond with lightning speed skimming the water's surface to snag a fly on wing. With a swift maneuver of its slate grey wings my avian friend flashed the splendor of his orange-breast feathers as he soared up across the pond and lighted on my shoulder.

I first saw this magnificent bird as a limp, featherless, bleeding swallow chick that had fallen from its nest in the eaves of my neighbor Ben's barn. I gently lifted it, cradled it in my palm, and took it home to live in a shoebox in my bedroom. As I painted Mercurochrome on its cut that matched its red skin, it opened its flat yellow beak chirping for food. My sister Fran named it Peeper. We read in the encyclopedia that swallows ate bugs rather than seeds like our canary. We spent our days catching flies, small moths, and crickets and digging for worms to feed the insatiable appetite of our small friend as his wound healed.

My drawings of Peeper documented his down growing to cover his nakedness and the splendid sprouting of his feathers. As flying lessons, I would hold him high above my bed and drop him. Days of plopping down onto my bed unaware of the function of his wings inspired me to make imaginary paintings of him flying free. He learned quickly once he discovered what wings were for. What an awesome sight to see him fly through the house at lightning speeds making ninety-degree turns around corners. This sleek swallow soon learned to exit from my bedroom window, soar up towards the clouds and swoop down to the pond behind our house where Fran and I swam with the newts, frogs, and minnows. Our utter amazement at seeing the graceful flight of our wounded swallow was transformed into joy each night when he would fly back to roost on the edge of the shoebox by my bed.

Although I enjoyed making drawings and paintings, I sensed that my artwork of greater significance was the actual act of nurturing a swallow chick on the verge of death and participating in its transformation into a beautiful bird of swift undulating flight. In his book on the blurring of art and life, Allan Kaprow (1993) contrasts art-like art to life-like art. My life-like art was living with a swallow. My art-like art was documenting my life with a swallow as well as imagining how it could be. My life-like art seemed to reach a higher spiritual plane than my art-like art. Perhaps the biblical injunction against making graven images is a warning to avoid freezing the wondrous and mysterious flow of living life into a static still life, *nature morte*, dead life.

Albert Einstein proposes that the miraculous encounter with the mysteries of our physical world is the fairest thing we can experience.

> It is the fundamental emotion which stands at the cradle of true art and true science. He who knows it not and can no longer feel amazement is as good as dead, a snuffed-out candle…But the Jewish tradition also contains something else, something which finds splendid expression in many of the Psalms – namely, a sort of intoxicated joy and amazement at the beauty and grandeur of this world, of which man can form just a faint notion. It is the feeling from which true scientific research draws its spiritual sustenance, but which also seems to find expression in the song of birds. (Einstein 1949: 5, 91)

Daily joy and amazement formed the core of my integral summer learning that was lost in my winter learning in the dreary grayness of Queens. What my winter school in the city forced into distinctly different disciplines had been integrally one in my summer learning in the Catskill Mountains. Thinking the world apart rather than experiencing it holistically broke my soul apart.

The joy of my holistic summer learning that honored my combination of spatial, naturalist, and spiritual intelligences was crushed by the fragmented learning of winter school that only valued those students endowed with linguistic and logical-mathematical intelligences. Although I was left with no choice but to develop linguistic and logical-mathematical intelligences, two of ten intelligences identified by Harvard psychologist Howard Gardner (1999), it is my innate spatial, naturalist, and spiritual intelligences that I had developed though my soul-soaring summers immersed in art-science learning that I needed most in my adult work as biologist and artist.

This experience of awesome immersion in the creative process is powerfully expressed by Rabbi Abraham Isaac Kook (1978):

Whoever is endowed with the soul of a creator must create works of imagination and thought, for the flame of the soul rises by itself and one cannot impede it on its course...The creative individual brings vital, new light from the higher source where originality emanates to the place where it has not previously been manifest, from the place that "no bird of prey knows, nor has the falcon's eye seen." (*Job* 28: 7), "that no man has passed,nor has any person dwelt" (*Jeremiah* 2: 6).

My childhood curiosity about what went on under logs and rocks in the forest followed me to college where I studied biology and wrote my thesis on the ecology of terrestrial isopods. Terrestrial isopods were my old summer friends – sowbugs – land-adapted crustaceans breathing with gills, surviving in the damp habitat under decaying logs. I found that they even lived under discarded cabinet doors on an empty lot in Queens. My scientific studies on the interrelationships between sowbugs and other organisms in their shared environment refined my systems thinking and ecological perspective that permeates my work as an artist.

## Learning through Playful Exploration

After earning degrees in biology and science education, I began doctoral studies in cognitive psychology at Yeshiva University, which I soon left to study painting at the Art Students League. I returned to my doctoral studies at New York University where the art department chairman, Howard Conant, had the daring to facilitate my earning an interdisciplinary degree in art, science, and psychology; rare four decades ago. My 1969 doctoral dissertation, *A Unitary Model of Aesthetic Experience in Art and Science*, was based on the analysis of my interviews of scientists (Nobel laureates and members of the National Academy of Sciences) and prominent artists who described their creative processes to me.

When the first computer plotter became available in 1965, I began creating vector drawings at NYU's Courant Institute of Mathematical Sciences that I transformed into sensuous encaustic paintings. One of these early high-tech/high-touch artworks exploring the physics of noise control was reproduced as the cover of *International Science and Technology* (April 1966). Working with nuclear physicists at Brookhaven National Laboratories, I created a series of paintings exploring the paths of subatomic particles moving in a bubble chamber. My representation of motion of subatomic particles developed into presentations of motion in real space-time through my kinetic participatory "Multiform" artworks. Spectators became active collaborators in creating the artwork by manipulating knobs to reveal different colored surfaces of multifaceted prisms. In 1967, I had a solo exhibition, *Multiform of 531,441 Paintings*, at the Art Gallery of Adelphi Suffolk College on Long Island.

During the ten years between my master's degree and doctorate, I earned my living as a science educator while studying painting at the Art Students League and NYU. I worked on Long Island as science teacher at Louis Pasteur Junior High School in Little Neck, science supervisor of the Manhasset Public Schools, and assistant professor of science education at Adelphi University. I directed one of ten test centers for American Association for the Advancement of Science curriculum project, *Science: A Process Approach*, funded by the National Science Foundation. My papers on scientific inquiry were published in *School Science and Mathematics* (1962) and in *Biosciences: Journal of the American Institute of Biological Sciences* (1969). My paper "The Binary System and Computers" appeared in the National Science Teachers Association journal, *Science and Children* (1964). I developed educational materials for the American Iron and Steel Institute, American Chemical Society, and the Leukemia Society of America. At the 1967 American Film Festival, I won the award for art direction for my film on leukemia.

Perhaps the most significant events at this time were my marrying my wonderful Miriam, experiencing the birth of our first three children and participating in their early childhood explorations. We realized that opportunities for them to experience the awesome immersion that I had enjoyed in my childhood would come through their playful explorations. I set up opportunities for them to play with everyday things around our house that became equipment and materials for simple scientific experiments. Seeing their enthusiasm and joy engaged in these playful explorations prompted me to share them with parents of other young children. I wrote them up as my monthly "Science Fun" feature in *Humpty Dumpty Magazine for Little Children* that appeared for several years and led to the publication of my best-selling children's books of hands-on science experiments for exploring the senses, *Sound Science* (1969) and *Light and Sight* (1970). I created an androgynous outer-space-looking creature who invites children on a playful romp to discover how their senses of sight and hearing reveal the secrets of light and sound. My daughter Iyrit named the creature a "Gloop. " The jacket flap copy for *Light and Sight* reads: "If you would like to work and learn as a scientist does, then follow the Gloop through *Light and Sight*. Have you ever wondered why you look so funny when you see yourself in the fender of a car? Or, why some shadows are large and some are small? You can find out about the world of light and sight from mirrors, water, light bulbs, or even your mother's cookie sheet."

The intrinsic reward from being immersed in the open-ended process of playful exploration was beautifully expressed by philosophy of science professor David Hawkins in his talk "Messing About in Science" at a meeting I attended at AAAS headquarters in Washington for directors of *Science: A Process Approach* test centers. He quoted from the Water Rat in the classic children's book *The Wind in the Willows*.

> "Nice? It's the only thing," said the Water Rat solemnly, as he leaned forward for his stroke. "Believe me, my young friend, there is nothing – absolutely nothing – half so much worth doing as simply messing about in boats. Simply messing," he went on dreamily, "messing – about – in – messing – about in boats – or with boats...in or out of 'em. It doesn't matter. Nothing seems really to matter, that's the charm of it. Whether you get away, or whether you don't; whether you arrive at your destination or whether you reach somewhere else, or whether you never get anywhere at all,

you're always busy and never do anything in particular; and when you've done it there's always something else to do." (Grahame 2003, first published in 1908)

As editor of *The American Biology Teacher* issue on educating young children, I quoted the Water Rat's words in my paper "Biology Education in the Elementary School: The First Task and Central Purpose" (Alexenberg 1967). My decade of work in awakening in children the sense of joy and excitement in the scientist's ways of asking questions and seeking answers to them has colored my subsequent work as an art educator. In teaching artists, I continue to emphasize the Water Rat's philosophy of playful exploration as a vital route to meaningful learning and creative expression. Scientist Jacob Bronowski in his book *Science and Human Values* compares the creative activities of artists and scientists to the play of children and young animals.

> In science and in the arts the sense of freedom which the creative man feels in his work derives from what I call the poetic element: the uninhibited activity of exploring the medium for its own sake, and discovering as if in play what can be done with it. The word play is in place here, for the play of young animals is of this kind – an undirected adventure in which they nose into and fill out their own abilities, free from the later compulsions of need and environment. Man plays and learns for a long time (he has a longer childhood) and he goes on playing into adult life: in this sense of free discovery, pure science is (like art) a form of play. (Bronowski 1965: 76)

## Learning through Aesthetic Creativity

To understand creativity in science and art at its highest level, I interviewed twenty scientists identified as the most creative by their peers – Nobel laureates and members of the National Academy of Sciences – and artists in *Who's Who in American Art* having their artworks in the collections of major museums. Through content analysis of my interview transcriptions, I found that the creative process in both art and science share a common aesthetic core. Although it is obvious that art and aesthetics go together, my study revealed the significance of aesthetic joy in the research process in the physical and biological sciences. For my 1981 book, *Aesthetic Experience in Creative Process*, I sent the transcripts of my interviews to the artists and scientists I had interviewed and asked them to edit the transcripts for inclusion in my book. Below are excerpts from two of the interviews, those of sculptor Richard Lippold and geophysicist Maurice Ewing. I interviewed sculptor Richard Lippold in his studio on Long Island and geophysicist Maurice Ewing at Columbia University's Lamont Geological Observatory of which he was director.

Richard Lippold is best known for his wire sculpture *The Sun* in the collection of the Metropolitan Museum of Art and his monumental *Orpheus and Apollo* hovering over the entire entry lobby of Lincoln Center's Philharmonic Hall. He dismisses things that are static and emphasizes how the constantly changing universe affects our lives and the artistic process. "If I sit down to make a sketch one day, surely it will be different from one I make another day. I feel different. We never feel the same from moment to moment; we are changing every moment. We are reshaping ourselves." He wrote in an article for the book *Structure in Art and Science* (Kepes 1965) that "chance is an accident of order and order is an accident of chance." He described to me his making *New Moonlight*, his first wire sculpture that became the ancestor of *The Sun* at the Met:

> The process involves the materials, the concepts, the feelings, and the physical making of the thing. Then anything can happen. It's charged with possibilities, with excitement, and with involvement. It's a little like making love. All the excitement is going on while it's going on. There is something comparable to an orgasm. It doesn't have quite this physical manifestation. But there is a sudden moment when I know it has come. I didn't mean to say it that way; it's the same word! Actually, this is what it is. You know that then everything has come together...The first time I made a work in which this happened, it happened quite mysteriously because I wasn't conscious of it. When the finished work arrived, appeared, the material and the technique came together in what struck me as an exquisite balance. The feeling didn't dominate; the concept didn't overwhelm; the form wasn't a technical exercise. Everything contributed to the meaning. It was a total balance which transcended all its parts that together seemed a spiritual totality – an ecstatic event. It impressed me so that I couldn't sleep for a couple of days. I thought, "What have I wrought? I didn't determine all this. It happened through me; I was the medium for it. I was surprised. I was astonished, surprised and delighted. (Alexenberg 1981: 109–110)

Maurice Ewing was America's foremost geophysicist, the first recipient of the Vetlesen Prize that honors leaders in the earth sciences the way scientists in other fields are honored with Nobel Prizes. While he was talking to me, he moved through a labyrinth of paper pillars composed of stacks of charts, heaps of data records, and piles of scientific papers. When not pulling graphs for me to see from these pillars and checking ticker-tape communication from his research ships, he sat at a desk cluttered with mementos of his far-flung journeys while his aging dog sat at his feet.

Ewing had been studying relationships between ocean waves and the waves in the ground under the ocean by making explosions in the water and measuring the results with seismographs. He dreamed about exploring these relationships at the global level rather than at the local level. Ewing had no idea how to do it since there was no way he could make explosions great enough to shake the whole planet. The solution popped into his consciousness from his childhood memories. He recalled a story he had read in his fourth-grade reader about the great eruption of the volcano Krakatoa and suddenly realized that such an enormous explosion had actually occurred naturally. The eruption of a volcanic island between Sumatra and Java in 1883 made sea waves fifty feet high and killed nearly forty thousand Javanese. If he could have been there then and known in advance that such a massive explosion would occur, he thought, he would have placed tide gauges, seismographs, and barometers strategically around our planet. He could then have measured the waves in the ocean, waves in the ground under the water, and waves in the air above and established mathematical relationships between them on a global scale.

On a shelf in his laboratory, he had an old book, *The Eruption of Krakatoa and Subsequent Phenomena*, published in 1888 by the Royal Society of Great Britain. When he looked in this book, he realized that all the information he needed was there. It was fortuitous that the eruption occurred when Venus was eclipsed by the moon. Scientists throughout the world had placed tide gauges to measure the effect of the transit of Venus on the oceans. They knew that the alignment of the moon and Venus would cause extra-high tides. Ewing enthusiastically explained the beauty and simplicity of integrating information recorded by different people seventy years earlier into a unified theory of resonant coupling. "It was possible in that one night to move into the study of surface waves, to understand it fully, to write the classic paper on it, to type it up, to put it in the mail. All in one night! Well, my friend, that is living. I don't know any thrill that anybody can have that will compare with that. Do you?" (Alexenberg 1981, p. 158)

### Learning through Morphological Analysis
In 1969, I submitted my research on the psychology of aesthetic experience in art and science to my interdisciplinary doctoral committee at NYU: Prabha Sahasrabudhe, art education professor; Janice Gorn, psychology professor; and Morris Shamos, physics professor and president of the National Academy of Sciences. A week after having earned my doctorate, I was on an El Al plane to Israel with my wife and our three children to accept a teaching and research position at Tel Aviv University. Except for a week in Holland two years earlier, this was my first trip abroad.

We rented a cottage set in an orange grove in a small town north of Tel Aviv. Our new neighbor's young daughter, Zahava, came to our door welcoming us with two large pita-like breads, one in each hand. They were still warm and surrounded by the welcoming aroma of fresh-baked bread. Our neighbors were Yemenite Jews who had ascended to Israel from the tip of the Arabian Peninsula a decade earlier. Having returned to their biblical homeland, they continued to bake flat round bread in a wood-burning, underground oven dug in their back yard as they had done in Yemen. Jews had lived in Yemen for nearly two thousand years in a style of life that changed little from biblical times.

I was struck by the contrast between the whole, two-dimensional, circular breads that Zahava brought us and the supermarket bread that I had been used to buying on Long Island. Supermarket bread is a three-dimensional, rectilinear, cold, white loaf fragmented into slices and kept at a distance from the consumer by a sealed plastic wrapper that cuts off olfactory and tactile contact. This quick lesson in the morphological analysis of visual culture became the core of my research, curriculum development, and teaching at Tel Aviv University. I realized that the morphology of pre-industrial mythological cultures is shaped by two-dimensional, undifferentiated, circular space, and cyclical time as symbolized by pita-like breads. On the other hand, three-dimensional rectilinear space and linear time sliced into discrete units is symbolized by the supermarket bread of industrial logical culture.

I asked myself, "How will my children, fourth-generation American Jews of European background, and Zahava's siblings build a common future?" In studying the Israeli educational system and visiting schools throughout the country, I learned of the significant gap in achievement between children from European backgrounds and those from Islamic lands. The school system was created by educators from industrial Europe to develop a logical structure of consciousness which was alien to children from pre-industrial lands with a mythological structure of consciousness. It was easy to understand the failure of those children in an unfamiliar, foreign learning environment. It was made ever easier to understand this problem when I passed by my neighbor's house coming home from my day at the university. Zahava's father was sitting on his porch reading a newspaper that he was holding upside-down. "Shmuel," I asked, "why are you reading upside-down?" "It's more comfortable for me that way," answered Shmuel, who went on to explain how he had learned to read sitting on carpets with other children around a handwritten scroll. His regular place was sitting at the top of the scroll. Therefore, he learned to read upside-down. When I joined him in his synagogue on the Sabbath, some men sat around the room against the four walls while others sat around the reader's platform with their backs to him as he chanted words that he read from a scroll. In sharp contrast, the typical American synagogue that I knew had seating in rows all facing in the same direction like the classrooms in Israeli schools.

In Shmuel's world of mythological perspective, people experience an auditory world listening to the retelling of the oral tradition – their communal mythology as handed down to them by word of mouth. They sit as a community surrounded by a sphere of sound. The auditory experience of space is encircling, involving, and soft-edged. Time is felt as cyclical and pulsating. The nature of the auditory experience is derived from the physics of sound. Sound generated in air produces spherical waves that surround the point of origin and engulf anyone within its sphere. A cross section of a sound-sphere would appear like the concentric circles that surround a pebble when it is tossed in a pond. When people sit within a sound-sphere of pulsating air, they cannot help hearing the message. They feel that sound surrounds them and involves them. They can neither turn away from it nor close their ears to it. Ears have no anatomical analogues to eyelids. Unlike the visual world where light sources can be accurately pinpointed, the auditory world is soft and fuzzy at both its core and edges. In the logical world of European culture shaped by the single-point Hellenistic perspective revived in the Renaissance, one gets to know the world visually, from rays of light traveling to one's eyes in straight lines from definite points in Euclidean space. Ecological perspective derives from a kinesthetic integration of auditory and visual senses in experiencing dynamic interrelationships between parts of a whole that are more than the sum of its parts. Space and time are unified in a four-dimensional world of events experienced through movement and interaction expressed in art through lively narratives.

I realized that the attempts to acculturate the mythological Jews in schools whose aim was to develop a logical structure of consciousness was foolhardy at a time when the logical structure of the Industrial Age had no future. I proposed that both the auditory mythological and visual logical minds can meet in a new shared multi-sense ecological structure evolving in a post-industrial electronic era. My research revealed that not only did both the mythological and logical Jews need to develop an ecological perspective to succeed in the electronic future together, but they also shared a past with a common deep structure of Jewish consciousness which is an ecological structure that creates an integral worldview. The ecological structure of Jewish consciousness remained embedded as a deep structure during the Jews' centuries in Islamic lands when a mythological perspective was plastered on. European Jews, too, had their ecological structure of consciousness and integral worldview distorted by the overpowering logical perspective of a Western culture shaped by Hellenism.

My research on the morphologies of mythological, logical, and ecological structures of consciousness that are revealed through space-time structures of visual culture formed the theoretical basis for my curriculum project, "From Science to Art" (Alexenberg 1974, 2006b). Beyond the theoretic underpinnings of the project, morphological analysis of natural and cultural systems became the subject matter of the curriculum aimed at bridging the gap between mythological and logical youth by stimulating their interdisciplinary imagination and developing their ecological perspective. The "From Science to Art" curriculum project had parallel explicit and implicit morphological aims.

Although I began this curriculum project in 1969, it is even more vital today in our era of globalization and intercultural conflict to educate artists in morphological analysis of visual culture. After all, artists have always shaped worldview by their perspective inventions. Renaissance artists renewed the Greek logical perspective by visually representing three-dimensional space from a single point of view and time as a cross section of a one-way linear path. Most people in the industrialized world continue to see the world through the eyes of these Renaissance artists. Most Third World people, however, continue to see their world through a mythological perspective of two-dimensional space and cyclical time. Artists today are once again reshaping humanity's worldview by inventing art of ecological perspective and integral consciousness in a multi-dimensional space-time continuum.

### Learning through Interdisciplinary Imagination

"From Science to Art" encouraged junior high school students to develop their interdisciplinary imagination, ecological perspective, and integral consciousness through morphological analysis of periodicity and rhythmic structures, threshold phenomenon, bilateral and rotational symmetries, spiral and branching systems, and stochastic processes and asymmetries.

In the unit of study on periodicity and rhythmic patterns in nature and culture, students rolled out ink on a glass plate, pressed their fingers on it, and printed their fingerprints on uninflated white balloons and on tracing paper. They enlarged their fingerprints by blowing up the balloons and by placing the tracing paper in 35 mm slide holders and projecting them. They compared their fingerprints to each other to appreciate the uniqueness of each person. They saw that no two people have the same fingerprint pattern. Students compared their own fingerprints to fingerprints of chimpanzees. They learned that although there was a wide range of variation in human fingerprints, fingerprints from another species were outside that range. After students created classification systems for their classmates' fingerprints, a police officer was invited to the classroom to explain the international system of fingerprint taxonomy. Students taped paper to the wall and projected their fingerprints on it while they drew the lines. They made paintings from their drawings. They enlarged fingerprints on a copy machine and printed them out on acetate sheets that they placed on top of one another to create moiré patterns. They discussed optical illusions and the psychology of human perception.

Students looked at reproductions of the "op art" of Bridget Riley and of Henry Pearson whose artwork was inspired by his drawing topographical maps in the army. Students studied topographic maps of the Israeli landscape. They observed the generation of rhythmic wave patterns in a ripple tank used in physics classes. What were the connections between ripples in water, geologically formed topographies, and their own fingerprints?

They watched a National Geographic film on zebras that showed how a pregnant zebra removed herself from the herd so that the newborn would only see her pattern of stripes. The baby zebra would memorize its mother's unique pattern of stripes so that it could recognize her in the herd. A zebra that could not find its mother for nursing would perish. Does the supermarket laser recognize the bar code stripes on cans and cartons like a baby zebra recognizing its mother? Bar codes are the secret language of the digital age. We are all illiterate before the stripes that supermarket lasers can read.

Students examined the variety of stripe patterns on the *talit* prayer shawls worn by Jews in synagogue. They looked at Marc Chagall's paintings of men wearing a *talit*. The unsymmetrical sequencing of the parallel stripes on each *talit* looks like a bar code. They studied the biblical verses about Joseph's striped coat (*Genesis* 37: 3–4) and read commentaries on the symbolism of the striped coat. Some watched the video of Andrew Lloyd Webber's musical *Joseph and his Amazing Technicolor Dreamcoat*.

Students went out onto the school playground on a sunny day, unrolled paper on the ground, cut it into long pieces, one for each student, and taped them down. Working in pairs, students drew around their classmate's two feet and shadows. They returned to their drawings and placed their feet in the same places every hour for the duration of the day having their shadow drawn each time. The set of shadow drawings one on top of the other were visually linked to topographic maps and fingerprints. They painted overlapping serial self-portraits on their shadow drawings that had documented Planet

Earth's rotation. "Conceptualizing the changing relationship of sun and earth, relating that dynamics to the form of one's personal shadow, and communicating these relationships in a serial painting – his squat noontime body form to a late afternoon elongated body form – moves the students toward an integral structure of consciousness by unifying time-space, subject-object, man-environment, and science-art" (Alexenberg 1974: 151).

Interdisciplinary imagination sees fresh relationships between disparate realms of experience. In linear logical thinking, phenomena are trapped within narrowly defined boundaries. "From Science to Art" invited questioning that leads to experiencing a diaphanous world in which boundaries lose their opacity. How does one connect one's own fingerprints with op art, topographical maps, ripple tanks, zebra stripes, supermarket bar codes, prayer shawls, Joseph's technicolor dreamcoat, one's shadows and the rotation of Planet Earth? Interdisciplinary imagination couples the cognitive act of matching, of creating relationships/connections/congruencies, with a concomitant affective response of joy/amazement/elation so that "the energy of all one's discordant impulses creates a single image connecting varieties of experience" (Bruner 1963: 70).

After four years in Israel, I returned to the States to accept a position as Associate Professor of Art and Education at Columbia University, where I introduced an interdisciplinary graduate course, "Morphodynamics: Design of Natural Systems," that I had first taught at the Bezalel Academy of Arts and Design in Jerusalem. I coined the word "morphodyanmics" to describe the processes that give rise to form rather than "morphology" which has a more static tone. In these courses, my students further expanded the units in the "From Science to Art" curriculum project to develop their interdisciplinary imagination through exploring evolving patterns in nature (Alexenberg 2005a).

I extended this pattern-thinking into the realm of culture in the research methods course at Columbia that I team-taught with anthropologist Margaret Mead, in my subsequent research and teaching at Bar-Ilan University in Israel, in "Morphological Perspectives: Space-Time Structures of Visual Culture," the second chapter of my book *The Future of Art in a Digital Age: From Hellenistic to Hebraic Consciousness* (Alexenberg 2006b), and in my paper "Biblical Fringes: Biomorphic Consciousness through Ancient Ritual" presented at the 2006 Consciousness Reframed conference at the University of Plymouth.

## Learning through Morphodynamic Beauty

Parallel with my teaching at Columbia University, I explored in the laboratory of the New York Botanical Gardens and in my studio in Teaneck, New Jersey, morphodynamics expressed in the cellular growth of plants. I found hidden within leaves a vital inner beauty that rivals the beauty of the outer forms of plants and their flowers. I sought to reveal this hidden beauty through encaustic paintings on photomicrographs of leaf cross sections.

I prepared microscope slides of leaf cross sections, photographed their elegant cellular patterns through a microscope, enlarged them 600 times, mounted them on shaped panels, and painted on the photographs with vibrant pigments suspended in molten waxes. The shapes of the panels are the outer shapes of the leaves, shapes emerging from the dynamic interplay between the cells within. Nothing is more important to us than what happens inside leaves. Without the vital process of photosynthesis occurring within leaves, we would not exist and there would be no life on our planet. Leaf cells, using sunlight and chlorophyll, take water flowing up into leaves from roots in the earth and carbon dioxide blowing into leaves from the surrounding air and transform the water and carbon dioxide into food and oxygen.

My focus on the inner beauty of the photosynthetic process and the cellular organization within leaves rather than the outer beauty of the plant is not only inspired by my background in biology and art, but by my Jewish consciousness. Unlike the Hellenistic art revived in the Renaissance that sees beauty in the imitation of external form, Judaism honors the inner dynamics of living systems. The growth process by which the outer form of a leaf is created by the organization of the cells within reveals an inner beauty known as *tiferet* in Judaism. *Tiferet* is the innermost node interconnected with nine others in the "Tree of Life" metaphor for the spiraling of divine light into our everyday world of space and time. This metaphorical way of seeing beauty as the dynamic harmony between multiple forces is called <u>h</u>okhmat hanistar (hidden wisdom), another name for *kabbalah*, Judaism's esoteric tradition.

This aesthetic enthusiasm for revealing the elegant cellular growth patterns hidden within leaves began with large oil paintings that I made when I was a 22-year-old science teacher at Louis Pasteur Junior High School on Long Island and tactile collages that I made as a student at the Art Students League of New York when I was science supervisor for the Manhasset Public School. This enthusiasm was renewed as the central focus of my artwork during my four years as art professor at Columbia when I equipped a studio for encaustic painting. I installed ventilation hoods to remove the fumes generated when I made paints by suspending powdered pigments in a combination of molten beeswax, microcrystalline wax, and dammar resin. I designed and built special equipment combining soldering irons and funnels with touch values for painting on photomicrographs that I mounted on shaped panels. Light waves reflected from within the depths of the translucent encaustic paints rendered the cells vibrancy unattainable with oil or acrylic paints.

At the laboratory of the New York Botanical Gardens, I replaced the water in plant cells with alcohol and then xylol and liquid paraffin so that they would be firm enough when refrigerated to be cleanly cut with a microtome into cross sections one-cell thick. I prepared microscope slides through which I photographed the cellular patterns creating the outer form of the leaf. In the darkroom at Columbia, I printed these photographs in black and white to mount on the shaped panels that I prepared in my Teaneck studio.

Three decades later, I am taking a break from writing this book to mount an exhibition at the Jerusalem Botanical Gardens of these shaped encaustic paintings of cellular patterns within leaves alongside the actual living plants that invite visitors to the exhibition to embark on an aesthetic journey from the whole plant into the beautiful world hidden within it. I exhibited these botanical paintings in a botanical gardens, a site-specific venue, rather than in a neutral white-box environment of an art gallery or museum.

## Learning through Semiotic Communication

In response to my students at Columbia being confused by the multiple directions that art was taking in the 1970s, I attempted to make sense out of this confusion using semiotics, the study of how signs communicate significance. As a starting point, I turned to the pioneering work on semiotics of American logician and mathematician Charles Pierce (1960). He identified three classes of signs: icon, symbol, and index. These categories can describe how significance is created in representational art of premodernism and modernism. They were insufficient, however, to describe postmodern presentational forms of art that my students were encountering.

Representational art forms show after-the-fact signs of what was. Presentational art locates art in the present and future in contrast to *r*epresentational art that locates art in the past. Presentational art forms required an expanded semiotic taxonomy (Alexenberg 1976). I identified three classes of presentation: identic, prioric, and dialogic. Identic art gains meaning by presenting what is. Prioric art presents what can be. And dialogic art gains meaning through dialogue, collaboration, and interaction in dynamic responsive processes.

My semiotic taxonomy provides a theoretical framework and pedagogical tool for educating artists in understanding how contemporary art forms and those that will evolve in the future create significance. I expanded the paper I had written when I was teaching at Columbia three decades ago by applying my semiotic taxonomy to new media art in my chapter "Semiotic Redefinition of Art in a Digital Age" in the book *Semiotics and Visual Culture: Sights, Signs, and Significance* (Alexenberg 2004).

Iconic art, the first category of representational art, represents the surface appearance of things. It gains meaning by looking like something that we see in the real world. Computer users know the word "icon" as the blank sheet of paper with its corner folded down, the floppy disc, the file folder, the printer, and the scissors icons on the toolbar of computer screens. These computer icons, Redon's painting of a vase of flowers, Michelangelo's Adam reaching out to touch the hand of God, Picasso's *Three Musicians*, and a road map are all icons with different levels of iconicity.

Symbolic art represents things or ideas through signs that are assigned meaning maintained by convention, by the agreement of community. Unlike an icon that bears a likeness to what it signifies, a symbol bears no direct or necessary connection to what it signifies. A red traffic light, for example, signifies a command to stop, while a green light signifies go. These are assigned meanings agreed upon by community consensus. Had the opposite assignment been made, green would signify stop. I have shown a slide of Larry River's painting *Last Civil War Veteran* when I lectured in Israel, Holland, and Japan. No one could identify the subject of the painting that shows the Confederate and Union flags behind a person in a bed. They all recognized the Union flag as the flag of USA, but none could recognize the flag of the Confederate states. On the other hand, when I showed this same slide in the USA, everyone could identify the subject of the painting.

The third class of representational art is indexic. If a painting that looks like a man walking on the beach is iconic art, and words MAN WALKING ON BEACH painted on a canvas are symbolic art, then the actual footprints in the sand indicating that a man had walked on the beach can be perceived as indexic art. Indexic art represents occurrences by presenting direct physical evidence that they occurred. The word "index" is used as in its original derivation from Latin *indicare*, meaning to indicate, to point out as an index finger does. Although indexical signs are felt strongly in Van Gogh's paintings as his impasto brushstrokes, he continued to maintain iconicity in them. The full abandonment of the icon in painting and its replacement with pure index occurred most powerfully in action painting. A Jackson Pollack painting is indexic art that displays symptoms of the artist's having dripped paint, as well as a documentary map and after-the-act choreographic score of the movement of his body over a canvas floor. There is a direct physical connection between the artist dripping paint and the dripped paint on the canvas. Indexic art represents by correspondence, directly connecting what was to what is.

Photographs, at first impression, would seem to be the epitome of iconic art, the zenith of iconicity, since they represent the most accurate visual likeness of an object or event. On closer scrutiny, however, it becomes clear that the very high iconicity results from the photographic image being produced by point-to-point correspondence between light rays coming from what is being represented and a chemically or electronically sensitized plane. From this point of view, photographs are indexic art forms, documentary records produced by direct physical connection between what was and what is. Indexic pictures that render the invisible visible play a vital role in contemporary science. The work of many scientists involves reading symptoms of natural occurrences from X-rays, MRIs, electrocardiograms, spectrograms, scintigrams, seismograms, voiceprints, and numerous other technologically generated indexic pictures.

Categories of representational art signify what *was* by illustration, symbolization, and documentation. Presentational art forms signify what is, what can be, and what is becoming. The first category of presentational art, identic art does not look like something else, nor does it symbolize or indicate something other than itself. It is form and color presented as form and color; it is a real thing presented as itself, it is a real-time electronic transmission of an event, and it can be an everyday event that is presented as life being lived.

Prioric art is the presentation of a proposal or plan for a potential event, an *a priori* statement of what can be. It often employs iconic and symbolic modes of signification for presenting itself. The prioric form is more common in art forms other than the visual arts. It can take the form of scores in music and dance, scripts in theater and film, or architectural plans. Like these forms, visual artists can propose artworks that they do not make themselves. Musicians perform music created by composers, dancers move to choreographers' notations, actors enact a script written by playwrights, and building contractors convert architectural drawings into buildings. Visual artists act more like composers, choreographers, playwrights, and architects in creating prioric art. New media artists in a networked world have the unprecedented power to create prioric artworks to disseminate their proposals globally. My Internet artwork described below in the section "Learning through Moral Courage," www.futureholocaustmemorials.org, is a prioric artwork that makes outlandish proposals as a call to action to confront bigotry, hatred, terrorism, genocide, and cults of death and destruction with moral outrage.

Dialogic art comes into being through dialogue. It exists as the interrelationship between people. The difference between identic and dialogic forms of art can be described by philosopher Martin Buber's two primary words: I-It and I-Thou. I-It is the experience of something; it describes identic art. I-Thou, however, is not the experience *of* something, but rather an interrelationship that has its own existence. I-Thou comes into being through dialogue, the interactive shared sphere between people, a sphere of spiritual intensity. "The participation of both partners is in principle indispensable to this sphere...The unfolding of this sphere Buber calls 'the dialogical.' The meaning of this dialogue is found in neither one nor the other of the partners, nor in both taken together, but in their interchange." (Freidman 1960: 85, 241)

### Learning through Cybersomatic Interactivity

After four years at Columbia, I returned to Israel as founding president of a regional college in the Negev Desert and as Associate Professor at Bar-Ilan University. I established an art school at the college in which the students joined me in creating conceptual and environmental artworks in the desert environment that addressed ecological, spiritual, and cultural issues. In 1984, after seven years of desert life, I returned to the States as Research Fellow at MIT's Center for Advanced Visual Studies. I taught the graduate seminar "Art, Technology and Culture" and developed a workshop for artists, scientists, and engineers, "Mindleaping: Developing Creativity for the Electronic Age." In collaboration with MIT's Center for Advanced Visual Studies director, Otto Piene, and our MIT colleagues, I created a major exhibition, *LightsOROT: Spiritual Dimensions of the Electronic Age*, for Yeshiva University Museum in New York. Harvard University psychologist Rudolf Arnheim wrote the catalog introduction. The *ARTnews* critic wrote: "Rarely is an exhibition as visually engaging and intellectually challenging."

We created 25 artworks using laser animation, holography, fiber optics, biofeedback-generated imagery, computer graphics, interactive electronic media, spectral projections, and digital music. My cybersomatic interactive system was born in my realization that the Hebrew words for face, *panim*, and for inside, *p'nim*, are written with the same four letters *PNIM*. I knew that I needed to create portraits which create a dialogue between the outside face and inside feelings.

As an MIT artist with access to electronic technologies, I designed a system for creating digital self-generated portraits in which internal mind/body processes and one's facial countenance engage in dialogue. I constructed a console in which a participant seated in front of a monitor places her finger in a plethysmograph, which measures internal body states by monitoring blood flow, while under the gaze of a video camera. Digitized information about her internal mind/body processes triggers changes in the image of herself that she sees on the monitor. She sees her face changing color, stretching, elongating, extending, rotating, or replicating in response to her feelings about seeing herself changing. My artwork *Inside/Outside: P'nim/Panim* created a flowing digital feedback loop in which *p'nim* effects changes in *panim* and *panim*, in turn, effects changes in *p'nim* (Alexenberg and Peine 1988).

Educating artists in a digital age should provide opportunities for learning to create artworks that are systems of cybersomatic interactivity that forge a vital dialogue between mind and body and between human consciousness and digital imagery. Significant developments in future art will occur at the interface between cyberspace and real space where virtual worlds interact with our bodies moving in our physical environments to shape consciousness. New directions in aesthetic creativity are being realized through elegant cybersomatic feedback loops that flow between dry pixels and wet biomolecules, between silicon-based cybersystems and carbon-based biosystems to create, what Roy Ascott (2000) calls, "moistmedia artworks."

## Learning through Global Connectivity

While creating the *LightsOROT* exhibition at MIT, I accepted the position as Professor and Chairman of Fine Arts at Pratt Institute and became a frequent flyer on the Boston–New York shuttle. At Pratt, I introduced and taught the first computer graphics course there, "Fine Arts with Computers," and began my digitized homage of Rembrandt series exhibited in my solo show, *Computer Angels*, at the Art Gallery of the State University of New York at Stony Brook. More than forty museums worldwide added my serigraphs, lithographs, and etchings exploring digital technologies and global systems to their collections. I was Art Editor of *The Visual Computer: International Journal of Computer Graphics* that published my paper "Art with Computers: The Human Spirit and the Electronic Revolution" (Alexenberg 1988).

A powerful force shaping the digital age is globalization, free trade, and the free flow of information and the range of human reactions to them. Thomas Freidman (2000) argues in *The Lexus and the Olive Tree: Understanding Globalization* that the challenge in this era of globalization is to find a healthy balance between preserving a sense of identity, home, and community and doing what it takes to survive within the globalization system. Digital-age art has the power to negotiate connections between global and local, between high tech and high touch, between Lexus and olive tree.

My global telecommunications artwork had its origins in a very local setting. It began in a small <u>H</u>asidic synagogue in Brooklyn while I was listening to the chanting of the weekly biblical portion from the handwritten *Torah* scroll. I listened to the ancient Hebrew words, translating them into English in my mind. They told of the prototypic artist Betzalel being filled with divine spirit, wisdom, understanding and knowledge, and talent for all types of craftsmanship to make all manner of *MeLekHet MakHSheVeT* (*Exodus* 35: 33). Usually translated as "artistic work," it literally means "thoughtful craft." In a sudden flash of insight, it dawned on me that the biblical term for "art," *MeLekHeT MakHSheVeT*, is feminine and that its masculine form, *MaLakH MakHSheV*, literally means "computer angel." Art is a computer angel when biblical Hebrew meets modern Hebrew in a digital age. As soon as the synagogue service came to an end, I ran to my wife and explained to her that as a male artist my role in life is to make computer angels.

I went to the print room of the Metropolitan Museum of Art where I selected angel images from Rembrandt's drawings and etchings to digitize. I wanted to applaud Rembrandt by having his winged angels wing their way around the world. I phoned AT&T and asked if I could use their telecommunications satellites to send a cyberangel on a circumglobal flight. "You have *what* to send around the globe?" was the response as I was transferred from office to office. Incredulity was turned to interest when I reached the public relations people who liked the idea. AT&T agreed to sponsor my memorial faxart event.

I flew to Amsterdam to meet with Eva Orenstein-van Slooten, Curator of Museum het Rembrandthuis, the artist's home and studio. With trepidation, I proposed having a fax machine placed on Rembrandt's 350-year-old etching press to receive the angel that would fly there from New York. She thought it was a wonderful idea. It would make her museum, a quiet place, come alive as a virtual Rembrandt angel rematerialized in the place he had originally created it.

On the morning of October 4th, the angel ascended from the Chippendale top of the AT&T building in New York. It flew to Amsterdam to Jerusalem to Tokyo to Los Angeles, returning to the former New Amsterdam on the same afternoon. It took an hour in each city to receive 28 pages of angel fragments and fax them on to the next city. After a five-hour flight around the planet, the deconstructed angel was reconstructed for the fifth time at its starting point. When it passed through Tokyo, it was already the morning of October 5th. The cyberangel returned to New York on the afternoon of October 4th, five hours after it had left. It had entered tomorrow before flying forward into yesterday.

The cyberangel was received at Rembrandt's house seconds after it left New York. Ms. van Slooten fed the 28 sheets back into the fax machine on Rembrandt's etching press and dialed the fax number of the Israel Museum in Jerusalem. She then assembled all the fragments into a whole 4 x 6 foot angel.

Jerusalem was the appropriate next stop since it is an angel from a biblical scene. It was evening when the cyberangel arrived. Amalyah Zipkin, Curator of European Art at the Israel Museum, sent me a description of the angel coming and going. She wrote:

> There is something appropriate in the illogic of the event: here we were in Jerusalem, the Holy City of 4000 years of turbulent history, huddled next to a fax machine in the mail room of the Israel Museum. It was a few days before Yom Kippur. Somewhere out there in technological space, a disembodied angel – computerized, digitized, enlarged, quartered, and faxed – was winging its way towards us from Amsterdam. This angel had been drawn in the 17th century by a Dutch artist with the instantly-recognizable mass-media name of Rembrandt van Rijn, and had undergone its electronic dematerialization 320 years after the artist's death at the hands of a New York artist and technology freak who had the audacity to make the connections: Rembrandt, the Bible, *gematria* [Hebrew numerology], the electronic age, global communications, the art world, and the fax machine. Like magic, at the appointed hour the fax machine zapped to life and bits of angel began to materialize in Jerusalem. Photographs and the attendant PR requirements of contemporary life were seen to, and the pages were carefully fed back into the machine. We punched in the Tokyo phone number and the angel took technological flight once more.

It was almost dawn on October 5th when the angel arrived in Tokyo in the Land of the Rising Sun where fax machines are made. Ikuro Choh of Tokyo National University of Arts and Music received the angel and revealed its full image by assembling the 28 sheets on the ground among the ancient pillars in Ueno Park. He then disassembled them and attached all the sheets end-to-end in a long ribbon ascending the stairs and entering into a centuries-old religious shrine built in traditional pagoda style. The old Tokyo site was selected to carry a spiritual message of electronic age homage to tradition. With the sun rising over Japan to begin a new day, the faxart angel rose over the Pacific Ocean to fly into yesterday. It arrived in the City of the Angels at 2:40 p. m. on October 4th. The angel came together once again at the Museum of Contemporary Art in Los Angeles on the day before it had visited Tokyo. Cyberangels can not only fly around the globe, they can fly into tomorrow and back into yesterday. They reshape our concepts of time and space.

## Learning through Polycultural Collaboration
In 1990, I was invited to be Dean of Visual Arts of New World School of the Arts in Miami, a new school created by the Florida State Legislature as "A Center for Excellence in the Arts," a joint venture of University of Florida, Miami-Dade College and Miami-Dade Public Schools. As part of a B.F.A. program in environmental public art that I created at NWSA, I collaborated with Miriam Benjamin on an intergenerational art project, *Legacy Thrones* (Alexenberg and Benjamin 2004). My wife, Miriam, is a high-

touch counterpart to my high-tech leanings, with an M.F.A. in ceramic sculpture from Pratt.

Elders from the three largest ethnic communities in Miami worked together with art students under our artistic direction to create three colossal thrones reaching twenty feet high and weighing more than two tons. We brought together African-American elders from the Greater Bethel AME Church, Hispanic elders from Southwest Social Services Program, and Jewish elders from the Miami Jewish Home for the Aged to work with New World School of the Arts students to create three *Legacy Thrones* facing Biscayne Bay in Miami. Through aesthetic dialogue between these elders and young people, valued traditions of the past were transformed into artistic statements of enduring significance. Together, young hands and old shaped wet clay into colorful ceramic relief elements collaged onto three monumental thrones, works of public art constructed from steel and concrete.

Elder-student dyads collaborated creatively with Miriam and me one day each week for a full academic year. All sixty participants worked simultaneously in one huge studio space. At their first meeting, each student listened to an elder tell about her life experiences and cultural roots. Life review methodologies facilitated elders looking back and reaching inward to trigger reminiscences of events and images of personal and communal significance. The challenge at the next meetings was to explore ways of transforming reminiscences that reveal cultural values into visual images that can be expressed through clay. The eminent psychologist Erik Erikson (1986) explains: "For the ageing, participation in expressions of artistic form can be a welcome source of vital involvement and exhilaration...When young people are also involved, the change in the mood of elders can be unmistakably vitalizing."

Working parallel to each other in one large studio, the three culturally different groups of elders continually engaged in dialogue with each other, an opportunity that rarely exists outside of the studio. African-American, Hispanic, and Jewish old people in their ethnically specific homes for the aged and senior centers seldom encounter one another. Working alongside each other and learning about each other's cultures, they came to realize how much they shared in experiences and in values. In *Mixed Blessings: New Art in a Multicultural America*, Lucy Lippard (1990) describes our art project's values: "I am interested in cultural dissimilarities and the light they shed on fundamental human similarities...in art that combines a pride in roots with an explorer's view of the world as shared by others."

The elders worked with clay to make relief sculptural statements of images from their personal and collective past. They painted them with colorful glazes creating numerous collage elements that were cemented to the thrones until the sculptural surfaces were entirely clad in ceramics. Our role as the artists was to integrate all the elements into aesthetically powerful expressions of each ethnic community. Although the elders had no prior experience working with clay, they developed their technical prowess and aesthetic judgment during their year of participation. While the students facilitated the elders' growth artistically, the young people's lives were enriched through creative collaboration with partners blessed with a long life of fertile experiences. By sharing their stories with the students, transforming them into artistic images, and leaving a legacy for future generations, the elders added deeper layers of meaning to their lives.

## Learning through Ecological Perspective

In my ten years living in Miami, it became clear to me that polyculturalism and ecological perspective are related. Both promote multiple views of the whole and of dynamic interrelationships in growing ecosystems that embrace nature, society, and media. Twenty-two young artists in the senior class of the NWSA high school worked on an art project, *Miami in Ecological Perspective*, with me and biologists from the Everglades National Park (Alexenberg 1994). These Miamians and their parents were born on five continents, in sixteen countries, and in twelve states. Miami is a lively international city framed by the mangrove swamps of Biscayne Bay and the wide saw grass river of the Everglades. Its future is related to how its ethnic communities bring their numerous viewpoints together in a common enterprise and how it protects and honors its natural environment, its primary source of revenue. Thousands leave a shivering winter of snow and ice to sun themselves on the palm-studded beaches, swim in warm blue waters, and marvel at the flight of flocks of great white egrets and the movements of giant alligators in the Everglade's waters.

Under the guidance of the Everglades biologists, the students waded through the Everglades, a shallow river 60 miles wide flowing 300 miles from the Kissimmee River to Florida Bay. It was the time of year that the waters receded leaving fish no choice but to find refuge in waterholes that alligators had dug under the water. When birds came to eat the fish concentrated in the waterholes, the alligators could choose the birds or fish for their breakfast. The students documented the dynamic interrelationships of the numerous species of animals and plants to each other and their environment using observational drawing, photography, and verbal and statistical notation. These studies became the raw material for artworks. Their scientific study of ecology was coupled with artistic explorations that expressed ecological perspective in relation to their environment and their place in it and with social action cleaning up trash thrown in the water by tourists in the national park.

> The ecological perspective begins with the view of the whole, an understanding of how the various parts of nature interact in patterns that tend towards balance and persist over time. But this perspective cannot treat the earth as something separate from human civilization; we are part of the whole too, and looking at it ultimately means looking at ourselves. (Gore 1993)

The students created mixed-media artworks that were published in a book, *Miami in Ecological Perspective* (1994), that integrated their field work in the Everglades with their studies of how artists shape worldview by their perspective inventions. As I discussed in the "Learning through Morphological Analysis" section of this chapter, the artists of the Renaissance created logical perspective by visually representing three-dimensional space from a single point of view and time as a cross section of a one-way linear path. Most people in the industrialized world continue to see the world through the eyes of these Renaissance artists. Before Renaissance perspective spread from Italy throughout Europe, artists employed a mythological perspective that arises from an auditory experience of space as two-dimensional and of time as cyclical. People from most pre-industrial cultures continue to experience space and time from a mythological perspective. Today, artists have an opportunity and responsibility of once again reshaping humanity's worldview by inventing an art of ecological perspective.

> Whereas the aesthetic perspective oriented us to the making of objects, the ecological perspective connects art to its integrative role in the larger whole and the web of relationships in which art exists. A new emphasis falls on community and environment…The ecological perspective does not replace the aesthetic, but gives a deeper account of what art is doing, reformulating its meaning and purpose beyond the gallery system, in order to redress the lack of concern, within the aesthetic model, for issues of context or social responsibility. (Gablik 1991)

As the students were creating artworks expressing ecological perspective, they studied ecological works of other artists. They were inspired by the work of Helen and Newton Harrison, Mierle Ukeles, Alan Sonfist, and Mel Chin. These artists and others had their work shown in the *Fragile Ecologies* exhibition at the Queens Museum of Art near the empty lots where I studied sowbugs for my thesis on the ecology of terrestrial isopods four decades earlier. The curator of *Fragile Ecologies* wrote in the exhibition catalog:

> Artists are in a unique position to effect environmental changes because they can synthesize new ideas and communicate connections between many disciplines. They are pioneering a holistic approach to problem solving that transcends the narrow limits of specialization. Since art embodies freedom of thought, spirit, and expression, its creative potential is limitless. Art changes the way people look at reality. (Matilsky 1992: 3)

### Learning through Responsive Compassion

I returned to Israel in 2000 to accept a professorship at Ariel University Center of Samaria where I taught the courses "Space-Time Systems in Nature and Culture" to architecture students and "Art in Jewish Thought" to students of humanities, sciences, and engineering. I also headed the studio arts programs in fine arts and graphic design at Emunah College of the Arts in Jerusalem and was appointed by the president of Israel to the Council of the Wolf Foundation which grants the prestigious Wolf Prizes in the arts and sciences.

I created a responsive artwork, *Cybersight*, linking Internet technology with a digital device that provides haptic opportunities for blind people to "see" computer images through their fingers. It attempts to create art that transcends the distanced formality of aesthetics and responds to the cries of the world. It creates art rooted in the responsive heart, rather than the disembodied eye, not as a solitary process it has been since the Renaissance but as something we do with others (Gablik 1991).

*Cybersight* responds to these cries by reaching out to human beings lacking the primary sense required to encounter art as defined by Western culture. *Cybersight* offers blind people opportunities to experience imagery through their sense of touch using unique digital technologies developed in Jerusalem. They can gain tactile access to those things they would most like to see. Through the Internet, access is extended globally to the blind as websurfers contribute images that generate funds for research to fight blindness. *Cybersight* is the embodiment of "the next historical and evolutionary stage of consciousness, in which the capacity to be compassionate will be central not only to our ideas of success, but also to the recovery of both a meaningful society and a meaningful art" (Gablik 1991: 182).

*Cybersight* is responsive art that gives eyes to the blind and systems art that gives hands to art. Art of the past may have expressed social and humanitarian concerns, but it hangs insularly on a museum wall disengaged from the issues that define it. In a sense, that art is handicapped. It possesses no hands to help the cause it is advocating. Responsive systems art plugs art into the real world transforming its audience into active participants. It has hands to reach out and invite people to collaborate in fixing the world. When art has hands for receiving and giving, art gains a soul.

The genesis of *Cybersight* was a discussion with my son, Ari, about extending into the social realm the human-machine interaction in our bio-imaging artwork, *"Inside/Outside: P'nim/Panim,"* that we had created at MIT. Our work at MIT led us to see how art of the future will more deeply explore interfaces between real space and cyberspace. We began brainstorming about how actions in cyberspace could effect changes in people's lives in real space, how the Internet can bring people together to help one another, how digital technologies can be used for fixing the world by filling it with loving kindness, and how web art could actually generate charity. We sought ways to move beyond making art *about* compassion and charity, to creating art in which actually performing acts of compassion and charity provide the aesthetic experience

Ari suggested that he could build a website in which people worldwide would be invited to contribute pictures to the site. Like the funding of walkers in a walkathon, we could get corporate sponsors to donate money to a charity each time an image is contributed. We began by asking people who were born blind or became blind at a young age: "What are four things that you would most like to see if you had vision?" We interviewed blind people in Israel, the Czech Republic, and United States and sent questionnaires worldwide to associations and schools for the blind. We received responses from countries as disparate as Australia, Ethiopia, Fiji, India, Korea, Lebanon, Lithuania, Niger, Poland, Slovenia, Zambia, and the United Kingdom. The similarity of responses from such diverse cultures teaches us about the common vision of humanity. Ari created the website on which we posted the results of our cross-cultural research to invite web surfers to contribute pictures of things that blind people most want to see.

The next stage was to link the Internet to innovative digital technologies that enable blind people to "see" pictures through the sense of touch. A special computer mouse was developed in Jerusalem that gives blind people direct access to pictures on a computer monitor. Beneath fingers placed in indentations in this specially designed mouse, there is a grid of pin-like protrusions that move up and down independently to trace the image on the computer monitor onto the blind person's fingertips. I drove up to Jerusalem to meet with Dr. Roman Guzman, inventor of this digital system, to discuss how his innovative technology could facilitate developing aesthetic experiences for blind people. With this new technology, blind people worldwide could access pictures from the image bank at our website.

In my years of dialogue on art and technology with the Lubavicher Rebbe, the twentieth century's foremost leader of Hasidic Jewry, I learned that the sweeping technological changes we are experiencing today are described in ancient kabbalistic texts. They relate how the outburst in scientific knowledge and technological advancement would be paralleled by an increase in sublime wisdom and spirituality. Integrating the wisdom of the mind and the wisdom of the soul, which is the role of the artist, can begin to usher true unity into the world.

> The divine purpose of the present information revolution, which gives an individual unprecedented power and opportunity, is to allow us to share knowledge – spiritual knowledge – with each other, empowering and unifying individuals everywhere. We need to use today's interactive technology not just for business or leisure but to interlink as people – to create a welcome environment for the interaction of our souls, our hearts, our visions (Schneerson 1995: 191).

**Learning through Spiritual Emergence**
Wassily Kandinsky (1977) explored the spiritual nature of the emerging modern art movements at the beginning of the twentieth century in his classic book *Concerning the Spiritual in Art*. He saw modern art as movement away from the representation of the material world to a more spiritually elevated world of abstraction. He symbolized this spiritual ascent by a moving triangle with its apex leading it *forwards and upwards*. Complementing modernism's movement of art to a higher spiritual realm of pure color and form, twenty-first-century art forms promote the movement of art down into everyday life and out across the planet. This spiritual movement *downward and outward* can be symbolized by a second triangle moving into the future through the wisdom of the past with the apex pointing downwards. The two triangles intertwined symbolize the teaching of the Lubavicher Rebbe that it is not enough to rest content with our own spiritual ascent, the elevation of our souls in closeness to God. "We must also strive to draw spirituality down into the world and into every part of our involvement with it –

our work and our social life – until not only do they not distract us from our pursuit of G-d, but they become a full part of it" (Schneerson 1986: 320).

The final project for my students in the colleges in Ariel and Jerusalem was to photograph God. I created a blog, www.photographgod.com, where I posted instructions and some of the most interesting sequences of photographs. The first question the students asked was, "Where do we find God?" I responded with the teaching of Rabbi Joseph B. Soloveitchik (1983), one of the foremost thinkers of the twentieth century, that they should not direct their glance upward but downward, not aspire to a heavenly transcendence nor seek to soar upon the wings of some abstract, mysterious spirituality, but to fix our gaze upon concrete, empirical reality. Look for God in the marketplace, the street, the factory, the house, the mall, and the banquet hall. "For God your Lord walks in the midst of your camp. " (*Deuteronomy* 23: 15) God permeates into every nook and cranny of life.

In his book, *Seeing God*, Rabbi David Aaron uses kabbalistic insights to illuminate how we can see divine light all around us. He shares my discomfort using the word "God," a Germanic word conjuring up images of some all-powerful being zapping us if we step out of line. Hebrew speakers call God *Hashem*, literally "The Name" in Hebrew, the name of the nameless One encompassing all of reality and beyond.

> Hashem does not exist in reality – Hashem is reality. And we do not exist alongside Hashem, we exist within Hashem, within the reality that is Hashem. Hashem is the place. Indeed, Hashem is the all-embracing context for everything. So there can't be you and God standing side by side in reality. There is only one reality that is Hashem, and you exist in Hashem...Everything is in Hashem, Hashem is in everything, but Hashem is beyond everything...Seeing God is all about getting in touch with reality (Aaron 2001: 14).

In *God is at Eye Level* (2000), photographer Jan Phillips quotes from Rabbi Elimelech:

> My eyes find God everywhere, in every living thing, creature, person, in every act of kindness, act of nature, act of grace. Everywhere I look, there God is looking back, looking straight back...Whoever does not see God in every place does not see God in any place.

In his acclaimed novel, *The City of God* (2001), E. L. Doctorow echoes these thoughts:

> If there is a religious agency in our lives, it has to appear in the manner of our times. Not from on high, but a revelation that hides itself in our culture, it will be ground-level, on the street, it'll be coming down the avenue in the traffic, hard to tell apart from anything else. It will be cryptic, discerned over time, piecemeal, to be communally understood at the end like a law of science. They'll put it on a silicon chip.

We learn divine attributes from the biblical passage "You Hashem are compassion, strength, beauty, eternity, splendor, and everything in heaven and on earth" (*Chronicles* 1:29). Like the spectral colors that make up white light, we can see the spectrum of divine light emerging everywhere we look. My students' charge was to photographically document processes that reveal these six divine attributes, a divine spectrum filtering down into their everyday lives:

*Compassion*: Largess/Loving All
*Strength*: Judgment/Setting Limits
*Beauty*: Aesthetic Balance/Inner Elegance
*Eternity*: Victory/Success
*Splendor*: Gracefulness/Magnificence
*Integration*: Foundation of Everything/Gateway to Action

On my blog, www.photographgod.com, I posted my students' work and invited worldwide participation. On the blog, I posted Karen's photographic sequence expressing *compassion* as a process that begins with hungry feral cats, hungry for love and food, surrounding an elderly gentleman who has seen much in his life who chose to respond to their hunger. He pets them in one photograph, satisfying their hunger for love and in the next photograph portions out food for each of them making sure there is enough for all. Sharon sees *compassion* as the divine loving kindness bestowed upon a bride on her wedding day. Her photographs show a beautiful bride, her eyes closed in contemplation, enveloped in the aura of her new husband's love, as they stand close together under a wedding canopy.

Dalia sees *success* as the *victory* of good over evil and the love of the Jewish people for its Torah for *eternity*. As a participant, she photographed the "March of the Living" to Nazi death camps in Poland in order to never forget the horrible nightmare and unimaginable suffering of millions of Jews brutally murdered there. On her return home to Israel, she photographed *strength* as her brave peers, soldiers defending their country against its current enemies seeking to destroy it. They are wrapped in prayer shawls reading from a Torah scroll in an open field marking the beginning of their dangerous day.

Esti documents avian *strength* in a photographic sequence showing a parrot chick pecking its way out of its egg and avian *splendor* as the metamorphosis of the young parrot, a strange-looking earthbound creature with stubby feathers, into a magnificent bird in flight. Roni's photographic sequence shows the birthing of a calf at a dairy farm on Israel's coastal plain, an awesome event expressing *beauty* as helping bring new life into the world. It reveals *beauty* as the vital balance between the farmer's *compassion* aiding a cow in labor and the *strength* of his arms pulling the calf through the birth canal. The biblical prophet Zechariah envisioned a beautiful future during the depths of despair when Jerusalem was razed by its enemies and the Jewish people exiled. Tzipi sees Zechariah's vision being realized in our day after two millennia of bitter exile. "Thus said God: I will bring My people from the land of the east and from the land where the sun sets to dwell within Jerusalem...We will see the wondrous vision of elderly men and women once again sitting in the streets of Jerusalem and the streets of the city will be filled with boys and girls playing." (*Zechariah* 8: 6–7) Tzipi photographed *beauty* as she and her brother sat with their great-grandparents, both 91 years old, in their home in Jerusalem. Her grandparents have 7 children, 47 grandchildren, 170 great-grandchildren, and 6 great-great grandchildren – in total 230 offspring!

## Learning through Moral Courage

In the kabbalistic schema, beauty is the balance between compassion and strength. This vital balance teaches that it is not enough for artists to rest content with their compassionate responses to the cries of the world through their artworks. They must gain the strength and moral courage to use art to confront hatred, bigotry, racism, terrorism, genocide, and cults of death and destruction. There are artists in the past who have exhibited the moral courage to confront evil through their paintings, drawings, and prints, from the etchings of Goya recording the horrors of Napoleon's invasion, George Grosz's drawings of the catastrophe of World War I – the disabled, crippled, and mutilated – and his caricatures ridiculing Hitler and his Nazi henchmen, Ben Shahn's *Passion of Sacco and Vanzetti* painting exposing bigotry, to Picasso's *Guernica* crying out against the bombing practice by Hitler's burgeoning war machine killing hundreds in a little Basque village in northern Spain as a prelude to WW II and the Holocaust.

In the tradition of *Guernica*, I created www.futureholocaustmemorials.org, an Internet artwork to warn the world of Iranian president Ahmedinejad's quest for a nuclear bomb to "wipe Israel off the map. " Just as the world's acquiescence to Hitler's raining bombs on Guernica gave him the license to proceed with preparing for WW II and exterminating the Jews of Europe on his way to global conquest, the world's indifference to the thousands of rockets launched against Israel by Iran's proxy armies, Hamas and Hizbullah, are empowering Ahmedinejad to incinerate the Jews of Israel as a prelude to his global jihad.

The nations that did little to prevent the murder of six million Jews in Europe or collaborated with the Nazis in their extermination have built memorials to honor those dead Jews. They are once again doing little to prevent a Second Holocaust. As a wake-up call to today's apathetic world, I propose designing in advance Holocaust memorials honoring the six million Jews in Israel incinerated by an Iranian nuclear bomb. I also propose redesigning, embellishing, and enlarging existing Holocaust memorials to pay tribute in a single artwork to all the twelve million murdered Jews. The Holocaust monument in Berlin, for example, is a sprawling field of 2,700 stone slabs for Holocaust One. I propose doubling its size by adding 2,700 more stone slabs as a future memorial for Holocaust Two. A total of 5,400 stone slabs for twelve million Jews murdered by the world's indifference.

The Islamist hatred for the Jews is so intense that they are willing to incinerate millions of Arab men, women, and children living among the Jews in the Land of Israel. I am inviting an Arab artist to collaborate with me in creating a memorial in advance for this collateral damage from Iran's nuclear bomb.

My web proposal for designing "Memorials for a Second Holocaust" is an artist's attempt to  make the world see that the dangers that face Israel are dangers faced by the whole  free world.   The world's indifference to Hitler's murderous attacks on the Jews encouraged  him to  attack Europe and America. Iran's nuclear ambitions and aggressive intent goes beyond incinerating Israel. It is a program of global conquest in the service of a mad ideology.

Today, the global reach of a networked planet gives artists unprecedented power to express their moral outrage as a worldwide call to action against these evils. The Internet is a powerful art medium that can reach out across our planet screaming, "Never Again!" On seeing www.futureholocaustmemorials.org, Kenneth Treister, artist/architect of the acclaimed Holocaust Memorial in Miami Beach, responded: "I do not remember being struck so sharply, like a thunder strike, by a work of art, in any form. It is so powerful. In a simple way, you tell a message that is both urgent and so sad. Reality is staring us in our face and we are blind...I never thought that contemporary art could speak clearly of important things. Your work has changed that perception."

### Learning through Holistic Integration

Holistic education is described in an online encyclopedia of education as learning that nurtures a sense of wonder, of the wholeness of the universe, of intrinsic reverence for life, and of passionate love of learning. Holistic education is based on the premise that each person finds identity, meaning, and purpose in life through connections to community, the natural world, and spiritual values. The art of holistic education lies in its responsiveness to diverse learning styles (Online Encyclopedia 2006).

In a special issue of *Visual Arts Research* devoted to holistic approaches to art education, its editor, Peter London, writes:

> Holism posits that at any moment in time we are the sum total of the prevailing states of our mind, body and spirit. This is the dynamic phenomenon, the being who is actively engaged in creating their life moment by moment, and their art, project by project. It is therefore addressing and ultimately integrating mind, body, and sprit, that holistic art education is after (London 2006, p. 8).

I have the opportunity to put holistic art education theory into practice by creating a new School of Art and Multimedia at Netanya College in Israel in which students redefine art in creative ways at the interdisciplinary interface where new technologies and scientific inquiry shape cultural values of a Jewish state in an era of globalization. The educational model for the new college is derived from my nearly five decades of experience as artist/researcher/teacher, my research on higher education in America, and ancient kabbalistic wisdom that has special relevance for the future of higher education in Israel (Alexenberg 2006a).

My research study in higher education, presented at the SIGGRAPH 2005 conference on computer graphics and interactive media in Los Angeles, analyzes degree requirements, curricula, and course offerings in theoretical studies and studio practice in B.F.A. and M.F.A. programs in sixty American art colleges and university art departments that have a range of cognate titles: digital art, multimedia design, art and technology, computer art, conceptual information arts, new media, electronic art, interactive media, science technology art, electronic imaging, interdisciplinary computing and the arts, arts computation engineering, interactive telecommunications, and others (Alexenberg 2005b).

In my book *The Future of Art in a Digital Age: From Hellenistic to Hebraic Consciousness* (Alexenberg 2006b), I explore the confluence between new directions in art and kabbalah, Judaism's ancient esoteric tradition. Kabbalah provides a symbolic language and conceptual schema that facilitates understanding the dynamics of the creative process in technoetic art – art that arises from the intersections of art, science, technology, and consciousness research. The kabbalistic model of creative process is a metaphorical way of thinking derived from the deep structure of biblical consciousness. It is a choreography of the mind that reveals a progression that draws inspiration down into the material world from a higher source where originality emanates.

Based upon a biblical passage, (*Isaiah* 43: 7), the kabbalistic schema posits worlds of Emanation, Creation, Formation, and Action, realms of spirit, mind, and body flowing from intentions, thoughts, and feelings to their realization through creating something original. The creative process aims "to liberate those who are blind though they have eyes and deaf though they have ears" (*Isaiah* 43: 8). Educating artists for the future requires a liberating curriculum to open the eyes and ears of students to their continually expanding range of learning options in these four worlds.

*Emanation* is the precognitive realm of consciousness/spirituality/intention.
*Creation* is the cognitive realm of insight/conceptualization/inquiry.
*Formation* is the affective realm of emotions/aesthetic experience/artistic expression.
*Action* is the space-time realm of working with materials/technologies/media and the space-time realm of creating through one's body/local community/global culture.

Holistic integration is the vital flow between these worlds that weaves together realms of learning at the intersections of art, science, technology and culture: awesome immersion, playful exploration, aesthetic creativity, morphological analysis, interdisciplinary imagination, morphodynamic beauty, semiotic communication, cybersomatic interactivity, global connectivity, polycultural collaboration, ecological perspective, responsive compassion, spiritual emergence, and moral courage.

## Works Cited

Aaron, D. (2001), *Seeing God*, New York: Berkley Books.

Alexenberg, M. (1962), "Teaching the Scientific Method with the Pendulum," *School Science and Mathematics*.

Alexenberg, M. (1967), "Biology Education: The First Task and Central Purpose," *The American Biology Teacher*, vol. 29, no. 3.

Alexenberg, M. (1969), *Sound Science*, Englewood Cliffs, NJ: Prentice-Hall.

Alexenberg, M. (1969), "Teaching Children Science: An Inquiry Approach," *Biosciences: Journal of the American Institute of Biological Sciences*, vol. 19, no. 7.

Alexenberg, M. (1969), *A Unitary Model of Aesthetic Experience in Art and Science*, doctoral dissertation, New York University.

Alexenberg, M. (1970), *Light and Sight*, Englewood Cliffs, NJ: Prentice-Hall.

Alexenberg, M. (1974), "Toward an Integral Structure through Science and Art." *Main Currents in Modern Thought*, vol. 30, no. 4.

Alexenberg, M. (1981), *Aesthetic Experience in Creative Process*, Ramat Gan: Israel: Bar-Ilan University Press.

Alexenberg, M. (1988), "Art with Computers: The Human Spirit and the Electronic Revolution," *The Visual Computer: International Journal of Computer Graphics*, vol. 4, no. 1.

Alexenberg, M. (1994), *Miami in Ecological Perspective*, Miami: New World School of the Arts.

Alexenberg, M. (2004), "Semiotic Redefinition of Art in a Digital Age," *Semiotics and Visual Culture: Sights, Signs, and Significance*, D. L. Smith-Shank (ed.). Reston: VA: National Art Education Association.

Alexenberg, M. (2005a), "From Science to Art: Integral Structure and Ecological Perspective in a Digital Age," *Interdisciplinary Art Education: Building Bridges to Connect Disciplines and Cultures*, M. Stokrocki (ed.), Reston: VA: National Art Education Association.

Alexenberg, M. (2005b), "Educating Artists in a Digital Age," ACM-SIGGRAPH 2005 Conference Poster Presentation. Full Conference DVD-ROM. Los Angeles: Association for Computing Machinery.

Alexenberg, M. (2006a), "Ancient Schema and Technoetic Creativity," *Technoetic Art: A Journal of Speculative Research*, vol. 4, no. 1.

Alexenberg, M. (2006b), *The Future of Art in a Digital Age: From Hellenistic to Hebraic Consciousness*, Bristol, U.K.: Intellect Books.

Alexenberg, M. and Benjamin, M. (2004), "Legacy Thrones: Intergenerational Collaboration in Creating Multicultural Public Art," *Community Connections: Intergenerational Links in Art Education*, A. M. La Porte (ed.), Reston: VA: National Art Education Association.

Alexenberg, M. and Blaney, R. B. (1964), "The Binary System and Computers," *Science and Children*, vol. 2, no. 3.

Alexenberg, M. and Peine, O. (1988), *LightsOROT: Spiritual Dimensions of the Electronic Age*, Cambridge, MA: MIT Center for Advanced Visual Studies and New York: Yeshiva University Museum.

Bronowski, J. (1965), *Science and Human Values*, New York: Harper & Row.

Bruner, J. (1963), *On Knowing: Essays for the Left Hand*, Cambridge: MA: Belkap Press of Harvard University Press.

Doctorow, E. L. (2001), *City of God*, New York: Plume.

Einstein, A. (1949), *The World as I See It*, New York: Philosophical Library.

Erickson, E., Erickson, J. M., and Kivnik, H. Q. (1986), *Vital Involvement in Old Age*, New York and London: Norton.

Friedman, M. S. (1960), *Martin Buber: The Life of Dialogue*, New York: Harper and Row.

Freidman, T. (2000), *The Lexus and the Olive Tree: Understanding Globalization*, New York: Farrar Straus Giroux.

Gablik, S. (1991), *The Reenchantment of Art*, New York and London: Thames and Hudson.

Gardner, H. (1999), *Intelligence Reframed: Multiple Intelligences for the 21$^{st}$ Century*, New York: Basic Books.

Gore, A. (1993), *Earth in Balance: Ecology and the Human Spirit*, New York: Plume.

Grahame, K. (2003), *The Wind in the Willows*, (first edition 1908), New York: Henry Holt.

Irwin, R. and de Cosson, A. (2004), *A/r/tography: Rendering Self though Arts-Based Living Inquiry*, Vancouver: Pacific Educational Press.

Kaprow, A. (1993), *Essays on the Blurring of Art and Life*, J. Kelley (ed.), Berkeley: University of California Press.

Kandinsky, W. (1997), *Concerning the Spiritual in Art*, M. T. H. Sadler. New York: Dover.

Kepes, G. (1965), *Structure in Art and Science*, New York: George Braziller.

Kook, A. I. (1978), *Abraham Isaac Kook: Lights of Holiness*, B. Z. Bokser (trans.), New York: The Classics of Western Spirituality, Paulist Press.

Lippard, L. R. (1990), *Mixed Blessings: New Art in a Multicultural America*, New York: Pantheon.

London, p. (2006), "Towards a Holistic Paradigm of Art Education: Mind, Body, Spirit," *Visual Arts Research*, vol. 32, no. 1.

Matilsky, B. C. (1992), *Fragile Ecologies: Contemporary Artists' Interpretations and Solutions*, New York: Rizzoli in association with The Queens Museum.

Online Encyclopedia (accessed Nov. 4, 2006), Holistic education@the encyclopedia of informal education. www.infed.org/biblio/holisticeducation.htm.

Phillips, J. (2000), *God is at Eye Level: Photography as a Healing Art*, Wheaton, IL and Chennai, Madras, India: Quest Books.

Pink, D. (2006), *A Whole New Mind: Why Right-Brainers Will Rule the Future*, New York: Riverhead Books.

Schneerson, M. M. (1986), *Torah Studies*, J. Sacks (ed.), London: Lubavitch Foundation.

Schneerson, M. M. (1995), *Toward a Meaningful Life: The Wisdom of the Rebbe*, S. Jacobson (ed.), New York: William Morrow.

Soloveitchik, J. B. (1983), *Halakhic Man*, Philadelphia: Jewish Publication Society of America.

# About the Authors

**Shlomo Lee Abrahmov** is an artist and a lecturer on art and photography. After receiving a B.F.A. from University of California Santa Barbara in painting and M.F.A. from University of California Irvine in studio art, he worked and exhibited in California while living in Los Angeles. Among his projects were an environmental art piece for the Museum of Contemporary Art and independent research on surrealist photography for the Department of Photography at the J. p. Getty Museum. In recent years, he has moved back to Israel where he teaches in Holon Institute of Technology and Shenkar College of Engineering and Design. His main focus of enquiry is how levels of meaning are developed in photographs and other visual media. Abrahmov has been developing e-Learning pedagogies, strategies, and platforms for visual education. One of the approaches he developed was the double blend approach that combines face-to-face learning with online instruction and the tandem teaching of theory and practice. In 2005, he received a research grant from Israel's Ministry of Education in order to develop an e-Learning approach to teaching visual literacy. He earned his Ph.D. at Anglia Ruskin University in the UK.

Email: artman2002@yakum.co.il

**Mel Alexenberg** is editor of this book and author of *The Future of Art in a Digital Age: From Hellenistic to Hebraic Consciousness*. He lives in Israel where he is Founding Dean of a new School of Art and Multimedia at Netanya College, head of art and design at Emunah College in Jerusalem, and former professor at Bar-Ilan University and Ariel University Center in Samaria. In the USA where he was born and educated, he was Dean at New World School of the Arts in Miami, Professor and Chairman of Fine Arts at Pratt Institute, Associate Professor of Art and Education at Columbia University, and Research Fellow at MIT's Center for Advanced Visual Studies. His artworks exploring digital technologies and global systems are in the collections of more than forty museums worldwide, including: Metropolitan Museum of Art in New York, Baltimore Museum of Art, High Museum of Art in Atlanta, Malmo Museum in Sweden, Museum Moderner Kunst in Vienna, Gemeentemuseum in The Hague, Victoria and Albert Museum in London, Museo de Art Contemporaneo in Caracas, and Israel Museum in Jerusalem. He has written numerous papers on art, science, technology, and culture and their interrelationships as well as the books: *Aesthetic Experience in Creative Process, Light and Sight,* and with Otto Piene, *LightsOROT: Spiritual Dimensions of the Electronic Age.* He was art editor of *The Visual Computer: International Journal of Computer Graphics* and assistant editor of *The American Biology Teacher.*

Alexenberg earned degrees in biology and science education and was awarded an interdisciplinary doctorate from New York University in art, science, and cognitive psychology.

Email: melalexenberg@yahoo.com
Website: www.melalexenberg.com

**Mark Amerika**, who has been named a "Time Magazine 100 Innovator," has had four retrospectives of his digital artwork. He is an Associate Professor of Art and Art History at the University of Colorado at Boulder. His net art, DVD surround sound installations, and VJ performances have been exhibited and featured internationally at many world-renowned venues including the Whitney Biennial, the ICA in London, and the Walker Arts Center. He is the author of two cult novels, *The Kafka Chronicles* and *Sexual Blood* (Fiction Collection 2: University of Alabama Press), and has edited three published anthologies. He is the founder and publisher of the Alt-X Online Network, a net art and new media writing site started on the Internet in 1993 (www.altx.com) as well as the publisher of the electronic book review (www.electronicbookreview.com). His forthcoming book of artist writings, entitled *META/DATA: A Digital Poetics*, will be published by MIT Press later this year.

Email: mark.amerika@colorado.edu and amerika@altx.com
Website: www.markamerika.com

**Roy Ascott** is founding president of the Planetary Collegium and Professor of Technoetic Art, University of Plymouth, England, and Visiting Professor in Design/Media Arts at UCLA. He was Vice-President and Dean of San Francisco Art Institute, California; Professor of Communications Theory, University of Applied Arts, Vienna; Professor of Fine Art, Minneapolis College of Art; and President of Ontario College of Art, Toronto. He served on the Art and Media Panel of the Arts and Humanities Research Council (2001–2004). Pioneer of telematic art, Ascott has shown at the Venice Biennale, Electra Paris, Ars Electronica Linz, V2 Holland, Milan Triennale, Biennale do Mercosul, Brazil, European Media Festival, and has initiated many online projects, including the seminal work of "distributed authorship," *La Plissure du Texte: a planetary fairytale* (1983). Founding editor of *Technoetic Arts*, he's also on editorial boards of *Leonardo*, *LEA*, and *Digital Creativity*. He has advised new media centers and festivals in Europe, Australia, Brazil, Canada, China, Japan, Korea, and the USA, as well as the CEC and UNESCO. He convenes the annual international *Consciousness Reframed* conferences. See: Ascott, R. 2003. *Telematic Embrace: visionary theories of art, technology and consciousness*. Edited with an introduction by Edward A. Shanken. Berkeley: University of California Press.

Email: roy.ascott@planetary-collegium.net
Website: www.planetary-collegium.net/people/detail/ra

**Michael Bielicky** is a new media artist who has participated in numerous international exhibitions, festivals, and projects that experiment with navigation, video communication, virtual reality technologies, and large-scale urban animated projections. His innovative artworks shown worldwide include: Sao Paulo Biennale in Brazil, Seoul Biennale in South Korea, *Infermental 7* in Tokyo, Fundacio Joan Miro in Barcelona, *Ars Electronica* in Linz, Anthology Film Archives in New York, Musee National d'Art Moderne, Centre Georges Pompidou in Paris, Museum for Contemporary Art in Warsaw, Kunstmuseum in Dusseldorf, ZKM Museum fur Neue Kunst in Karlsruhe, the Gallery for Contemporary Arts in Milan, and the Jewish Museum in Prague. He has also been honored with solo exhibitions in Paris, Amsterdam, Bucharest, and Berlin.

Bielicky has been Founding Head of the School of Media Arts at the Academy of Fine Arts in Prague for sixteen years and currently Professor of New Media at Hochschule fur Gestaltung linked to the ZKM Center for Art and Media in Karlsruhe, Germany. He has been advisor in culture and technology to the Soros Center for Contemporary Art through Eastern Europe from Bucharest, Odessa, and Moscow to Alma-Ata in Kazakhstan, to the Council of Europe in Strasbourg, and to Chiang Mai University in Thailand where he is involved in establishing a new Media Arts Department.

Email: x@avu.cz

**Dr. Ron Burnett** is President of the Emily Carr Institute of Art and Design in Vancouver, Canada, and Artist/Designer at the New Media Innovation Center. He is the author of *How Images Think* published by MIT Press in 2004 and of *Cultures of Vision: Images, Media and the Imaginary* published by Indiana University Press in 1996. Burnett is also the author of over 150 published pieces in books, journals, and magazines. He was the Director of the Graduate Program in Communications at McGill University and is an Adjunct Professor in the Graduate Film and Video Program at York University. He is the Chair of the Board of Knowledge Network, recipient of the Queen's Jubilee Medal for service to Canada and Canadians, member of the Royal Canadian Academy of Arts, and is presently working on two new books and a film/video installation.

Email: rburnett@eciad.ca
Blog: www.eciad.ca/~rburnett/Weblog

**Dr. Carol Gigliotti** is Associate Professor of Interactive Media and Environmental Ethics at Emily Carr Institute of Art and Design in Vancouver, BC, Canada. She has been presenting and publishing about ethics and technology for the last fifteen years. She recently spoke at *Kindred Spirits* at Indiana University, one of the first academic conferences in the humanities on human-animal studies. Recent activities: an essay in the June 2005 issue of *Parachute* on "Artificial life and the lives of the non-human," guest-editing a special issue on "Genetic Technologies and Animals" for the January 2006 issue of the journal *AI and Society*. In the last few years, she has spoken on art, ethics, and the non-human world in keynotes at NEW FORMS 2005: Museum of Anthropology in Vancouver, BC, Interactive Futures 2005: Victoria International Independent Film Festival, as well as talks at University of the Arts, Philadelphia, PA, and University of California, Los Angeles (UCLA). She is presently working on a book, entitled *Wildness and Technology*, and is Co-Chair of the Research B Cluster at University of British Columbia's Innovative Centre for Interactive Sustainable Research.

Email: carolgigliotti@mac.com
Website: www.carolgigliotti.net

**Diane Gromala** is Professor and Associate Director of the School of Interactive Arts and Technology (SIAT) at Simon Fraser University in the greater Vancouver area. An artist, designer, theorist, writer, performer, and curator, Gromala's work has been exhibited, performed, and published around the world. Gromala has developed new media curricula in a school of fine arts, a school of communications, and a literature department in the USA. As part of a Fulbright grant, Gromala also co-developed curricula between a design school and a computer science department in New Zealand. With Jay Bolter, Gromala is co-author of *Windows and Mirrors: Interaction Design, Digital Art and the Myth of Transparency*, MIT Press. Gromala's *Meditation Chamber*, co-created by Drs. Larry Hodges and Chris Shaw, is in use at Virtually Better, a health clinic for the treatment of psychological disorders. Her current work and long-time interests concern pain, addiction, visceral embodiment, and the artistic deployment of biomedical technologies. Her grants were awarded by the (U.S.) National Science Foundation, UNESCO, and numerous corporations. Gromala is affiliated with the Planetary Collegium and holds an M.F.A. from Yale University.

**Wengao Huang** is Associate Professor of Media Art, College of Information Science and Engineering, Shandong University at Weihai, China. He is an artist with many years of experience in scientific, engineering, and design fields. His broad artistic interests include painting, writing, video, computer graphics, and animation that all come together at the interface between art, science, technology, and culture. He received B.Sc. in Automated Control Systems from University of Science and Technology of China, M.Sc. and Ph.D. in Biomedical Engineering from Zhejiang University, China. He was a post-doctoral researcher at Planetary Collegium, Institute of Digital Art and Technology at the University of Plymouth, UK, working in the transdisciplinary field of art, technology, and consciousness research. He worked as an engineer for the Chinese Ministry of Aviation, as Lecturer at the Industrial Design Institute at Zhejiang University, and as a post-doctoral researcher at China's State Key Lab of CAD & CG. Throughout his complex journey, Professor Huang has been striving to maintain a balance between art and science. His art has evolved from early pastoral painting to complex video artworks and fantastic artificial life animation. He has been exploring multiple forms of media to embody his artistic ideas that interweave Western science with Eastern philosophy and Chinese poetry.

Email: ggart@sohu.com

**Eduardo Kac** (pronounced "Katz") is Professor and Chairman of the Art and Technology Department at the School of the Art Institute of Chicago. He is author of *Telepresence and Bio Art: Networking Humans, Rabbits and Robots* (University of Michigan Press, 2005); editor of *Signs of Life: Bio Art and Beyond*, MIT Press, 2007 and editor of *Media Poetry* (Intellect Books, 2006). He is internationally recognized for his interactive net installations and his bio art. A pioneer of telecommunications art in the pre-Web '80s, Eduardo Kac emerged in the early '90s with his radical telepresence and biotelematic works. His visionary combination of robotics and networking explores the fluidity of subject positions in the post-digital world. His work deals with issues that range from the mythopoetics of online experience (*Uirapuru*) to the cultural impact of biotechnology (*Genesis*); from the changing condition of memory in the digital age (*Time Capsule*) to distributed collective agency (*Teleporting an Unknown State*); from the problematic notion of the "exotic" (*Rara Avis*) to the creation of life and evolution (*GFP Bunny*). At the dawn of the twenty-first century, Kac shocked the world with his "transgenic art" – first with a groundbreaking installation, entitled *Genesis* (1999), which included an "artist's gene" he invented, and then with his fluorescent rabbit called Alba (2000). Kac's work has been exhibited internationally.

Email: ekac@artic.edu
Website: www.ekac.org

**Lucia Leão** is an interdisciplinary artist that has been leading researches in art and technologies since 1989. She received her M.A. and Ph.D. degrees in Communication and Semiotics: Information Technology from PUC – SP Sao Paulo Catholic University, Brazil and has Post Doctoral Degree in Arts from UNICAMP, Sp. Lucia Leão is Professor at PUC-SP and SENAC. Leão's work has been exhibited internationally at venues such as Museum of Contemporary Art, São Paulo and Campinas; ISEA 2002, Paris; XV International Biennial of São Paulo, Brazil; II International Biennial of Buenos Aires; ArtMedia

– OLATS, Paris; File – International Festival of Electronic Art (2002); Arte Digital Rosario 2003; Cinético Digital Itaú Cultural (2005), SP; Mostra SESC de Artes (2005), SP and FILE RIO (2006). Leão is author of "The labyrinth of hypermedia: architecture and navigation on cyberspace" (1999), "The labyrinth aesthetics" (2002), "Interlab: labyrinths of contemporary thought" (2002), "Derivas: cartografias do ciberespaço" (2004), and "O chip e o caleidoscópio: reflexões sobre as novas mídias" (2005).

Email: lucia@lucialeao.pro.br
Website: www.lucialeao.pro.br

**Aaron Marcus** was educated in physics at Princeton and in graphic design at Yale. He studied computer programming in 1966 and became a researcher in 1967 at AT&T Bell Telephone Labs, Murray Hill, NJ, becoming the world's first graphic designer to be involved full-time in computer graphics. He programmed a prototype desktop publishing application in 1969 to 1971 for Bell Labs, programmed virtual reality art in 1971 to 1973 while a faculty member at Princeton, and directed an international team of visual communicators as a Research Fellow, East-West Center, Honolulu, in 1978. He exhibited his computer graphics and conceptual artwork beginning in the 1960s. His works are in the collections of the Princeton University Art Museum and the Victoria and Albert Museum, London. In 1980, after teaching in universities for more than ten years, he became a Staff Scientist at Lawrence Berkeley Laboratory. In 1982, he founded AM+A. Mr. Marcus received the National Computer Graphics Association award for achievement in Industry in 1992, and in 2007, the American Institute of Graphic Arts named him a Fellow for his work in cross-cultural design. Mr. Marcus has written/co-written over 250 articles and five books, including *Human Factors and Typography for More Readable Programs* (1990), *Graphic Design for Electronic Documents and User Interfaces* (1992), and *The Cross-GUI Handbook for Multiplatform User Interface Design* (1994), Reading, Addison-Wesley. He has also published two monographs of his computer graphics and conceptual art, *Soft Where, Inc.*, West Coast Poetry Review Press, Reno, 1975, 1982. Mr. Marcus continues to do user-interface design and information visualization for computer technology.

Marcus, Aaron (2008). "My Journey: From Physics to Graphic Design to User-Interface/Information-Visualization Design" in Alexenberg, Mel (Ed.), Educating Artists for the Future: Learning at the Intersections of Art, Science, Technology and Culture. Bristol, UK; Chicago, IL, USA: Intellect, 2008 , pp. 229–242. ISBN 978-1-84150-191-8.

Email: aaron.marcus@amanda.com
Website: www.amanda.com

**Jill Scott** was born in Melbourne, Australia, and currently lives in Switzerland. Her most recent publication, *artists-in-labs Processes of Inquiry:* 2006 Springer/Vienna/New York, maps the results and experiences of fourteen artists inside nine Swiss science labs (physics, life sciences, and computer/engineering). She has written many articles in books and catalogues about media art, interactivity, and philosophy. In 2002, a monograph was published entitled *Coded Characters 2003.* Ed. Marille Hahne, Hatji Cantz, which covers 28 years of her media artwork. She has exhibited many video artworks, conceptual performances, and interactive environments in the USA, Australia, Europe, and Japan. Currently, she is Professor for Research in the Institute Cultural Studies in Art, Media and Design at the Hochschule für Gestaltung und Kunst (HGKZ) in Zurich, Switzerland, where she is leader of the AIL (artists-in-labs) research program and Vice Director of the Z-Node of the Planetary Collegium – a collaborative Ph.D. program with the University of Plymouth, UK. She also serves on the board of Sitemapping, the media project awards for the Ministry of Culture in Switzerland. She has held professorial posts at University of New South

Wales, Australia; Academy of Art, Saarbrucken, Germany; Medienmuseum at the Zentrum fur Kunst und Medien Technology (ZKM) in Karlsruhe; and Bauhaus University in Weimar, Germany. Her education includes a degree in Art and Design from the Prahran Institute of Technology, Melbourne, a master's degree in communications from San Francisco State University, USA, and a Ph.D. in philosophy from the University of Wales, UK.

Email: Jill.Scott@hgkz.ch
Website: www.jillscott.org

**Bill Seaman** received a Ph.D. from the Centre for Advanced Inquiry in Interactive Arts, University of Wales, 1999. He holds a M.S.visS. degree from MIT, 1985. His work explores an expanded media-oriented poetics through various technological means. Seaman is Department Head of Digital+Media at Rhode Island School of Design. His works have been in many international shows where he has been awarded two prizes from Ars Electronica in Interactive Art (1992 &1995, Linz, Austria); International Video Art Prize, ZKM, Karlsruhe; Bonn Videonale prize; First Prize, Berlin Film/Video Festival for Multimedia in 1995; and the Awards in the Visual Arts Prize. Seaman was given the Leonardo Award for Excellence in 2002. Selected exhibitions include 1996, Mediascape Guggenheim, NYC; the premiere exhibition of the ZKM in Karlsruhe, Germany; 1997, Barbican Centre (London); 1997, C3 – Center for Culture & Communication, Budapest; in 1998, Portable Sacred Grounds, NTT-ICC Tokyo; Body Mechanique, The Wexner Center, Columbus, Ohio, 1999; David Winton Bell Gallery, Brown University, 2004. Seaman contributed a video set for SLEEPERS GUTS by Ballett Frankfurt. He has been commissioned on a number of occasions. He is currently working on a series of installations and research papers in conversation with the scientist Otto Rössler.

Email: bseaman@risd.edu
Website: www.billseaman.com

**Jinsil Seo** is a Ph.D. candidate at the School of Interactive Arts and Technology at Simon Fraser University where she teaches classes in immersive, responsive, environmental installations. She holds an M.F.A. (Computer Art) from School of Visual Arts in New York and an M.F.A. (Media Art) from Kyung Hee University in Korea. Seo creates media artworks that interlace space with human body and mind. Her artwork *Sky Reverie*, initiated at SVA, refined at SFU, and exhibited in New York and Los Angeles, won the top award at the Advanced Computing in Entertainment Conference. Seo's artworks have been exhibited in the U.S., Canada, and Korea. Her research has been presented at numerous art and technology conferences.

Email: dgromala@sfu.ca and jinsils@sfu.ca

**Edward Shanken** is a senior researcher at the UCLA Art|Science Center and Lab, Los Angeles, CA and Professor of Art History, Savanah College of Art and Design, Georgia, USA. He edited a collection of essays by Roy Ascott, entitled *Telematic Embrace: Visionary Theories of Art, Technology and Consciousness* (University of California Press, 2003). His essay "Art in the Information Age: Technology and Conceptual Art" received honorable mention in the Leonardo Award for Excellence in 2004. He edited "Artists in Industry and the Academy: Interdisciplinary Research Collaborations," a special series of essays in Leonardo 38: 4 and 38: 5 (2005). His scholarship has appeared in journals including *Art Journal, Art Byte, Art Criticism, a minima, Leonardo,* and *Technoetic Arts* and has been translated into French, Polish, and Spanish. He has lectured at conferences including the Association of Art Historians, the College Art Association,

Consciousness Reframed, Cyberart Bilbao, ISEA, and SIGGRAPH. Dr. Shanken earned his Ph.D. in Art History from Duke University (2001) and his M.B.A. from Yale University (1990). He has been awarded fellowships from the National Endowment for the Arts and the American Council of Learned Societies, co-chairs the Leonardo Education Forum and serves on the CAA Education Committee. His book *Art and Electronic Media* is forthcoming from Phaidon Press.

Website: http://artexetra.com

**Yacov Sharir** is Professor at the University of Texas at Austin where he teaches courses in virtual reality/cyberspace, multi-disciplinary art and technology, as well as dance, improvisation, and choreography. He is a frequent keynote speaker at arts and technology conferences worldwide on wearable computers/devices, technologically charged interactive systems, virtual reality, interactive video art/games, and the creation of computer-animated cyber-human performers. He was the founder of the American Deaf Dance Company, which pioneered the inclusion of deaf artists in professional dance. He subsequently founded Sharir Dance Company, for which he choreographed and created over thirty original technologically mediated compositions. Sharir was awarded the Career Research Excellence Fine Arts Award at the University of Texas and was inducted into the Austin Arts Hall of Fame. He was awarded the National Foundation for the Advancement in the Arts Award for Innovative Use of Instructional Technology and is a multiple recipient of the National Endowment for the Arts Choreographic Awards. He has served on arts councils in the United States, Israel, Spain, Portugal, Japan, China, Brazil, and France. He is a contributor to numerous journals and books on interdisciplinary arts and technology. Sharir graduated from the Bezalel Academy of Art in sculpture and ceramics and continued his studies in dance at the Rubin Academy of Music and Dance in Israel. He is currently enrolled in the Planetary Collegium Ph.D. Program at University of Plymouth, UK.

Email: sharir@mail.utexas.edu

**Ismail Ozgur Soganci** worked as an art teacher at Turkish public schools and contributed to various painting exhibitions in Turkey's capital city, Ankara. In 1999, he completed his MA degree in art education at Arizona State University as a government-sponsored scholar. His master's thesis was a micro-ethnographic study of a pre-service art education class at an American state university. He earned his PhD degree in art education at the same US institution in 2005 with a dissertation on the curricular negligence in Turkish art schooling toward issues regarding the aniconic Ottoman visual culture. His current work deals with images, icons, symbols, and representations focusing on a set of attitudes spanning from iconophobia to idolatry and the kinds of relationships people construct with respect to them. He is a book artist and faculty member of the department of fine arts education at Anadolu University in Turkey.

Email: iosoganci@anadolu.edu.tr

**Stefan Sonvilla-Weiss** is professor of eLearning in Visual Culture and head of the international M.A. program ePedagogy Design – Visual Knowledge Building at the University of Art and Design Helsinki. He studied philosophy, graphics, art and design education, and communication theory in Salzburg and Vienna where he earned his Ph.D. During the 1980's and 90's he worked as artist, media designer, educator, project manager and author of numerous publications in the context of art, new media and education.

He has contributed widely to future developments of European Higher Education in the Media, Erasmus and eLearning program and he has steered the interdisciplinary and international ePedagogy Design curriculum development. His current interrelated research includes the following topics: "Envisioning new interfaces in cooperative media culture"; "Scale-free networks - the realm of the social"; "Mobile technologies - mobile thoughts?" Stefan Sonvilla-Weiss is currently working on his new book (In)Visible. Learning to act in the metaverse, to be published by Springer Vienna/New York in August 2008.

Email: stefan.sonvilla-weiss@taik.fi
Website: http://epedagogydesign.uiah.fi

**Robert W. Sweeny** is Assistant Professor of Art and Art Education at Indiana University of Pennsylvania, where he also serves as coordinator of the Art Education program. He has published widely on the topics of digital visual culture, new media art education, and the relationships between surveillance technologies, artistic practices, and pedagogy. He has also presented at numerous national and international conferences, most recently delivering a preliminary version of the contributed chapter at *Digital Art and Culture* 2006, Copenhagen, Denmark. He is Educational Director of FLUX, a not-for- profit digital art center located in the Bronx, New York City. He is also a practicing artist and musician, creating mixed-media works based on complexity theory and network structures. He earned his M.F.A. from Maryland Institute, College of Art, in 2000, and completed his Ph.D. in Art Education at the Pennsylvania State University in 2004. He previously taught art at the middle-school and high-school level in Montgomery County, Maryland.

Email: sweeny@iup. ed

**Dr. Vinod Vidwans** is a Senior Designer (Professor) and an Ex-Vice Chairman (Research) at National Institute of Design (NID), Ahmedabad, India. He also headed the Departments of New Media and Software User Interface Design. Dr. Vidwans is a cognitive philosopher, a designer, and a portrait painter. He holds a Ph.D. in Cognitive Philosophy and a master's degree in Design from the Indian Institute of Technology, Mumbai, India. He has also topped in the examination for M.F.A. He is a recipient of the Junior Research Fellowship in Fine Arts from University Grants Commission, India. His doctoral work postulates a new paradigm called 'Design Intelligence' and characterizes creativity from a new perspective. He carries nineteen years of eventful professional and research experience with him. While working in the industry and managing content design and development projects, he explored various facets of New Media Design. He has developed '*Sharada*,' multilingual technology for Indian languages. He has also developed a computational theory of Indian classical music. At NID, Dr. Vidwans teaches Instructional Design, Information Design, Design Cognition, System Design, and Creative Composition.

Email: vidwans@nid.edu

**Stephen Wilson** is a San Francisco author, artist, and professor who explores the cultural implications of emerging technologies such as biosensors, gps, and artificial intelligence. His award-winning interactive installations & performances have been shown internationally in galleries and SIGGRAPH, CHI, NCGA, Ars Electronica, and V2 art shows. He has been artist-in-residence at various think tanks including Xerox PARC. He has published numerous articles and books including the latest *Information Arts: Intersections of Art, Science and Technology* (MIT Press, 2002). He directs the Conceptual/Information Arts Program at San Francisco State University, which prepares artists to work with emerging technologies.

Email: swilson@sfsu.edu
Website: http: //userwww.sfsu.edu/~swilson/